Rethinking Evil

Contemporary Perspectives

T0381293

T0373102

EDITED BY

María Pía Lara

UNIVERSITY OF CALIFORNIA PRESS
Berkeley · Los Angeles · London

To Richard Hecht,
for his faith in this project

University of California Press
Berkeley and Los Angeles, California

University of California Press, Ltd.
London, England

© 2001 by the Regents of the University of California

Henry E. Allison's essay, "Reflections on the Banality of
(Radical) Evil: A Kantian Analysis," is from *Idealism and
Freedom: Essays on Kant's Theoretical and Practical Philosophy*,
© 1996 Cambridge University Press. Reprinted with permission of Cambridge University Press.

Library of Congress Cataloging-in-Publication Data

Rethinking evil : contemporary perspectives / edited by María
    Pía Lara.
        p.   cm.
    Includes bibliographical references and index.
    ISBN 0-520-22632-1 (alk. paper) — ISBN 0-520-22634-8
    (pbk. : alk. paper)
    1. Good and evil.   I. Lara, María Pía

BJ1401 .R48 2001
170—dc21   2001041450

Manufactured in the United States of America
10   09   08   07   06   05   04   03   02   01
10   9   8   7   6   5   4   3   2   1

The paper used in this publication meets the minimum
requirements of ANSI/NISO Z39.48–1992 (R 1997) (*Permanence
of Paper*).

CONTENTS

ACKNOWLEDGMENTS

This book is the product of two important events organized by the people who participated in this volume. The first event took place in Mexico City in January 1999, and thanks to the Universidad Autónoma Metropolitana, Iztapalapa, we had the possibility to sit down and discuss seriously about the issues concerning evil in a friendly and interdisciplinary way. We would like to thank Dr. Luis Mier y Terán (chancellor of UAM-I), Dr. José Lema (dean of social sciences and humanities at UAM-I), and Dr. Carlos Illades (chair of the Departament of Philosophy at UAM-I) for helping us financially to develop this project. We would also like to thank Alessandro Ferrara, who first thought of organizing a special workshop on the problem of evil during the Prague colloquium sponsored by the Czech Academy of Social Sciences in May 1999. We owe special thanks to Richard Hecht, who became the poet and the bard of our group and who helped us launch the possibility to publish this book with the great support of the University of California Press. We are also indebted to Stanley Holwitz, our editor, whose strong support allowed us to complete this book and to deliver our promise to open a new space for the discussion of the problem of evil.

I would also like to thank my two students, Arturo Cano and Felipe Gaytán, for helping me with the technical elements of the book. In addition, I wish to thank the Institute for Research on Women and Gender at Stanford University for having me as a visiting scholar in the academic year 1998–99, the year I started organizing this project. And last but not least, I would like to thank Jeffrey C. Alexander for the enormous support he gave me in encouraging me to organize the conference, then in working hard with me to make the conference a success, and finally, in helping me to make an important and coherent synthesis of all our efforts to publish this book.

The essays are all written for this volume, except Henry Allison's contribution, which he kindly gave us permission to reprint. We thank Cambridge University Press for allowing us to reprint Dr. Allison's essay, published originally in his volume *Idealism and Freedom*.

Introduction

Contemporary Perspectives

María Pía Lara

In fear and trembling, have they finally realized of what man is capable—and this is indeed the precondition of any modern political thinking. Such persons will not serve very well as functionaries of vengeance. This, however, is certain: Upon them and only upon them, who are filled with a genuine fear of the inescapable guilt of the human race, can there be any reliance when it comes to fighting fearlessly, uncompromisingly, everywhere against the incalculable evil that men are capable of bringing about.

HANNAH ARENDT,
"ORGANIZED GUILT AND UNIVERSAL RESPONSIBILITY"

The past hundred years have been a long succession of genocides, mass killings, systematic rapes, ethnic cleansings, and tortures in many places around the world, including Europe. These events have seemed to threaten our belief in the possibility of moral and democratic institutions. The need to understand what has happened and to look for ways of fighting such destruction cannot wait any longer. With this book, we want to fight back by recovering the category of evil for contemporary thought, constructing a postmetaphysical theory that can support the moral and political claims to human rights around the world.

"Evil" as a philosophical concept has never been clarified in a manner that allows us to specify what we mean, morally speaking, when we talk of "evil deeds." The problem lies not so much in a lack of philosophical attention, but rather in how philosophers have interpreted the meaning of evil when they discuss it. Since Plato, the concept of evil has grouped together a wide range of problems.[1] Natural disasters *(physical)*, accidents and sicknesses, which have been interpreted as metaphysical disasters *(metaphysical)*, and cruelty, murder, and human failures *(moral)* have been conceptualized and organized as if they all belonged to the same kind of "moral" phenomena (see Susan Neiman's essay in chapter 2). Theodicies, for example, were attempts to anthropomorphize God, and thus their goal was to justify the existence of God while discussing the "presence" of evil in the suffering, the human losses, and the disasters of the world (see Isabel Cabrera's essay in chapter 1). Metaphysical conceptions of evil have mixed physical phenomena, such as hurricanes and earthquakes, with human accidents, such as sudden deaths; and with human actions aimed at cruelty against others, such as murder, rape, and torture. This lack of conceptual clarity has led to various attempts to conceptualize evil in religious, naturalistic, and psychological terms, but these have failed to bring us closer to the concept of evil and to answering the question of whether it is possible to argue that such a concept has any relevance for philosophy, and more concretely, for moral and political philosophy (see Peter Dews's essay in chapter 3).

The religious link between evil and God played a major role in earlier struggles to conceptualize evil. Attempts to justify the existence of both evil and God were not seen as addressing theoretical or moral problems, but rather as a religious burden to explain why suffering is possible if God exists. Thus, philosophies of religion and their theodicies were failed attempts to anthropomorphize nature and God,[2] without really confronting why evil seems to be a definite part of human nature, and why it is necessary for us to take this reflexive step if we are to find a way of accepting human weakness, our dark side, or as Martha Nussbaum would say, our own "fragility."[3] The challenge is to create a meaningful account of evil that allows us to comprehend why we are capable of exercising cruelty[4] upon our fellow human beings.

Absolutely central to considering the problem of evil is its relation to human agency. Evil belongs to the domains of action where agency is related to moral and political responsibility. Cabrera rightly argues that the measure of evil cannot be suffering because not "all suffering makes for a moral wrong." Rather than suffering per se, a concept of "evil," can only be conceptualized as "evil deeds," that is, as the result of intentional human actions (see Sergio Pérez's essay in chapter 11). We are not responsible for natural disasters, nor are we guilty of creating diseases or causing accidental deaths. These unintended sources of suffering do not address humanity's darkest side, which concerns to the fundamental question of why we humans are willing to destroy other humans.

Metaphysical philosophy conceptualized evil through the lens of suffering, but as we shall see, the most important aspect of evil is not suffering per se, but the fact that groups of humans exercise cruelty against others who are incapable of defending themselves—so suffering becomes an important, desired result of "evil actions." As Cabrera argues, "to attribute a wrong of a moral character to someone, three conditions must be satisfied: that the subject is responsible for his actions; that his action has harmful consequences (i.e., it produces suffering in others or in himself); and, finally, that this suffering is unjustified." Moral responsibility and political agency are the two main conceptual sources that can allow us to focus on evil in a different way.

With this book, we aim to provide the necessary tools to conceptualize evil in a philosophical framework that avoids the dead ends of metaphysical and religious conceptions. Many of the contributions start with Kant's transition from a metaphysical perspective to a moral one. Richard J. Bernstein (chapter 4) reconstructs Kant's conflicts in conceptualizing evil in the realm of freedom—moral, political, and practical. In *Religion within the Limits of Reason Alone,* Kant attempts to separate the physical and metaphysical dimensions from the moral ones. Kant clearly recognizes that "nothing is morally evil (i.e., capable of being imputed) but that which is our *own* act."[5] It is "at this point," as Joan Copjec has argued, that evil "ceases to be a religious or metaphysical problem"[6] and becomes a subject of human agency and moral choice. This conceptual revolution that Kant brought to the territory of philosophical reflection, Richard J. Bernstein concludes, allows him to become "the first major modern thinker to deal with the problem of evil in a manner that does not depend on *cognitive* claims about the existence or attributes of a supreme being." This is the point of departure for our book. Our essays allow readers to step away from earlier notions of evil. From a postmetaphysical understanding, we develop a perspective on evil that relates it to the historical catastrophes of the twentieth century. We establish a space where our consciousness of evil can—indeed, must—be drawn from such tragedies as the Holocaust, and we delineate the ways in which such tragedies have allowed us to learn about and reconsider the concrete meanings of evil deeds. As Neiman argues, "'Auschwitz' . . . stands for all we mean when we use the word 'evil' today: absolute wrongdoing which leaves room for no account and no expiation."

Some of the essays in this book (Allison, Bernstein, Cooke, and Leyva) also stress the importance of Kant's concept of evil because it presents an approach to human nature that emphasizes the permanent conflict at its core created by what Kant called our "evil heart," *(Bösartigkeit)*[7] the space where the "evil principle" *(böses Prinzip)* is situated as an exact opposite of the morality principle *(gerades Widerspiel des Prinzips der Sittlichkeit).* This explains why evil illuminates the basic frailty of human nature. Bernstein's essay illustrates the struggles that Kant undergoes in trying to preserve free human agency and in searching for some coherence between his moral theory and his idea of evil. Bernstein shows that in the end Kant does not make use of the explanatory power of his new concept of "radical evil." If Kant did redress previously failed conceptualizations of evil, he himself could only acknowledge that all he could say is that "there is in man a natural propensity to evil."[8] Bernstein's essay clarifies how Kant, because of his rather simplistic psychology, is incapable of explaining further that propensity.

If we follow Kant in his insistence that we should pay "attention to the actual evil of given actions with respect to its inner possibility—to what must take place within the will if evil is to be performed,"[9] then it seems necessary to configure or recover some psychological territory that seems slippery in Kant's own work. It is in this sense that Maeve Cooke's essay (chapter 7) develops her basic insight from Kant's work, *Religion within the Limits of Reason Alone,* transforming Kant's intuitions into a systematic conceptualization of evil, one that aims to provide a perspective on moral evil that permits a nonarbitrary condemnation of it without denying its connection to human motivation, agency, and praxis. Cooke makes her strongest criticism against Habermas's discourse ethics, and against Alessandro Ferrara's authenticity alternative to Habermas, claiming that neither theory is equipped to provide an adequate conception of evil. Cooke argues that, while Habermas shares with Arendt a reluctance to relate moral evil to moral character, neither his nor Ferrara's theory is able to conceptualize evil in a manner that allow us to discriminate among different types of evil or different degrees of evil; nor does either theory explain the "perversion of moral character" that seems to play such an important role in our understanding of human cruelty. Cooke argues that Ferrara's alternative, while better equipped to deal with validity and identity, fails to provide an adequate conception of moral identity because of its overly subjectivistic criteria. Thus, argues Cooke, it is "Kant's starting point," with his assumption of a "predisposition *(Anlage)* to want to obey the moral law," that makes our "predispositions" the essential feature of our moral character. Cooke concludes that Kant's notion of "evil heart" explains the perversion or corruption of the "human heart that results from a faulty moral disposition."

On the other hand, Kant's concept of evil and moral agency, which explicitly denies the existence of a "diabolical will," elevates his concept of freedom as the philosophical category within which to thematize evil and judgment. This is where it is important to seek Kant's concerns about what happens when we are confronted with choosing evil and deciding to act against the moral law. Henry Allison's essay (chapter 5) attempts to give an answer to this question from Kant's own point of view. Allison claims that in thematizing evil, Kant develops further his initial formula that the source of evil deeds comes only from a "propensity to subordinate moral considerations to those stemming from self-love," a feature that Allison calls an "empirically based moral anthropology."[10] This connection, argues Allison, helps relate Kant's theory to Arendt's own thematization of evil in her book *Eichmann in Jerusalem: A Report on the Banality of Evil.* Furthermore, argues Allison, with this move Kant inaugurates a whole new paradigm when he connects evil to culture and he defines evil as rooted in self-love, a feature that produces hatred when we find ourselves immersed in competitive social contexts. Kant claims, according to Allison, that the "bare propensity to evil" can easily be related to "extreme evil as a cultural phenomenon" when we crave our own superiority to others and allow jealousy and rivalry to be the driving forces that dominate and lead our moral character. In my opinion, Allison's interpretation opens up the possibility to seek an interesting, cultural understanding of the political phenomena of evil by focusing on the symbolic constructions of our desire to be superior to others. Pointing out the historical events of the twentieth century, it is possible to relate those experiences to a symbolic understanding of how evil actions such as genocide, ethnic cleansing, and rape, are products of symbolically constructed enemies in terms of race, religion, or ethnicity. However, Allison warns us not to forget that "Kant's story about the social conditioning of vice must be understood against the backdrop of transcendental freedom," therefore, it is important to understand "cultural phenomena" not only as contextually constructed, but also as sources of moral values, otherwise, "freedom" could be erased from this view and nothing morally relevant would have been accomplished in Kant's own postmetaphysical search for conceptualizing evil within the territory of human responsibility.

Gustavo Leyva's essay, "The Polyhedron of Evil" (chapter 6), goes from Kant to Schelling and extends from there to Hegel, agreeing with Neiman's view that both Schelling and Hegel went back to a metaphysical account of evil, Schelling through God, Hegel through his own theory. Neiman describes Hegel's effort as a new theodicy, and his concept of the Spirit *(Geist)* as allowing him to present the stages of the Spirit—self-consciousness—as a teleological narration that regards past evils as necessary steps in the spirit's process of self-knowledge.

Peter Dews's essay (chapter 3) offers us a different approach to the problem of evil from our contemporary perspective. Is it possible to secularize a concept like evil that has always been linked to God? Is it necessary for us to understand that the link between evil and theodicies is a structural problem related to the same effort to conceptualize evil? In reconstructing Wellmer's failed attempt to secularize Jonas's conception of evil, Dews raises pertinent questions, since what we are trying to do is to offer a renewed effort to understand evil. Dews explores Wellmer's critical emphasis vis-à-vis Jonas's effort to situate goodness and badness as two important and necessary binomies related to God. In contrast, Wellmer thinks of the concept of "radical finitude" as the only alternative to connecting God and evil in order to overcome the problematic stance of this failed attempt to describe God and evil. The only way to interpret Jonas's effort as something still valuable to us, according to Wellmer, is to regard it as a mythical tale, and in that sense, as a literary "image."[11] Dews claims that Wellmer's effort to dispel the problem of metaphysics generates its own problems, for he "makes no attempt to explain how the radically evil is to be distinguished from the merely evil or the non-good, so as to avoid such a morally destructive interdependence." Dews's essay raises the question of whether it is really possible to detach the conceptualization of evil from "its previous theological and metaphysical contexts," for it would lose the quality of "absolute irruption that is essential to it." Perhaps the only alternative can be developed through an understanding of why we humans need to relate the darkest sides of our actions with a culturally embedded idea of absolute goodness. It is clear, however, that some of the essays in this volume attempt to reframe the problem raised by Dews's interpretation by drawing an interpretative horizon of our cultural and symbolic elaborations of evil meanings and why they have been conceived as such.

In the second part of this book, the essays concentrate on more contemporary efforts to draw a plausible conception of evil. In order to understand this point of departure, we need to go back to Arendt's legacy and try to understand some of her efforts to comprehend evil.

ARENDT'S RECOVERY OF KANT IN HISTORICIZING (CONTEXTUALIZING) EVIL

Richard Bernstein quoted Arendt's statement that "the problem of evil will be the fundamental question of postwar intellectual life in Europe,"[12] in order to illuminate the error in this judgment. In reading those lines again, however, the irony is that the events in our twentieth century seem to give her judgment some support after all. Arendt observed that, in the face of evil deeds, "we actually have nothing to fall back on in order to understand a phenomenon that nevertheless confronts us with its overpowering reality and breaks down all standards we know."[13] She was the first thinker to push further what Kant had left unexplained, writing that, while Kant was "the only philosopher" who "suspected the existence" of this evil, "he immediately rationalized it in the concept of a 'perverted ill will'" (see Allison's essay).[14] Arendt's initial recovery of "radical evil" not only was totally different from Kant's notion of it, but it was meant to exemplify a concrete historical example of something that Arendt thought to be unprecedented, namely, the systematic dehumanization of human beings. This specific kind of *political evil,* Arendt called it *radical evil* to distinguish it from all other forms of domination by political regimes. Not only did Arendt appropriate Kant's moral notion of radical evil in order to use it differently, in a political theory of evil, but she also employed Kant's notion of judgment as a new hermeneutical tool to describe a political understanding of totalitarianism.[15] She justified her arbitrary use of the term "radical evil" by arguing that Kant had discovered a concept that was essential for evil, that is, *judgment—* the idea of becoming a disinterested, impartial, observer of worldly affairs. What seems extraordinary, however, is that in her search for a possible connection between an aesthetic dimension (taste) and a moral one (judging), Arendt had to go all the way back to Kant, and not Heidegger, to recover a fundamental condition for judging evil deeds. While she tried to correlate these realms in her historical examples, a space for the interaction between the two spheres—where political and moral judgment should interact with each other—she developed a "dialogue"[16] with her historical moment, with totalitarianism, placing some of its features at the center of her analytical frame. Judging became for Arendt a technique of getting rid of the familiar in order to step into the realm of the unprecedented "horrors" of our times, this was the place where she needed the help of the power of imagination, "a fearful imagination" to bridge the "abysses of remoteness until we can see and understand everything that is too far away from us as though it were our own affair."[17] Arendt seemed to be connecting her ideas of judgment taken from Kant with a new notion of imagination clearly linked to her own hermeneutics. Arendt turned to the aesthetic dimension where "imagination" belongs, claiming that she needed it because it "is concerned with the particular darkness of the human heart and the peculiar density which surrounds everything [that] is real."[18]

At the same time, Arendt developed this hermeneutics of her times as a political theory that allowed her to disconnect the features of totalitarianism from other historical moments of domination and cruelty. Her exercise of hermeneutical judgment needed here to concentrate on what was truly unique about the concentration camps and the terror implemented in them. She described her initial understanding of evil as an effort to grasp why "systematic torture and systematic starvation *create an atmosphere of permanent dying, in which death as well as life is effectively abstracted*" making the normative idea of human beings become superfluous.[19] This description of evil points to how the technologies of terror seemed to constitute a dehumanization that eradicated all human capacities to react, suppressing spontaneity, which is one of humanity's most precious features. Here Arendt's descriptions of what happened in the Holocaust have proven capable of leading us into the creation of new tools to understand tragedies that we face in our contemporary horizon (see Robert Fine's essay in chapter 8). "Radical evil" meant for Arendt a specter of "the danger of the corpse factories and the holes of oblivion, with populations and homelessness everywhere on the increase, [where] masses of people are continuously rendered [as] superfluous."[20] She took the examples of two totalitarian regimes and described their specific features, grasping that terror was their very essence. By renaming the features of evil deeds performed by human beings on those who had no power to defend themselves, Arendt stumbled into the space of the "darkness" where "the use of terror" is the weapon "to prove that there are no limits to human power, and that there is nothing built-in or permanent about human dignity."[21] The Nazi structures weighed so heavily that the dehumanizing effect was felt simultaneously by the perpetrators and their victims.

Arendt is thus able to configure a new theory of political judgment which enables her to visualize a postmetaphysical theory of evil. In her innovative concept of a principle of "totalitarian terror," she describes a system capable of "total domination" that deals entirely with new goals of destroying humanity to recreate it again, in order to prove that domination can make humanity something to be programmed.

Thus, even if Arendt's conceptual path to evil is filled with gaps, it has stimulated newer interpretations such that her conceptual legacy has become a fruitful site for finding tools that can be clarified and renewed. It is not surprising, then, to find that most of the essays in this volume make creative use of her concepts. Carlos Pereda (chapter 13), for example, employs the term "banality of evil" to describe how military governments in South America, giving up their power in the face of social and economic bankruptcy, brought their societies to moral collapse, forcing them afterwards to "forget and forgive" on the grounds that raising legal claims against the military threatened social destabilization. The most well-known case is Argentina, where the military officers were found guilty at a criminal trial but were set free because of the fear created by the proliferation of military coups, which ceased only when leaders were promised a general amnesty.[22] Subsequently, under the presidencies of Alfonsín and Menem, Argentinians created first a special "law" to liberate the perpetrators, a law that justified their murderous actions on the grounds that as soldiers they had to obey the orders, and then, with Menem, all militaries enjoyed a general amnesty. Chile waited patiently until the dictator stepped out of power, guaranteeing his own amnesty by transforming the constitution and naming himself a "senator for life," so that his office immunity spared him of legal recrimination. Pereda uses the notion of "banality" to describe how easily societies give up their moral claims and bury their memories of evil in order to secure a peaceful transition to democracy.

On the other hand, Arendt's conceptualizations were products of her experiences and her two concepts of evil crystallized different issues of her time. They are also related to Arendt's effort to exercise moral and political judgment, both of which had to break new conceptual grounds because the existent philosophical and political traditions did not offer any help in rethinking human cruelty, especially after the Holocaust (see my essay, chapter 15, on the connection between storytelling and judgment; Susan Neiman's view, chapter 2, of Arendt's stories as new theodicies, and Robert Fine's essay, chapter 8, about Arendt's conception of understanding the Holocaust).

One of the first things Arendt did was to use the concept of "evil" in a totally different sense from the one we have just seen. Arendt's second effort to conceptualize evil made her transition between her idea of political judgment, as Ronald Beiner has well explained,[23] and her late theory of judgment related more to a moral dimension of the individual spectator. The now well-known exchange of opinions between Karl Jaspers and Arendt that took place immediately after the war, when they were both grappling with how to conceptualize evil, seems a good starting point for our historical reconstruction. Jaspers was writing his *Schuldfrage (The Guilt Question)* and Arendt had began to elaborate a concept of "radical evil" to describe what had happened in totalitarian regimes. Much has been written about the correspondence between the two authors,[24] and this specific exchange, and specialists have discussed the process by which Arendt moved from her initial theory to her later, more polemical, theory on the "banality of evil."[25] There has been growing interest in this exchange precisely because it reflects our own puzzlement about the possible meanings of evil. What happened was that Jaspers criticized Arendt's use of the idea of "monstrousness" in regard to the Nazis, objecting that it suggested a "greatness" at odds with what Jaspers believed to be the Nazis' "prosaic triviality."[26] Arendt accepted Jaspers's criticism and later reformulated her ideas while attending the Eichmann trial, finally describing Eichmann as a particular exemplar of the figure she coined as embodying the "banality of evil." Arendt performed her own particular judgment, only this time, she did it strictly *on moral grounds*.

What happened in Arendt's mind between these two different periods is the subject of different and even contradictory interpretations.[27] In Richard Bernstein's last book on Arendt,[28] for example, we find a strong claim about the influence Jaspers's exercised in Arendt changing her mind. However, we are only starting the process of revising Arendt's legacy and this subject will be open to new hermeneutic exercises that will undoubtedly compel us to revise our views. It seems clear, however, that Jaspers could only have exerted such an influence on Arendt if she had already understood why "radical evil," the Kantian term, could give a wrong connection between human deeds and otherworldly monstrousness, which alerted her as something not from this world, something "nightmarish" and not human. An interpretation that necessarily gave great weight to the perpetrators' demonic powers instead of focusing on the core of a conscious mind when choosing to do an evil action (see Ferrara's essay in chapter 10). Arendt drew apart from a metaphysics of evil but much of her contemporaries were still trying to sort their way out of that. Already in her 1945 review of Denis de Rougemont's *The Devil's Share*, Arendt expressed her disdain at his "desperate attempt not to be confronted with this nightmare in spiritual nakedness." Rougemont instead, "picks up from the great and beautiful arsenal of time-honored figures and images that seems to correspond to or to interpret the new shocks that rock old foundations" and leaves us with traditional views of evil. Thus, Arendt concludes, "instead of facing the music of man's genuine capacity for evil and analyzing the nature of man, he [Rougemont] in turn, ventures into a flight from reality and writes on the nature of the

Devil, thereby, despite all dialectics, evading the responsibility of man for his deeds."[29] Seeing evil as she later does—as a banality that is exemplified by a subject who cannot rid himself of his own clichés in rendering some coherent explanation of his actions—seems to lead to a more complex interpretation of human nature. Arendt's subtle view of what we are as humans led her to perceive a different kind of dehumanizing perspective than the one she had suggested earlier. Instead of seeing this radical evil through the strategies of dehumanizing humans, through a permanent technique of instilling fear and constant suffering, she turned to the agents' incapacity for moral reflection. What she was searching for is to enter into the mind of a particular perpetrator in order to learn what impeded him from thinking in moral terms and on "individual grounds" without banisters. It was this incapacity that she meant when she used the term "banality of evil."

This later attempt to come to terms with "evil" implicitly elided two different kinds of problems. One problem was naming "evil deeds" by attributing agency and responsibility. Arendt did this by using her "judgment" of a concrete human being—Eichmann.[30] For Eichmann, doing evil was a job, a matter of discipline, and how he justified himself, his crooked moral criteria, and his own distortions in his judgment are the pieces that Arendt links together for us in her account of the trial. At the same time, however, Arendt is also motivated by a second problem, namely, how to develop and apply her own "personal moral judgment," a reflective judgment. This second problem is something Arendt failed to explain to her critics. For the "banality of evil" is not only a *reflexive term* that Arendt used to call attention to her interpretation of evil as the *shallowness* of an individual, but an empirical description of the actions of a concrete human being. This effort introduces a new understanding of evil agency, one that relates the loss of Eichmann's perspective to a wrong "moral" judgment, and seems to shift away from her previous political emphasis on earlier "collective" strategies of evil (e.g., in *The Origins of Totalitarianism*). This is the reason why Arendt refused to accept Mary McCarthy's criticism that she had used the term "banal" in a wrong way. McCarthy insisted that the English term "banal" means "trivial," something "light."[31] Arendt wanted to transform this meaning, linking it to the story of her personal experience of listening to such a man while exercising the irony of a detached impartial spectator, of her very own reflective judgment. Arendt trusted language and its disclosive critical capacities. But Arendt failed to offer a consistent perspective on this new meaning to her critics, and the two different levels in which judgment was being offered are confused and intermingled in the minds of her critics.

Arendt's description of the trial draws another important distinction. As Dana Villa has well argued, this new analytical distinction is only possible when Arendt understands Eichmann's failure to confront his own responsibility, a fact that situates Eichmann's explanation of his deeds as a conflation between obeying the law and obeying his moral duty. This detected distinction between "morality with legality"[32] allows Arendt's theory to become an important source for the reflection of evil when related to political and legal responsibilities. Most of the evil actions performed by militaries seem complicated to judge legally because of their claim that they were only obeying their orders, or they were following the wicked laws of their times (such as the Nazis). On one level, Arendt refers simply to Eichmann's mistaken judgment, in his account of why he felt compelled to obey the "Nazis' laws."[33] As Maeve Cooke and Richard Bernstein remind us in their essays, this level is consistent with a reading of Kant's morality. On a second level, the important distinction of one's capacity for moral judgment becomes a crucial feature of one's possibility to distinguish right and wrong, a problem that Eichmann could not understand because he did not distinguish between his moral and his legal duties.

Despite Arendt's failure to defend herself against her critics, she takes an important step beyond Kant in the creation of a postmetaphysical theory by offering us some new material for thinking about the possible mediation between freedom, agency, and individual responsibility with historical judgments, which help us create new moral, political, and legal vocabularies. She does so by developing two specific figures of evil, and by drawing a *historical* connection between evil and the reflective horizon of two different roles of judgment, a political one (analyzed in *The Origins of Totalitarianism* and in the concept of "criminal responsibility" that she describes when attending the Eichmann trial), and the moral one (when describing Eichmann as having lost his sanity in terms of his morality because he had confused it with obeying the Nazi "criminal" laws).[34]

On another level, however, Arendt emphasized that judgment might also have to do with describing evil experiences with new words. Only by creating new vocabularies can we grasp things that otherwise would remain opaque. For Arendt, it is important to stress that her theory of evil implied the connection between the disclosive capacities of language and the situating of descriptions of evil deeds in a historical context and as particular exemplars of reflective judgment. In this way, a moral and political frame is made possible only through the words that she coined. Arendt wanted to distort the ordinary meanings of words by using them in a totally different way, in order to describe something that could not even be thought before. She wanted to use words to give a violent shock, illuminating the novelty of the catastrophe. The missing link is Arendt's own explicit justification for this emphasis, a failure that can be ascribed to her own lack of consciousness about the interrelation between language, understanding new meanings against the backdrop of tradition, and interpretation, her own exercise of a hermeneutics of evil. This is evident in the description she offered of her role in writing about the Eichmann trial—"just describing facts"—as she wrote to Mary McCarthy, while she was doing much more than that,[35] she was *interpreting* those facts by virtue of her own individual judgment.

This evidence of Arendt's final failure to gain clarity about her own efforts to conceptualize evil clearly has impeded the effort to come to an agreement about her political and philosophical legacies. This is the reason why many of the essays in this volume not only develop her ideas further but criticize the contradictions in her work. Whatever these criticisms and elaborations are, Arendt seems to be a necessary point of reference for any consideration of evil today.

POSTMETAPHYSICAL APPROACHES FOR A THEORY OF EVIL

The essays by Jeffrey C. Alexander, Alessandro Ferrara, Sergio Pérez, and Manuel Cruz (chapters 9 to 12) contribute further to the development of a theory of evil. Although the essays have some shared interests (i.e., the concern about why Habermas has not offered a perspective on this problem, with the legacies of Arendt), they offer different and even contradictory perspectives. Ferrara's approach is to gain clarity about "radical" evil as opposed to "ordinary" evil, and to develop his particular approach to judgment in relation to evil. Ferrara's strongest claim is that Arendt was right in not wanting to declare "evil" as something "monstrous," because "a demonic view of what happened at Auschwitz and other such places as the embodiment of evil would amount to a posthumous vindication of a Hitlerian understanding of the moral world as the theater of a deadly confrontation between good and evil."[36] Ferrara uses his criteria of authenticity and judgment to situate "radical evil" as "paradigmatic evil" (i.e., the Holocaust). It is through our judgments that we are able to grasp how inconsistent the principles of radical evil are with our universal notions of "humanity." "The grounding of such principle," argues Ferrara, "rests on nothing else than the fact that we could not regard us as ourselves anymore, as Western moderns of the twentieth and twenty-first centuries, if we embraced a view of the moral life that did not include it." A second stance Ferrara takes is to argue for the normative role of a concept such as "humanity" which must be present in any idea of a political democratic community. Ferrara develops a Durkheimian approach to "radical evil" by claiming that "the criterion for the radicality of radical evil ought perhaps to be internal to us, the moral community, rather than external, objective. Evil then is perhaps best conceived as a *horizon* that moves with us, rather than as something that stands over against us."

This is where the cultural approach of Jeffrey C. Alexander becomes a relevant contribution to the social sciences and to philosophy in particular. If we think of the tasks of moral judgment as a moral education through a careful hermeneutic reading of how we have created different historical meanings about who the evildoers are, then we will understand that people construct their own ideas of identity and of what is valuable against what is not. "Evil can never be eliminated from the social world," argues Alexander; thus, we must become aware of how we build up our identities and of the need to defend normative conceptions and critical readings that allow us some reflexivity and knowledge. "Good and evil" should be seen, argues Alexander, as products of our cultural understanding. From the point of view of the social sciences, this definitely seems to be a starting point, and Ferrara's essay supports this claim. The challenge becomes, then, to stress that what matters are the collective spaces where democratic societies teach their civil societies the normative contents of moral values and how they all relate and begin with justice and solidarity as forces against cruelty. Democratic societies can help us cope with our "human frailties" by creating institutional mechanisms (legal, moral, and political) that make us aware of how we tend to construct the "good and bad" as mechanisms of exclusion by defining ourselves "against" others. The implicit idea that "otherness" is "bad" seems to be an element to analyze critically. Democratic societies should commit themselves to a notion that the good implies aligning justice with concrete ways of establishing solidarity, that the idea of "equal respect to all humans" is not just a phrase but the way we all must behave and feel. In short, we must build up a strong universalistic moral culture. Alexander, thus, would agree with Arendt's idea that the tasks of storytelling allow the readers to become reflexive about how we build and construct our notions of what is evil as mechanisms of identity and exclusion. As with Ferrara, the core of Alexander's contribution in this volume is his interpretation of Durkheim's legacy through a reading of "the sacred and the profane" as the two basic ways that humans construct meanings in our world. Alexander stresses that only through contrasts are we able to develop our notions of the good: "For every effort to institutionalize comforting and inspiring images of the socially good and right, there is an interlinked and equally determined effort to construct social evil in a horrendous, frightening, and equally realistic way." Thus we need to be conscious of what a democratic, moral culture should offer against our own weaknesses.

The final section concentrates on the impact of narratives for theorizing evil. Narratives present themselves as ways to cope with evil only if they are also related to reflective moral judgment (see my essay, chapter 15), for only in this manner can narratives become forms of learning from the past, which project a different future for societies that have confronted destruction. While Carol Bernstein dedicates her essay to tracing the complexities of the preservation of memory, she insists, by contrast, on the impossibility of communicating the horrors of lived experiences in the Holocaust: "The very language the survivors used—their difficulty in speaking words for ordinary things, which had become extraordinary, or their inability to speak, sometimes for decades—challenges the authority of the storyteller and his responsibility for communicating both the suppressed stories of the immediate past and the now-distant stories of an unreachable past." Bernstein's aesthetic knowledge shows the reader how impossible it is, after the Holocaust, to continue our lives as if nothing happened. Stories and descriptions after the Holocaust must suffer total transformations. Aesthetic discourses are the first to devote themselves to the search for something different. Bernstein's historical reconstruction allows us to understand that the idea of "narrative" itself would never have survived if it were not linked to evil, for as she says, "without some forms of evil, we are not likely to have encountered many if not all of the dominant forms of narrative. Insofar as narrative is a vehicle for cultural memory, the latter has long been on familiar terms with evil." The problem here is not simple, for Bernstein alerts us to the fact that there are witnesses who are not alive to relate their experiences. There are also formal elements that seem contradictory to the idea of narrative closure, for many experiences of evil seem impossible to ever settle completely. For Bernstein, what is meaningful in stories is that "memory confronts its double and its antithesis: it knows, knowing that it does not know."

We need to find ways for the consciousness of evil deeds to become a way of learning about our fragility, part and parcel of a shared humanity that compels us to seek institutional protections to counterbalance human destruction. Thematizing evil should begin by alerting us to our human ways of dehumanizing others. As this introduction comes to an end, it is necessary to point out the paths that one can find to think of evil as situated on postmetaphysical grounds. As seen with the paradigmatic thinker that Hannah Arendt has become, especially when thinking about evil, one can analyze evil through a moral theory, a political one, or a legal theory. These fields are all interrelated, but they are not the same. By developing some insights of these perspectives, our book claims that if it is possible for humans to show that we have learned from our mistakes, this effort at understanding evil in these three areas must surely be one of our main concerns. If we can construct moral and political concepts that best comprehend the meaning of evil deeds, and the agency and responsibility of cruelty, then legal institutions must proceed to translate these meanings into the realm of positive law, by configuring a set of rights to defend humans against other humans and to seek accountability and legal responsibility in democratic laws. Only then will we make our experiences of tragedies like the Holocaust, the genocides of Armenia, the Balkans, Cambodia, and Rwanda, and the ethnic cleansings in Sebrenice and Kosovo, the historical examples that can lead us to configure a collective moral frame—a step needed as a new stage of *moral learning* of the historical textures of our times, a collective memory that should remind us always of our fragile and imperfect moral selves.

PART ONE

A Critical Review of Evil

Is God Evil?

Isabel Cabrera

If we ask a believer in the Judeo-Christian religious tradition[1] if God is evil, he would most likely answer: "No, on the contrary, God is good, infinitely good." For some, the claim that God is good is even a truth that emerges from an analysis of the concept of God. Nevertheless, as we know, the acceptance of this truth (regardless of whether it is analytic) generates the question of the theodicy: If God is good, then why does God permit evil? Throughout the centuries, many authors in the Judeo-Christian tradition have attempted to answer this difficult and painful question; and arguably none has truly succeeded.

The purpose of this essay is not to solve the problem of the theodicy, but to dissolve it by arguing that, on the one hand, the stock solutions turn out to be unsatisfactory and, on the other, the problem is generated by the acceptance of a conception of God that is not the only possible one nor even the most attractive one. To that end, I divide the essay into four sections. The first makes explicit two presuppositions of the question of the theodicy: the conception of God as a moral subject whose purposes, actions, and omissions can be morally judged; and the idea of unnecessary suffering as the measure of moral evil. The second section briefly examines the four most common responses to the problem of the theodicy, highlighting their weaknesses. The third section seeks to question the conception of God as a being endowed with purposes and will, contrasting it with a concept of the sacred that is rooted in religious experience, a conception in which God is not thought of as a moral subject. Finally, the fourth section attempts to find a role for anthropomorphic language about God that comports well with this alternative conception and that consequently does not allow the problem of the theodicy to reemerge.

It seems to me that everything I have written here is already present in the Book of Job, albeit read from a certain standpoint that I will not defend in detail here. In any case, this essay may be considered as a gloss on Job.

I. SOME PRESUPPOSITIONS OF THE QUESTION OF THE THEODICY

When we describe some intention, action, or conduct as morally bad, what are we calling attention to? First and foremost, that the action in question is incorrect, that it deviates from a norm or principle that we accept as a moral rule. Yet how do we know what are the rules from which we should seek deviations? Faced with this difficult question, one of the most commonly employed criteria is suffering: someone does something morally bad if he causes harm, that is, if he produces unnecessary suffering in others. Typically, then, the index of evil is suffering; indeed, we always can—and usually do—argue that there is no moral wrong where there is no harm. Nevertheless, it is obvious that not all suffering makes for a moral wrong. In order for it to do so, two further conditions must be satisfied: there must be a person responsible for the evil, and the person responsible must lack motives that justify it. The doctor who sets a dislocated bone produces pain in the patient, but his conduct is not morally reprehensible; on the contrary, in this case the pain is necessary and consequently justified, so the suffering produced does not constitute a moral wrong. On the other hand, if there is no one to whom the harmful action can be attributed, then the suffering involved will not reflect a wrong of a moral character. If a plague of locusts destroys crops and produces famine, we say that there was a wrong, but we cannot say that it is of a moral nature, since although the locusts were the cause, it is obvious that we cannot attribute moral responsibility to them. In order to attribute moral responsibility we need a person, someone endowed with at least a certain degree of consciousness and will, who acted in a certain manner while being able to do otherwise. It is for this reason that in order to judge that someone did wrong, we must be able to credit him with, if not an explicit intention, at least carelessness or negligence.

In short, in order to attribute a wrong of a moral character to someone, three conditions must be satisfied: that the subject is responsible for his action; that his action has harmful consequences (i.e., that it produces suffering in others or in himself); and, finally, that this suffering is unjustified. So it is that when someone tries to exonerate himself of an evil that is attributed to him, he typically avails himself of one of three ways out: he claims either that his action was innocuous and lacks harmful consequences; or that he did it because he considered it necessary for a greater good; or that he did it unintentionally, without realizing it, or because he could not do otherwise, which is to say that he acted either unwittingly or involuntarily.

With this in mind, I would now like to return the concern of the theodicy: how is it that God, being infinitely good, allows evil? There can be no doubt that the world is full of it; crimes, injustice, wars, illnesses, and natural catastrophes are part of our everyday reality. And this evil results daily in suffering which rarely comes back upon those who cause it. For the religious believer, the conspicuous existence of evil raises painful questions. There is no doubt that, as the Judeo-Christian tradition has pointed out time and again, a great deal of this evil is our fault. Nevertheless, there is a portion of these evils—a portion that is not at all inconsiderable—that cannot be the responsibility of humans: the majority of illnesses and natural catastrophes harm us without our having done anything to bring them about. But if human beings are not responsible, is this evil the responsibility of God? Is God to blame for the evil we do not cause?

Let us pause for a moment, however. According to what we saw at the outset, to describe some action that we attribute to God as morally wrong implies three things: that God is responsible for his actions, that certain of God's actions produce suffering, and finally, that this suffering is unnecessary (i.e., that it is not justified). The first idea, the attribution of responsibility to God, is something very few theists in the Western tradition put in doubt. Usually, the believer thinks that God is responsible for his creation, and besides being good, God is omniscient. We suppose, then, that he does everything knowingly and freely, so that there is no way to maintain that God acts unintentionally. As far as the second point is concerned, there is no room for doubt: the evil that we do not produce also harms us; everyday, catastrophes and illnesses take many lives and generate a great deal of human suffering. And although God does not directly produce or cause this evil, he does indeed seem responsible for permitting it, since (according to the traditional theist) all that happens, happens with God's consent. What about the third claim? Might it be that God does not always have good reasons for doing what he does and permitting what he permits? Or is it possible that God permits suffering for good and just motives? Answers to the problem of the theodicy have usually followed the latter path. So it is that the problem of the theodicy has been transformed into the problem of the meaning of suffering.

II. FOUR CLASSIC REJOINDERS TO THE PROBLEM OF THE THEODICY

Let us briefly consider those answers to the problem of the theodicy that leave untouched the assumption that God can be judged morally and instead focus their attack on the other assumption, namely, that the suffering God permits is unnecessary. And to show that this suffering is justified, believers defend (and occasionally combine) the following four answers: (1) suffering is a punishment; (2) suffering is a test or trial; (3) suffering is the prelude to eternal life; or (4) suffering is a mystery.

The first response is very ancient. The idea that comes from the Old

Testament is that Yahweh punishes those who do not obey his will, making them suffer. The blessings of the Jewish god bring peace and well-being; his curses, tribulation and loss. To avoid suffering, the believer must obey, respect the terms of the Covenant, and not transgress the mandates of his god. This idea, which forms the traditional theory of retribution found in the Old Testament and is crystallized in Deuteronomy,[2] is maintained almost unaltered until the Book of Job, where it is argued that suffering is not always deserved. Indeed it rarely is, as we would now say; God appears to punish the righteous and the wicked indiscriminately. The manifest presence of innocent suffering renders this first response exceedingly weak. To think that suffering is a punishment is to suppose that any afflicted person is guilty—even a newborn—and we cannot accept that this should be so. The question is posed anew: if God permits evil in order to punish, why does he allow those to suffer who do not deserve punishment? It is obvious that neither illnesses nor mudslides choose to carry off only the guilty.

The second response—that suffering is a test—is the most common way of handling such unresolved cases. If innocent people suffer without deserving it, then there are cases where God sends suffering not to punish but rather to test. But to test what? Celebrated passages from the Old Testament give an answer: to test one's fear of God and one's fidelity to him. This is what the author of Ecclesiasticus (among others) preaches: "Accept what is brought upon you, and in changes that humble you be patient. For gold is tested in the fire and acceptable men in the furnace of humiliation."[3]

Thus the Judeo-Christian tradition has repeatedly called attention to the courage of Abraham and other patriarchs, to the patience of the celebrated Job, and to Christ's acceptance of the cup of bitterness. All of them accepted a painful fate out of fear or love of their god. Yet what is God trying to accomplish when he tests a righteous person by means of suffering? On this issue, Maimonides thinks that Yahweh seeks to bequeath an example that will inspire bravery in others (as in the case of Abraham and perhaps that of Job). Other thinkers, mainly Christians, believe, moreover, that God's purpose is to perpetuate a message of redemption and salvation (as in the case of Jesus Christ). In this vein, a Protestant theologian writes:

The Son of God suffered unto the
Death not that men might not suffer, but
That their sufferings might be like His.[4]

First Yahweh, and later God the Father, have good reasons for permitting such tests; what is more, the biblical texts that refer to them usually include an ending in which God rewards those who have submitted to his tests with a greater good. However, does it really happen that all who suffer are being tested? And is it actually the case that those who pass the tests are compensated? How can this be if many do not even have time to react, let alone receive compensation, because they die as a result of the test? Suffering crushes them without serving any educational purpose. The second response also leaves unresolved cases. So we come, it seems to me, to the third possibility: the view that suffering is a prelude to eternal life.

In contrast to the Hebraic doctrine of retribution, the Christian tradition proposes that there exists another life where the injustices of the present one are remedied. God permits the suffering of the righteous because he is keeping for them the reward of another life. Sometimes suffering is even regarded as the price we must pay to make ourselves worthy of the other life. God thus appears to be justified in permitting evil because he has reserved for us a greater good, which we obtain if we expiate our sins as much as if we submit ourselves to testing. I believe that here we come up against a hope that at times we cannot share. What if there is no other life in which God compensates us for the wrongs suffered in this one? What is more, this response contains a danger that has been pointed out elsewhere: to resolve the injustices of this life with the promise of another is to depreciate and devalue this life, and to induce resignation and passivity. This means that for a believer who is unwilling to renounce the value of this life or who does not believe in eternal life, the suffering of the innocent continues to demand an explanation and threatens to leave us with a god indifferent to injustice.

Finally, the fourth response consists in saying that what we regard as evil is in reality not evil, but good. We have a limited and fragmented perspective of things, and for that reason cannot completely understand what an event means; the particular evil (for us) is in fact, when seen from the correct perspective—which is to say, the perspective of God—a general good (for the universe). God knows why he does things, although for us this remains a mystery. God acts knowingly and freely, but his reason and his will are unfathomable mysteries. Pointing out this possibility leaves us just as we were: without understanding and without being able to help thinking that the suffering we undergo, and for which we as a species are not responsible, is a senseless evil that appears entirely gratuitous. We are told that we cannot blame God for this; but we are not told why not. This response offers no explanation; it merely points out a limit, and tells us that the problem has no solution.

On the basis of the foregoing, none of the classic solutions to the problem of the theodicy turns out to be completely satisfactory. Once we allow that God can be judged morally—once we accept that the usual concepts of moral good and evil are applicable to what God does and permits—then the question of whether God is responsible for any evil inevitably arises, and it is not clear that we can exonerate him of all wrongdoing. This is why, when we are faced with the problem of the theodicy, the best alternative may well be not to try to answer the question, but to avoid it. Yet how can it be avoided?

III. THE SHIFT FROM GOD TO THE SACRED

Earlier, we noted that to hold someone responsible for an evil of a moral character, we needed to consider him as a person—although not necessarily human—endowed with consciousness and will. We also observed that the majority of thinkers in the Judeo-Christian tradition assumed this conception of God. Consequently, if we reject this conception of God as a moral subject like us—a conception that is ultimately anthropomorphic—then it is not clear how the problem of the theodicy could be formulated. However, this apparently implies the abandonment of the Judeo-Christian tradition. Both the god of Abraham and the god of Jesus are lawmakers and are thought of by the greater part of the faithful as analogous to a king or a father, which is to say as a person (albeit not a human one). Nevertheless, there is an underlying element in the religious experience of the very same tradition that allows us to set aside the conception of God as a transcendent being endowed with thought and will, and directs us to another, more fundamental conception, one in which the deity cannot be the subject of our moral judgments.

Rudolf Otto suggests that the conception of God as a moral subject is a subsequent rationalization of the original object of religious experience.[5] The tremendous mystery that is the object of the original numinous experience is converted into a personal god as the rational idea of divine justice gradually pervades and infiltrates this experience. However, to maintain that God has purposes that we can judge as just or unjust is to think, as Spinoza said, of a god in the image and likeness of human beings.[6] And why should one think God is something analogous to a person? Why not assume, once and for all, that moral evaluations and judgments only concern human beings? Why not transcend the anthropomorphism that has permeated almost all of Western theology by reclaiming an archaic but ultimately basic conception of the sacred? Once again, however, if we dispense with the traditional conception, what is to take the place of a god endowed with will and thought? Does it not become empty for the believer? When Spinoza proposes to abandon the anthropomorphic conception of God, he replaces it with a conception of an immanent god who is usually indistinguishable from Nature. Has God then been dissolved among the fragments of the universe in this way?

It seems to me that the phenomenology of religion is right about a central issue: in order to answer the question, "What is God?" we need to start with god as the intentional object of human beliefs, experiences, and practices that have been considered and are considered religious. Yet the idea that the Judeo-Christian religious texts reveal—especially where they make an experience explicit or stress certain practices such as sacrifice—is not always that of a god-person. So it is that many contemporary humanists belonging to the same Judeo-Christian tradition prefer to speak of "the sacred" and not of "God," with the aim of referring to the intentional object of religious experience. In this way, a hasty conclusion is avoided: whereas the term "God" suggests a person, "the sacred" carries no such association (although it does not exclude it). Furthermore, "the sacred," in virtue of being an adjective, is conceived analogously to "the beautiful" or "the good." This means that religion, like aesthetics or morality, seems to represent a sphere of values that can be grasped and appreciated by human beings.

The tradition that starts with William James, and even more clearly with Rudolf Otto, has attempted to characterize the sacred in many different ways, though all these characterizations are related.[7] Here I shall try neither to review them nor to privilege any one of them. Despite this, I allude to them because I believe that all of them—and in a certain sense, each taken on its own—constitute an alternative conception of the sacred, in which God is not regarded as a moral subject. To bring this section to a close, I would merely like to give an example of what I mean: the dissolution of the problem of the theodicy as a result of a change in the conception of God. And I know of no better example than the Book of Job.

Throughout the bulk of the poem that makes up the text of Job, it is clear that when Job asks Yahweh for an explanation, he thinks of Yahweh as someone who is capable of providing him with it. His god is the god of the Covenant, who has agreed to be responsible for the fate of his creatures. Thus, as Fingarette has pointed out,[8] Job addresses God in legalistic language in which Yahweh is at times a prosecutor, at times a judge, and is always an ardently desired but absent defender. As all readers of the book know, Yahweh never gives the eagerly awaited explanation and yet there comes a moment when Job—who until then has seemed relentless—ceases to question. The final chapters of the book tell of the religious experience that supposedly convinced Job and extinguished his indignation. Yahweh is revealed as a power, creator of an enormous natural diversity, of an universe both astonishing and sublime, but devoid of moral purposes. The Voice from the Whirlwind, that answers Job does not speak—as Otto and Fingarette have noted—either of good ends nor of reasons that explain the innocent suffering of Job; in this sense, the Voice from the Whirlwind does not resolve Job's problem, but instead dissolves it, since it discloses a deity that is not subject to moral evaluation. If the universe is not responsive to human expectations, why should God be? And justice and morality, I am afraid, are concerns that are fundamentally human.[9]

But if we do not conceive of God as a transcendent being who can be judged morally, then we can find in him neither the meaning of suffering nor the explanation of the evil that engulfs us. Job remains speechless, but his suffering remains without an answer. He will no longer need to seek the answer in God, but this does not mean that the answer has been found.

Related to the conception of God as moral is the idea that religious faith somehow gives suffering a meaning. Indeed, as we noted earlier, the classic responses to the problem of the theodicy are also responses to the problem of the meaning of suffering. But how can this question be reformulated with respect to the sacred? How can room be made for the consolation the believer seeks in God when he is tormented by the senselessness of suffering? The alternative conception of the sacred seems alien and indifferent to these concerns. In this sense, the sarcastic dialogue Robert Frost imagines taking place years later between Job and Yahweh is very much to the point. There God says to Job,

> Too long I've owed you this apology
> For the apparently unmeaning sorrow
> You were afflicted with in those old days.
> But it was of the essence of the trial
> You shouldn't understand it at the time.
> It had to seem unmeaning to have meaning.
> And it came out all right. I have no doubt
> You realize by now the part you played
> To stultify the Deuteronomist
> And change the tenor of religious thought.
> My thanks are to you for releasing me
> From moral bondage to the human race.
> The only free will there at first was man's
> Who could do good or evil as he chose.
> I had no choice but I must follow him . . .
>
> I had to prosper good and punish evil.
> You changed all that. You set me free to reign.
> You are the Emancipator of your God . . . [10]

Once again, however, if God is freed from concerning himself with the human yearning for justice, then in what sense can religious faith help to resolve the problem of the meaning of suffering? Religion, it seems to me, can give only a partial answer, in a way similar to that in which other things also help us quell this anxiety: beauty, love, and solidarity are also partial responses to the problem of the meaning of life and the meaning of suffering. They are responses inasmuch as they give us another perspective, and remind us that in this life there are other things besides pain. However, there may well be no point in seeking more consolation than this from a religious faith that is directed to a god that is not considered a morally responsible agent but a tremendous mystery.

IV. THE PLACE FOR ANTHROPOMORPHIC LANGUAGE

Finally, I would like to say something about a problem that is, in my view, important. It might be said that imposing a conception of the sacred on the idea of a transcendent God means ignoring the bulk of what has been said about God within the Judeo-Christian tradition. There is no doubt that the majority of religious texts use anthropomorphic language and speak of God as if they were dealing with a transcendent being who establishes covenants with his creatures and even, according to some, becomes incarnate in the figure of Jesus. What is one to say about this?

Some analyses of religious experience have underscored the presence of a feeling of closeness, of a connection, often intimate, with the sacred; this element of connection or closeness is necessary to give meaning to prayer, worship, invocation, and other religious practices. The believer not only perceives or experiences something as sacred but also believes that he can establish a personal relationship with it, and he usually establishes it by means of these religious practices. As Buber acutely observes, the believer typically believes in a God whom he can address as a Thou. It is no accident that the very word "religion" has its origin in this idea of a relation or link with the sacred. But this need for closeness does not necessarily commit us to a conception of God as something analogous to a person. There are transcendent deities endowed with intellect and will that are nevertheless remote: we may think of the unmoved mover of Aristotle, the demiurge of Plato, or the god of some of the English deists. On the other hand, there are religious conceptions that are immanent, and that maintain that God is not something analogous to a person, but which nevertheless permit a close relationship: we may think of the archaic religious framework centered on manna, or of the way in which Goethe speaks of and to Nature, to mention a few of the examples Buber gives in his *I and Thou*.

Given this fact, namely that the need for closeness and for a relation with the sacred is an element present in most religious experiences, phenomenological analyses normally interpret religious language as being analogical instead of descriptive. When the author refers to God as the Lord of the Armies, as a king or as a father, he is not describing who God is; instead, he is expressing the sort of feelings and experiences aroused in him by the sacred. In fact, in many places the texts refer to God using images that, if interpreted descriptively, make Yahweh a ferocious animal, a whirlwind, a desert storm, or a poisoned dart; here, too, it is clear that there is an analogical use of language.

In any case, it seems that to renounce anthropomorphic language is to renounce intimacy with God. Conceiving of God as a person who can share certain of our concerns opens up the possibility of talking with him, and hence of praying. On the other hand, the sacred—which I suggested as an alternative conception—does not seem to be something with which we could communicate in a personal way. In this sense, the form of expression is not irrelevant; to the believer, it matters whether an anthropomorphic language or a set of cosmic symbols is employed, because the form facilitates the invocation of God and thus the sensation of closeness to God. What matters is not simply successfully referring (however vaguely) to God, to the Wholly Other, it is also important to establish a certain sort of relationship with it.

But the sacred seems liable to evaporate and dissolve more easily than does a personal god. For this reason (among others), religions have personalized their deities, and virtually no believer would pray to or speak with a god who had a name other than the god in whom he believes. Thus if, as is usually the case, the believer is not inclined to forgo a personal relationship with the sacred, he may succumb to the natural temptation of treating it as a "You," but always knowing on some level that this is merely a manner of speaking. It seems to me that the reflections of Eckhart, the anguish of Luther, the poetry of San Juan de la Cruz, or the *Stabat Mater* of Vivaldi are all different ways of speaking with God—of praying—that assume a god who is close and personal; and this leads us back for the most part to the anthropomorphic language that they use to address the sacred. Nevertheless, I believe that here is the key: it seems permissible to be sceptical if anthropomorphic language is supposedly used for the purpose of speaking *of* God, or of describing him; but it is not valid to reject it when it is being used to speak *with* God. For ultimately, as Gómez Caffarena has noted, the goal is not to formulate a theory about a personal god, but to live God personally, to be able to address the ultimate mystery as a loving You.[11]

2

What's the Problem of Evil?

Susan Neiman

This essay introduces themes that are developed at length in my forthcoming book, *Evil in Modern Thought*. My work on the subject began with the recognition that the eighteenth century used the word "Lisbon" roughly as we use "Auschwitz." How much weight can one word carry? Here all one need do is name a place to mean the collapse of all that gives us trust in the world, the grounds that make civilization possible. I no longer remember when I learned that the names had been used in similar ways, but I do recall my reaction, which was one of simple envy: lucky the age to which an earthquake can do so much damage.

For those who don't know the story: What "Lisbon" referred to, for a good half century, was the 1755 earthquake that destroyed the Portuguese capital, and several thousand of its inhabitants, in a couple of minutes. But that was something less than the damage it seemed to do the Enlightenment itself. *Dichtung und Wahrheit* records the six-year-old Goethe's reaction to the flood of discussion that swirled around him, his first conscious doubt, his first intellectual *event*. Academies across Europe devoted essay contests to the questions of justice and sense that it seemed to engender: did the citizens of Lisbon deserve to be punished more than those of London or Paris? (Let us note that the earthquake that destroyed Port Royal, Jamaica, fifty years earlier, had produced no intellectual shockwaves; less, I think, because Jamaica was even farther from the center of European discourse than Lisbon, but because even its own inhabitants viewed it to be full of half-bred buccaneers and women of easy virtue, who must have had it coming.) For Voltaire, Lisbon proved that law was impossible and philosophy vain. Rousseau found another occasion to quarrel with him over it, but the earthquake was not confined to the best minds in Europe. Popular reaction ranged from sermons to eyewitness reports to very bad poetry. Only in

Prussia, it seems, were the consequences said to be less than earthshaking. Frederick the Great thought it was overdoing things to cancel carnival preparations months after the disaster. And an unknown *Privatdozent* named Immanuel Kant wrote three essays on earthquakes that make Dr. Pangloss sound reserved. Those concerned with the damage done by the disaster, he tells us, need only look at its bright side: the earthquake also brought into being several springs of mineral water known to possess healing properties. And those who see the avenging hand of God, rather than a thoroughly explicable natural process, can perform a small experiment: Kant advises his readers to take twenty-five pounds of sulfur and twenty-five pounds of iron filings, mix them together, and bury them in the ground to produce a little earthquake themselves. This shows you need no supernatural explanation to find everything transparent to laws of reason—Kant later said these were the only essays of which he was ashamed.

Kant's shame makes more sense than anything else in this story, for it looks like the beginning of the modern. At best, their reaction seems quaint. What exactly do you believe if you find your world undermined by an earthquake? That no sparrow falls in creation without God's wise, unseen hand? Something like a traditional picture of Providence does seem presupposed: belief in a vast, fine order that grounds and fills the world as a whole. To be sure, we do not see all of it, but none of it is in principle obscure. Since the order is at once a natural and a moral order, its author can be none other than God himself. To say that we live in a postmetaphysical world is to say that we have lost all this, and nearly everything else that seemed certain as well. What becomes of philosophy in a time when it is no longer tied to, or supported by, metaphysics is a far-reaching question. What becomes of the problem of evil in postmetaphysical thinking is, of course, a part of this more general question, but the question itself reveals unspoken assumptions. One, I suspect, is an implicit acceptance of Comte's division of the history of thought into theological, metaphysical, and scientific stages. Oddly enough, this picture of progress—or anyway, movement—is often taken for granted by those who have nothing else in common with positivism.

If one assumes this sort of picture, postmetaphysical thinking about the problem of evil ought to mean anything that happened after Leibniz. For Leibniz was clearly the last major thinker to try to give a metaphysical, as opposed to a purely theological, account of evil, before philosophy deemed both to be out of bounds. For those unconvinced by the pathos of the poem on the Lisbon disaster, Voltaire made the point with satire in *Candide:* God ran out of credit at Lisbon. For those who want philosophical proof instead of any variety of literary persuasion, Kant spent half a lifetime making it clear: neither God nor his purposes can be objects of philosophical discourse. Since Kant, even those wanting to maintain private belief in God have moral as well as epistemological grounds to keep him out of the realm of explanation. Since Rorty, words like "order" and "foundation" are used mostly in scare-quotes, the grammatical equivalent of a sneer. Thus it is easy to view the reactions to Lisbon as something childish, the birthpangs of a sadder but wiser age which has learned to live on its own.

We can make the point stronger: there is a perspective from which comparing Lisbon to Auschwitz seems simply mistaken. The mistake is thought to lie in accepting the eighteenth-century use of the word "evil" to cover both acts of human cruelty and instances of human suffering. It's a mistake that came naturally to theists, who were willing to leave the responsibility for both in God's hands, but it shouldn't confuse the rest of us. Postmetaphysical thinking (and/or analytic philosophy) on this view ought to teach us that "Lisbon" and "Auschwitz" designate two completely different kinds of events. "Lisbon" refers to what insurance companies call "natural disasters" or "acts of God" to take them out of the sphere of human action. This means that we not only absolve human beings of the responsibility for causing or compensating for them, but even for thinking about them, except in pragmatic and technological terms. Earthquakes and volcanoes, famines and floods inhabit the borders of human meaning. We want to understand just so much about them as might help us gain control. Only the most traditional of orthodox theists would seek significance in them. "Auschwitz," by contrast, stands for all we mean when we use the word "evil" today: absolute wrongdoing, which leaves room for no account and no expiation.

So nothing will strike us as more different. If there is a problem of evil engendered by Lisbon, it will occur only for orthodox theists: how can God allow breaks in the natural order that cause innocent suffering? The problem of evil posed by Auschwitz looks like another problem entirely: how can human beings behave in ways that so thoroughly violate what Rawls called both the reasonable and the rational—all dictates of moral value, and all interests of instrumental reasoning? It may seem unobjectionable to engage in *moral* theory in a postmetaphysical world; thinkers like Rawls and Habermas have done it perfectly well. But moral theory is more comfortable with categories like right and wrong, good and bad. "Evil" carries theological resonance even when explicit theological foundations are rejected. And if the definition of evil as absence, which the Middle Ages inherited from Augustine, seems inadequate to express anything about contemporary horror, no other metaphysical definitions have been—perhaps mercifully—proposed. We know without having to argue it that an attempt to give a scientific account of evil not only will end in failure, but threatens something worse: a category mistake of such proportions that it may veer toward the evil itself. Thus neither theological, metaphysical, nor scientific discussion seems available for dealing with what we designate as the problem of evil. Perhaps the problem itself, as a philosophical problem, has been overcome by attention to distinctions that the eighteenth century confused?

Examples of progress in philosophy are sufficiently rare that it is tempting to take whatever instances come our way. But we should pause before congratulating ourselves for conceptual maturity on this score. If the history of philosophy has anything to teach us, it's not to take ourselves for granted. Looking anew at the history of philosophy should show our distinctions to be anything but obvious. For Job, whose statement of the problem of evil remains not only the first but the most powerful, this distinction makes no difference: death and suffering are death and suffering, whether at the hands of marauding Chaldeans or a great wind blown from the desert. Of course, Job was a theist, and we may be tempted to dismiss him as a poet—not even a metaphysical, but a premetaphysical thinker. Before doing so we should listen to Kant, whose essay "On the Failure of All Attempted Philosophical Theodicies" describes Job as the first Kantian, that is, postmetaphysical thinker. Job is postmetaphysical, for Kant, because he lives without foundations: whatever faith he maintains is based on his moral character, not the other way around. His friends, by contrast, are metaphysicians worthy of Leibniz and Wolff. Their attempts to prove what cannot be proved, and ignore what cannot be ignored, are undertaken not only in their own defense, but in the hope, Kant says, that God will be eavesdropping.

I will return to Kant, but use him, for the moment, in an appeal to authority. It was Kant, after all, who is supposed to have revolutionized philosophy by rejecting all such traditional questions as transcending the bounds of human reason. What is he doing discussing them, or identifying with the figure of Job? If writers as modern as Kant or Dostoyevsky return us to Job, and if Elie Wiesel calls him "our contemporary," he cannot be a simple anachronism. The Book of Job and the traditional problem of evil will strike us as a knot in need of unraveling, but modern attempts to do so have the effect of cutting all the cords rather than disentangling them. The separation of the problem of evil into a moral problem that belongs to philosophy and a cosmological one that does not is an attempt to find a clarity that proves to be false. The distinction between moral evil and natural suffering, which now seems self-evident, was born around the Lisbon earthquake and nourished by Rousseau. But for all his and later attempts to separate them, the questions remain entwined.

The distinction that might be thought to end the traditional discussion of the problem of evil was itself a part of that discussion. I will suggest that the distinction is as little obvious as the discussion itself is obsolete. The Comtean categories that I suspect to have pervaded modern historiography of philosophy imply that the problem of evil must have ended with the end of classical metaphysics. In fact, it was *after* Leibniz that discussion of the problem really began in earnest. It was because of his solution to the problem of evil that Kant designated Rousseau as "Newton of the mind."[1] Nor was it the effect of Hume's discussion of causality on the future of natural science but its effect on future understanding of God, so devastatingly argued in the *Dialogues Concerning Natural Religion,* which disturbed Kant's dogmatic slumber.[2] These are but references to the major figures contained in any current canon of the history of philosophy. A glance at minor ones, and at works more easily reckoned to literature, will show that—far from exuding the shallow, confident optimism with which it is frequently charged—the eighteenth century was preoccupied with the problem of evil.

If the problem of evil was central to eighteenth-century thinkers, it may be said to have dominated the nineteenth. I suspect this is one reason that the anglophone history of philosophy has tended to collect thinkers as vast and disparate as Hegel, Kierkegaard, Marx, Schopenhauer, and Nietzsche under the rubric "nineteenth-century philosophy" and teach them, if at all, in one quick semester. Taking them at length and in depth would have demanded revision of the standard narrative of the history of philosophy, oddly accepted, in broad outline, by philosophers on both sides of the Atlantic. According to that narrative, our subject concerns a development from metaphysics to epistemology. If early modern philosophy's goal was to interpret the world, later philosophy examined the foundations of interpretation. Kant, it is taught, was the focus of change, shifting philosophy from the interesting but impossible project of tracing the nature of reality to the modest but possible one of tracing our knowledge of it. In broad outline, this narrative has seemed self-evident even to those most critical of the project itself. Rorty, for example, would rather abandon philosophy itself than abandon this reading of its history.

On literary grounds alone, this reading deserves to be abandoned. It's a less interesting narrative than others, for it lacks what is central to dramatic movement anywhere, a compelling motive. Except for a thoroughly anachronistic desire to distinguish themselves from natural scientists, these philosophers act without intention. There is no good reason for the history of philosophy to have consisted of this story: as Descartes himself would tell us, none but madmen *really* think our representations might be dreams. Throughout the *Critique of Pure Reason* Kant says that something must explain all the effort philosophers make for a subject which brings no results. He tells us it cannot be speculation alone: the work is too hard and too frustrating to be driven by purposes and problems which are not urgent.

Kant concludes that speculative interests must be moved by practical ones, but we should not read this narrowly. For the very last thing I want to claim is that in addition to epistemology, the history of philosophy was *also* concerned with ethics. (It was, of course, as excellent contemporary work on the history of ethics has shown, but this is another story.[3]) Like no other question, the problem of evil shows how hopeless it is to try to divide philosophy into areas which may or may not be connected. We can see this in the most skeptical of empiricists like Hume as in the most devoted of holists like Hegel. Would you care to decide if their works are more about ethics than epistemology? The fact that the world contains neither justice nor meaning equally threatens our ability to understand the world and to act in it. It is not only undecidable if this problem is ethical or metaphysical; in some moods it is hard to view it as a philosophical problem at all. For stated with the right degree of generality it is but unhappy description; this is our world. That might be a cry, but it is not a question, so it is all the less surprising that philosophy has been unable to give it an answer. And yet philosophy has been repeatedly moved to try in ways which have driven the most creative thinking the subject has known.

If we ignore enough texts, or decide they are peripheral, we can fit the major figures of eighteenth-century philosophy into the narrow schema that is supposed to capture the history of modern philosophy. With a masochistic effort that confines us to the most badly written texts as well as the most recondite ones, we can make Leibniz, Hume, and Kant tell a very dull story—once philosophy wanted to prove the existence of God and certain general propositions about the nature of his world. Under the pressure of science and skepticism, it would now be content to prove the existence of that world at all. (To tell this story one must argue that Rousseau, for example, was not really a philosopher but a neurotic genius who could not help himself from making certain contributions to literature and political theory, so this is where—notwithstanding Kant's estimation—his books have been taught.) In this narrative modern philosophy involves a massive shrinking act; not just objects of philosophy, but all our expectations for it, disappear with every passing decade. If you hold shriveled expectations to be a sign of maturity, you will see such a narrative as a sign that philosophy has come of age.

The nineteenth century is a stumbling block for the attempt to fit its major figures into a debate about epistemology—which has not stopped some philosophers from trying. In addition, even a superficial look at central nineteenth-century authors leaves us with glaring questions which would not only bely all hopes for progress in thought, but make history look stubbornly regressive. Hegel wrote that philosophy must become theodicy. Marx wrote that the criticism of religion is the first premise of all criticism. Schopenhauer wrote that speculative theology is the main subject of philosophy. Let us call these but headlines which emerge from the first half of the nineteenth century. Open any volume of Schelling, Feuerbach, Kierkegaard, or Nietzsche and you may add your own. That is, all subjects which were thought to be excluded from traditional philosophy since Kant (as Mendelssohn complained) destroyed it, turned out to be very much present. Did the nineteenth century simply fail to understand those lessons we now take as elementary?

In his preface to the (not incidentally titled) *Geschichte der Religion und Philosophie in Deutschland* Heinrich Heine wrote:

> Der Deismus lebt; er ist nicht tot, und am allerwenigsten hat ihn die neueste
>   deutsche Philosophie getoetet.
> Diese spinnwebige Berliner Dialektik kann keinen Hund toeten, wie viel
>   weniger einen Gott. Ich habe es
> am eigenen Leibe erprobt, wie wenig gefaehrlich ihr Umbringen ist; sie
>   bringt immer um, und die Leute
> bleiben dabei am Leben.[4]

> Deism lives; it isn't dead; and the last thing that killed it was recent German
>   philosophy.
> This cobweb, Berliner dialectic, couldn't kill a dog, much less a God. I
>   experienced
> the harmlessness of its killing first-hand; it isn't always killing, and the
>   targets
> always stay alive.

Heine gives no explanation for the resistance of deism, and deist-inspired themes, to classical attempts to do away with them. One way of understanding that resistance will appeal to a simple account of human needs: it is so hard to grow up and face life without theological foundations that traditional beliefs in religion inform even the bravest of attempts to live without them. On some readings of Nietzsche, such attempts are shadows inevitably cast by the dead god long after he has become obsolete, but no more substantial than shadows. The classic claim that Marxism is but displacement of human needs for traditional religion was stated more attractively than usual in Walter Benjamin's *Theses on the Philosophy of History*.[5]

The story is told of an automaton constructed in such a way that it could play a winning game of chess, answering each move of an opponent with a counter-move. A puppet in Turkish attire and with a hookah in its mouth sat before a chessboard placed on a large table. A system of mirrors created the illusion that this table was transparent from all sides. Actually, a little hunchback who was an expert chess player sat inside and guided the puppet's hand by means of strings. One can imagine a philosophical counterpart to this device. The puppet called "historical materialism" is to win all the time. It can easily be a match for anyone if it enlists the services of theology, which today, as we know, is wizened and has to keep out of sight.[6]

Benjamin's figure is more elegant than most, but it is no less reductive. For the automaton he describes is a fake. The robot that looked like a genuinely modern invention turned out to be an ordinary human, and an old Byzantine one at that. If philosophy of history is driven by theology as the chess player is moved by the hunchback, its results are just as deceptive, and fully without autonomy. Benjamin's metaphor, like his little hunchback itself, works behind the scenes of that discussion known as the secularization debate. That debate began with the recognition of enormous similarities between nineteenth-century ideas of progress and earlier ideas of Providence. It thus seemed natural to conclude that various claims about progress which fuel attempts to construct philosophies of history are derived from theology, not metaphysics.[7]

I cannot enter this rich debate in detail here, but want merely to distinguish my own view from ones that are better known. Much of the debate, like Benjamin's metaphor, oddly depends on the Comtean idea that intellectual history can retain clear divisions between theological, metaphysical, perhaps even scientific stages, and on some sort of genealogy between them. A much simpler and less reductive view is common to Kant, Hegel, and even Marx. This is the claim that some questions are prescribed by the very nature of reason itself. They are expressed and answered in different forms at different times. We may or may not make progress in resolving them, but whatever appears to be progress in forgetting them will be nothing but repression. Here ideas of progress and of Providence will be alternative ways of working out the same sort of problem. Neither can be reduced to or derived from the other, since they stem not from historical accident (even a major historical accident, like the Judeo-Christian notion of a personal God) but from something about human nature itself.

Certainly aspects of our problem of evil are new and distinctly modern. Others may be unthinkable without two millennia's worth of monotheistic assumptions. On occasion it may prove important to trace the theological sources of secular constructions. Such genealogies can be of interest quite apart from debates in the history of ideas. Consider Adam Smith's view that an invisible hand regulates individual economic self-interest so as to lead to the good of the whole. It bears unmistakable traces of the doctrine of Providence, as any eighteenth-century reader would have recognized.[8] There may be political contexts in which this should be stressed: to suggest, for example, that unless we actually rely on full-blown trust in Providence, the invisible hand will require guidance and intervention from visible ones. But it would be drastic to suppose that pointing to theological undertones in *The Wealth of Nations* would suffice to undermine the foundations of capitalism. All the more so as it is possible to argue the reverse: the problem of evil may gain force during the modern period through the growth of particular economic assumptions. The more reward and desert came to seem directly linked through modern economic arrangements, the more their connection in the universe as a whole was demanded. Reduction seems as pointless in one direction as another. My intention is therefore not to endorse it, but to underline questions which were ignored not because they *derived* from theology, but because they were *framed in theological language.* Misplaced respect for Kant treated those questions as undigested remainders of those he banned from philosophical discourse. His strictures are better read as banning theological solution of certain problems—not the attention to the problems themselves.

It is precisely by looking at theological formulations of the problem of evil that we can see why it is not, or not only, a theological problem. Here is the traditional problem of evil, as a classical theist would state it:

1. God is omnipotent
2. God is benevolent
3. Evil exists

We cannot maintain rules of reasoning and accept all three premises at once. Something has to go. Orthodox theism tends to find a way to reject (3): though it *looks* as if evil exists in abundance, behind the appearances, sanity reigns. For what looked like unbearable evil was necessary in order to achieve some greater good. This is the route taken by Leibniz, Hegel, and other friends of Job. It makes no attempt to account for the facts, but rather denies their substance: more important than appearances is the unseen order behind them. Rejecting the second premise is a solution taken only by Sade, and not even he took it consistently; the possibility that the world and all its creatures were produced by something less than benevolent is, after all, Descartes's nightmare. Rejecting the first seems the best option. Even if painful, it is less frightening to deny God's omnipotence than his benevolence. We can keep the appearances by making God into a large and long-living parent: well-intentioned but bounded, he does all the good that is in his power, but runs up against the limits of other forces. Those who choose to personify those forces will take this route to Manichaeanism; for asserting the reality of a good and an evil principle seems truer to faith, as well as fact, than denying either the second or the third of the claims.

There is another alternative. Rather than maintaining the rules of reason, and trying to decide which of the three propositions it is easier to live without, one can jettison reason itself. Is the combination of these three claims unintelligible? So much the worse for intelligibility. In the early Enlightenment, this is the route taken by Pierre Bayle as well as his admirer David Hume. The problem of evil is Hume's strongest weapon in the struggle to prove that human reason is worse than useless. Our inability to understand causality or induction is nothing next to our ability to make sense of this one: how one small change or another might have produced a design which contained far less misery, yet the world was created as it was. Does reason demand something different? This just proves that the possession of reason is not only no help in navigating the world; it constantly puts us at odds with it.

What is important to note here is the deep similarity of views like Hume's and Bayle's—though one is as cheerful an atheist as ever graced a salon, and the other the embodiment of fideism: one who believes *because* it is absurd. You can look at the facts and take whatever position about God's existence that you choose. This was proved once again by Friedrich Jacobi, who used Hume's arguments to invent the term "leap of faith" he bequeathed to Kierkegaard. God's existence is compatible with any position you like about the problem of evil; conversely, the problem of evil is compatible with any position you like about God's existence. What is not so easy to manage is a belief in the intelligibility of his Creation. Some believers are happy to live without this; many an atheist is troubled by its absence. Perhaps it is a question of temperament; but it is this, and not theism, that is at stake in the problem of evil.

Understanding this allows us to understand Leibniz's long-winded attempt to convince Bayle that this world is the best of all possible ones (otherwise known as the *Theodicy*) for something other than the foolishness Voltaire mocks in *Candide*. Leibniz's claim can seem to express an optimism which is at best empty, and at worst cruel; for any fact, however awful, can be made to fit the claim that this world is the best of all possible. Two hundred years after Voltaire, Bertrand Russell reformulated his charge, "Leibniz seems to imply that existing *means* belonging to the best possible world. . . . If these are the consolations of philosophy, it is no wonder that philosophers cannot endure the toothache patiently!"[9] But Voltaire and Russell miss the point. Leibniz is not insisting on the goodness of the world but on its comprehensibility. In so doing he may seem to be ignoring the fear and pain which drives people to seek a theodicy, but in fact he is speaking to another—the fear and pain of being left in the dark. I suspect he believes this the worst place in hell: to add to all the world's evils the torment of not understanding it would be unendurable. Russell is right, of course, to remind us that the claim that this world is the best one is not based on evidence. Evidence leads you elsewhere: if I had to pick a destination, I would probably follow Bayle and view Manichaeanism as the hypothesis that makes most sense of the facts. But evidence is not decisive; traditional views of Providence were built not on evidence, but in spite of it. Nor do you have to be a believer to defy those particular appearances. Thus Horkheimer tells us that reason itself "rebels against the thought that the present state of reality is final and that undeserved misfortune and wrongdoing—and not the self-sacrificing deeds of men—are to have the last word."[10]

Now it is Kant who best explains the grounds for reason's rebellion. The problem of evil is, for him, the most important of those questions which are prescribed by the very nature of reason itself, yet which reason is unable to answer. For nature and reason have claims which are equally pressing, it is just as important to recognize the way the world is as to demand that it be otherwise. Though nothing is more crucial than distinguishing between "ought" and "is," all our hopes are directed to joining them. Whether we try to make the world intelligible by understanding it or changing it, we are guided by an idea of the unconditioned—a world which would be transparent to human reason. For if everything were as it should be, we could make no more demands, theoretical or practical. The world would be the best of all possible ones. For Kant, unlike many, this set of assumptions is neither foolish nor psychological. It expresses what he calls a need of reason, which is presupposed in all our attempts to make sense of the world. And yet, as he tells us, it is a need which cannot be met. The gap between "is" and "ought" is systemic, not accidental. It cannot be bridged by history, or obscured by stoic attempts to convince us that all we need is a satisfied mind. Kant, along with common sense, insists that virtue and happiness are two different things, and any connection between them in our world is accidental. We need not read *Candide* to know that, at Lisbon and elsewhere, the righteous may be drowned, the vicious saved. This is something like the first experience of moral consciousness itself. For those of a certain temperament, it is the experience which provides the urge to metaphysics. Elsewhere I have argued that Kant's notion of reason, and other crucial features of the Critical Philosophy, were developed in order to respond to these questions in a way that resists the metaphysical impulse.[11]

Yet the *Critique of Pure Reason* tells us that "We can be sure that however cold or contemptuously critical may be the attitude of those who judge a science not by its nature but by its accidental effects, we shall always return to metaphysics as to a beloved with whom we have had a quarrel" (A849/B878).

To ask about evil in a postmetaphysical age is to ask about maintaining tormented love. It isn't news that we're not going to reach the objects of metaphysics; in the case of theodicy, there's good reason to think we shouldn't try. I believe that much of modern philosophy is about one such obsessive narrative; an attempt to answer a problem of evil which is difficult enough to state, and probably impossible to answer. I cannot, therefore, recommend any course of action but this one: that we cease rewriting the history of philosophy in the attempt to make its objects more accessible. (The search to provide firm foundations of knowledge has, after all, proved equally problematic despite its limited scope. This may suggest that philosophy's goal is not to solve problems at all; but that must remain the subject of another discussion.) Here I wish to give the briefest sketch of the alternative narrative of philosophy's history which is developed in more detail in my forthcoming book.

Let us take the modern to begin with Pierre Bayle, whose claim that history is the history of the crimes and misfortunes of the human race is one way the eighteenth century begins. The Enlightenment can be seen as opening under pressure to answer Bayle's challenge. Crimes and misfortunes are a way to divide the world into moral and natural evils, as Leibniz would do. He drew a clear distinction between Judas's betrayal of Jesus (for Leibniz, the paradigm of moral evil) and all the facts of death, disease, and suffering he calls natural. As God's advocate, Leibniz set himself the task of defending his client's goodwill, and maintained that natural evil is just punishment for moral evil, as we would know if we could know their author's design. Although this defense seemed less than decisive, it was uneasily accepted for a number of decades. Leibniz's accounts of truth and freedom were built in service of it. The account may have partly inspired Alexander Pope's wonderful "Essay on Man," which seems to give a more poetic and acceptable version of the *Theodicy* until it hits the bottom line: "Whatever is, is right." Pope was Kant's favorite poet, and it was this line that he suggested when he called Rousseau the "Newton of the mind." What could the sage of Konigsberg have meant?

Rousseau's account of evil was directed at the wave of despair which overtook much of Europe at midcentury. Voltaire expressed it in his poem "On the Lisbon Earthquake" which attacks attempts like Pope's and Leibniz's to maintain that the distribution of happiness and virtue is just. Natural evils as punishments for moral ones? For what, precisely, were the babies left shattered in their mothers' arms being punished? It need not, of course, have been Lisbon; few causes seem so clearly occasional. Nor was Voltaire's question a new one; as already suggested, it goes straight back to Job. New was the Enlightenment's reluctance to accept the general promissory note Leibniz had offered: with infinite time, and nearly as much patience, we will come to understand the order behind those appearances which made Voltaire say the world exists to drive us mad. After Lisbon, the claim that the order is *in principle* intelligible came to seem simply hollow. Someone had to fill in the details, to do the work involved in showing intelligibility, not just stating it. So it fell to Rousseau, most unorthodox of philosophers, to provide tools which could be used to defend orthodox claims.

"Everything is good as it leaves the hands of the Author of nature, everything degenerates in the hands of men." This is the first sentence of Rousseau's masterpiece *Emile,* and it could stand as his central thought. Most of Rousseau's work can be read as an attempt to explain how that degeneration occurred through natural causes, and how it might, therefore, be cured by them. It is an explanation which tries to determine a distinction between moral and natural evils without appealing to original sin, hence to punishment; and it is brilliant, detailed, and naturalistic enough to deserve Kant's judgment: Newtonian. Rousseau's account might be said to invent the notion of history itself, on which the nineteenth century would rely. Yet before this could happen, Kant would fix the division between moral and natural evils into metaphysics. This is, if you like, the distinction between reason and nature itself, the fundamental dualism which splits us all in two. The gap between the demands of reason and the claims of nature is one we cannot overcome. Kant decisively rejected the notion of evil as punishment: he may be the first of Job's readers to find him unambiguously innocent. (Most of the previous commentary on Job is devoted to showing some reason for Job's suffering after all.) Kant insisted that Job is as righteous as he seems, an insistence on remaining with the awfulness of appearance: happiness and virtue are indeed not in balance. But his justification of our outrage came at a price: the imbalance is writ in the universe itself, framing the structure of the human condition.

The *problem* is set by the wavering Enlightenment: in the years between Lisbon and Jena, the old models of Providence had broken down, without anything clear to replace them. The nineteenth century can be seen as a race to provide a model. Determined to find a science which would make the moral order as transparent as the physical one, it tried, alternately, history, biology, economics, and psychology. Animating all those attempts was an assurance of intelligible order behind the moral chaos we do not understand. The nineteenth century was so bent on solving the problem in one form or another that it can look dogmatic next to those, like Kant and Rousseau, who were struggling to formulate the breakdown itself. Their period can remind us of our own: in the half century that has elapsed since Auschwitz, it has become clear that earlier notions of progress will not help us. This must explain the decline in postwar Hegelianism in left- and right-wing versions, but we have, as yet, no alternative. The difference between wanting to understand the world and wanting to change it can seem to be all the difference, and in some contexts, of course, it is. But it is also the case that both Hegel's and Marx's determination to find the world's evils intelligible hark back to classical rationalist traditions as far as Maimonides. And the leap of faith offered by writers like Kierkegaard and Dostoyevsky is equally a return to a willingness to live without comprehension. Among the things we share with the late eighteenth century is an inability to believe all the ways in which tradition found meaning in evil, and an inability to accept that it has none at all. Where this changes, nihilism wins.

It is a word which was invented in the course of the *Pantheismusstreit* [Pantheism Controversy], the eighteenth century's fiercest debate about the meaning of enlightenment, but it takes us straight to Nietzsche. In a chronological sketch as general as this one, I can do no more than remind you that Nietzsche's attempt to go beyond good and evil was undertaken in the most conscious of theological service. His doctrine of eternal return is an attempt to smash the residue of redemption he sees lurking in the Philistine insistence on progress. Without a point beyond time to redeem or condemn us, humankind must transform itself. Nietzsche is perfectly right in underlining the significance of this thought, and perfectly prescient in thinking it would take generations to comprehend. One can understand Heidegger's view that something about philosophy seems to end there.

Instead of philosophy ending, it merely divided. For want of a satisfactory characterization of the split within twentieth-century philosophy, recent philosophers have tended to deny it. The division of philosophy into "analytic" and "continental" has come to seem far too crude, and recent decades have seen an interest in celebrating what philosophers have in common. Surely earlier attempts to describe the differences were not simply crude but false attempts to articulate the vague sense that analytic philosophy cared less about the world, and continental philosophy less about being clear in it. But it would be nonsense to say that the Vienna circle's concern with the political was less genuine or salutary than Heidegger's, or that Rawls's contribution to ethics will prove less important than Sartre's. Nor is it easy to describe Moore as more incisive than Arendt, or Brentano as less serious about science than Austin. But the impression of deep difference between philosophers on both sides of the Atlantic is not thereby dispelled, as it is not by pointing to the many differences within each tradition.

I suggest that for all the real contrasts between them, what unites philosophers as different as Arendt, Benjamin, Camus, Marcuse, Schmitt, or Levinas is a concern with the problem of evil which radiates throughout their work, and which is absent in philosophers as different as Russell, Quine, Carnap, or Austin. Through Hegel, what came to be known as continental philosophy found a way of inheriting themes which earlier belonged to theology. This allowed it to take history and historical events as objects of philosophical concern. Analytic philosophy found no way to do so, which affected its treatment of the history of philosophy as well. Here I refer not only to the common complaint that the history of philosophy was not viewed as part of philosophy proper for many decades. No doubt as a result, that history which was undertaken focused so squarely on those questions it considered legitimate that it simply failed to notice texts and authors which were guided by other ones. Devastating in this sort of historiography was not the commitment to naturalism, which united most philosophers for more than a century, but the simple way it construed that commitment. For the naturalist impulse itself can arise from, and be maintained in service of, questions which began in theology—as can be seen in writers as different as Rousseau, Nietzsche, and Arendt.

Both traditions began by reacting to Kant. One can locate the split between analytic and continental philosophy not in geographical but in textual space, with answers to the question: What happens after the transcendental deduction? When everything that can be known has been proven, what becomes of all the rest? For analytic readers, what is important is what you *can* say after Kant; for continental readers, just the opposite. For the latter, the things we cannot know are those on which our lives depend. For analytic philosophy, good sense and good taste demand they drop out of the picture. Analytic philosophy views Kant as concerned with restricting our discourse lest we stray into the realm of the inexpressible. Continental philosophers seek other ways to articulate it. They divide over the question: Is the urge to move beyond experience something central to experience itself? Is the desire for transcendence a piece of psychological or logical equipment? I suggest that continental philosophers are united by conviction that experience is conditioned by a moment which points beyond itself, and that such a moment is itself tied to a concept of redemption. The hope of redemption is the hope that, appearances to the contrary, there is meaning in the world—which cannot be wrested by force nor revealed on demand.[12]

In the foregoing I have sketched an argument designed to suggest that the questions about moral evil that haunt us today are part of the same problem which animated the earlier discussion of natural evils. Both stem from the need to find order within those appearances so unbearable that they threaten reason's ability to go on—in the theoretical or the practical sphere. The need to make the world as a whole intelligible cannot neatly be reckoned to theological, metaphysical, or scientific discourse, though it has been framed in all of them. I have further claimed that this need is the problem which drives modern philosophy, though most current historiography of philosophy has repressed it in the belief that Kant taught us such questions make no sense.

The most serious reproach which could be made to the claims I have sketched has not yet been considered. This is the claim that our refusal to view the events embodied in the word "Auschwitz," or discourse about them, as part of an older tradition, is a moral, not a conceptual, reaction. To compare Lisbon to Auschwitz seems to risk viewing the latter as one more or less natural disaster, in a way bound to exonerate its architects; or to liken the Creator to human criminals of the highest order. Even atheists are loathe to violate certain images of God, or to contemplate an understanding of, say, Rudolf Hess, which would open the way for his redemption. There is thus very good reason to be moved to reserve. One contrast with Lisbon is relative reticence: Auschwitz stuns us. Here essay contests seem not just ludicrous but obscene. We have been flooded with historical reports, but philosophical reflection has been slow in coming—and most of it exhorts us to silence.

I want to try to answer this charge by showing that there are, very broadly, two sorts of positions which can be taken toward the problem of evil, and that both have been taken toward Auschwitz as toward Lisbon. Each stems from moral, not metaphysical, grounds. One holds it indecent to attempt to explain the existence of evil. For, protests to the contrary, to explain something is to justify it—at least to a point. Now this is the view Voltaire expressed in his poem on the Lisbon disaster. The idea that Auschwitz was so absolutely evil that it *should* defy our capacities for comprehension has been maintained by a number of contemporary thinkers, but none better than Jean Améry.[13] His account of the intellectual at Auschwitz is one of the most deep and chilling left by any survivor, and it may lead us to conclude that this is an event of which we should not make sense. Before doing so we should note his works which claim that, for example, the natural process of aging and death seemed to him more horrible than anything he observed at Auschwitz, for death is absolutely unreasonable.[14] Such claims and many others place his work self-consciously within a traditional debate which has little to do with traditional theology. Améry's work wrestles with questions of meaning which straddle the range from metaphysics to morals. His answers are inconclusive, but they raise at least a warning: where events call the value of reason itself into question, we should be wary of the urge to comprehension. Even Kant found the idea of theodicy to be noxious: *solving* the problem of evil would be a moral mistake.

Now the other sort of discussion maintains something close to the contrary. It runs from Rousseau to Arendt, and as much as the previous one, this line is moved by moral considerations. It holds the attempt to explain past evils to be our only hope of preventing future ones, and views the urge to leave the question unanswered in silent moral horror to be a dangerous form of mystification. This claim is central to understanding, in particular, Arendt's work. I have argued elsewhere that much of the controversy surrounding *Eichmann in Jerusalem* can be understood when the book is placed within traditions of philosophical theodicy.[15] For much of the controversy is still driven by the question: whose trial was it? Arendt charged that the state of Israel was busy trying the history of anti-Semitism rather than the particular deeds of a particular criminal, as justice demands. Her critics found her introduction of the *Judenräte* [Jewish councils whom Nazis used to help organize deportations] even worse: her insistence on discussing their role in the Holocaust seemed to suggest that not Eichmann but the victims were on trial. I suggest we consider that what was on trial, for Arendt, was not simply German war crimes, or Jewish complicity in them, but in a sense very nearly as sure as that of Leibniz, Creation itself. This explains why Arendt's critics were right to challenge her claim to be doing nothing more than simple journalism; there is no doubt that she also was defending something whose justification should make us uneasy. It was not, however, Adolf Eichmann, but a world which contained him.

Eichmann in Jerusalem opens by accusing both prosecutor and defense attorney of Hegelianism and bad history. Arendt will not accept a response to evil that would excuse or redeem it. And yet, she suggests, we cannot neglect the project Kant undertakes in lieu of theodicy: asking whether human beings fit into the world in the face of the evil within it. Arendt seeks to show us that we do by seeking a way to find our place in the world without making us too comfortable in it. For this you need a naturalistic account of its evil. To claim that evil is comprehensible in principle is not to claim that any instance of it is transparent. It is rather to deny that supernatural forces, divine or demonic, are required to account for it. It is also to say that while natural processes are responsible for evil, natural processes can be used to avoid it: the faculty of judgment we were given to guide us is fundamentally sound.

In the famous letter to Scholem, Arendt compares evil to a fungus: "Evil possesses neither depth nor any demonic dimension. It can overgrow and lay waste the whole world precisely because it spreads like a fungus on the surface." Though this is a metaphor which comes from natural science, Arendt is far too sophisticated to suggest that evil could really be given a scientific explanation. But the metaphor expresses Arendt's attempt to defuse the *conceptually* threatening element in the novelty of modern evil. The fungus metaphor thus signals evil which can be comprehended. It also shows an object in which intention plays no role. Here Arendt's discussion most radically diverges from philosophical tradition. Intention has been seen as the heart and soul of action, the thing that determines its very meaning. She argues that Eichmann's intentions were not wicked, in the sense of stemming from wicked motives; they were also thoroughly disconnected from the consequences of his actions. To shut your eyes to Nazism and even to profit from it was not to intend the chain of events which ended at Auschwitz. The Holocaust was nevertheless the result of a series of discrete actions whose agents could have done otherwise. "Wir haben es nicht so gemeint"[We didn't meant it that way] is just as true, and just as unacceptable, as "Wir haben es so nicht gewusst" [We didn't know about it]. So much the worse for intention.

That is to say, Arendt hardly tried to mitigate the guilt of Eichmann, or anyone like him. On the contrary, she insisted on the need for moral theory which locates guilt and responsibility in something besides intention. It is the observation of what she called the total moral collapse of European society which made that need acute. For if a good will were unconditionally valuable, there would be nothing wrong with what became known in the Third Reich as "inner immigration." Classical moral theories, like Kant's, which locate morality in intention do, of course, distinguish good will from merely wishing; but his critique of consequentialism emphasizes the way in which the consequences of action may be out of our hands. Kant's claim that the good will can thus become useless comes perilously close to Eichmann's tale of hard luck. As in her discussion of inner immigrants, Arendt insists that sincerity is insignificant. What is important is not whether claims to have been inwardly opposed to the Final Solution were genuine, but the complete irrelevance of inner states in determining moral guilt and innocence.

I believe that it is concern to show the irrelevance of intention which led

Arendt to the very controversial discussion of the *Judenräte,* whose place in the book cannot otherwise be explained. Nor is it accidental that she discusses their behavior with that of the "inner immigrants" in one breath. The point is not to equate their intentions, but to show the equal irrelevance of intention. The members of the *Judenräte* acted from motives which were positively admirable, and Arendt never questions them; she merely points out that their well-intended actions had the result of enabling the murder to occur with an efficiency it would otherwise have lacked.

It is this sort of data that leads Arendt to conclude that intention cannot be the issue. In questioning Eichmann's sincerity, she maintains that the judges missed the greatest moral and legal challenge of the case. For legal judgment rests on the assumption that intention is the locus of praise and blame. The difference between manslaughter and murder rests on the defendant's ability to convince a court that he didn't really mean it—where "meaning it" signifies both that he neither acted from base motives nor intended the consequences of his actions. Trials like Eichmann's make us conclude that the lack of bad intentions does not even mitigate—it plays exactly no role.

Time and again Arendt rejects the notion of collective guilt as just sentimental: it substitutes an attempt at sincerity for a search for truth. Where everyone's guilty, no one really can be. It is worse than ironic that her denial of the moral relevance of intention was taken to erase responsibility, or show that evil is "merely structural." For replacing intention with judgment is precisely the attempt to fix the gap between the actual crimes of Eichmann and the potential crimes of others which makes guilt and innocence matters not of feeling but of fact.

Arendt's work is thus an attempt to undermine the sense of the distinction between what came to be known, among historians, as the functionalist and intentionalist approaches to understanding the Holocaust. Functionalists focused on the systematic developments that created the structures that enabled genocide. Intentionalists charged that this reduced mass murder to negligence and focused on finding evidence of felt anti-Semitism as a means of assigning moral responsibility. This can look like a conflict between history and philosophy, even descriptive and normative assertions themselves. Functionalist explanations seem most able to capture what actually happened with accuracy and nuance. Intentionalists, by contrast, occupy moral high ground at the price of falsifying particular experience. Arendt, I suggest, wants to suggest that these positions are mutually exclusive. If she takes up the sort of explanation which came to be called functionalist, it is not to evade moral judgment but to realize it.

If it is possible to show how the very greatest crimes can be carried out by men who have none of the marks of the criminal, it is possible to make evil intelligible without denying its full force. In this sense, Arendt's project continues that of Rousseau and Kant. To deny that reason leaves us helpless when confronted with horror is at once a validation: our natural faculties are corruptible but not inherently corrupt. Nor are they principally impotent. We have means both to understand the world and to act in it. Substituting judgment for intention provides no guarantee for the results of moral reasoning, but it does save the prospect of it. And this is to save a great deal. Our capacity to comprehend what seemed incomprehensible is evidence for the idea that we and the world were made for each other. And this, as Kant showed us, is as close to the argument from design as we should ever come. To give a naturalistic account of the development of evil, and the forces which allow us to resist it, is to show that evil is not demonic. Arendt's contrast between the banal and the demonic is perhaps her most important, and she was conscious of her predecessors. Writing about the problem of evil in 1946, she described gnosticism as the most dangerous and attractive heresy of the future.[16] To deny that evil has depth or dimension is to say that gnosticism is false. But then, as she wrote to Kurt Blumenfeld: "The world as God created it seems to me a good one."[17]

Alluding, as often, to Kant, Arendt describes understanding the world as providing orientation in it.[18] This is something less than justification and something more than hope. Améry called it trust in the world, and he never got it back. The task undertaken by Arendt is a naturalist project which began as early as Rousseau. As I suggested, the line of thought which opposes it is equally driven by deep moral conviction. The idea that there are things we should be uneasy about understanding is an idea I believe ought to guide inquiry into the problem of evil, but not preclude it.

There is a question implicit in the title of this book. To ask about evil from a postmetaphysical perspective is to ask whether we can talk about evil at all—except, of course, to say that it is wrong. Writers like Arendt show that we can. I believe her most famous book must be read not as elevated journalism, but as a dialogue with philosophical tradition dating back at least to Leibniz. (There are others, of course, but Arendt's contribution to that dialogue is the most important of the twentieth century.) Looking at that tradition lets us turn the question around. The issue is not whether there is room to examine the problem of evil without classical metaphysics, but whether we should allow the examination of the problem of evil to change our understanding of the history of philosophy.

"Radical Finitude" and the Problem of Evil

Critical Comments on Wellmer's Reading of Jonas

Peter Dews

In the past few years there has been a resurgence of interest among philosophers in the question of evil. The revival of this venerable philosophical topic, which had fallen into disrepute throughout much of the twentieth century, must no doubt ultimately be attributed to an intensifying sense of the twentieth century as a "dark century." It has now become clear that recent generations have lived through an era in which the scale and scope of the human capacity to inflict death and suffering on other human beings has been exhibited in ways unimaginable in earlier times. Any philosophically reflective response to such events will almost inevitably gravitate toward the concept of evil. And this move will in turn give rise to a renewed interest in the writings of major thinkers of the past who have reflected on the topic. In this context, the works that have attracted the most new attention are Kant's *Religion within the Limits of Reason Alone* and Schelling's *Philosophical Investigations into the Essence of Human Freedom*—the first an investigation of the boundary between moral and religious experience, the second a dizzying speculative exploration of the ontological wellsprings of evil.[1] Recently, some of the most adventurous re-readings of these works have come from contemporary authors influenced by Lacanian psychoanalysis, most notably those of the Slovenian philosopher Slavoj Žižek and his school.[2]

It could be argued, however, that much of this new literature is flawed by its failure to pose a basic preliminary question. For the problem of evil, as traditionally understood in Western thought, arose from the difficulty of reconciling the benevolence and omnipotence of God with the existence of unmerited suffering and gratuitous destruction in the world. And insofar as most contemporary philosophers would regard themselves as inhabiting a "posttheological"—and even a "postmetaphysical"—intellectual universe, one must ask why evil should be regarded as a problem at all.[3] The pain of human existence and the horrific behavior of which human beings are capable may call forth all kinds of existential, moral, and political responses. But insofar as these phenomena are no longer regarded as blemishing a divinely ordained cosmos, it is hard to see what specifically *philosophical* difficulty there might be in coming to terms with them.

To put this in another way: it would seem that the problem of theodicy, of justifying the ways of God to a suffering world, should have disappeared for us, who live after Nietzsche's proclamation of the death of God. And yet, as the recent burgeoning of philosophical literature on the topic of evil suggests, the problem of theodicy seems in some sense to have outlived the explicit belief in a divine creator that first gave rise to it.

Some leading contemporary thinkers, such as Jürgen Habermas, seem to assume that this may not be so great a problem as it first appears. In a number of more recent essays, Habermas has affirmed that contemporary moral discourse must be able to orient itself by drawing on the semantic resources of the religious tradition. He has stated, "I do not believe that we, as Europeans, can seriously understand concepts like morality and ethical life, person and individuality, or freedom and emancipation, without appropriating the substance of the Judeo-Christian understanding of history in terms of salvation."[4] However, for Habermas, such appropriation should take the form of a conceptual translation that renders the ethical content of religious discourse universally accessible, no longer dependent for its validity on belief in privileged sources of revelation. Presumably, from this point of view, contemporary philosophers concerned with the concept of evil should be engaged in translating the core of religious responses to the problem of evil into a form that can be fed into our general, secular moral discourse. But we may wonder if this is in fact what contemporary thinkers are doing, or could do. Is such a translation of the problem of evil possible? Or, alternatively, could the use of the concept of evil be disconnected, in principle, from the theodicy problem? It is these questions that are raised in a particularly vivid form by the response of Albrecht Wellmer to Hans Jonas's famous essay, "The Concept of God after Auschwitz."[5]

Another prominent representative of the Critical Theory tradition, Wellmer endorses Habermas's conception of the need for a secularizing translation of religious discourse. Indeed, in some respects he is even more insistent about this than Habermas, since he now regards the latter's regulative notion of an "ideal speech situation" as a metaphysical residue in his thought.[6] Jonas's work therefore presents a particular challange to Wellmer, since it is notable for its refusal of any neat separation of philosophical and religious dimensions. In fact, the implication of much of his writing is that the problem of evil in our time cannot be addressed in purely secular terms. Let me be more specific. In some of his later writings, Jonas developed a speculative and confessedly mythical account of the interrelation of the divine and the human that intended to disrupt many of the basic structures of Western "onto-theology." Jonas's studies in biology and cosmology led him to the view that it is impossible to account for the evolution of life— from its most primitive stages up to the fully reflexive consciousness of human beings—without presupposing that some implicit spark of freedom and awareness was already present at the beginning of creation. Hegel too, of course, had this idea, with his conception of nature as the extreme point of the self-alienation of spirit. But for Jonas, Hegel's account of the ensuing world process is intolerably optimistic: "The disgrace of Auschwitz," he affirms, "is not to be charged to some all-powerful providence or to some dialectically wise necessity, as if it were an antithesis demanding a synthesis or a step on the road to salvation."[7] In contrast to Hegel's account, Jonas suggests that at the very beginning of things God "abandoned himself and his destiny entirely to the outwardly exploding universe and thus to the pure chances of the possibilities contained in it under the conditions of space and time. Why He did this remains unknowable. We are allowed to specu-late that it happened because only in the endless play of the finite, and in the inexhaustibility of chance, in the surprises of the unplanned, and in the distress caused by mortality, can mind experience itself in the variety of its possibilities. For this the deity had to renounce His own power."[8]

One consequence of this conception of crucial importance to Jonas is that God cannot be reproached for the failure to prevent the horror which befell the Jewish people in the twentieth century, summarized in the word "Auschwitz." For God has handed over responsibility for history to human beings, and both the nameless evil of the Holocaust and the solitary acts of devotion and sacrifice which mitigated against it must be attributed to human beings alone. This does not mean, however, that God stood by indif-ferently as the moral catastrophe occurred, like the divine watchmaker of eighteenth-century deism. On the contrary, Jonas's God is not merely a suf-fering and becoming but also a caring divinity. Jonas writes: "this I like to believe: that there was weeping in the heights at the waste and despoilment of humanity . . . 'The voice of thy brother's blood cries unto me from the ground': Should we not believe that the immense chorus of such cries that has risen up in our lifetime now hangs over our world as a dark and accus-ing cloud? That eternity looms down upon us with a frown, wounded itself and perturbed in its depths?"[9]

As I have already indicated, Albrecht Wellmer's essay, "Jonas's Myth of the Suffering and Becoming God," can be regarded as an attempt on the part of one Critical Theorist to carry out Habermas's translation program in miniature. Wellmer focuses on Jonas's essay, "The Concept of God after Auschwitz," seeking to show that, despite its mythico-religious language, it is susceptible to a secularizing translation. Wellmer's basic argument runs as follows. Since, as Jonas admits, the mythic imagery of his account cannot be transformed into a new metaphysics which could actually provide *support* for moral claims, it is more plausible to interpret Jonas's speculations as the "metaphorical expression of an ethical self-understanding, rather than as its possible foundation."[10] Wellmer writes, "my suspicion is that, insofar as it can be retrieved in philosophical-conceptual terms, Jonas's myth of a God caught up in becoming is indistinguishable from a position of radical finitude. What makes this myth of a becoming God who externalizes himself in the world so convincing—by contrast with all positive theology—is that it takes the finitude of human beings seriously and thereby takes up basic themes of the modern, post-Nietzschean critique of metaphysics."[11] Thus, for Wellmer, Jonas's account of a God who surrenders to plurality and contingency can be translated into what he calls a "thesis of radical finitude," namely that "it is intrinsic to the concept of mind that it be connected to individuated—finite—particular beings; indeed, in such a way that the conditions of naturalness and finitude are not merely a limit of the human mind and human possibilities, but at the same time and in unison with this, indicate the conditions of everything which we can term 'mind,' 'knowledge,' 'truth,' 'goodwill,' or even 'linguistic meaning.'"[12]

Wellmer finds confirmation of this interpretation in certain arguments which Jonas develops in "The Concept of God after Auschwitz," which are directed against the onto-theological conception of God. For example, Jonas suggests that the notion of absolute power is logically incoherent, since "power meeting no resistance in its relatum is equal to no power at all: power is exercised only in relation to something that itself has power."[13] Similarly, Wellmer argues, all the idealizing notions of metaphysics— absolute power, absolute freedom, even Habermas's ideal speech situation—must succumb to a thought of radical finitude in which contingency and negativity remain essential, insuperable conditions of the positive and the ideal.

Toward the end of his essay, Wellmer tries to show that, if followed through, the thought of radical finitude—which he takes Jonas to be expressing in mythical form—must block the possibility of transforming Jonas's images into a conceptually coherent metaphysical position.[14] For example, Jonas obviously has to concede that the possibility of evil is contained in God, since God is the Creator of all. But Jonas insists that this evil is only a *possibility*, since otherwise the notion of God's goodness—which he regards as indispensable—would be lost.[15] But, Wellmer enquires, why does Jonas speak only of the possibility of evil? In accordance with the thought of radical finitude, must one not think of the *reality* of evil, in order to get any experiential grip on the thought of a countervailing goodness?[16]

This question raises crucial issues concerning the relation between mythical and conceptual modes of discourse, and how exactly an equilibrium can be struck between them. Jonas often appears to believe that merely advertising the mythical character of his speculations will immunize them against conceptual dissection and criticism. Yet it is undeniable that his myth gives no adequate account—to take one example—of the relation between mere finitude and contingency on the one hand, and positive evil on the other. However, once we have seen what is at issue in Jonas's thought, the question of finitude can also be turned back against Wellmer. For, in the last analysis, there is something strangely complacent in his "position of radical finitude."

As we have seen, Wellmer writes as though the decoding of Jonas's myth would result in an unproblematic conception of naturality and finitude as both limiting and providing the conditions of possibility for the human mind and human cognitive and moral capacities. But to put matters in this way not only reveals a surprising insensitivity to the concerns of earlier thinkers; it seems almost to represent an abandonment of philosophy as such. For surely it is precisely the existence of finite, natural beings who are capable of grasping truths which appear to transcend any spatial or temporal context, of understanding meanings whose objectivity seems independent of any psychological process of comprehension, and so on, which through the ages has aroused the perplexities with which philosophers have grappled. Extravagant and abstruse Jonas's speculations may be, but it requires only a little intellectual sympathy to see that their elaboration is driven by the pressure of authentically philosophical problems.

Against this it might be objected that however genuine and enduring *some* of Jonas's problems may be, his central concern of reconciling evil and the existence of God must surely be regarded as generated by outmoded theistic assumptions—that, to take up the terms of my opening remarks, in our post-Nietzschean world there can no longer *be* a problem of evil in the traditional sense of the problem of theodicy. So it is crucial to note that Wellmer's "position of radical finitude" in fact generates its own a version of the theodicy problem. As we have seen, Wellmer suggests that the reality of evil—or the existence of the "non-good," as he terms it—is implied by the "finitude of the conditions under which alone we are able to use the concept of the ethically good."[17] But he also hastens to add that we cannot include something so "radically evil" as Auschwitz in this reality, for this would make it a condition of the good. Yet Wellmer makes no attempt to explain how the radically evil is to be distinguished from the merely evil or the non-good, so as to avoid such a morally destructive interdependence. (And in a significant lapse into religious terminology, Wellmer himself employs the word "blasphemous" to describe such an interdependence.)

Thus, the purely contrastive conception of good and evil which Wellmer proposes seems to run up against a limit. It appears that we cannot accept such a contrastively constituted world as *justified* or *morally tolerable*—or at least to do so would require an intellectual and existential effort far greater than Wellmer is prepared to put in. Indeed, if Wellmer is not prepared to make events such as Auschwitz part of the general chiaroscuro of good and evil, then we need to review the range of options which remain available to him. For Wellmer is implicitly confronted with the task of making philosophical sense of his feeling that there is something which we must term "radical evil," something which lies outside what he portrays as the usual contrast of the morally good and the morally bad.

One obvious difficulty which arises here is that of *recognizing* radical evil in the first place. Since Wellmer insists that our recognitional capacities are contrastive, yet also affirms that radical evil lies outside everyday good and evil, he would seem to be faced with an intractable dilemma. For if he argues that we recognize radical evil through some capacity for direct moral intuition, then he has to abandon the assumption that all our awareness of moral features (indeed, of all features) is based on contrast. On the other hand, if Wellmer wanted to retain both the contrastive thesis and the notion of radical evil, then he would be obliged to posit the existence not only of radical evil, but also of an opposing radical good. But such a move would in fact generate an even worse philosophical quagmire. For the radically evil and the radically good would then have to be conceptualized as *simultaneously* contrastive and noncontrastive: noncontrastive because radical (or absolute), and contrastive because recognized through their opposition to each other.

By this point it will be clear that the difficulties which Wellmer's response to Jonas generates are in fact remarkably similar to the traditional problems of evil and theodicy. For, from one perspective, the theological problem of evil can be seen as the problem of how evil can be *opposed* to God, since he is absolute *goodness,* yet not *ultimately* or *irreducibly* opposed to him, since he is *absolute* goodness. Furthermore, Jonas's speculations are at least an explicit attempt to approach this problem, by arguing that God is not absolute in every respect, whereas Wellmer stumbles across it by accident, as it were.

My conclusion is that the notion of evil cannot be as readily detached from its previous theological and metaphysical contexts as some contemporary thinkers assume. For it is hard to see how evil can be thought of as both relational and radical (or absolute), contrastive and noncontrastive, without drawing on conceptual resources such as those deployed by German idealism. Not to think of evil in this way would deprive it of the quality that Paul Ricoeur, formulating the same paradox, describes as an "absolute character of irruption."[18] For Ricoeur this quality is crucial to our sense of evil. Furthermore, to take evil seriously, as Wellmer inadvertently discovers, is to run up against the limits of any morally relativizing view of the world, including his own "position of radical finitude." In general, it is far from clear that the concept of evil can be entirely naturalized and secularized. On the contrary, the revival of interest in this concept may ultimately bring metaphysical and theological questions which were once assumed to be outdated back onto the philosophical agenda.

PART TWO

Evil and Moral Philosophy

Radical Evil

Kant at War with Himself

Richard J. Bernstein

*The problem of evil will be the fundamental question
of postwar intellectual life in Europe.*

HANNAH ARENDT, 1945

It is inherent in our entire philosophic tradition that we cannot conceive of a "radical evil," and this is true both for Christian theology, which conceded even the devil himself a celestial origin, as well as for Kant, the only philosopher who, in the word he coined for it, at least must have suspected the existence of this evil even though he immediately rationalized it in the concept of a "perverted ill will" that could be explained by comprehensible motives. Therefore, we actually have nothing to fall back on in order to understand a phenomenon that nevertheless confronts us with its overpowering reality and breaks down all standards we know. . . . Totalitarian solutions may well survive the fall of totalitarian regimes in the form of strong temptations which will come up whenever it seems impossible to alleviate political, social, or economic misery in a manner worthy of man.

HANNAH ARENDT, 1951

It was really as if an abyss had opened. . . . This ought not to have happened. And I don't mean just the number of victims. I mean the method, the fabrication of corpses and so on—I don't need to go into that. This should not have happened. Something happened there to which we cannot reconcile ourselves. None of us ever can.

HANNAH ARENDT, 1964

I have begun with these three epigraphs from Hannah Arendt because they help to orient my discussion. The first quotation appears in a review that Arendt wrote just at the end of World War II; the second is from her closing remarks in *The Origins of Totalitarianism;* and the third is from a television interview that she gave in 1964 in which she recalls her shock when she first discovered (in 1942) what has taking place in the Nazi death camps.[1] Although Arendt's reflections set the context for my inquiry, my primary concern is with Kant. Ever since Kant used the expression "radical evil" in his *Religion within the Limits of Reason Alone*,[2] it has been a source of fascination and perplexity: fascination, because it has struck many of his readers (including Arendt) that Kant was dimly aware of a type of evil that exceeds our traditional conceptions; perplexity, because it is not clear just what Kant means by radical evil—and how it fits (or does not fit) with his moral philosophy. I want to examine the meaning of radical evil, the philosophic context in which Kant explores its significance, and how radical evil is related to his moral philosophy. Is it true, as Arendt suggests, that Kant "immediately rationalized it in the concept of a 'perverted ill will'"?

Now it would be anachronistic to expect that Kant anticipated the horrors of the twentieth century. But Kant is certainly a thinker whose moral philosophy has altered the way in which we think about morality in the modern world. And despite the many critiques of Kant's conception of morality, we are presently living through a resurgence of interest in, and novel appropriations of, Kant's moral philosophy. So it is eminently appropriate to ask whether Kant's reflections on radical evil help to guide our thinking about the evil that we witnessed in the twentieth century.

Like Arendt, I too think that with Auschwitz "it was really as if an abyss had opened. . . . Something happened there to which we cannot reconcile ourselves." An outbreak of evil occurred that poses a challenge to all previous conceptions of evil. When we consider the forms of cruelty and suffering that occurred in the twentieth century, not just in Nazi Germany but throughout the world, we desperately want to call them "unspeakable" forms of evil that exceed what we ordinarily mean by immoral behavior. It appears that we are confronted with phenomena that are qualitatively different than anything that has ever happened before in history. There have been many detailed and moving descriptions—especially by victims—of what happened at Auschwitz, the Gulag, the killing fields of Cambodia and Rwanda. But the philosophic issue is to reflect upon what we mean by evil and what is our justification for calling occurrences, acts, and persons evil. What are we really saying when we judge something to be evil? Are there different types of evil? And how are they to be distinguished? The larger question looming in the background is whether our philosophic tradition— especially the modern philosophic tradition—is rich and deep enough to enable us to comprehend what we are asserting when we judge something to be evil. Or are we—as the emotivists tell us—only expressing a noncognitive emotional reaction of extreme horror.

Before proceeding with the critical analysis of Kant, a word of caution is required. When philosophers or theologians speak about the "problem of evil," they are frequently referring to a very specific set of issues. The problem of evil is understood to be the problem of how to reconcile the existence (or the apparent existence) of evil with the existence of an omniscient, omnipotent, and beneficent God. If God is the creator of the universe, and if evil really exists in this world (physical or moral evil), is God responsible for the existence of evil? If he is not, then what kind of account can be given of evil—especially the evil committed by human beings—that is compatible with the existence of such a deity. Typically it is assumed that what counts as evil is relatively clear, for example, gratuitous cruelty, intentional humiliation, the extreme suffering of innocents. It is not so much the precise character that is at issue but rather how any evil (whatever we take to be the exemplar of evil) can be reconciled with our religious convictions about God. But this is not my primary concern—and it was not Kant's primary concern. Soon after completing the *Critique of Judgment* and two years before he published *Religion within the Limits of Reason Alone* in 1793, Kant wrote "On the Failure of All Attempted Philosophical Theodicies."[3] The very title of this essay is significant. For insofar as the traditional problem of evil presupposes that there is or can be some theoretical or speculative knowledge about God (no matter how partial, analogical, or fallible), all theodicies must *necessarily* fail. For Kant claims to have demonstrated that such knowledge is impossible. Consequently we cannot even coherently raise the issue of theodicy as a *theoretical* issue.[4] The most significant consequence of Kant's rejection of all theodicies is that he is the first major modern thinker to deal with the problem of evil in a manner that does not depend on *cognitive* claims about the existence or attributes of a supreme being.

The primary analysis and discussion of radical evil is to be found in *Religion within the Limits of Reason Alone.* The opening sentences of the preface reiterate and emphasize Kant's fundamental conviction that "for its own sake morality does not need religion at all."

> So far as morality is based upon the conception of man as a free agent who, just because he is free, binds himself through his reason to unconditioned laws, it stands in need neither of the idea of another Being over him, for him to apprehend his duty, nor of an incentive other than the law itself, for him to do his duty. At least it is man's own fault if he is subject to such a need; and if he is, this need can be relieved through nothing outside himself: for whatever does not originate in himself and his own freedom in no way compensates for the deficiency of his morality. Hence for its own sake morality does not need religion at all (whether objectively, as regards willing, or subjectively, as regards ability [to act]); by virtue of pure practical reason it is self-sufficient. (Rel 3)

Kant not only asserts the independence of morality itself, but it is also clear from this passage that human beings are fully accountable and completely responsible for what they do as free moral agents—whether they do their duty and obey the moral law or whether they fail to act in accordance with the moral law. If we are to understand the meaning of radical evil, then our first task is to understand what Kant means by evil. He tells us that good or evil must "lie only in a rule made by the will *[Willkür]* for the use of its freedom, that is, in a maxim" (Rel 17). Consequently we can say that all moral good and evil has reference to the *maxims* of human volition. We can already see how the *Religion* clarifies a troubling ambiguity in Kant's moral philosophy. This concerns his understanding of the will. For in the *Groundwork*, Kant identifies the will with pure practical reason itself. But if this were a strict identity, then one wonders how it would ever be possible for someone to commit an immoral or evil act. The identification of the will with practical reason was criticized during Kant's own lifetime by his younger contemporary Reinhold, and this is an objection reiterated by many subsequent critics of Kant.[5] But the *Religion* makes it eminently clear that Kant has a more complex and subtle understanding of the faculty of volition. This is indicated by distinction that he introduces between *Wille* and *Willkür* (which unfortunately are frequently both translated in English as "will").[6] When Kant refers to the will as the capacity to *choose* between alternatives, he typically calls it *Willkür*. It is an *arbitrium liberum*. The human *Willkür* (as distinguished from the *Willkür* of brute animals) is the faculty of free spontaneous choice. Or more accurately, it is that aspect of the faculty of volition that involves unconstrained free choice. As Kant tells us, "the freedom of the will *[Willkür]* is of a wholly unique nature in that an incentive can determine the will *[Willkür]* to an action *only so far as the individual has incorporated it into his maxim* (has made it the general rule in accordance with which he will conduct himself); only thus can an incentive, whatever it may be, coexist with the absolute spontaneity of the will *[Willkür]* (i.e., freedom)" (Rel 19). The *Willkür*, the name that we give to the capacity to freely choose alternatives is not then intrinsically good or evil: rather it is the capacity by which we choose good or evil maxims. What becomes clear in the *Religion* is that *Wille* (in its more technical and narrow sense) does not act at all; it does not make decisions. It refers to the purely rational aspect of the faculty of volition. Henry Allison states the point succinctly: "Kant uses the terms *Wille* and *Willkür* to characterize respectively the legislative and executive functions of a unified faculty of volition, which he likewise refers to as *Wille*."[7] And John Silber gives a lucid description of the *Wille* and its relation to *Willkür*:

> [The *Wille*] is the source of a strong and ever present incentive in *Willkür*, and, if strong enough to be adopted by *Willkür* into the maxim of its choice, *Wille* "can determine the *Willkür*" and then "it is practical reason itself." *Wille* expresses the possibility of autonomy which is presupposed by transcendental freedom. The *Wille* represents the will's own demand for self-fulfillment by commanding *Willkür*, that aspect of the will which can either fulfill or abnegate its freedom, to actualize its free nature by willing in accordance with the law (and condition) of freedom. The most important difference between *Wille* and *Willkür* is apparent here. Whereas *Willkür* is free to actualize either the autonomous or heteronomous potentialities of transcendental freedom, *Wille* is not free at all. *Wille* is rather the law of freedom, the normative aspect of the

will, which as a norm is neither free nor unfree. Having no freedom of action, *Wille* is under no constraint or pressure. It exerts, instead, the pressure of its own normative rational nature upon the *Willkür.*[8]

Now it is vital to see why Kant makes this all-important distinction between *Wille* and *Willkür.* When Kant seeks to introduce and clarify what he means by the categorical imperative in the *Groundwork,* one seems to be left with an awkward consequence. For if will is completely identified with practical reason, then it is not entirely clear where choice enters into moral decisions. But Kant's account of morality requires that we are agents who freely choose to follow (or disobey) the moral law. To have the capacity to choose freely does not, of course, mean that we are indifferent. On the contrary, to the extent that we respond to what the *Wille* as the moral norm—as the law of freedom—dictates, we are autonomous. As Silber emphasizes, we must also be able to make heteronomous choices. Nothing determines the *Willkür* unless the *Willkür* itself chooses to be so determined. In this sense to be a human being is to be radically free—that is, to be an agent that can choose good or evil maxims.

But what precisely is an evil maxim? Before addressing this question directly, it is important to emphasize that Kant is perfectly clear that it is not our natural inclinations that are the source of evil. On the contrary, Kant does not even say that the existence of natural inclinations is neutral (neither good not evil) but they are actually good! (Later we shall consider in what sense they are good.) Kant emphatically declares: "Natural inclinations, *considered in themselves,* are *good,* that is, not a matter of reproach, and it is not only futile to want to extirpate them but to do so would also be harmful and blameworthy. Rather, let them be tamed and instead of clashing with one another they can be brought into harmony in a wholeness which is called happiness" (Rel 51).

Kant explicitly repudiates the caricature that is so frequently drawn of him. He is frequently, but mistakenly, criticized for claiming that it is our natural inclinations that are the origin of human evil. What is so misleading about this is that it obscures what is perhaps the most fundamental point of his understanding of practical freedom and morality—that human beings by virtue of their faculty of volition are completely accountable and responsible for their good and evil deeds. In *this* respect, there is no original sin or original *moral* goodness. To put the point positively, all sins, vices, and virtues originate in a (free) *Willkür.* The primary issue for Kant is always *how* we choose to *respond* to the different and sometimes conflicting incentives with which we are confronted. But let us return to the question of what precisely is an evil maxim.

In the *Groundwork,* in order to clarify the nature of duty and the moral law, Kant emphasizes those situations in which there is a conflict between our inclinations and our moral duty. Indeed, his infamous examples tend to suggest that it is only when there is an overt clash between our natural inclinations and the moral law that we have the paradigm situations in which we can be said to act not simply in accordance with duty but for the sake of duty. And here there arises another persistent caricature of Kant—that we are only "truly" moral when we are acting *against* our natural inclinations. But this is also misleading, and once again the *Religion* repudiates this caricature and helps to clear up the misunderstanding. The primary issue for Kant in determining whether a maxim is good or evil is not whether it "contains" the incentive to follow the moral law or to follow our inclinations or desires. Rather, the issue is how these various incentives are *ordered*.

> Hence the distinction between a good man and the one who is evil cannot lie in the difference between the incentives which they adopt into their maxim (not in the content of the maxim), but rather must depend upon *subordination* (the form of the maxim), i.e., *which of the two incentives he makes the condition of the other.* Consequently man (even the best) is evil only in that he reverses the moral order of the incentives when he adopts them into his maxim. He adopts, indeed, the moral law along with the law of self-love; yet when he becomes aware that they cannot remain on a par with each other but that one must be subordinated to the other as its supreme condition, he makes the incentive of self-love and its inclinations the condition of obedience to the moral law; whereas on the contrary, the latter, as the *supreme condition* of the satisfaction of the former, ought to have been adopted into the universal maxim of the will *[Willkür]* as the sole incentive. (Rel 31–32)

As Allen Wood emphasizes,

> all maxims of finite rational volition (be they good or evil) contain both the incentives of moral reason and of sensible inclination; every maxim must contain both these incentives if it is to be the principle from which a finite rational subject acts, since both incentives belong to the predisposition of such a subject. . . . The maxim of the good man differs from that of the evil man only in that the former conditions the incentives of inclination by those of duty, whereas the latter reverses the moral order of incentives, and makes it a rule to do his duty only on the condition that it is consistent with the pursuit of inclination.[9]

Consequently I can and frequently do act in a manner that is consonant with my sense of what is morally required and with what I naturally desire to do. I do not have to frustrate my natural inclinations. The issue of the moral worth of an agent depends exclusively on how these different incentives are ordered in the maxim that I freely adopt.

Although this understanding of the difference between a good and evil maxim (and a good and evil human being) clears up a persistent misunderstanding about the role of inclinations in our maxims, it does have some

drastic (Kant would say "rigoristic") consequences for Kant's characterization of an evil maxim. If we consider the example from the *Groundwork* of
the shopkeeper who feigns honesty because this is the most profitable and
advantageous policy, we can understand how in his maxim there is an
ordering of incentives where it is his desire to increase his wealth that has
primacy. This is his reason for acting as he does. He acts in accord with duty
but not for the sake of duty. But let us consider the more difficult example
of the person whose primary motivation is his sympathy. Kant tells us that
there are persons "so sympathetically constituted that without any motive or
vanity or selfishness they find an inner satisfaction in spreading joy and
rejoice in the contentment of others which have made this possible."
Although actions performed on this basis are "dutiful and amiable" and
"deserve praise and encouragement," they do not evince moral worth
because they are not done from duty. Christine Korsgaard has given a very
sensitive and insightful analysis of this example.[10] She notes that Kant clearly
distinguishes this example, where one acts "from direct inclination (performs an action because one enjoys it)" from the merchant example, where
"one acts from indirect action (performs an action as a means to an end)."[11]
Kant tells us that the sympathetic person is "without any motive of vanity or
selfishness." In explicating what Kant means, Korsgaard writes:

> Therefore, when Kant says that the difference between the sympathetic per-
> son and the dutiful person rests in their maxims, the contrast he has in mind
> is this: although the sympathetic person and the dutiful person both have the
> purpose of helping others, they have adopted this purpose on different
> grounds. The sympathetic person sees helping as something pleasant, and
> that is why he makes it his end. The morally worthy person sees helping as
> something called for, or necessary, and this is what motivates him.[12]

I think that this is exactly right and that Korsgaard perceptively states
Kant's main point. But consider the consequence of this analysis when we
put it together with Kant's analysis of good and evil maxims in the *Religion*.
Korsgaard tells us that "Duty is not a different purpose, but a different
ground for the adoption of a purpose. So Kant's idea here is captured better by saying that the sympathetic person's motive is *shallower* than the
morally worthy person's: both want to help, but there is available a *further*
stretch of motivating thought about helping which the merely sympathetic
person has not engaged in."[13] Korsgaard's interpretative suggestion is eminently reasonable, but she is ignoring a consequence of Kant's "rigorism."
For she describes the motivation of "the merely sympathetic person" in a
way that clearly indicates that his maxim is one in which he is ordering his
incentives to give priority to his inclinations (his sympathy) rather than to
his moral obligation to help others. And this is the *paradigm* of what Kant
takes to be an *evil* maxim. This is the troubling point. The person who

gives priority to the incentive of sympathetic feelings in his maxim is not just "shallower" than the moral person, he is evil—he is adopting an evil maxim.[14]

Yet Kant himself does not flinch from drawing this conclusion. In the *Religion* he emphatically endorses such a rigoristic analysis. He tells us that we call a man evil not because he performs actions that are evil, "but because these actions are of such a nature that we may infer from them the presence in him of evil maxims" (Rel 16). Furthermore Kant accepts the exclusive disjunction that "man is . . . either morally good or morally evil" (Rel 17). Kant admits that although "experience actually seems to substantiate the middle ground between these extremes," nevertheless it is "of great consequence in ethics in general to avoid admitting, so long as it is possible, of anything morally intermediate. . . . Those who are partial to this strict mode of thinking are usually called rigorists (a name which is intended to carry reproach, but which actually praises) . . ." (Rel 18). Whoever incorporates the moral law into his maxim and gives it priority is morally good—and whoever does not do this, but gives priority to other incentives (including sympathy) is morally evil. And to drive home his point, Kant tells us:

> Neither can a man be morally good in some ways and at the same time morally evil in others. His being good in one way means that he has incorporated the moral law into his maxim; were he, therefore, at the same time evil in another way, while his maxim would be universal as based on the moral law of obedience to duty, which is essentially single and universal, it would at the same time be only particular; but this is a contradiction. (Rel 20)

Allison provides a succinct statement of Kant's grand Either/Or—his rigorism. He tells us:

> Starting with the premise that respect for the law is an incentive, Kant reasons that since the freedom of the will *[Willkür]* entails that an incentive can determine the will only if it is "taken up" into a maxim, it follows that the failure to make the thought of duty or respect for the law the sufficient motivation for one's conduct, must be regarded as resting on the adoption of an alternative principle of action. But since the adoption of an alternative principle involves an explicit deviation from the law, such an act must be characterized as "evil."[15]

So following the logic of Kant's rigoristic analysis, there does not seem to be any way to avoid the conclusion that a benign sympathetic person (who gives the incentive of sympathy priority over the moral law in his maxim), Hitler, and even Eichmann (whose maxims presumably did not give priority to respect for the moral law) are *all* morally evil. Kant would acknowledge that there are certainly differences among them. Despite his "official" doctrine, Kant recognizes these differences. Nevertheless, given the exclusive rigoristic disjunction—good or evil—we must judge them to be evil.

What they share in common is "the failure to make the thought of duty or respect for the law the sufficient motivation for one's conduct."

Thus far, I have been addressing the question of what Kant means by evil—and specifically what constitutes a morally evil maxim, but I have not said anything about radical evil. How does Kant's understanding of radical evil condition and/or supplement what he has told us about evil maxims? More generally, we want to know how radical evil is compatible with his moral theory.[16] We will see that despite the striking connotations of the term "radical" Kant is not speaking about a special *type* of evil or evil maxim. Kant would not agree with Arendt when she declares that radical evil is a phenomenon that "confronts us with its overpowering reality and breaks down all standards we know."[17] And he certainly does not mean anything like what Arendt means when she claims that "radical evil has emerged in connection with a system [totalitarianism] in which all men have become equally superfluous."[18] But what then does Kant mean, and why does he introduce this tantalizing concept? The answer is complex, and we need to clarify a number of issues and important distinctions in order to grasp what Kant is claiming.

To set the context for our analysis, we must first briefly consider the sharp distinction that Kant makes in his Critical Philosophy between phenomena and noumena. This distinction, which is so central for Kant's understanding of freedom and his moral theory, has proved especially troublesome. There are many passages in Kant that seem to suggest that this is a "two world" theory in which there is no (and can be no) interaction between them. If this were really so, if noumena and phenomena referred to two "ontologically" different worlds, then there would be no way to make sense of his moral philosophy, human freedom, and responsibility. But recently a number of sympathetic commentators have argued that there is a way of interpreting and/or correcting Kant to show that he is not committed to a rigid ontological or metaphysical distinction between two entirely different worlds. Although they approach the issue in a variety of ways (not all of which are fully compatible with each other), these commentators, including Silber, Allison, Wood, and Korsgaard, have presented a strong case that Kant is not committed to a "two world" theory. For example, Silber claims that: "Although he asserted that the two realms exist 'independently of one another and without interfering with each other' he found it impossible to speak of moral problems without presupposing their complete interaction. The experience of moral obligation is a prime example of thorough interaction. If the same human being (and therefore, the same *Willkür*) were not both moral and natural, existing fully and simultaneously in both realms, moral experience would be impossible."[19] And Korsgaard argues that the confusions about the "two world theory" stem from "a failure to appreciate the radical nature of Kant's separation of theoretical and practical reason, and their respective domains of explanation and deliberation. When these domains are separated in the way that Kant's philosophy requires, the problems about responsibility disappear, and we see that Kant's theory of freedom does not commit him to an ontological dualism."[20] Although these commentators have not cleared up all the problems that arise from the distinction of noumena and phenomena, I do think that they have been successful in showing that Kant is not committed to an extreme ontological or metaphysical dualism, and that Kant does have a unified conception of a human agent who is both free and conditioned by natural causality.

In the *Religion*, Kant does not abandon the noumena/phenomena distinction, but he plays down its significance. In the preface to the second edition he says:

> To understand this book in its essential content, only common morality is needed, without meddling with the *Critique of Practical Reason*, still less with the theoretical critique. When, for example, virtue as skill in *actions* conforming to duty (according to their legality) is called *virtus phaenomenon*, and the same virtue as an enduring *disposition* towards such actions from *duty* (because of their morality) is called *virtus noumenon*, these expressions are used only because of the schools; while the matter itself is contained, though in other words, in the most popular children's instructions and sermons, and is easily understood. (Rel 12–13)

The reason it is so important to see that Kant is not committed to a two world theory is because his analysis of radical evil presupposes the intelligibility of speaking about a "human nature" which cannot simply be identified with our phenomenal nature (or with our noumenal selves). "Nature" and "human nature" are used in the *Religion* in a manner that is strikingly different from the typical use of these terms in the *Critique of Pure Reason* and the *Critique of Practical Reason*. "Human nature" encompasses what we are as phenomenal and moral beings.

This becomes evident when, for example, Kant tells us that human nature possesses three "predispositions *[Anlagen]* to good." To be more precise, these are three divisions or elements "in the fixed character and destiny *[Bestimmung]* of man: (1) the predisposition to *animality* in man, taken as a *living* being; (2) the predisposition to *humanity* in man, taken as a living and at the same time a *rational* being; (3) the predisposition to *personality* in man, taken as a rational and at the same time an *accountable* being" (Rel 21). It is perfectly clear from this passage that Kant is speaking about "human nature" in a way that encompasses what he has previously classified as phenomena and noumena. When Kant speaks of "man" here he is not referring to a specific individual or even the entire set of single individuals. He is referring to man—or rather human beings—as the human race. As he tells us, "The man of whom we say, 'He is by nature good or evil,' is to be understood as not the single individual (for then one man could be considered good, by nature, another as evil), but as the entire race . . ." (Rel 21). We must be careful not to misinterpret what Kant is affirming here. We may be tempted to think that these three divisions of the original disposition to good in human nature (especially the predisposition to personality) are constituents of a predisposition to be *morally* good. But Kant explicitly denies this.

> Man *himself* must make or have made himself into whatever, in a moral sense, whether good or evil, he is or is to become. Either condition must be an effect of his free choice *[Willkür]*; for otherwise he could not be held responsible for it and could therefore be *morally* neither good nor evil. When it is said, Man is created good, this can mean nothing more than: He is created *for good* and the original *predisposition* in man is good; not that, thereby, he is already actually good, but rather he brings it about that he becomes good or evil, according to whether he adopts or does not adopt into his maxim the incentives which this predisposition carries with it ([an act] which must be left wholly to his own free choice). (Rel 40)

But if this is so, then in what sense can we say that the original predisposition is a predisposition *to* or *for good*.

Allen Wood is helpful in clarifying what Kant means:

> These predispositions all belong to "human nature" in the sense that they are "bound up with the possibility of human nature." They are predispositions *to good* in the sense that they are considered in themselves "not a matter of reproach" and that through them man is created "for good."
> No man, says Kant, is actually good or evil on account of his possession of these predispositions. Hence, if man is to be said to be "by nature" good or evil, this goodness or evil cannot consist in the predispositions bound up with the possibility of human nature. The very concept of morally good and evil involves, rather the actual use man makes of his capacities, and prevents us from regarding these capacities themselves as morally good or evil.[21]

I think Kant might have expressed himself more clearly, if he had simply said that human beings as a species have a predisposition to *become* morally good (or evil), but that we are not actually *born* morally good; human nature is not innately morally good. Human beings can only become morally good if they freely choose to act according to the moral law; if they adopt good maxims and act accordingly.

Before proceeding with our analysis of radical evil, we must clarify what Kant means by a disposition *(Gesinnung)* and a propensity *(Hang)*. They are the basis for understanding radical evil. But these concepts are not be confused with what Kant calls a predisposition *(Anlage)*.[22]

Silber claims that "the development of *[Gesinnung]* is, perhaps, the most important single contribution of the *Religion* to Kant's ethical theory, for by means of it he accounts for the continuity and responsibility of ambivalent volition, as well as the basis for its complex assessment."[23] We can appreciate why Silber makes this strong claim. On the basis of the *Groundwork* and the *Critique of Practical Reason,* it has not been entirely clear how Kant deals with the continuity of moral agency. In part, this is because he has primarily focused on the role of maxims and acts of choice in making moral decisions. But the individual who makes these choices, who adopts maxims, who does his duty for duty's sake is not simply a collection of discrete choices and maxims. Nor is he simply a timeless noumenal self. As Silber perceptively notes: "The disposition *[Gessinung]* is thus the enduring aspect of *Willkür;* it is *Willkür* considered in terms of the continuity and fullness of its free expression. It is the enduring pattern of intention that can be inferred from the many discrete acts of *Willkür* and reveals their ultimate motive." And he adds: "Continuity in disposition *[Gessinung]* is essential to moral self-identity."[24] This certainly helps to clarify the "work" that the concept of *Gesinnung* is intended to perform, and why it is so essential for Kant's analysis of moral agency. As long as we stay at this general abstract level, we do not encounter difficulties. But the more closely we examine the details of what Kant says about *Gesinnung,* the more problematic this concept becomes. Initially, we might think that Kant is finally coming to recognize the importance of what Aristotle recognized long ago—that by disposition, Kant means something that approximates what Aristotle meant by *hexis*—the disposition to act virtuously, which is acquired by proper education. Or we might think that by disposition, Kant means something that approximates what logical empiricists called "dispositional properties" that we ascribe to entities. But neither of these understandings of disposition is compatible with what Kant explicitly says about *Gesinnung.* For whether we are dealing with the Aristotelian tradition of the virtues, or with the more contemporary analyses of dispositional properties, we are dealing with dispositions that exist prior (conceptually and temporally) to any act of deliberative choice. But Kant explicitly says that "this disposition *[Gesinnung]* itself *must have been adopted by free choice [Willkür]"* (Rel 20, emphasis added). The full passage from which this is cited is even more perplexing because Kant says that, although this disposition is acquired, it "has not been acquired in time."

> To have a good or an evil disposition *[Gesinnung]* as an inborn natural constitution does not here mean that it has not been acquired by the man who harbors it, that he is not author of it, but rather, that it has not been acquired in time (that he has *always* been good, or evil, *from his youth up*). The disposition, i.e., the ultimate subjective ground of the adoption of maxims, can be one only and applies universally to the whole use of freedom. Yet this disposition itself must have been adopted by free choice *[Willkür],* for otherwise it could not be imputed. (Rel 20)

This is an extremely perplexing and obscure passage, and we will have to keep it in mind as we proceed. But, for all of its obscurity, there is no ambiguity that Kant is saying that a good or evil disposition *(Gesinnung)* is adopted by free choice. (This is perhaps the most significant difference between a predisposition *[Anlage]* and a disposition *[Gesinnung]; a Gesinnung* is adopted by a free choice *[Willkür]*, but a predisposition *[Anlage]* is *not* chosen; it is a constituent of our human nature; it is bound up "with the possibility of human nature.") This has led one critic to suggest that Kant's concept of *Gesinnung* is an unstable combination of the Aristotelian *hexis* and the Sartrean *project fondamental.*[25] We see how radically Kant's notion of a *Gesinnung* departs from any ordinary or traditional concept of a disposition when Kant tells us that "it has not been acquired in time" and that this *Gesinnung* must itself be conceived as a maxim—a supreme maxim that provides orientation to the moral life of an agent viewed as a whole (even though it is also possible for an agent to alter this disposition).[26] One might feel that Kant here comes close to being incoherent. He seems to get himself entangled in a vicious circle—a good or evil disposition *(Gesinnung)* is adopted by *Willkür,* but the *Willkür* itself presupposes this disposition.

Without underestimating these problems, I do think that we can give a sympathetic account of *Gesinnung,* which at least approximates what he wants to say (and is compatible with much of what he actually does say). For the moment, let us set aside the problems arising from the noumenal-phenomenal distinction, and what is and is not "acquired in time." We frequently do distinguish persons with good and evil dispositions in the following sense. There are persons whom we can trust or count on to do the right thing in difficult moral situations. They exhibit an overall pattern of beliefs, intentions, and actions which provide a basis for our (fallible) judgment that when they confront difficult moral choices, they will do what duty requires. Or to phrase the issue in a Kantian manner, they will adopt good maxims, maxims that give priority to the moral law. And, of course, there are persons who are so selfish or narcissistic, they are most likely to do anything to avoid acting for the sake of duty. Here there is no difficulty in drawing a distinction between a person's disposition or overall moral character and the specific actions or maxims that they adopt. Although their patterns of action are the basis for making inferences about their character, we do make judgments about their moral character—a character that informs the maxims they adopt. We also recognize that the relation between their moral character and their specific actions is neither strictly causal nor strictly logical. A person with a basically good disposition or character may occasionally adopt a maxim in which he gives priority to some natural inclination. And a moral scoundrel may occasionally do what duty requires (honor among thieves). Viewed in this manner, we can understand why such a disposition may be characterized as the subjective ground for the adoption of individual maxims. For such a disposition *informs* but does not (causally) determine the maxims that are adopted in specific concrete situations of moral conflict. We can also understand the sense in which we are responsible for our dispositions or characters. It is not that at a specific moment in time, we "choose" such a disposition. But rather the disposition itself is a result of the type of (free) moral decisions and maxims that we adopt. We are not born morally good or morally evil, we *become* morally good or evil by virtue of the choices we make and the maxims that we adopt. If we press further and ask why one person develops a disposition that leads him to adopt good maxims and someone else adopts evil maxims, there is much we can say about background and social circumstances, but we cannot give an ultimate answer to this question: it is inscrutable. Such an answer would require us to be able give a *theoretical* account of human freedom. And this is precisely what the Critical Philosophy shows us that we *cannot* provide. Ultimately, we cannot *know* why one person chooses to follow the moral law and another person does not. Nevertheless, from a practical point of view, this does not prevent us from postulating that as free moral agents we have the capacity to choose good or evil maxims. We are responsible for our individual choices and for our overall moral character. Furthermore, this disposition or character is not to be thought of as a fixed determinate essence. A good person can become evil, and an evil person can become good. "For man, therefore, who despite a corrupted heart yet possesses a good will *[Wille]* there remains hope of a return to the good from which he has strayed" (Rel 39).

I do not want to suggest that this understanding of a *Gesinnung* clears up all the problems and difficulties that Kant's discussion involves, but it helps to show the plausibility of the idea of a *Gesinnung*, why the notion is so important for Kant's mature theory of moral agency. There is one major difficulty with my analysis that cannot be avoided. For if my description approximates what Kant means by a *Gesinnung*, then it is applicable to both good and evil dispositions. And most of the time, Kant writes in a manner that would lead us to think that there are good and evil dispositions. Yet when Kant explicitly turns to the notion of radical evil and characterizes it as a propensity *(Hang)*, he neglects this symmetry between good and evil dispositions. Most of the time Kant writes as if there is no significant difference between disposition *(Gesinnung)* and propensity *(Hang)*, but he *never* speaks about a propensity to good, but only a propensity to evil. He explicitly tells us that "man is evil by nature" (and he means "man" as a species) — although we will see that this does not quite mean what we think it does. For Kant also insists that although "the character (good or evil) distinguishing man from other possible rational beings . . . is *innate* in him . . . , we shall ever take the position that nature is not to bear the blame (if it is evil) or take credit for it (if it is good), but that man himself is its author" (Rel 17).

Although there are many obscurities and problems concerning this crucial notion of *Gesinnung*, we can appreciate why Kant gets himself entangled in these difficulties. It stems from one of the most admirable and important features of Kant's moral theory. Despite the caricatures of him, Kant certainly acknowledges that an individual's temperament, background, social circumstances, and moral training influence his moral character and choices. But the primary issue for Kant is always responsibility and accountability. Our moral freedom is never compromised by external events or by our natural inclinations, desires, character, or our acquired dispositions. Kant might have made himself clearer if he had forthrightly said that a disposition *(Gesinnung)*—whether an individual or species disposition—is *never* sufficient to determine our moral choices instead of saying that a good or evil disposition "must have been adopted by free choice *[Willkür]*." Kant himself appears to be aware of the awkward way in which he has characterized a *Gesinnung*. For he characterizes it as "the ultimate subjective ground of the adoption of maxims," and immediately says, "But the subjective ground or cause of this adoption cannot be further known (though it is inevitable that we should inquire into it)" (Rel 20).

But let us put aside these difficulties in giving an intelligible account of what Kant means by *Gesinnung* and explore how the introduction of this concept enables us to understand what he means by "radical evil." On the basis of what we have learned about the "original predisposition to good in human nature," we at least know what radical evil is not. Radical evil is not to be identified with natural inclinations. Nor is it to be identified with some intrinsic defect or corruption of our human rationality. The third division of our original predisposition to good provides an essential clue to the meaning of radical evil. This aspect of the predisposition to good enables us to understand what Kant calls "the propensity *[Hang]* to evil in human nature." Consider Kant's characterization of the predisposition to personality.

> The predisposition to *personality* is the capacity for respect for the moral law as *in itself a sufficient incentive of the will [Willkür]*. This capacity for simple respect for the moral law within us would thus be moral feeling, which in and through itself does not constitute an end of the natural disposition except so far as it is the motivating force of the will *[Willkür]*. Since this is possible only when the free will *[Willkür]* incorporates such moral feeling into its maxim, the property of such a will *[Willkür]* is good character. The latter, like every character of the free will *[Willkür]*, is something which can only be acquired; its possibility, however, demands the presence in our nature of a predisposition on which it is absolutely impossible to graft anything evil. We cannot rightly call the idea of the moral law, with the respect which is inseparable from it, *a predisposition to personality;* it is personality itself. . . . But the subjective ground for the adoption into our maxims of this respect as a motivating force seems to be an adjunct to our personality, and thus to deserve the name of a predisposition to its furtherance. (Rel 22–23)

There is nothing startlingly new here that could not have been inferred from the *Groundwork* or the *Critique of Practical Reason*. But there is a new emphasis insofar as Kant isolates the predisposition to follow the moral law from the actual decision to follow the law. Kant seeks to clarify the conditions for the possibility of being moral. Having this predisposition is constitutive of what it is to be a human being (a finite rational being).

But if this predisposition to good is constitutive of our very nature as human beings, how are we to account for the fact that we do not always follow this predisposition; that we do not always do what we morally ought to do. We are tempted *not* to follow the moral law, to adopt evil maxims—maxims that give priority to incentives other than those of respect for the moral law. It is this tendency or propensity *(Hang)* that Kant seeks to isolate with his introduction of the concept of radical evil. But what does Kant mean by a propensity *(Hang)*? He tells us that "by *propensity (propensio)* I understand the subjective ground of the possibility of an inclination (habitual craving, *concupiscentia*) so far as mankind in general is liable to it" (Rel 23–24). And how are we to distinguish a propensity *(Hang)* from a predisposition *(Anlage)*? "A propensity is distinguished from a predisposition by the fact that although it can indeed be innate, it ought not to be represented merely thus; for it can also be regarded as having been acquired (if it is good), or brought by man upon himself (if it is evil)" (Rel 24). We get a clearer idea of what Kant means by turning to his shocking footnote.

> A *propensity [Hang]* is really only the predisposition to crave a delight which, when once experienced, arouses in the subject an inclination to it. Thus all savage peoples have a propensity for intoxicants; for though many of them are wholly ignorant of intoxication and in consequence have absolutely no craving for an intoxicant, let them but once sample it and there is aroused in them an almost inextinguishable craving for it. (Rel 24)[27]

"Radical evil" is not the name of a special type or form of evil. It is certainly not a form of evil that "we cannot conceive." On the contrary, we can clearly conceive it, and what it names is simply the propensity *(Hang)* not to do what duty requires, not to follow the moral law. Kant does distinguish three distinct degrees of this "capacity for evil," but they are all related to the failure to adopt good maxims.

> First, there is the weakness of the human heart in the general observance of adopted maxims, or in other words, the *frailty* of human nature; second, the propensity for mixing unmoral with moral motivating causes (even when it is done with good intent and under maxims of the good), that is, *impurity,* and third, the propensity to adopt evil maxims, that is, the *wickedness* of human nature or of the human heart. (Rel 24)

We may think that "wickedness" names some horrendous form or degree of evil. And certainly Kant's rhetoric makes it sound this way.

Third: the wickedness *(vitiositas, pravitas)* or, if you like, the corruption *(corruptio)* of the human heart is the propensity of the will *[Willkür]* to maxims which neglect the incentives springing from the moral law in favor of others which are not moral. It may also be called the *perversity (perversitas)* of the human heart, for it reverses the ethical order [of priority] among the incentives of a *free* will *[Willkür];* and although conduct which is lawfully good (i.e., legal) may be found with it, yet the cast of mind is thereby corrupted at its root (so far as the moral disposition is concerned), and the man is hence designated evil.

It will be remarked that this propensity to evil is here ascribed (as regards conduct) to men in general, even to the best of them; this must be the case if it is to be proved that the propensity to evil in mankind is universal, or, what here comes to the same thing, that it is woven into human nature. (Rel 25)

Let us reflect carefully on Kant's characterization of the "third degree" of the capacity for evil with reference to the example of the sympathetic person that I discussed earlier. Let us suppose that such a person—even when it is pointed out to him—makes a conscious decision to continue to give priority to his feelings of sympathy for his fellow human beings (rather than "incentives springing from the moral law"). And let us also grant—as Kant says we may—that his conduct is "lawfully good." He acts in accord with duty, although not for the sake of duty. On the basis of Kant's characterization of wickedness, such a self-consciously motivated sympathetic person whose actions are "lawfully good" is a paradigm of wickedness. He has a cast of mind that is corrupted at the root, and he must be "designated as evil." And the reason for this judgment is that he has given priority to an incentive based upon his natural inclinations rather than to the incentive of following the moral law. But to judge such a person to be an exemplar of wickedness; to judge his maxims—in respect to the degree of evil—to be in the same category as those of the mass murderer is much more than awkward consequence of a rigoristic analysis; it is morally perverse.

But we must face still greater problems. Kant's characterization of radical evil as a propensity that is "woven into human nature" actually obscures (rather than clarifies) a cardinal point in his moral philosophy. The very concept of a propensity *(Hang)* is one that is parasitic upon our notion of causality. A propensity presumably has *causal efficacy.* Thus in Kant's unfortunate example of savages who have a craving for intoxicants, we think of this as a propensity with an overwhelming causal power. Such a craving demands satisfaction unless it is forcefully resisted in the strongest possible manner. But the propensity to evil cannot be thought of in this way. It is *not* an active force "pushing" or tempting us to be morally evil. For there is no moral evil unless we *freely* adopt evil maxims. And a *Willkür* that adopts these maxims is not causally determined by anything but itself; it is a spontaneous manifestation of our freedom.[28]

It may be objected that the example of the craving for intoxicants is mis-leading because Kant himself makes a sharp distinction between a physical (natural) propensity and a moral propensity.

> Every propensity is either physical, i.e., pertaining to the will *[Willkür]* of man as a natural being, or moral, i.e., pertaining to his will *[Willkür]* as a moral being. In the first sense there is no propensity to moral evil, for such a propen-sity must spring from freedom. . . . Hence a propensity to evil can inhere only in the moral capacity of the will *[Willkür]*. But nothing is morally evil (i.e., capable of being imputed) but that which is our own *act*. (Rel 26)

Kant realizes that if by the concept of moral propensity we mean "a sub-jective determining ground of the will *[Willkür]* which precedes all acts," this cannot be an act itself. To clear up this point, he introduces two meanings of "act." In the first sense "act" refers to the exercise of freedom whereby the supreme maxim—the subjective determining ground of the will is adopted by the *Willkür.* The second refers to specific acts performed on the basis of this supreme maxim. But these distinctions do not alter the main point that I want to emphasize; they reinforce it. The alleged propensity to intoxicants is neither universal nor necessary; it is not a propensity of humans as a species. It need not even lead to the adoption of evil maxims. In all these respects, it differs from a moral propensity to evil. But if a moral propensity to evil "springs from freedom," one may begin to wonder whether—and in what sense—there really is such a propensity. Why? Because if the propen-sity springs from freedom, the very existence of such a propensity depends upon "the exercise of freedom whereby the supreme maxim . . . is adopted by the will *[Willkür]* . . . "(Rel 26). But the *Willkür* is the capacity for choos-ing maxims freely. Consequently it is not conditioned (causally influenced) by any propensity—physical or moral.

We can specify Kant's problem from a slightly different perspective. Kant insists on making two claims which, although not necessarily incompatible, nevertheless seem to undermine the very idea of a propensity to moral evil. The first claim is that this propensity is itself the result of an *act* understood as the exercise of freedom whereby the supreme maxim is adopted by the will *(Willkür)*. The second claim is that we, as free moral agents, can always resist this alleged propensity (which we have adopted by the exercise of our freedom). But if both these claims are true, it is difficult to understand what is left to the very idea of a "propensity to moral evil." It is extraordinarily paradoxical (if not incoherent) to claim that there is a "natural propensity to evil" that is universal, necessary, and "as it were, rooted in our humanity," and yet "we must, after all, ever hold man himself responsible for it" (Rel 28). Yet this is precisely what Kant affirms. Kant unambiguously declares that we call this "*radical* innate *evil* in human nature (yet none the less brought upon us by ourselves)" (Rel 28). Furthermore, Kant is quite emphatic that "we must not, however, look for an origin in time of a moral character *[Beschaffenheit]* for which we are held to be responsible; though to do so is inevitable if we wish to *explain* the contingent existence of this character . . ." (Rel 38).

Why, we may ask, does Kant get himself entangled in these difficulties and paradoxes? It looks like Kant wants to have his cake and eat it too, and in a way he does. Or to switch metaphors, Kant is at war with himself. For, on the one hand, Kant never wants to compromise one of the most basic claims of his moral philosophy—human beings are free moral agents who are completely and solely responsible for their moral choices and for the maxims that they adopt. If we become morally good or evil, this is a consequence of our own doing—our own free will. But, on the other hand, Kant also wants to affirm that all human beings have an innate propensity to moral evil. In order to have his cake and eat it too, Kant is driven to claim that even though this propensity is woven into the fabric of human nature, it is a propensity that springs from our freedom; a propensity for which we are responsible.

Furthermore, the more we focus on the details of Kant's analysis of radical evil, the more dubious the concept seems to be.[29] After making the apparently dramatic claim that "man is evil by nature," Kant, as I have previously indicated, writes "Man is evil, can mean only, he is conscious of the moral law but nevertheless adopted into his maxim the (occasional) deviation therefrom" (Rel 27). But we do not need the *Religion* or any special concept of radical evil to know this. The *Groundwork*—indeed the very project of Kant's moral philosophy—is based upon the idea that we do not always do what we ought to do; we do not always follow the moral law. Presumably the introduction of the concept of radical evil is intended to explain (from a practical point of view) *why* we deviate from following the moral law. We do not always follow the moral law *because* all human beings have a propensity to moral evil. What is the explanatory role of this "because"? It simply reiterates the obvious fact that human beings who are conscious of the moral law occasionally (freely) deviate from it. In short, radical evil—the alleged propensity to moral evil which is presumably a universal characteristic of human beings—does not have any explanatory force (practical or theoretical) at all. It simply restates the obvious—that we sometimes (freely) deviate from the moral law, and that no matter how morally good we actually become, we never escape from this possibility.

I have no doubt that Kant intended to make a much more forceful claim, that he thought he was showing something fundamental when he asserted that human beings are by nature evil, that this active "propensity is so deeply rooted in the will *[Willkür]*" that we are justified in calling it "radical," that human beings—even the best of them—*cannot* escape the temptation to violate the moral law because this propensity is innate and inextricable. My argument, however, is that when we scrutinize carefully what Kant actually *says*, when we see how "radically" he qualifies his key claims, when we realize that we are responsible for this propensity to evil because it issues from our freedom, and that it is always within our power to resist this temptation to violate the moral law, and that even the most wicked person with the most entrenched evil disposition can be "reborn," it is difficult to avoid the conclusion that Kant himself completely eviscerates his doctrine of radical evil.

But we have not yet come to the end of our difficulties with the concept of radical evil. I have already noted that radical evil is a species concept; it is universally applicable to all human beings; it is woven into the very fabric of human nature. It is not then a contingent characteristic of *some* human beings or even of *all* human beings. But now we must ask, what is the justification for this universal claim? What is the basis for claiming that the propensity to moral evil is a species concept, one which is woven into the very fabric of our human nature? If there is one lesson that we should have learned from the Critical Philosophy, it is that genuinely synthetic universal claims can *never* be justified by appeals to experience; their justification requires a deduction. Yet when Kant comes to that crucial stage in his argument where, after explaining what he means by radical evil as a species concept, we expect some sort of formal proof that it is a universal characteristic of human beings, no such proof is forthcoming. Kant says, "That such a corrupt propensity must indeed be rooted in man need not be formally proved in view of the multitude of crying examples which experience *of the actions* of men puts before our eyes" (Rel 28).

Kant follows this assertion with a set of empirical observations based upon (dubious) anthropological evidence, "melancholy" observations about "civilized" peoples, and casual remarks about the international behavior of nation-states (Rel 28–29).[30]

Allison states the problem here quite clearly—and even attempts to do what Kant failed to do—to provide an a priori deduction to justify the claim that there is a universal propensity to moral evil.

> Kant insists not only that there is a propensity to evil but that it is "rooted in humanity itself" and therefore, universal. What grounds, we may ask, does Kant offer for this apparently audacious claim?
>
> Kant's official answer to this obvious question is quite disappointing. . . . Instead of offering a "formal proof" of the universality of the propensity to evil, he simply asserts that the necessity for such a proof is obviated by "the multitude of crying examples which experience of the actions of men put before our eyes.". . . In short, he seems to treat it as an unproblematic empirical generalization. But clearly, even if for the sake of argument one accepts Kant's appeal to some rather selective anthropological evidence, the *most* that this evidence can show is that evil is widespread, not that there is a universal propensity to it. Moreover, since Kant insists that this propensity concerns only the ultimate subjective ground of one's maxims and is perfectly compatible with a virtuous empirical character, it is difficult to see what could conceivably

falsify this claim. Consequently, it is also difficult to take seriously the suggestion that it is intended as an empirical generalization.[31]

When we examine what Kant means by radical evil, and his justification (or rather lack of justification) for claiming "man is evil by nature," we become acutely aware of the disparity between his dramatic rhetoric and the innocuous content of what he is saying. Even if we accepted the doctrine that there is "propensity to evil in human nature," the existence of such a propensity does not tell us anything about whether human beings will become actually good or evil. At times, it seems as if "radical evil" is only a fancy way of reiterating the obvious, that is, human beings do not always follow the moral law, they do not do what they ought to do. If we ask—using Kant's own words—*why* human beings who are "conscious of the moral law" nevertheless adopt into their maxims "the (occasional) deviation therefrom" (Rel 27), the appeal to radical evil does not really offer any account or explanation. Ultimately, the reason why some persons adopt good maxims and some adopt evil maxims is "inscrutable." Furthermore, we do not have any proof, deduction, or justification that the propensity to evil is a universal characteristic of the human species.

It almost seems as if Kant is caught in something like a "dialectical illusion." For starting with the obvious fact that human beings sometimes adopt good maxims and sometimes adopt evil maxims (i.e., sometimes adopt maxims in which we give priority to moral incentives and sometimes adopt maxims that give priority to nonmoral incentives), we seek to explain why human beings do not always follow the moral law, why they do adopt evil maxims. We do this by appealing to the concept of radical evil, the presumably universal propensity that is "rooted in humanity itself." But once we carefully analyze what this means, we discover only that although it is always possible for human beings to adopt good maxims, sometimes they do not. The illusion here is that we think that radical evil is a concept that enables us to explain (at least practically) why we are tempted to adopt evil maxims, but it does not explain anything about our actual moral choices. Indeed, given Kant's account of freedom, we realize that in asking *why* we freely adopt good maxims rather than evil maxims, we are asking an impossible question. For we are, in effect, asking for a theoretical understanding of what constitutes human freedom. Ironically, Kant himself comes very close to saying something like this at the very beginning of the *Religion*.

> When we say, then, Man is by nature good, or, Man is by nature evil, this means only that there is in him an ultimate ground (inscrutable to us) of the adoption of good maxims or of evil maxims (i.e., those contrary to law), and this he has, being a man; and hence he thereby expresses the character of his species. (Rel 17)

And to drive home the point that this is *inscrutable*, Kant adds the following footnote:

> That the ultimate subjective ground of the adoption of moral maxims is inscrutable is indeed already evident from this, that since this adoption is free, its ground (why, for example, I have chosen an evil and not a good maxim) must not be sought in any natural impulse, but always again in a maxim. Now since this maxim also must have its ground, and since apart from maxims no *determining ground* of free choice *[Willkür]* can or ought to be adduced, we are referred back endlessly in the series of subjective determinations, without ever being able to reach the ultimate ground. (Rel 17–18)

It is difficult to resist the conclusion that the concept of radical evil is a dialectical illusion. It seduces us into thinking that we can explain something that we—as finite rational beings—cannot *possibly* explain, the ultimate subjective ground for why we freely choose good or evil maxims. This ultimate subjective ground is inscrutable.

My aim in this essay has been to understand what Kant means by radical evil. But I also want to see if Kant's reflections on evil help us to comprehend the forms of evil that have broken out in the twentieth century—including the evil evoked by the word "Auschwitz." John Silber (and many would agree with him) says that Kant is "the most important writer on ethics since Aristotle" and that he intended "to set forth doctrines that were not just theoretical in nature but were intended to guide everyday conduct."[32] But despite Kant's language of "wickedness," "corruption," and "perversity," his analysis of evil is disappointing. "Evil" primarily designates *any* immoral maxim, any maxim that gives priority to nonmoral incentives—no matter how benign these may be. A "wicked" person is someone who has a disposition (for which he is responsible) to adopt evil maxims. And this disposition is itself like a supreme maxim (and consequently freely adopted) that disposes us to adopt specific evil maxims. I have argued that when we scrutinize the meaning of "radical evil," it turns out to be little more than a way of calling attention to the fact that human beings have a propensity (for which *they are responsible*) to adopt immoral maxims. (When one subordinates a moral incentive to a nonmoral incentive, the result is an immoral maxim.) This is a propensity or temptation which can and ought to be resisted. Everyone can and ought to adopt good maxims even though human beings never escape the temptation to adopt evil maxims. But some of Kant's reflections on duty—especially the "absolute" duty of a citizen to obey the sovereign power and the duty of a soldier to obey the orders of a superior—are more than disappointing; they are extremely disturbing. Consider the case of Adolf Eichmann, who cited Kant (with reasonable accuracy) at his trial in Jerusalem in order to justify his conduct in sending victims to death camps.[33] We cannot blame Kant, the great champion of human dignity, for this perverse appropriation of the categorical imperative. Nevertheless, as Silber points out: "It may seem outrageous to find Kant's ethical doctrine, grounded as it is in the dignity of the moral person as end-in-himself, used to exculpate a confessed accomplice to mass murder. But it should come as no surprise to Kant scholars, for Kant's views on the citizen's obligation to the sovereign strongly support Eichmann's position."[34] Kant's "official" doctrine is that the ban on resisting any supreme lawmaking is *absolute*, and also that a soldier must always obey the orders of a superior. (Let us not forget that for all the violence of the Nazis, "Hitler was made Chancellor in a constitutionally proper manner.")[35] I want to quote just three of the many passages that Eichmann might have cited from Kant to justify his acceptance of the *Führerprinzip*.

> [A]ny resistance to the supreme lawmaking power, any incitement of dissatisfied subjects to action, any uprising that bursts into rebellion—that all this is the worst, most punishable crime in a community. For it shatters the community's foundations. And this ban is *absolute*, so unconditional that even though that supreme power or its agent, the head of state, may have broken the original contract, even though in the subject's eyes he may have forfeited the right to legislate by empowering the government to rule tyrannically by sheer violence, even then the subject is allowed no resistance, no violent counteraction.
>
> [T]here is no right of sedition (*seditio*) much less a right of revolution (*rebellio*), and least of all a right to lay hands on or take the life of the chief of state when he is an individual person on the excuse that he has misused his authority. . . . It is the people's duty to endure even the most intolerable abuse of supreme authority.[36]
>
> Thus it would be ruinous if an officer, receiving an order from his superiors, wanted while on duty to engage openly in subtle reasoning about its appropriateness or utility; he must obey.[37]

I certainly do not want to judge Kant by the way his statements have been misappropriated and distorted—especially when they are taken out of context. Nor is it fair to criticize Kant for his failure to anticipate the type of systematic terror and violence practiced by the Nazis. (It is difficult to think of any philosopher whose ethical doctrines have not lent themselves to gross distortions.) And I have no doubt that Kant would find ample grounds to condemn the conduct of the Nazi regime. Nevertheless, the consistency and even harshness with which Kant opposes any active resistance against "the supreme lawmaking power," no matter how tyrannical and violent it may be, should at least make us question his rigorism—and his insistence that this ban is *absolute* and *unconditional*.[38]

The Eichmann question concerns the issue of a citizen's duty to obey the law of the land, even if it is the Führer's law, and a soldier's duty to obey orders, but what about the Führer himself? How does Kant's moral theory apply to the person who is ultimately responsible for giving the orders? Does Kant's understanding of evil and radical evil help us to understand and judge the conduct of Hitler?[39] I cannot explore the complex historical question of discerning Hitler's actual motives and behavior. I refer to Hitler solely in order to raise some questions about Kant's understanding of evil that I have not yet squarely addressed. To raise these questions we need to return to some of the details of Kant's analysis of evil. Let us recall that in the *Religion* Kant makes it perfectly clear that it is not our natural inclinations, our sensuous nature, that is the source of evil. Furthermore, our faculty of volition and our reason are not intrinsically (morally) evil or corrupt. In this respect, Kant stands squarely in the theological tradition that can trace its lineage back to Augustine—a tradition which affirms that the faculties of human beings (God's creatures) are not intrinsically evil; rather moral evil arises when human beings misuse their faculties. We, and we alone, are responsible for evil maxims that we adopt. In a famous passage in the *Religion*, Kant categorically rejects the possibility of thinking of man as "a devilish being *(einem teuflifchen Wesen)*."

> In seeking, therefore, a ground of the morally-evil in man, [we find that] *sensuous nature* comprises too little, for when the incentives which can spring from freedom are taken away, man is reduced to a merely animal being. On the other hand, a reason exempt from the moral law, a *malignant reason* as it were (a thoroughly evil will *[Wille]*) comprises too much, for thereby opposition to the law would itself be set up as an incentive (since in the absence of all incentives the will *[Willkür]* cannot be determined), and thus the subject would be made a devilish being. *Neither of these designations is applicable to man.* (Rel 30, my emphasis added to the final sentence)

But why cannot human beings be considered to be devilish beings? Why is the idea of a "malignant reason" rejected? Why does Kant simply rule this out as being "applicable to man"? Seeking answers to these questions takes us to the heart of Kant's moral philosophy, and indeed, to his understanding of moral evil. There are reasons why Kant does reject these possibilities. But before we can evaluate his rejection, we need to understand these reasons.

How are we to interpret the above passage, which rules out the possibility of man's being a devilish being? If we recall that in dealing with radical evil, Kant is primarily concerned with man as a species (and not with the character or disposition of individual human beings), then we can certainly understand why he makes the above claim. If it were true that a malignant reason is constitutive of human nature, if man as a *species* were intrinsically devilish, then there would be no morality. The reason is clear. Morality presupposes freedom and choice. If one claims that man as a species is devilish, that a malignant reason is *constitutive* of his very nature, then there is no possibility that he could act otherwise. It makes no sense to speak of human beings as (freely) adopting good or evil maxims. We can see the parallelism with why there would be no morality (according to Kant) if man as a species were simply and exclusively a sensuous natural being, that is, a nonhuman animal. The possibility of morality presupposes freedom and choice, and this means that a moral agent has the capacity to (freely) choose which maxims are adopted; he is not predetermined to choose only evil maxims.

But what about the possibility that *some* human beings are devilish beings. Once again, if this is interpreted to mean that some but not all human beings are *innately* devilish, then the same considerations would apply. For this would mean that some human beings are not really fully human—they do not have the capacity to (freely) choose good or evil maxims.

But suppose we consider the case of someone who is not innately (in the strong sense of innate) diabolical but *becomes* diabolical, that is, who acts in a manner so that we infer that he has a disposition whereby his supreme maxim is to defy the moral law—someone who refuses to acknowledge the authority of the categorical imperative. Kant addresses this possibility:

> Man (even the most wicked) does not, under any maxim whatsoever, repudiate the moral law in the manner of a rebel (renouncing obedience to it). The law, rather, forces itself upon him irresistibly by virtue of his moral predisposition; and were no other incentive working in opposition, he would adopt the law into his supreme maxim as the sufficient determining ground of his will [*Willkür*]; that is, he would be morally good. (Rel 31)

But this passage is ambiguous: it is open to at least two radically different interpretations which must be carefully distinguished from each other. In order to bring out this ambiguity, we need to return to our discussion of the *Wille/Willkür* distinction. Kant emphasizes (especially in the *Religion*) that *Willkür* is that aspect of the faculty of volition by which we make free choices. Even when we recognize the moral law as the norm to which our maxims may or may not conform, we are nevertheless free to obey or disobey it; we are free to adopt good and bad maxims. The *Wille* itself (in its narrow technical sense) is practical reason; it is the moral law, the supreme moral norm. The *Wille/Willkür* distinction is one that is made within a *unified* faculty of volition (sometimes also referred to as *Wille*). In short, there is no *Wille* without a *Willkür*, and there is no (human) *Willkür* without the *Wille*. *Wille* and *Willkür* are codependent, although we can distinguish their different functions. Allison crisply states the difference: "Thus, it is *Wille* in the narrow sense that provides the norm and *Willkür* that chooses in light of this norm."[40] When Kant says that "the law . . . *forces* itself upon [man] *irresistibly*," he is not making a causal claim but rather a moral claim; he is asserting that man as a finite rational agent *recognizes* the objective moral law as the norm to which his maxims ought to conform. We cannot avoid *acknowledging* the categorical imperative regardless of whether we choose to obey it or not. This is the sense in which it is perfectly accurate for Kant to declare: "Man (even the most wicked) does not, under any maxim whatsoever, repudiate the moral law in the manner of a rebel (renouncing obedience to it)." To be a human being, to be a finite rational agent, is to be person who recognizes the authority of the moral law, regardless of whether we *choose* to follow or not to follow the categorical imperative.[41]

But now we can specify the ambiguity in the above passage. Even if we accept the claim that human beings as a *species* are not devilish beings, and that no matter how wicked a person may be he cannot avoid acknowledging the authority of the moral law, this does not address the issue of whether someone can repudiate the moral law in the sense that he freely chooses to defy it. I want to argue that not only is this possible, but on Kant's own analysis of the *Willkür* (free choice) this *must* be possible. It *must* be possible for an individual to become a devilish being. It must be possible for an individual to repudiate the moral law in such a manner that he freely adopts a disposition *(Gesinnung)* in which he consistently seeks to repudiate the moral law.

To bring out the significance of what I am claiming, I want to examine Silber's fundamental criticism of Kant's treatment of radical evil. Silber thinks that Kant's refusal to consider the possibility that individuals can defy the moral law reveals a fundamental weakness in his moral philosophy. This is the primary reason why Silber claims that Kant's ethics is not adequate to account for Auschwitz.

> Kant's ethics is inadequate to the understanding of Auschwitz because Kant denies the possibility of the deliberate rejection of the moral law. Not even a wicked man, Kant holds, can will evil for the sake of evil. His evil, according to Kant, consists merely in his willingness to ignore or subordinate the moral law when it interferes with his nonmoral but natural inclinations. His evil is expressed in abandoning the conditions of free personal fulfillment in favor of fulfillment as a creature of natural desire. . . . [Kant denies] the possibility of a person knowingly doing evil for its own sake. By insisting that freedom is a power whose fulfillment depends upon rationality and that its irrational misuse is merely impotence, Kant proposed a theory that rules out the contravening evidence of human experience.[42]

Several commentators have sought to defend Kant against Silber's objection. Allen Wood, for example, addressing himself to an earlier expression of this criticism by Silber, says, "This, however, is a fallacy endemic to philosophical criticism: the supposition that by pointing to 'facts' (which no one disputes) that one can give a philosophical justification of the manner in which one has expressed the facts."[43] It is, of course, true that philosophical claims rarely are resolved by "pointing to 'facts,'" and that the crucial issue frequently turns out to be the *interpretation* of the so-called facts. Nevertheless this dismissal strikes me as rather cavalier for two reasons. In the first place, Kant himself—as we have noted—certainly seems to support his thesis about the universality of radical evil by "pointing to 'facts.'" But secondly, this is not quite what Silber means when he says "Kant's insistence to the contrary, man's free power to reject the law in defiance is an ineradicable fact of human experience" (Rel cxxix). Silber is not referring to the "facts" and "experience" in the *restricted* sense that these terms are used in the *Critique of Pure Reason,* where they refer to the phenomenal realm. He is using these terms more broadly, in a manner consistent with Kant when he himself speaks of the "experience *[Erfahrung]* of the actions of men" in the *Religion* (Rel 28). Silber's claim is that there are persons who knowingly do evil for its own sake, who deliberately reject the moral law, who freely use their (practical reason) to reject reason—and that Kant's moral theory does not account for this.[44] Silber would have been more precise if he had phrased his point in a slightly different manner. The locus of evil is to be found in the maxims that an agent adopts. An individual is judged to be evil if he "chooses" a disposition—a supreme, overarching maxim—to adopt evil maxims. We do not directly "observe" maxims, we infer them from the actions that human beings perform.[45] And such an inference is always (in principle) fallible. Nevertheless, despite this fallibility, we do judge persons to be evil (or good) on the basis of their actions. We *infer* their disposition *(Gesinnung)* on the basis of the pattern of their actions. So Silber might have said that on the basis of their actions and their general behavior we infer and judge that there are some persons who do not simply give priority to incentives based upon their natural inclinations, but who act in such a manner that they do evil for evil's sake; they *systematically* defy the moral law. And this is the possibility that Kant fails to consider.

We still have not come to the heart of the matter—to what Silber is getting at in his criticism of Kant. For Silber is not arguing that man as a species is devilish, that being devilish is constitutive of human nature. And he is not even denying that human beings as rational moral agents must acknowledge the authority of the moral law. On the contrary, his criticism depends on affirming this claim. Rather he is underscoring something that Kant does not seem to really consider—that there are some persons (and characters in fiction) who—to use the Kantian terminology, adopt as a primary incentive the incentive to defy the moral law, to do evil for evil's sake.[46]

Although I agree with Silber that Kant does not squarely deal with this possibility, ironically, his moral theory—as developed in the *Religion*—*can* deal with it.

In a revealing and significant footnote, Kant writes:

For from the fact that a being has reason it by no means follows that this reason, by the mere representing of the fitness of its maxims to be laid down as universal laws, is thereby rendered capable of determining the will *[Willkür]* unconditionally, so as to be "practical" of itself; at least not so far as we can see. The most rational mortal being in the world might still stand in need of certain incentives, originating in objects of desire, to determine his choice *[Willkür]*. He might, indeed, bestow the most rational reflection on all that concerns not only the greatest sum of these incentives in him but also the means of attaining the end thereby determined, without ever suspecting the possibility of such a thing as the absolutely imperative moral law which proclaims that it is itself an incentive, and indeed, the highest. Were it not given us from within, we should never by any ratiocination subtilize it into existence to win over our will *[Willkür]* to it; yet this law is the only law which informs us of the independence of our will *[Willkür]* from determination by all other incentives (of our freedom) and at the same time of the accountability of all our actions. (Rel 21)[47]

Although Kant's phrasing is a bit turgid his basic point is clear. Reason by itself is not sufficient to determine what we choose to do. There must be a *moral incentive*. Our moral feeling, our respect for the law, is a sufficient incentive. But our *Willkür* may *choose* to defy the moral law. If the moral law serves as an incentive, there can always be a counterincentive. As human beings, with a *human Willkür*, we are *radically* free in choosing which incentives to follow, and we are accountable for these choices. We *can* choose to be "perverse," we *can* choose to be "devilish," we *can* choose to defy what reason tells us we ought to do. If we are told that to act in such a manner is irrational, or self-destructive, or even that acting in this manner negates our human freedom, it does not follow that we *cannot* do this. On the contrary such a possibility is intrinsic to a *human Willkür*. There are no constraints—either external or internal—on what the *Willkür* can choose. For to say there are constraints is, in effect, to limit—and thereby to deny—freedom.

We can approach the issue of our radical free choice from a slightly different angle. Kant typically limits the type of incentives that can be adopted into a maxim (good or evil) to two kinds: the moral incentive to conform to the moral law—the incentive that arises from "moral feeling"—and nonmoral incentives that arise from our natural inclinations. But why should we limit incentives to these two kinds, why should we identify—as Kant frequently does—nonmoral incentives with the incentives that arise from natural inclinations. Why not recognize that there can be incentives like the incentive to do evil for the sake of evil, or the incentive to defy the moral law, or the incentive to further the dominance of the "master race" which cannot be assimilated to what Kant classifies "natural inclinations."[48] These are not just abstract or theoretical questions. It is completely artificial and misleading to say that figures such as Hitler or Stalin, who are responsible for the murder and torture of millions, are evil because they privileged incentives based upon their natural inclinations; that they were motivated primarily by self-love or the desire for happiness. They are not comparable to shopkeepers who pretend to be honest because they want to increase their profits. The fault here is to be found in Kant's limited moral psychology, in the narrow range of *types* of incentives that Kant considers for adopting evil maxims. If one is really to distinguish different types of evil, then one must consider the full range of incentives that govern evil maxims. There are major differences among those who may be misguided because they give priority to their sympathetic feeling for their fellow human beings; those (like Eichmann) whose primary incentive for performing murderous deeds seems to have been advancing his career; those who mock and defy the moral law; and those who do evil for evil's sake. It obscures more than it illuminates to say in *all* of these instances (and many more which we can distinguish), that an agent is evil because he gives priority to "incentives of his sensuous nature" over "the moral incentive" to obey the moral law. There is no free choice *(Willkür)* unless there is the free choice to be morally perverse. And if we ask why do *some* persons choose to become good and others choose to become evil, let us not forget that it is Kant himself who tells us "that the ultimate ground for the adoption of moral maxims is inscrutable . . ." (Rel 17).

Silber criticizes Kant for being too "rationalistic," for linking reason and freedom so intimately that he cannot allow for the possibility of self-consciously defying the moral law. But if we follow out the consequences of Kant's analysis of *Willkür*, it is Kant himself who opens up the possibility that some individuals may become "devilish beings."

There is, however, a point to Silber's criticism, although I think it must be restated. Silber tries to locate what I take to be the deepest unresolved tension in Kant's moral philosophy and in his analysis of evil. There is the Kant who focuses on the dignity of human beings, on what it means to be a free autonomous being. Freedom and autonomy are achievements—the highest achievements that human beings can realize. There is the Kant who links freedom, autonomy, the moral law, and practical reason. This is the Kant who insists that in following the moral law we fulfill ourselves as (practical) rational beings. This is the Kant who seeks to give a deduction of freedom from the moral law which is based upon "the fact of reason."[49] And, on the basis of the *Groundwork* and the *Critique of Practical Reason,* this is the dominant Kant that emerges—and the Kant that has influenced so much of modern moral philosophy.

But there is another strand in Kant's thinking. Kant realized—especially in the *Religion*—that in order to give an adequate account of the will (*Wille* in the broad sense) he needed to carefully distinguish the *Wille* as practical reason, the *Wille* as the moral law, the norm that ought to guide the maxims that we adopt from our capacity to make free choices *(Willkür).* We cannot hold agents responsible for what they do unless we recognize that they are responsible for the maxims that they adopt. A moral agent can choose to follow the moral law or to disobey it. Kant's intellectual integrity is revealed in his insistence that *Willkür* must be radical. *Willkür* as free choice must be able to choose between good and evil. And ultimately there are no (and can be no constraints) on this *Willkür*. Kant's "official" position is that "man (even the most wicked) does not [indeed cannot] repudiate the moral law," but if we pursue the logical consequences of Kant's understanding of the *Willkür*, then the human *Willkür* certainly *can* repudiate the moral law. Individuals *can* become "devilish beings." And this possibility is not simply a contingent or accidental consequence of his moral philosophy, it is a necessary consequence. It is this tension between Kant's positive analysis of freedom as the highest achievement of finite rational agents and his insistence on the radical unconstrained character of free choice *(Willkür)* that is the source of the many paradoxical claims that he makes about evil and radical evil.

I want to return to my beginning—to the question that motivated this analysis: whether Kant's reflections on evil and radical evil help to guide our thinking about the evil that we have witnessed in the twentieth century. The answer is a mixed one—and we need to distinguish the strengths and weaknesses of his analysis. I do not think that Kant would have agreed with Arendt that "radical evil" is a type of evil that cannot be conceived. Nor do I think that it is accurate to say that he "rationalized" the existence of this evil in the concept of "a perverted ill will." At times, Kant seems to use the term "radical" simply to mean "rooted." I do, however, think that there are many problems in his concept of radical evil. I have argued that when we analyze what Kant means, the results are quite disappointing. Radical evil seems to be little more than a way of designating the tendency of human beings to disobey the moral law, not to do what they ought to do. There is a disparity between Kant's rhetoric—his references to "wickedness," "perversity," and "corruption," and the content of what he is saying. We are told that radical evil is a propensity rooted in our human nature. Yet we are also told that "the propensity to evil . . . is an act" in the sense that it is the "exercise of freedom whereby the supreme maxim . . . is adopted by the will *[Willkür]*" (Rel 26). Furthermore, this propensity, this tendency, no matter how forceful it may seem to be, can always be resisted. I have also argued that Kant's concept of an evil maxim is too limited and undifferentiated. The distinction between a good man and an evil man depends on whether or not he subordinates the "incentives of his sensuous nature" to the moral law as an incentive. Kant, by restricting the types of incentives to just two kinds fails to do justice to the range of types of evil maxims, and consequently to the different types of evil persons. Despite the striking claim that man is by nature evil, Kant does not give an a priori proof that this is constitutive of our human nature. (Indeed, he does not offer any sort of proof.) He violates one of his own cardinal doctrines—that the appeal to experience is never sufficient to establish universal claims. He offers some rather feeble observations about human behavior in "barbarous" and civilized conditions to support this universal claim—this claim about man's species character. And against Kant's explicit rejection of the possibility that man is (or can become) a devilish being, I have argued that the logic of Kant's own understanding of *Willkür* entails that individuals can become devilish. They can choose to defy the moral law for a variety of reasons.

But what is most important (and profound) is the reason why Kant gets tangled up in these double binds. I suggest that the primary reason has to do with one of the virtues of his moral stance. The most dominant and central motif in Kant's moral philosophy is his absolute insistence that human beings are solely responsible and accountable for what they do. Human beings as practical moral agents must take full responsibility for their acts, the maxims they adopt, and even their moral disposition *(Gesinnung)*. We cannot absolve ourselves (or others) from moral responsibility and accountability.[50] This uncompromising and dominant theme in Kant's moral philosophy certainly goes against a contemporary prevailing tendency to find all sorts of excuses for immoral behavior and moral lapses. Despite the criticisms I have advanced against Kant's understanding of evil maxims and radical evil, we can see how Kant's understanding of freedom—including the radical sense of freedom *(Willkür)* in which we can even defy the moral law—is illuminating for understanding Auschwitz. One of the most troubling issues that arises in trying to comprehend the evil that is epitomized by Auschwitz is the assigning of responsibility not only to the perpetrators—those who gave the orders and those who followed these orders (including such "desk murderers" as Eichmann)—but also to the so-called bystanders who actively or passively supported the Nazis. We do not have to say that all those involved are responsible in the same way. Kant would never endorse a notion of "collective guilt," but he would insist that each and every individual is morally responsible for what they did and did not do. It is not only in such extreme situations that Kant is helpful in pinpointing moral responsibility. We are living in a time when increasingly there is a temptation to undermine, soften, or mitigate claims about moral responsibility. There is a dangerous convergence in some of the fashionable intellectual tendencies which question the very idea of a subject to whom we can ascribe responsibility, and the popular tendency to find excuses for the most horrendous (and evil) deeds. In our own attempts to come to grips with the many faces of evil, Kant—despite the many problems with his analysis—is still vitally relevant.

5

Reflections on the
Banality of (Radical) Evil

A Kantian Analysis

Henry E. Allison

In her reply to Gershom Scholem's criticism of *Eichmann in Jerulsalem: A Report on the Banality of Evil*, Hannah Arendt writes:

> It is indeed my opinion now that evil is never "radical," that it is only extreme, and that it possesses neither depth nor any demonic dimension. It can overgrow and lay waste the whole world precisely because it spreads like a fungus on the surface. It is "thought-defying," as I said because thought tries to reach some depth, to go to the roots, and the moment it concerns itself with evil, it is frustrated because there is nothing. That is its "banality." Only the good has depth and can be radical.[1]

Arendt is here contrasting her post-Eichmann view of evil with that of her earlier work, *The Origins of Totalitarianism* (1951). In that work she had explicitly characterized the evil perpetrated by the totalitarian systems of Hitler and Stalin as "radical" in the sense of being "beyond the pale of human sinfulness."[2] In fact, this conception of radical evil underlies the central thesis of this work, namely, that the evil of those regimes is a peculiar phenomenon of the twentieth century, qualitatively distinct from anything that had preceded it in history, including the worst tyrannies of the past. As Young-Bruehl notes, Arendt there seems to have adopted three criteria for such evil: it must be unforgivable, unpunishable and rooted in motives so base as to be beyond human comprehension.[3] Appealing to the etymology of the term "radical," Arendt also contends that such evil must be viewed as rooted in some original fault in human nature. Finally, in the same context she asserts that the entire philosophical tradition was unable to conceive of radical evil. Interestingly enough, this includes even Kant, whom she says, "must have suspected the existence of this evil even though he immediately rationalized it in the concept of a 'perverted ill will' that could be explained by comprehensible motives."[4]

As Young-Bruehl makes clear, the change in the Eichmann book concerns mainly the matter of motivation (the third criterion). The Nazi atrocities remain both unforgivable and unpunishable; but instead of viewing them as stemming from inhuman, diabolical motives, Arendt now sees Eichmann's crimes (and by extension, those of the Nazi regime as a whole) as essentially motiveless. Thus, she notes at one point that far from being a Macbeth, Iago or Richard III, "[E]xcept for an extraordinary diligence in looking out for his personal advancement, he [Eichmann] had no motives at all."[5] And with the rejection of anything like diabolical motivation goes the need to assume some deep fault in human nature which could account for its possibility.[6] Accordingly, evil loses its depth dimension and becomes simply banal.

Ironically, by rejecting the notion of diabolical motivation Arendt came closer to the genuinely Kantian conception of radical evil than she was in her earlier work, in which she embraced the concept, if not Kant's understanding of it. She apparently failed to realize this, however, because of a misunderstanding of what radical evil meant for Kant and the systematic role it plays in his moral theory. Radical evil does not refer, as Arendt seems to have assumed throughout, to a particularly great or deeply rooted demonic evil.[7] It refers rather to the root of *all* moral evil, whatever its extent. In Kantian terms, it refers to the universal propensity *[Hang]* to evil, which serves as the precondition of the adoption of maxims contrary to the moral law and, therefore, of evil actions in the familiar sense. Moreover, properly construed, Kant's analysis of evil not only shares certain important structural features with the evil attributed by Arendt to Eichmann, it also provides a philosophical framework in which this latter account of evil can be further analyzed, if not fully understood. Or so I shall argue.

The discussion is divided into four parts. The first sketches the main features of Arendt's conception of the banality of evil as exemplified in the persona of Eichmann. The second considers Kant's denial of the possibility of a diabolical human will in relation both to his own theory and to Arendt's similar denial, which she erroneously takes as equivalent to a denial of radical evil. The third explores the connection between radical evil and self-deception, which is also an important feature in Arendt's account. Finally, the fourth briefly considers and rejects the objection that Eichmann cannot be condemned as evil by Kantian standards, since he scrupulously obeyed the law of the land.

I

According to Arendt, what was most striking about the defendant, Adolf Eichmann, and what created the greatest perplexity for the Israeli judges at his trial, was precisely his chilling ordinariness. Far from the moral monster,

the depraved, demonic anti-semite, driven by a passionate desire to exterminate Jews, which the prosecution attempted to depict him as being and
which the world had taken him to be, Eichmann appeared as a totally unre-
markable human being. As she succinctly puts it, "The trouble with
Eichmann was precisely that so many were like him, and that the many were
neither perverted nor sadistic, that they were, and still are terribly and terrifyingly normal."[8]

An essential feature of this terrifying normalcy is the claim to have lived
according to a moral code, indeed, by no less a code than the Kantian. Thus,
we learn that Eichmann repeatedly insisted that, at least up until the time at
which he was given the responsibility for carrying out the "Final Solution,"
he had followed the categorical imperative. And, as Arendt notes, in
response to the questioning of an incredulous judge, Eichmann was even
able to provide a passable characterization of the categorical imperative and
once remarked that he had read the *Critique of Practical Reason.*[9] How, then,
could such a person have committed such heinous crimes? And having done
so, how could he be so free of a guilty conscience? These are the questions
with which Arendt attempts to grapple without any appeal to the conception
of radical evil or any comparable philosophical or theological construct.

Now, one might argue that, objectively speaking, all of this is readily
understandable precisely in terms of the true nature of the "moral code" to
which Eichmann and presumably many other Nazis subscribed. Although
Eichmann claimed to be following the categorical imperative, it was clearly
a grotesquely distorted form of this imperative. According to Arendt, it
amounted to the principle "Act as if the principle of your actions were at the
same time that of the legislator or law of the land," which, she suggests, is
virtually equivalent to what Hans Frank, the Nazi governor in Poland, had
termed "the categorical imperative in the Third Reich": "Act in such a way
that the *Führer,* if he knew your action, would approve it."[10]

Moreover, this perverted understanding of duty was reflected in
Eichmann's legal defense. Thus, the central claim was not that he was
merely following superior orders, which he could not disobey without
putting himself in great danger (a matter of *casus necessitatis*), but rather
that he was obeying the *legal* order, the law of the land as manifest in the will
of the *Führer.*[11] Leaving aside, then, the perverted nature of the principles to
which Eichmann subscribed, it would seem that, in his eyes at least, these
principles provided an explicitly *moral* justification for his actions. He was
doing the morally required thing, not simply what he had to do in order to
survive or even to avoid seriously unpleasant consequences. More than that,
he was identifying his own will with the principle behind this law, which, in
his distorted understanding of the categorical imperative, is precisely what
morality requires.[12] No wonder, then, that he did not have a guilty con-

science; that while acknowledging his acts, he consistently proclaimed himself to be "Not guilty in the sense of the indictment."[13]

Nevertheless, far from clarifying matters, this serves merely to underscore the central problem, which is just how such a perverted moral standpoint is possible in the first place. At the heart of Arendt's answer, which is scattered throughout the book rather than located in a single section, is her claim that it was the "sheer thoughtlessness" of Eichmann, which she distinguishes from stupidity, which prevented him from ever fully realizing what he was doing and "predisposed him to become one of the greatest criminals of that period."[14] Moreover, for Arendt this thoughtlessness is hardly unique to Eichmann, since she seems to regard it as a characteristic of virtually all Germans of the Nazi period.[15] What differentiates Eichmann from the many like him, who took no overt part in the "Final Solution," are merely the circumstances in which he happened to find himself.

In order to understand what Arendt terms "the strange interdependence of thoughtlessness and evil,"[16] it is first of all necessary to determine the precise sense in which she construes "thoughtlessness." Clearly, we cannot take it in the usual sense in which thoughtlessness is regarded as a moral failure: as simple inconsiderateness. It would be a misstatement of grotesque proportions to claim that the problem with the Nazis was that they were "inconsiderate"! Equally clearly, it cannot mean a complete neglect of moral considerations. As we have seen, the enigmatic feature of Eichmann's character was not a total lack of moral reflection, but the truncated, grossly distorted form which that reflection took. If Arendt's portrait is accurate (and for purposes of this discussion I am assuming that it is), it would seem that the usual moral considerations regarding appropriate means were in place, but combined with a complete failure to question the nature of the end for which these means were intended. How else can one understand the fact that, while unconcerned about the morality of exterminating millions of Jews, Eichmann was apparently insistent about avoiding causing any unnecessary suffering?[17]

According to Arendt, the unique and pernicious kind of thoughtlessness underlying this attitude consists in a total incapacity to look at things from the other's point of view.[18] It is this incapacity, then, which perhaps one might characterize as an incapacity even to recognize that the other has a point of view, that accounts for Eichmann's peculiar form of moral blindness. And this makes perfect sense *as far as it goes,* for it surely must be a failure to recognize the personhood of the other, in Kantian terms the other's status as an end in itself, that underlies the unprecedented crime of genocide. Moreover, only such thoughtlessness, as contrasted with sheer maliciousness, could account for the above noted combination of a concern to avoid unnecessary suffering with a total unconcern about killing on a mass scale.

As is apparent from her posthumously published *Lectures on Kant's Political Philosophy*, Arendt's analysis of Eichmann's thoughtlessness in terms of an incapacity to recognize the point of view of the other has deep Kantian roots. These roots stem from the *Critique of Judgment*, however, rather than the *Critique of Practical Reason* or *Religion within the Limits of Reason Alone*. Arendt's project in these lectures is to expound and analyze Kant's "unwritten political philosophy," which she finds in the third *Critique*. Central to this philosophy is the account of reflective judgment, particularly the judgment of taste, which presupposes the capacity to abstract from one's own interest and consider the aesthetic object (or its representation) from a universal point of view. Basing her analysis largely on the account of the *sensus communis* in §40, Arendt takes the capacity to judge in this way or, in Kant's terms, to adopt the maxim of an "extended way of thinking," as essential not simply to aesthetics, but to moral and political life.[19] And viewed in this context, Eichmann's thoughtlessness can be seen as the extreme case of the failure of judgment, a failure which Arendt insists was endemic to the whole Nazi era.[20]

More germane to our present concerns, this inability to judge (at one point Arendt equates it with an inability to imagine[21]) is deemed inseparable from an inability to communicate (another familiar third *Critique* theme). In fact, one of the most striking features of Arendt's portrait of Eichmann, one to which she returns again and again, is his use of language. Eichmann could speak only in clichés.[22] This lent a certain comic quality to his performance before and during the trial, making him often seem like a clown, since he frequently expressed himself with ridiculous *non sequiturs*. But Arendt's deeper point is that the "language rules" used by Eichmann and his fellow Nazis were truly invidious rather than comic, playing a large role in blinding them to the moral implications of their acts. As Arendt's account indicates, it is not that they literally did not know what they were doing, it is rather that their use of language enabled them to take their own acts under descriptions which obfuscated their true moral status.[23] Nowhere, of course, is this more evident than in their use of the horrible phrase "Final Solution," which suggests that the extermination of millions of human beings is, at bottom, nothing more than a technical problem.

Given this analysis of thoughtlessness and obfuscation through language, it is not surprising that Arendt locates the real basis of Eichmann's attitude, and that of the Nazis as a whole, in self-deception. To be sure, at one point she asks rhetorically: "Is this a textbook case of bad faith, of lying self-deception combined with outrageous stupidity? Or is it simply the case of the unrepentant criminal . . . ?"[24] Nevertheless, her position is clear; she characterizes Eichmann's own capacity for self-deception as itself "criminal" and notes that, in general, the practice of self-deception by the Nazis had become so commonplace that it was "almost a moral prerequisite for survival."[25] Presumably, her point is that self-deception becomes "criminal" and a "moral prerequisite for survival" by enabling its practitioners to avoid facing both the true moral character of their deeds and their ultimate responsibility for them.

At this point, however, her analysis effectively stops. Although she does link Eichmann's self-deception to that of the German people as a whole, suggesting that the latter somehow made the former possible or at least easier, she does not really pursue the question of the grounds of individual responsibility for such criminal thoughtlessness and self-deception. Admittedly, this procedure is consistent with the historico-sociological, anti-metaphysical thrust of her book as well as with her views about evil. Clearly, if evil is truly banal in Arendt's sense, if it is a surface phenomenon without depth, then there is no need to pursue the topic any further.[26] Nevertheless, this refusal to continue really begs the question regarding radical evil, which is perhaps the point of Scholem's complaint that Arendt's appeal to the banality of evil in her discussion of Eichmann remained a mere "catchword," standing in need of philosophical analysis.[27] In any event, it seems to be worthwhile considering whether the Kantian conception of radical evil offers any resources for such an analysis. One reason to think that it might is that Kant, like Arendt, explicitly denies the possibility (at least for human beings) of a diabolical will.

II

Since Kant's rejection of a diabolical will is an essential feature of his account of radical evil, whereas Arendt appeals to it in her denial that evil can be radical, it is hardly surprising that they arrived at this shared view by quite different routes. For Arendt, it seems to have been largely a psychological claim, resulting from her experience of and reflection upon Eichmann, as well as her continued study of the literature regarding the Nazi period. For Kant, by contrast, it is clearly an *a priori* matter, following directly from his thesis that we must somehow still respect the categorical imperative even while violating it. Thus, already in the *Groundwork*, after noting that in the transgression of duty we do not actually will that our immoral maxim should become a universal law, but merely "take the liberty of making an exception to it of ourselves" (Gr 4: 424; 91), he goes on to reflect:

This procedure, though in our impartial judgment it cannot be justified, proves none the less that we in fact recognize the validity of the categorical imperative and (with all respect for it) merely permit ourselves a few exceptions which are, as we pretend, inconsiderable and apparently forced upon us (Gr 4: 425; 92).

In *Religion within the Limits of Reason Alone*, where Kant for the first time explicitly thematizes about evil, this all too human tendency to make exceptions for oneself, to quibble with the stern dictates of the law on behalf of self-interest, is inflated into an innate (yet freely chosen) propensity to evil. The propensity is not to reject the law altogether, to abandon all moral considerations (this is deemed incompatible with our predisposition to the good); it is rather the propensity to subordinate moral considerations to those stemming from self-love. In short, it is to reverse priorities or, in Kant's terms, "the order of incentives." The claim is not that we always in fact do this, but rather that even the best of us have such a tendency; that it is ineliminable or "rooted in human nature" and that we must constantly struggle against it. It is against this background of ideas that Kant writes:

> Man (even the most wicked) does not under any maxim whatsoever, repudiate the moral law in the manner of a rebel (renouncing obedience to it). The law, rather, forces itself upon him irresistibly by virtue of his moral predisposition; and were no other incentive working in opposition, he would adopt the law into his supreme maxim as the sufficient determining ground of his will [*Willkür*] (Rel 6: 36; 31).

This conception of radical evil is actually the logical consequence of the combination of two essential features of Kant's theory of freedom. One, which I term the "Incorporation Thesis," holds that inclinations themselves do not constitute sufficient reasons or incentives to act for a free agent. They only become such insofar as an agent takes one up or, as Kant puts it, "incorporates it into his maxim" (Rel 6: 23, 19), which means that an agent spontaneously makes it his rule to act on a given inclination in certain circumstances.[28] Otherwise expressed, inclinations do not come with an inherent motivational force, by virtue of which they can move us to act against our will. On the contrary, we are moved to act by means of or, better, on the basis of them only insofar as we allow ourselves to be. This feature of our agency accounts for our responsibility for heteronomous or inclination based action and explains why evil must be rooted in the will rather than in our given sensuous nature.

The other feature is Kant's affirmation of a reciprocal connection between the moral law and a free will (what I have termed the "Reciprocity Thesis").[29] This thesis precludes the possibility of a diabolical will, understood as one which explicitly denies the authority of the law, since it rules out the possibility of such a denial. The reasoning here is simple: if, as the Reciprocity Thesis maintains, the moral law necessarily is the law of a free will in the sense of providing the ultimate norm in terms of which its choices must be justified, then a free rational agent cannot reject the authority of the law without undermining its own agency. Combining both of these, we arrive at the result that evil must be rooted in a free choice against the law (a kind of inner voting in favor of inclination), which recognizes and respects the authority of the law even while contravening it.

At its maximum, evil, so construed, takes the form of wickedness [Bösartigkeit], which rather than choosing evil for its own sake intentionally subordinates moral considerations to those of self-love. And since even at this last stage of humanly possible evil the authority of the moral law is recognized, Kant indicates that this is only possible insofar as the agent engages in a kind of systematic self-deception. Basically, the idea is that one tells oneself that one is doing all that morality requires, as long as one's overt behavior (taken under some description) accords with the law. In fact, Kant points out that this stage may even coexist with a certain (ungrounded) moral self-satisfaction, which stems from the fact that one has been fortunate in avoiding circumstances that would have led to actual immoral behavior (Rel 6: 30; 25). In short, moral good luck is self-deceptively identified with virtue. Although Kant himself does not make the point, it would seem to be in accord with his analysis to add that insofar as wickedness leads to actually immoral behavior (which it does not necessarily do), this result is self-deceptively attributed to bad (moral) luck.

In spite of its considerable subtlety and accord with the basic principles of Kant's moral theory, this conception has seemed to some to stand in blatant contradiction with the facts. Thus, John Silber, in his otherwise highly appreciative account of Kant's views on morality and freedom, maintains that far from being an impossibility, the kind of defiant rejection of the moral law that Kant apparently rules out "is an ineradicable fact of human experience."[30] In support of this claim he appeals to the historical examples of Napoleon and Hitler, the authority of St. Paul, Kierkegaard, and Nietzsche, and even the fictional example of Melville's Captain Ahab. These examples and authorities strike quite different notes, but they presumably all bear witness to the fact that evil takes forms that transcend the narrow confines of the Kantian moral framework. More specifically, they suggest that evil cannot be understood simply in terms of the contrast between morality and self-interest, as the subordination of the former to the latter. Great evil, it would seem, can involve as much self-sacrifice (at least as it is usually conceived) and intensification of personality as great virtue. In the end, then, according to Silber, Kant remains very much a child of the Aufklärung (or Plato) and, as such, is incapable of recognizing the Dostoevskian depths to which humanity can sink.

Although Arendt could hardly accept Silber's essentially Dostoevskian conception of evil, she would certainly join with him in rejecting Kant's account in terms of the subordination of moral motives to those of self-interest. Indeed, as we have seen, in The Origins of Totalitarianism she criticized Kant for rationalizing evil, by which she presumably meant the attempt to account for it in terms of "comprehensible motives" such as self-interest, while in *Eichmann in Jerusalem* she explicitly linked the banality of evil to its motivelessness. Accordingly, it would seem that the Kantian conception is vulnerable to attack from both sides.

In an effort to deal with these difficulties, I shall first consider Silber's affirmation of genuinely diabolical evil and then the objection, shared by both Silber and Arendt, that evil of the quality of Eichmann's cannot be adequately accounted for in terms of motives such as self-interest. To begin with, it is not at all clear that the kinds of examples to which Silber alludes in support of his thesis really amount to choosing evil for the sake of evil. Certainly, we should be careful about identifying evil that seems manifestly counter-prudential (for example Ahab's single-minded, obsessive pursuit of Moby Dick) with evil chosen for its own sake. As we shall see, there are other alternatives.

Moreover, as Allen Wood has pointed out, Silber's whole line of criticism stems from a failure to consider Kant's claim in light of his conception of a predisposition to personality, which is just the capacity to be motivated by respect for the law. So considered, Kant's denial of a diabolical will is not a dubious bit of empirical moral psychology, but rather an *a priori* claim about the conditions of the possibility of moral accountability. Specifically, the claim is that in order to be accountable and, therefore to be *either* good *or* evil, it is necessary to recognize the validity of the moral law. Since a being who lacked this recognition and the concomitant feeling of respect would not be morally accountable, such a being could hardly be thought to have a diabolical will. On the contrary, it would have to be viewed as an unfortunate product of nature (rather than freedom), a non-person, since it lacked the defining characteristic of personality.[31] Thus, the very condition which makes morality possible at all, also rules out the possibility of a genuinely diabolical will.

Of itself, however, this analysis merely reconfirms the incompatibility of a diabolical will with the central principles of Kant's moral theory; thus, it certainly does not address the objection that Kant's moral psychology lacks the resources to account for the motivation (or lack thereof) of villains such as Eichmann. Accordingly, it is worth noting that Kant also has a story to tell (albeit a brief one) about how apparently selfless evil and even the "diabolical vices" *[teuflische Laster]* of envy, ingratitude and spitefulness *[Schadenfreude]* can be grafted on to the original propensity to evil. Moreover, it is at this juncture, which marks the move from *a priori* moral theory to an empirically based moral anthropology, that the Kantian account begins to make contact with Arendt's portrait of Eichmann.

The main thrust of this story, which has been helpfully analyzed by Sharon Anderson-Gold, is that the vices associated with man's inhumanity to man, which seem to differ qualitatively from the mere subordination of moral considerations to self-love, are actually grounded in this very self-love as it is affected by the competitive social context in which human beings find themselves.[32] Given this context, our judgments of personal happiness are essentially comparative, so that we measure our happiness by comparing our state with that of others. This, in turn, leads to a desire "to acquire worth in the opinion of others." Although originally merely a desire for equality, within the competitive context in which everyone else has similar aims, it gradually becomes transformed into the craving for superiority, with which come inevitably jealousy and rivalry. Finally, from these stem what Kant terms "vices of culture," since they only arise in a cultured or civilized state and themselves serve as further spurs to culture. At their most extreme, these vices of culture become the devilish vices (Rel 6: 27; 22n).

As Anderson-Gold indicates, by appealing to our social nature (what he elsewhere terms our "unsocial sociability"), Kant endeavors to show how the bare propensity to evil can account for extreme evil as a cultural phenomenon, without assuming the possibility of a diabolical will. Evil is rooted in self-love insofar as it refuses to limit itself by the moral law, even though in its advanced stages it takes forms that are hardly commensurate with the pursuit of self-interest. As a result of the competitive social context and the effect that it has on our self-conception, an initially innocent self-love can produce the most horrible crimes.

As Anderson-Gold also notes, this suggests "a certain parallel between Kant's concept of radical evil and Hannah Arendt's concept of 'banal' evil."[33] Although she does not expand on this point, except to remark that Arendt would reject what she terms the "species character" of evil (its universality), it is not difficult to see what she had in mind. In addition to their common rejection of any diabolical motivation, the main point is presumably the way in which Eichmann's character was supposedly molded and corrupted by his social context. Indeed, Arendt does remark that Eichmann was a product of a society in which mendacity had become an ingredient of the national character;[34] that evil in the Third Reich was so deeply ingrained as to lose the capacity to tempt;[35] and that Eichmann committed crimes under circumstances that made it virtually impossible for him to recognize that he was doing wrong.[36]

We must be careful, however, not to push this parallel too far. As already indicated, Kant's account operates at a different level than Arendt's, and this difference is due primarily to the characteristically Kantian emphasis on freedom. Accordingly, Kant's story about the social conditioning of vice must be understood against the backdrop of transcendental freedom. From the Kantian standpoint, if Eichmann truly lacked the capacity to recognize the criminality of his acts, then we must either absolve him of responsibility (as we would someone who has been genuinely "brainwashed") or acknowledge that in some sense his must have been a willful ignorance, a self-imposed thoughtlessness. In an effort to conceptualize such a possibility, we turn now to the notion of self-deception.[37]

III

Perhaps because he refers explicitly to it only in connection with his account of wickedness, the third and highest degree of evil, most interpreters have tended to either downplay or ignore completely the place of self-deception in the overall Kantian account of evil. A careful consideration of Kant's theory, however, suggests that it plays an absolutely crucial role at all levels. Consider the notion of moral weakness or frailty *[Gebrechlichkeit]*, which Kant characterizes as the first stage of evil. At this stage, Kant tells us, the good, which objectively considered is an inexpugnable *[unüberwindlich]* incentive, when considered subjectively turns out to be weaker in comparison with inclination (Rel 6: 29; 24). In other words, we recognize and desire to do our duty but find ourselves unable to do so because of powerful countervailing motives.

Now, although this phenomenon is all too familiar, it is by no means an easy matter to reconcile it with the Kantian conception of freedom. After all, how can a philosopher who has as his basic principle that "Man *himself* must make or have made himself into whatever, in a moral sense, whether good or evil, he is or is to become" (Rel 6: 44; 40) allow for a moral *weakness?* Insofar as it is an expression of evil, this weakness must be something for which one is responsible and, as such, an expression of freedom. Consequently, we cannot appeal to any form of constitutive moral luck in order to excuse our frailty (as if a weak will were like a weak heart). But a weakness for which one is responsible is no longer a simple weakness; it is rather a self-imposed or, as Kierkegaard might have put it, a "dialectically qualified" weakness.

The problem thus becomes how one is to understand a self-imposed weakness and here, I have argued, is where self-deception comes into play.[38] To begin with, this "weakness" must be identified with the bare propensity to evil, that is, the ineliminable tendency of even the best of us to subordinate the moral incentive to that of self-love. This expresses itself in moral experience as an openness to temptation, which is really nothing more than a susceptibility to just such a subordination. Self-deception then enters the picture as the means by which an agent transforms this openness into a brute, given fact, a part of one's nature, which one laments because it apparently stands in the way of becoming virtuous, but for which one does not hold oneself responsible. In short, a state of mind for which one is ultimately responsible is self-deceptively taken as a bit of bad moral luck. Similarly, in the case of impurity, the second stage of evil, self-deception explains how we can take ourselves to be acting from duty alone, when, in fact, we require some extra-moral incentive in order to do what duty dictates. Given this, together with the earlier analysis of wickedness, it seems reasonable to conclude that self-deception is already for Kant (as it was to become for Fichte[39] and in our century Sartre) the major mechanism that human beings make use of to evade their responsibility.

Admittedly, Kant does not explicitly argue in this way in the *Religion*, but it is nonetheless, I suggest, precisely how his account of evil must be understood, if it is to be made coherent. Moreover, he gives strong indication in his account of lying in the *Tugendlehre* that this is, indeed, precisely how he understands the situation. Not only does Kant there (in contrast to the various versions of his lectures on ethics) classify lying as a violation of duty to oneself rather than to others, he also puts prime emphasis on the inner lie. Thus, he concludes his account of lying with the reflection:

> But such insincerity in his declarations, which man perpetrates upon himself, still deserves the strongest censure, since it is from such a rotten spot (falsity, which seems to be rooted in human nature itself) that the evil of untruthfulness spreads into man's relations with other men as well, once the highest principle of truthfulness has been violated (MS 6: 430–31; 226–27).

Even granting this, however, it is still not clear that the Kantian conception of self-deception can be used to illuminate the phenomenon of Eichmann. Apparently standing in the way of such a use is Kant's well-known view that the difficulty in the moral life consists not in the recognition of what, objectively speaking, is one's duty (since this must be readily apparent to everyone), but in acting as duty dictates. After all, if Arendt's analysis is correct, we have in Eichmann a case of someone whose "thoughtlessness" somehow prevented him from recognizing the most basic obligation, who committed the most heinous crimes without a guilty conscience, and who lived by means of a perverted moral code. And it is by no means immediately obvious that such a possibility can be understood in Kantian terms.

As a first step in dealing with this problem, it must be noted that, in spite of his adherence to the Rousseauian principle that even the humblest intelligence is capable of distinguishing right from wrong, Kant does at times acknowledge the possibility of being mistaken about what is objectively one's duty. For example, in the *Tugendlehre*, while ruling out as an absurdity the notion of an erring conscience, he maintains that incorrigibility applies only to the "subjective judgment" of whether I have consulted my conscience, and that "I can indeed be mistaken at times *[bisweilen]* in my objective judgment as to whether something is a duty or not" (MS 6: 401; 202). Similarly, in his account of moral character as a matter of committing oneself to self-imposed practical principles in the *Anthropology*, he reflects that, "Though it is true that these principles might occasionally *[bisweilen]* be mistaken and imperfect, still the formal element of his volition in general— to act according to firm principles . . . —has something precious and admirable in it; and so it is also a rare thing" (Anthro 7: 292; 157).

Welcome as it is, however, this admission of human fallibility with respect to moral judgment and its principles is only a first step and is obviously not sufficient to deal with the problem at hand. For Kant's circumspect language in both passages (his use of the qualifier *"bisweilen"*) makes it clear that he views such mistakes as relatively rare occurrences, which might concern some of the "gray areas" of morality, such as are dealt with in the casuistical questions of the *Tugendlehre*, but not what is fundamental in the moral life. Moreover, insofar as such mistakes are "innocent" errors in moral judgment, it would seem that they do not involve self-deception, at least not in a major way. Accordingly, we find ourselves back at the original problem of trying to understand how Kant's analysis of radical evil can be applied to Arendt's portrait of Eichmann.

In order to make further progress in this direction, it is necessary to consider (albeit briefly) Kant's view of moral deliberation. As is clear to any reader of the *Groundwork*, this consists in subjecting one's maxim to the universalizability test in order to determine whether it can be universalized without contradiction. As is also clear to any student of the literature, however, this is precisely the place where Kant's moral theory is attacked by critics who charge that virtually any maxim, if suitably formulated, can be made to pass the test. Although I can hardly argue for it here, I believe that this much discussed difficulty points more to the failure to recognize the complexity of Kant's moral psychology than to the limitations of his moral theory. Suffice it to say that it is precisely the testing of maxims that provides the major occasion for self-deception, which here takes the form of disguising from ourselves the true nature of the principles upon which we act. In short, immoral maxims appear to pass the universalizability test only because they ignore or obscure morally salient features of a situation.[40] Thus, far from demonstrating the emptiness of the categorical imperative, this shows how the imperative can be misapplied by radically evil agents who continue to recognize its authority.

Let us consider an example which fits nicely into Kant's account of wickedness.[41] Suppose that I have a violent dislike for someone and have come into possession of a piece of information about him, which I know will cause him great pain if he learns of it. With the intent of doing so, I decide to inform him of the matter, but I justify the action on the grounds of his right to know. Accordingly, rather than being a vicious act of causing unnecessary pain, I represent it to myself (and perhaps others) as a laudable act of truth telling. Depending on the degree of my depravity, I might even half-convince myself that it is a sacred duty. In any event, this justificatory procedure is clearly based on self-deception, by means of which I am able to ignore my actual intention, which is here the morally salient factor, defining the very nature of the act.

Admittedly, this still does not quite fit the Eichmann case, since, if Arendt is correct, he was not a rabid anti-semite, who had to hide his true feelings from himself in order to maintain a clear conscience while sending Jews to their death. Even granting this, however, I would still contend that Eichmann can be viewed as a virtual limiting case of Kantian wickedness, on the grounds that his "thoughtlessness" represents an extreme example of the neglect of morally salient features. Once again, what could be more salient than the fact that one is dealing with human beings? And if this neglect is somehow willful, as it must be if it is to be imputable, then it is difficult to see how one can avoid attributing it to something like a propensity to evil.

IV

Up until this point the Kantian analysis has assumed Eichmann's criminality, and in so doing it might seem that we have neglected the obvious objection that in expressly obeying the law of the land, Eichmann was, as he claimed, really following Kantian principles. After all, Kant himself notoriously claimed that revolution and active rebellion are always illegitimate; that we have a duty to obey the most intolerable despot. Given this, Eichmann might seem to provide not so much an illustration of Kant's conception of radical evil as a *reductio* of his political philosophy, and since this supposedly rests on moral grounds, of the categorical imperative itself. Since this again is a large topic to which I can hardly hope to do justice here, I shall limit myself to two brief points.

First, it must be kept in mind that, in spite of his uncompromising views on obedience to the law, Kant did not advocate simple acquiescence to tyranny. On the contrary, as a zealous advocate of freedom of expression, of the "public use of reason" as a necessary condition of enlightenment, he subscribed to Frederick the Great's famous motto: "Argue as much as you will, and about what you will, but obey!"[42] As Arendt emphasizes, however, Eichmann not only failed to argue with his superiors, he apparently never even really questioned in his own mind the morality of the Final Solution. Accordingly, far from being compatible with Kantian principles, both Eichmann's actions and his pernicious thoughtlessness are clearly opposed to these principles.

Second, it should be noted that on occasion Kant introduced explicit and significant qualifications of the duty to obey.[43] Thus, in *Religion within the Limits of Reason Alone* Kant glosses the Biblical injunction: "We ought to obey God rather than men," to signify that "when men command anything which in itself is evil (directly opposed to the law of morality) we dare not, and ought not, obey them" (Rel 6: 99n; 90). And, in the appendix added to the second edition of the *Rechtslehre*, where, in response to the lengthy criticism of the original version by Friedrich Bouterwork, he affirms as a "categorical imperative" the principle: *"Obey the authority who has power over you* (in whatever does not conflict with inner morality)" (MS 6: 371; 176). Unfortunately, these qualifications of the demand of absolute obedience to the ruling pow-ers remain cryptic remarks, which Kant never integrated into his political theory. Nevertheless, if we assume, as I believe it reasonable to do, that Kant would have regarded the Nazi crimes as "directly opposed to the law of morality" or in "conflict with inner morality," they do suffice to deprive Eichmann of his presumed grounds for a so-called "Kantian defense."

6

The Polyhedron of Evil

Gustavo Leyva

In his *Esquisse d'un tableau historique des progrés de l'esprit humain* (1794), a kind of summation of the most relevant topics of the modern philosophy of history, Condorcet offers a view of history, reason, and human society which today we would consider naive. The model of rationality he presents is that offered by the mathematical sciences of nature, of which Newton's physics constitutes the nucleus. In it, according to Condorcet, he discovered "the true method of studying nature"; "observation, experimentation and calculation" are, from this perspective, the three instruments with which physics deciphers the enigmas of nature.[1] Physics thus becomes the paradigm of science in general. This concept of knowledge, developed according to the model of the natural sciences, questions the legitimacy of the religious, philosophical, political, and ethical ideas inherited from tradition. For Condorcet, it was perfectly coherent not only to trust in the critical potential of the sciences, but also to expect them to help answer central normative questions. Thus, he expressed a conviction that humanity would someday be able to elevate the moral sciences to the level achieved by the natural sciences. Framed within the program of the Enlightenment, Condorcet declared that progress could be expected both in the morality of individuals, as well as in the civilized forms of their coexistence. Just as Kant would later, Condorcet believed the progress of civilization lay in establishing a republic capable of guaranteeing civil liberties, in an international organization that ensured perpetual peace, and in a regime that would accelerate economic growth he also believed that technical advances would be able to do away with social inequalities, or at least compensate for them. Condorcet—and, with him, some of the most renowned figures of the Enlightenment—thought that the arts and sciences would not only promote controls on nature, but would also contribute to improving the interpretation of the world and the self-interpretation of subjects, moral progress, justice in social institutions, and even happiness.

It took a thinker such as Max Weber to radically question the suppositions of philosophers such as Condorcet and the Enlightenment program in general. Weber posed these questions in a fashion which is still relevant to us today. In his introduction to the collection of articles in *The Sociology of Religion*, Weber referred to the "problem of universal history," which he devoted his whole life to analyzing: the question of why outside of Europe, neither the evolution of science, nor that of the arts, politics, or economics, developed along the lines of rationality which characterized the Western world. In this context, Weber wrote of that plexus of phenomena that expressed the "specific nature of Western culture's rationalization": in the first place, modern science, which gives mathematical form to theoretical knowledge and puts it to the test by means of controlled experiments, systematic cultivation, and the universal organization of the scientific specialties; printed literature for the marketplace and the institutionalization of the cultivation of art through theaters, museums, magazines, and so forth; harmonic music taking the form of sonatas, symphonies, and operas, and performed on instruments such as organ, piano, and violin; the use of a linear and aerial perspective and the constructive principles of the great monumental edifices; the scientific systematization of the theory of law; the institutions of formal law (and a judicial system applied by officials specializing in law); the modern administration of states, with their rational organization of officials, operating on the basis of a enacted or positivized law; the predictability and the way that social businesses regulated by private law can be calculated; the capitalist enterprise that works for profit and assumes a separation between personal holdings and those of the company, utilizing a rational accounting, formally organizing free work from the point of view of its efficiency, and utilizing scientific knowledge to improve the apparatus of production and its own internal organization; and, finally, the capitalist economic ethic, which is part of a rational way of life *(rationale Lebensfürung)*.[2]

As we know, Max Weber explained these phenomena by reducing them to the rise, flowering, and domination of a process of rationalization that led to the conflictive and increasing division of law and morality, that is to say, the separation of practical and ethical ideas, of ethical and juridical doctrines, and the separation of the principles, maxims, and rules of decision-making from the cosmological, religious, and metaphysical worldviews in which they were originally embedded. This process of rationalization was also taken to be at the foundation of the rise of science and modern theory, just as art became autonomous from the sacred and cultural spheres in which it arose. Science, ethics, and art are thus differentiated one from another as autonomous value spheres, each one ruled by an abstract value judgment. As Weber himself explained:

the various value spheres of the world stand in irreconcilable conflict with each other. . . . If anything, we realize again today, it is that something can be sacred, not only in spite of not being beautiful, but rather because and in so far as it is not beautiful. . . . And since Nietzsche, we realize that something can be beautiful, not only in spite of the aspect in which it is not good, but rather in that very aspect. You will find this expressed earlier in the *Fleurs du Mal,* as Baudelaire named his volume of poems. . . . But all these are only the most elementary cases of the struggle that the gods of the various orders and values are engaged in.[3]

Reason is thus divided into several spheres that destroy its old unity, the unity of truth, beauty, and goodness. This is expressed in the form of a paradigm in the sphere of art, where a series of categories that no longer have to do directly with the beautiful and the sublime begin to be articulated. Indeed, in a thinker such as F. Schlegel we find clearly formulated the conviction that only art can adequately express the discontinuous nature of modernity and the modern experience of time. This argument is carefully explained in the categories of the fragmentary, allegory, or irony. Especially significant here is the juxtaposition between a reality seen as estranged and disintegrated on the one hand and the individual experience manifested in the work on the other. Likewise, in other authors, such as the aforementioned Baudelaire, we find a special attention given to shock, to the horrible and the grotesque, as an integral part of modern art, which liberates aesthetics from their platonic overtones.[4] All these categories point to an art made autonomous, which is part and parcel of a process of dissociation between the orders of truth, beauty, and goodness, and in which, for example, in terms of the problem we are dealing with, it is possible to include evil in the artistic experience.

The above is an attempt to smooth the way toward the problem of evil. I would like to approach this problem by beginning with some preliminary considerations, and then to examine three philosophers—Kant, Schelling, and Hegel—who have offered relevant interpretations of this issue, and finally to state some thoughts that do not at all aspire to be conclusive.

Various positions can be pointed out regarding evil and its relationship with good. Some of the most relevant ones in Western thought are found in Plato and especially in Neoplatonism, where good is identified with the eternal and harmonious principles that are the basis for unity of ideas and which in turn constitute the being. According to this position, the phenomena of space and time—with their inherent imperfections—lack reality. Evil thus possesses no real autonomy, but originates in the absence of good, that is to say, from a deficiency, a lack. Hence, evil is considered something not real, which is the consequence of the manifestation of Ideas in space and in time. We find another interpretation of evil in Christianity, where good is personified in the figure of God the Creator; and evil, in turn, is considered not so much an immediate consequence of the creation of a spatial-temporal world—as it is in Neoplatonism—but rather, as a consequence of original sin. As we know, this explanation leads to the theodicy problem, the question of how it is possible for God, all-powerful and all-good, to have allowed evil to arise.[5] In these positions—Platonism and Christianity—supreme reality is identified with the idea of good, or with God the good creator. In contrast, Manichaeanism conceived good and evil as two metaphysical principles of equal dignity, finding themselves in a perpetual battle in which human beings must constantly decide between one or the other. Finally, we might also mention that interpretation deriving from the sophist tradition, and reappearing later in thinkers such as Hume and Nietzsche, as well as in philosophers of the most diverse schools, such as positivism or existentialism, where good and evil are no longer viewed as metaphysical principles of equal rank, but rather as human interpretations of reality or reactions to it. In this conception, the world is neither good nor bad and, if human beings did not exist, there would be no good or evil. One important aspect of the interpretations offered here is that at the bottom of the concept of evil we find the basic experience of an impediment, an obstacle to the realization of life, a harming of happiness and salvation. We must also recall that the concept of evil is differentiated at times into a *malum physicum* (for example, pain and suffering), a *malum metaphysicum* (the imperfection of creation, evil as a deficiency, as a lack of being), and a *malum morale* (related to the evil and the guilt arising from human action). This division of meaning gives rise to a question regarding the origin and significance of evil, which is intimately linked to the question about the meaning of human life and the order of the world itself. In what follows, I intend to briefly develop three positions that I consider pertinent to evil, in the hope of reaching some general conclusions on this problem. First, I shall discuss Kant, then Schelling, and finally Hegel.

OVERCOMING RADICAL EVIL: KANT

Religion within the Limits of Reason Alone,[6] published in 1793, is considered part of Kant's late period. In it, as we know, Kant sets out to show how elements of the "religion of reason" *(Vermunftreligion)* are already contained in the Christian religion, or, to put it more emphatically, how Christianity can be understood as the set of fundamental truths of a "practical, rational faith" *(praktischer Vermunftglauben).* Kant summarized this in the following way: "Religion is (subjectively regarded) the recognition of all duties as divine commands."[7]

For Kant it is a matter of extracting the concept of God and the philosophy of religion from the field of traditional metaphysics in order to reconstruct them and give them a foundation in the sphere of pure practical reason. In this text Kant also deals with the problem of freedom, which brings up not only the tension between moral law and natural inclinations, but also what Kant calls the "evil principle" *(böses Prinzip)*, "the exact counterpart of the principle of ethical life" *(gerades Widerspiel des Prinzips der Sittlichkeit)*, to which Kant himself had already referred in the *Critique of Practical Reason*.[8] This is the maxim of action "against the law" *(gesetzwidrig)* "consciously" *(mit Bewußtein)* raised to the rank of principle inherent in human "nature" *(Natur)* as a natural propensity to radical evil *(Hang zum radikalen Bösen)*.[9] Thus, Kant outlined a permanent conflict between the "good" principle and the "evil" principle to attain "dominion over man" *(Herrschaft über den Menschen)*, the outcome of which would have to be decided entirely by free will. For the purposes of this paper, we might note how Kant, in the first part of this work, interprets the doctrine of original sin as "radical evil" *(das radikal Böse)* in human beings, as the propensity to evil that leads us to deviate from our maxims of action of moral law provided by practical reason. According to Kant, only through a "revolution in conviction" *(Revolution in der Gesinnung)*, a "transformation in the way we think,"[10] can we free ourselves from this propensity to evil, so that human beings can restore their original predisposition for good by deciding to be virtuous solely because we ought to be so. We then see that the framework in which Kant places his reflection on evil leads not to suppositions of a theological nature, nor to presuppositions of a variation on the latest ontological term, neither does it lead to biological explanations linked to a certain conception of human nature. It is, rather, a matter of approaching the problem of evil within a framework in which the concepts of liberty and reason—in this case, practical reason—are central. In this sense, we might note his statement that "nothing is morally evil (i.e., capable of being imputed) but that which is our own act."[11] All historical periods can provide a testimony of the inhumanity of man.[12] It is thus that Kant points out that "the history of freedom begins with evil, since this is a human act."[13] It is precisely by reason of this that Kant emphatically rejects all attempts to develop parameters for ethical action based on the factual use—or rather misuse—of freedom of which history provides such dramatic examples. Hence, in the interpretation of evil offered by Kant, a central position is given to the tension between moral law governed by reason, on the one hand, and history as the history of humanity's freedom, a still unfinished enterprise, on the other hand. This expresses an intimate connection between freedom and evil. Evil, to Kant, cannot be explained, as we said, on the basis of a biological set of human impulses and needs, nor from the point of view of biology or anthropology. Kant located the problem of evil, rather, in the midst of that tension between the moral law provided by reason in its variant of practical reason and the always inconclusive history of human freedom. If we wished to be even more precise regarding Kant's thoughts on evil, we could say that this philosophical effort was aimed at clarifying what is ethically bad, moral wrong *(das Moralisch-Böse)*. Therefore, he had to reject any attempt to explain the problem of evil by recourse to God or being, by relying on laws and limitations derived from nature—be it human or extra-human nature. "Evil could have sprung only from the morally evil *[Moralisch-Bösen]* (not from mere limitations in our nature); and yet the original predisposition (which no one other than man himself could have corrupted, if he is to be held responsible for this corruption) is a predisposition to good *[Anlage zum Guten]*."[14]

According to Kant, what the lone individual, society, and politics can and ought do concretely to at least diminish inhumanity, the presence of evil among human beings—which cannot be totally eradicated, since human beings are a twisted branch from which nothing straight can come—is the subject matter of ethics and politics, of practical philosophy.

THE COSMIC DRAMA OF EVIL: SCHELLING

Schelling's text *Philosophical Investigations into the Essence of Human Freedom,* published in 1809,[15] falls under this philosopher's efforts to reflect upon a "Real-Idealismus" oriented toward constructing the being *(Sein)* in its totality based on the powers of the "real" *(Reale)* and the "ideal" *(Ideale)*.[16] As we know, at least until 1806, Schelling's philosophical efforts had been directed almost exclusively toward the "ideal": the "real," nature, was seen as nothing without the "ideal," the spirit. The existence of the "real," however, had not yet been thematized explicitly and in detail. His reflection on the real took place within a reflection on human beings. It was obvious to Schelling that the human being was definitely marked by the "ideal." The question he asked himself was exactly what was "real" in human beings. To Schelling, it was not enough to identify the "real" in human beings with the corporeal, in the sense of a material, spatial being, but rather the vital force, the impulse of desire, which expresses something dynamic, a force of will that provides human beings with the essence of their action. Hence, while spirit and understanding give human beings the form (the ideal), the real is provided by mobility and force. The "real" appears mainly as a principle of contraction, a principle of movement "toward within." In this, Schelling's thinking converges with that of Jakob Böhme, in the conception of the real as a principle of contraction "toward within," making it into the force which in principle creates what exists and maintains it as *in-dividuum,* something that is by itself, something separate from the rest, and at the same time, undivided. This principle of contraction keeps the being from all rending, and makes it into something in and for itself. Thus, he created the "principle of existence" *(Grund der Existenz),* the fundament of existence itself, the fundament of the being itself, of the individual being. However, and this is where we find a turning in Schelling's thought, which again links up with Jakob Böhme's, this principle of contraction that makes it possible for the being to express itself as an individual being, takes place within a process in which the being is permanently endangered. The contraction of the being that allows it to articulate itself as such is constantly in danger of a rupture, a splitting of the being. Left to itself, this principle of contraction becomes the principle of a demonic closure, the "principle of egotism" *(Prinzip des Egoismus)* by which that which exists forbids all connection, all bonds, producing what Schelling calls a "demonic encapsulation." Thus the self, threatened by the "real," becomes possible thanks to a second principle, that of the "ideal," which prevents the being itself from splitting and destroying itself. The "ideal" principle is directed toward connection and ties, which is why Schelling calls it the power of love. Only the principle of the ideal as the force of love can tear the soul from the darkness and encapsulation of egoism *(Egoität)*, to which the contraction principle leads it.

It is within this vast drama, which is not only ontological but cosmic, that Schelling's thoughts on the problem of evil must be situated. Indeed, in the work we have been discussing, Schelling points out that all beings *(Wesen)* arising in nature express a "double principle within themselves," a double principle, which, as Schelling points out immediately afterwards, is one and the same principle viewed from two different perspectives.[17] The first principle is that "dark" principle of the "own will" *(Eigenwille)* of the creature. The second is the principle of light, of understanding *(Verstand)*. The dark principle is none other than a will that is incapable of establishing unity with the light—meaning the principle of understanding—and which therefore becomes mere appetite or desire, that is to say, "blind will" *(blinder Wille)*. Understanding, in this sense, is distinguished from and opposed to this "own will" in the form of a "universal will" *(Universalwille)*. Nonetheless, Schelling said, "that unity which is inseparable *(unzertrennlich)* in God, must be separable *(zertrennlich)* in human beings, and thus arises the possibility of Good and Evil."[18] Evil, or better yet, the possibility of evil, is then explained by a kind of flight from the center by the "own will" *(Eigenwille)* by virtue of which a breach occurs in "the bond of the forces" *(das Band der Kräfte)* which maintain the unity not only of human beings and nature, but of the whole cosmos. In its place, a "private will" *(Partikulärwille)* predominates, which, as Schelling put it, "being contrary to original will *[der ursprüngliche]*, cannot but unite the forces within itself, and therefore must strive *[streben]* to create a life of its own, a differentiated life, based on the separated forces of the indignant army of appetites and desires (insofar as each individual force is also a wish *[Sucht]* and a desire *[Lust]*)."[19] This life, formed by the joining of the separated elements, is possible because within evil there still exists the first bond of the forces *(das Band der Kräfte)*, the "fundament of nature" *(der Grund der Natur)*.[20] Such a life, however, as Schelling would be quick to say, cannot be a "true life" *(kein wahres Leben)*. Thus arises a false life, a life that is a lie, a plexus of disquiet and decomposition, the closest physical analogy of which is illness. The concept of evil outlined by Schelling rests, then, on an ontological and cosmic explanation which leads, in the final analysis, to an "inversion of principles" *(Verkehrtheit oder Umkehrung der Prinzipen)*.[21] In this regard, Schelling's treatment of evil shows similarities to that of Franz Baader, especially in terms of the analogies between evil and sickness.[22] What is important from the point of view of our reflections is that Schelling calls attention to the fact that it is human beings—the most perfect of all visible creatures—who are, at the same time, the only ones capable of doing evil. Therefore the fundament *(der Grund)* of evil cannot be explained by a lack or a deficiency, as Leibniz attempted, Schelling recalls, and as was suggested by Plato. Evil is not the result of an imperfection, nor should it be considered something negative. Its fundament resides not in an absence, but in a presence; it is not an empty negativity, but a full positivity.[23]

THE EVIL OF EMPTY SUBJECTIVITY: HEGEL

The *Phenomenology of Mind*,[24] as we know, bases its reflection on the opposition between the knowledge (certainty: "itself"; *Gewissheit: "für es"*) of consciousness and its object (truth: "itself"; *Wahrheit: "an sich"*) .[25] Experience is determined thus as "the dialectical movement that consciousness itself exercises both in knowing and in its object insofar as this leads to a new true object for it."[26] The goal of this path of experience is reached when consciousness does not have to go beyond itself, "where it finds itself and the concept corresponds to the object and the object to the concept."[27] The *Phenomenology of Mind* is precisely that reflection on the experience of consciousness that successively covers the figures of "consciousness," "self-consciousness," "reason," "spirit," and "religion" until it achieves its goal of "absolute knowledge." In many cases these figures of consciousness describe a particular view of the world or a historical period.

In the beginning of the chapter on spirit *(Geist)*, Hegel stresses that the configurations of consciousness analyzed up to that point are only analytical moments of the essence *(Wesen)*, of the spirit. The spirit, as "the universal work produced by means of everyone's deeds as its unity," becomes itself, that is to say, is realized, only through history *(Geschichte)*. It is at this point that a series of figures of consciousness appear corresponding to antiquity, modernity, and romanticism. In each of these figures, certain oppositions between the universal and the individual are renewed. Thus, for example, the moral unity of the *polis* is diluted by internal conflicts[28] to develop in the direction of the formalism of the Roman Rule of Law. In search of a reedification of the ethical life *(sittlich)*, the spirit estranged from itself builds the kingdom of culture with its fundamental values, to wit, the power of the state and the riches into which vain consciousness is separated and split. On this issue, Hegel points out that the concepts "good" and "evil" are inverted depending on general interest or private interest. Thus, he arrived at two specific configurations: on the one hand, that of faith as flight to a better world, and on the other hand, that which combats faith, the "pure vision" of the Enlightenment, which reduces things to their utility and proudly proclaims the freedom of the subject, emancipated from all types of bonds and, therefore, led to caprice *(Willkür)*. Because of the increase in this split, the spirit estranged from itself returns to itself insofar as it gives freedom a positive sense in ethics. In order to penetrate reality, ethical life must rise up over the duty without content of Kant's imperative and the isolated self-reflection of the beautiful romantic soul. Thus it will become "true morality" as the union of acting and judging consciousness in the horizon of a reciprocal recognition among people. It is in the experience of forgiveness, when the individual overcomes the strangeness of others and finds himself or herself again, that Hegel discovers the religious or absolute spirit.

These same problems reappear in an analogous framework in *Grundlinien der Philosophie des Rechts* (1821). Hegel's *Philosophy of Right*, as we know, is divided into three parts: morality is situated between abstract law and moral life *(Sittlichkeit)*. On these three levels, we can see a continuous development of the degree of actuality *(Wirklichkeit):* while abstract law is not sanctioned subjectively nor institutionally, and therefore lacks all actuality, in morality the subjective will makes it possible to achieve an existence of the concept *(Dasein des Begriffs):* "In this way, a higher ground *[Boden]* has been assigned to freedom; the idea's existential aspect *[Existenz]*, or its moment of reality *[reales Moment]*, is now the subjectivity of the will *[Subjektivität des Willens]*. Only in the will as subjective, can freedom or the implicit principle of the will be actual *[wirklich]*."[29]

This subjectivity is, however, a fluctuating terrain. As subjective individuality *(subjektive Einzelheit)* it is determined in opposition to the universal *(das Allgemeine)* (Right 33). The *concrete* analysis and development of morality then shows the contradictions of this subjectivity lacking in mediation. These contradictions arise from the fact that the norm this subjectivity applies to itself is abstract, an empty universal which cannot be mediated with individual obligations and oughts,[30] and, therefore, can only serve as a justification of private well-being (Encyc 509). The good *(das Gute)* in morality is a norm that remains purely internal. This implies a contradiction: "the absolute being, which, nonetheless, at the same time, is not" (Encyc 511). This contradiction is overcome, according to Hegel, through the ethical life *(Sittlichkeit):* the objective norm (the good) and subjective consciousness achieve *Sittlichkeit* in their coming together, in their harmony (Right 141). It is then that one goes beyond the mere *concept* and achieves the sphere of the *ideal,* in which determinations of both objectivity and subjectivity are integrated into a whole. The difference between ought *(Sollen)* and being *(Sein)* that characterized and determined abstract law and, reflexively, morality, is overcome: "The consciously free substance, in which the absolute 'ought' is no less an 'is'" (Encyc 514).

This development through the three parts making up the *Philosophy of Right* also refers to the *content* of each one of these levels. Thus, for example, in abstract law, we are dealing essentially with the relationship between the person and the natural objectivity of things. Although we already find ourselves also in the sphere of law, we are dealing with a legal, juridical relationship of the subject with objectivity, which is therefore intersubjectively recognized. This intersubjectivity—presupposed, moreover, throughout the *Philosophy of Right*—exists, nonetheless, only implicitly, and not for itself. This externality of the objects of the will corresponds to the abstract character of the own will. The particularity of the individual will does not play a role here (Right 37): "The thing is an abstract, external thing" (Encyc 490).

Certainly, in the sphere of abstract law, intersubjective relations are also thematized through the person-thing relationship. This occurs in the contract which "is the process in which there is revealed and mediated the contradiction that I am and remain the independent owner of something from which I exclude the will of another only insofar as in identifying my will with the will of another I cease to be an owner" (Right 72). The intersubjectivity of the contract, however, is deficient insomuch as it is not an end in itself, but takes place only for a thing and through the thing, and therefore expresses a reciprocal instrumentalization of people; to me, the other represents only a means for me to obtain a thing: "The thing *[Sache]* is the *means [Mitte]* by which the extremes meet in one *[sich zusammenschliessen].* These extremes are the persons who, in the knowledge of their identity as free, are simultaneously mutually independent" (Encyc 491).

The untrue *(unwahr)* nature of this instrumentalization which is immanent to the contract is finally shown in illegality *(Unrecht),* especially in deceit or fraud *(Betrug),* in passion or coercion *(Zwang),* and in crime *(Verbrechen),* in which it is possible to find a *first* level of articulation of evil. Evil appears here either as an absence or as a dissolution of intersubjective mediations that results, in turn, in a consciousness which, having turned on itself, turns against others. A *second* level of articulation of evil is found in the sphere of morality. Indeed, in morality it is no longer a matter of the objectivity of the thing, but rather of a relationship between the subject and himself or herself, in a self-determination as subjectivity *(Selbstbestimmung der Subjektivität)* (Right 104a). The subject, in this case, is infinite not merely itself but for itself, as Hegel put it (Right 105). In the sphere of morality, subjectivity has to do and deals only with itself: "The moral standpoint *[der moralische Standpunkt]* therefore takes shape as the *right of the subjective will.* In accordance with this right, the will recognizes something and is something, only insofar as the will is present to itself there as something subjective" (Right 107).

Certainly it is essential for the subject of morality to enter into relations with other individuals and to do so in a positive relationship *(positive Beziehung)* (Right 112–13). However, these intersubjective relations present deficiencies and lacks due to two reasons: (1) because the preoccupation for the welfare of another may easily be diverted to a calculatedly egotistical thought—thus, Hegel maintained, my welfare cannot exist in society without the welfare of others, it is that selfish *(eigennützig)* (Right 126); (2) because moral action requires the individual to constantly reflect on the fact that it is right to have acted as he or she acted, but that he or she could have acted differently or could have refrained from the action. This means that the ethical subject's action *is not institutionalized,* but simply left to the caprice of individual reflection (Right 26). This is why, for Hegel, morality leads to evil (Right 139), insofar as the individual has absolute independence with regard to all objectivity—with regard to the world of objects, to other subjects, and to the state. The ironic consciousness—the epitome of evil—can certainly observe the laws. However, it is based on and lives off the consciousness that it depends exclusively on caprice *(Willkür):* "You actually accept a law, it says, and respect it as absolute. So do I, but I go further than you, because I am beyond this law and can make it to suit myself" (Right 140).

Contrary to this, the essence of the ethical life *(Sittlichkeit)* as objectified subjectivity so that intersubjective relations have become an end in themselves, is subordinated neither to an interest in matters of abstract law, nor to morality's need to place emphasis on one's own particularity. In this case, what ought to count no longer depends on the interest or the caprice of the legal person, nor on the moral subject. In the sphere of the ethical life, the subject depends rather—both in self-consciousness and in being—on the *institutions of ethical life.* The ethical order, Hegel says, has "a stable content independently necessary and subsistent in exaltation above subjective opinion and caprice. These distinctions are absolutely valid laws and institutions" (Right 144). This is a double relationship between subjectivity and institutionality: the individual enters into and knows himself or herself to be part of the institutional network that frees the subject from the particularity of arbitrary private impulses and opinions (Right 149) and, at the same time, the substantiality of the institution is mediated and exists only by virtue of the mediation of subjectivity. "The objective ethical order *[das objektiv Sittliche]* . . . is substance made concrete by subjectivity as infinite form" (Right 144).

We could summarize and say that, for Hegel, evil is an expression of the dissolution of the bonds articulating ethical life *(Sittlichkeit),* which is the only place that ethical consciousness can be located and exists itself. Thus, Hegel conceived evil as arising from the collapse of the moral texture of society, which diluted the parameters of individual and collective action and, at its most extreme, continued in a progressive erosion of customs, moral and political habits and standards, impairing practical judgment and thinking, both on an individual and on a collective level. Thus, an apparently normal individual could become capable of the worst crimes.

FINAL CONSIDERATIONS

We could say that in all known societies human beings have attempted to overcome the problems arising from evil, both theoretically and practically. This has occurred by means of art, religion, theology, and even philosophy, as well as through social and political action. Included under the same generic name of evil, we find phenomena which, due to their origin and nature, are entirely different: suffering, malaise, the destructive force of nonhuman nature (e.g., earthquakes and other natural catastrophes), sickness, death, guilt, wars, injustice, as well as the deficiencies of the institutions governing human relations.

In the above considerations, evil is interpreted not so much from the point of view of the premises of the Judeo-Christian doctrine of creation and salvation, as something counterdivine. Neither is it conceived as non-being according to traditional ontology. Evil is not included in the framework of difference Leibniz established between *malum physicum* and *malum metaphysicum*. Evil, finally, is not presented only as a negation of the divine, but rather, in the form of a negation of humanity originating in the actions of human beings themselves. Evil is, thus, not a necessary moment in a theogonic process of creation of the absolute (as in Schelling and in Baader), nor a necessary moment in the history of the absolute or the being—which might diminish human responsibility for the presence of evil in the world of actions and human institutions. The aforementioned concepts, however, tend to show that reflections about evil appear always in a polyhedric field, one of the planes of which is given by Schelling's interpretation, where evil appears as the creative force of the universe itself, which it is impossible to escape. Another is given by Hegel, where evil is explained by the dissolution of bonds linking human beings within a community. And yet another by Kant, in which the origin of evil is traced to a drama which is more modest than Schelling's, but also perhaps more relevant to us: the drama of human freedom.

7

An Evil Heart

Moral Evil and Moral Identity

Maeve Cooke

The question of evil throws into relief the difficulties facing contemporary moral philosophy. Although these difficulties also confront it in its concern with moral *good*, they tend to do so in less immediate or obvious ways. I take moral philosophy to be concerned first with *moral* (good and) evil—that is, with (good and) evil as it results from the will, actions, or personalities of human agents to whom, by definition, some measure of intentionality and accountability can be imputed. Moral evil in this narrow sense is bound up with questions concerning cultural and social forms of evil, and with the problem of theodicy; nonetheless, it may be considered initially in abstraction from such questions. Even with this narrow focus, however, moral philosophy is confronted by a number of difficulties. To begin with, there are many types of moral evils and it is far from clear what they have in common, how they may be distinguished, whether they are comparable at all, and whether they should be graded and ranked. Moral philosophy thus needs to provide a perspective broad enough to encompass various types of moral evils yet be sensitive to differences of quality and degree.

Secondly, evil highlights the role played by feelings in the moral domain. Our reactions to evil tend to be passionate. An account of evil that ignored the feelings it evokes would disregard a vital dimension of moral experience. On the other hand, feelings can be unreliable. Moreover, the mere presence of a feeling is no guide to how it should be evaluated. Moral philosophy thus has to consider the weight it should attach to subjective feelings in accounts of moral evil.

Thirdly, evil calls more urgently than everyday moral action for an explanation of its causes—the question of how systematic acts of extermination come about demands an answer. Moral philosophy thus has to address the question of *how* moral evil results from the will, actions, or personalities of individual human agents. Here it must consider the importance of moral motivation, the impact on this of environmental and other external factors, and the ways in which moral motivation may be nurtured or corrupted. In addition, since moral motivation is not readily explicable without reference to moral persons, moral philosophy has to confront the question of the relationship between moral duty and moral identity and, more generally, between morality and the good life.

Finally, the problem of evil highlights the problem of moral critique. Evils such as genocide seem to call for unconditional condemnation. In the case of genocide, moral criticism that remains immanent to a contingent cultural context appears inadequate. Insofar as we want more than this, moral philosophy has to find some vantage point for adjudicating evil that transcends the local perspectives of specific cultures. At the same time, however, any such moral vantage point must be congruent with the normative views of knowledge, society, the self, and subjectivity that shape the interpretative horizons of (late) modernity.[1] For we are unavoidably shaped by a certain history and by certain traditions, which produce conceptions of rationality, of knowledge, and of human beings and their interrelationships, that shape our identities. This is not to dispute that there can be many diverging narratives of the historical development of a given culture. In the case of Western modernity, for example, one need think only of the very different narratives offered by Simmel and Nietzsche, or by Foucault and MacIntyre. Nor is it to dispute that these narratives compete with each other, but notwithstanding the differences, there is usually also a significant overlap. This is evidently the case for the rival narratives of Western modernity, where a number of points of agreement are readily discernible. To give one example, these rival narratives concur in the view that the development of Western modernity is characterized by a new attitude toward authority: the authority of tradition, and of those in positions of power and privilege, is no longer unquestioned, but is regarded as open to challenge and criticism by ordinary citizens. A further example, which is clearly connected with the first, is that of the contextuality of knowledge. Even the rival narratives of modernity share a view of knowledge as subject to the constraints of contextuality, as inevitably emerging from within historically specific contexts and as accessible only from contextually defined vantage points. A consequence of this view is that no authoritative standards independent of history and of cultural and social context are now available that could adjudicate competing claims to validity. The idea that knowledge is always tied to specific historical, cultural, and social contexts is one important strand in what is often referred to as "postmetaphysical" thinking.[2] At the same time, it is useful to note that the thesis of the contextuality of knowledge is not necessarily linked with an anti-metaphysical view.[3] Frequently, however, postmetaphysical thinking *goes beyond* recognition of the contextuality of knowledge to reject the need for—or meaningfulness of—metaphysical speculation about the essence of human beings and the world they inhabit. The approach to evil I propose here emphasizes the contextuality of knowledge as a key element of modern self-understanding; however, it requires no commitment to postmetaphysical—in the sense of *anti*-metaphysical—thinking.

The following discussion is guided by an awareness of the difficulties mentioned above, although it does not address all of them directly. Its aim is to open a perspective that is broad enough to cast light on a range of types of moral evil while permitting evaluative distinctions and gradations. Although it does not take up explicitly the question of the importance of subjective feelings in the moral domain, it does look sympathetically at one contemporary approach to questions of validity that focuses on feelings. Its central thesis responds to the need to make sense of moral evil. Its claim is that any convincing account of moral evil requires recognition of the connection between evil and individual moral motivation, and more generally, between evil and individual moral identity as a whole; at the same time, it acknowledges the relevance of environmental and other external factors. Finally, it offers a perspective on moral evil that combines a critical viewpoint with sensitivity to the influences of history and context on human interpretations and evaluations, and that is guided by the principle of the fallibility of knowledge.

The work of Hannah Arendt features prominently in contemporary endeavors to come to grips with the problem of moral evil. Indeed, an epigraph from Arendt seems to have become a mark of serious engagement with the topic. There are, of course, good reasons for this. Arendt is important not only because of her personal experiences and her contribution to the theory of totalitarianism, or even because of her concern with the specific forms of evil that arose within the Nazi regime in Germany, but also because her writings reflect how she grappled with the meaning of evil right up to her death in 1975.[4] In particular, the question of the banality of evil continued to perplex her—and has continued to perplex her commentators.

As has often been observed, Arendt's attempts to grapple with specifically twentieth-century forms of evil were complicated by her attendance at the trial of Adolf Eichmann, a Nazi war criminal, in Jerusalem in 1961. In encountering Eichmann, she was struck by the "banality of evil."[5] By this she meant the phenomenon of evil deeds, committed on a gigantic scale, which could not be traced to any particularity of wickedness, pathology, or ideological conviction in the doer.[6] According to her account, Eichmann, who stood accused of, and was sentenced to death for, mass destruction of Jews, was neither monstrous nor demonic. Furthermore, he seemed to have no motives at all for his role in the Nazi genocide. As she later summarized it:

"[Eichmann's] only personal distinction was a perhaps extraordinary shallowness . . . a curious, quite authentic inability to think."[7]

What interests me here is that Arendt herself blocked off one avenue that could have helped her to make sense of the peculiarly banal type of evil she attributes to Eichmann. This avenue leads toward a conceptualization of evil in terms of perversion of moral character. Despite the fact that she was struck by the banality of evil as a result of her encounter with Eichmann as a *person*, Arendt shied away from the conclusion that Eichmann himself was evil, restricting her use of the word "evil" to his actions and their effects.[8] Arendt seems to have resisted the idea that evil is related to the character of individuals, to the qualities possessed by "a man's nature" or "soul."[9] This is evident in her later discussion of the kind of thinking that she saw as a possible means of conditioning people against evildoing. Here she shows clear distaste for the conclusion that something like Plato's "noble nature" might be a prerequisite for the kind of thinking she advocates, although, as she herself admits, this is the conclusion demanded by the logic of her argument.[10]

In my view Arendt was wrong to reject the position that Eichmann himself was evil. Some of the advantages of the alternative path I propose are that it helps to make sense of banal types of evil and allows for a possible disjunction between moral personality and actions and their effects.

Arendt's reluctance to relate moral evil to moral personality in a robust sense is shared by an important strand of contemporary moral theory. This strand, for which I take Jürgen Habermas's discourse ethics as representative, attempts to reformulate a Kantian deontological approach to morality in light of late modern postmetaphysical thinking. From the point of view of the conceptualization of evil, the separation of moral evil from a robust sense of moral personality has a number of undesirable consequences. I mention in particular:

- a failure to provide a conceptualization of evil that permits discrimination between, and ranking of, types of evil;
- a failure to provide a conceptualization of evil that permits differentiation between degrees of evil;
- an inability to conceive of moral evil as a perversion of moral character that affects moral identity as a whole, and for which the individual concerned is ultimately responsible.

On the other hand, an alternative contemporary approach that does connect validity with identity as a whole is no better equipped to provide an adequate conceptualization of evil. My example here is Alessandro Ferrara's model of reflective authenticity, which seeks to rethink the concept of authenticity in postmetaphysical terms. Despite the strengths of Ferrara's approach, it is, I argue, ultimately too subjectivist. It lacks an adequate conception of moral identity.

I allege, therefore, that Habermas and Ferrara fail to come to grips with the problem of evil due to an inadequate treatment of the dimension of moral identity. Against this, however, it could be argued that there is a more fundamental reason for the inadequacy of their approaches. This is their commitment to postmetaphysical thinking. For, although Habermas and Ferrara offer somewhat divergent interpretations of the postmetaphysical orientation, they share a commitment to certain key elements. They share the view that it is neither possible nor desirable to retreat behind the threshold of Western modernity, of which the so-called linguistic turn is a defining feature;[11] furthermore, that there can be no binding sources of authority external to history, that we must be conscious of context, of our situatedness in history, and of the fact of human plurality, that we must be wary of claims to infallible knowledge and open to the findings of empirically based modes of inquiry; finally, that contemporary philosophy must abandon metaphysical speculation about the essential nature of human beings and the world they inhabit.

It could be argued that so long as they continue to follow postmetaphysical thinking, Habermas and Ferrara will never be able to conceptualize evil adequately. This argument does have some force. However, it is important to recognize the variety of impulses that motivate postmetaphysical thinking and to engage critically with each of its various strands. For example, as already indicated, I see no reason to abandon the postmetaphysical emphasis on the contextuality of knowledge; indeed, I regard it as a key formative element of the late modern self-understanding; jettisoning it would require a fundamental cultural reorientation. By contrast, I find Habermas's and Ferrara's rejection of metaphysical speculation as part of their moral theories less easy to defend,[12] though in the following discussion, I do not deal explicitly with the problems connected with that rejection. Indeed, I leave open the question of whether postmetaphysical thinking is the most adequate philosophical response to moral problems in late modernity. My thesis is rather that Habermas's and Ferrara's incapacity to come to grips with the problem of evil has to do with their failure to relate it to the individual subject's moral identity as a whole. In the case of Habermas, because his notion of moral identity is too thin, in the case of Ferrara, because he has no account of moral identity.

I shall summarize my main criticisms of Habermas and Ferrara before sketching an alternative conceptualization of moral evil.

As is well known, Habermas's discourse ethics is a proceduralist theory that views morality primarily as a means of social action-coordination.[13] This view, as he points out, is compatible with an anthropological perspective that sees morality as a protective mechanism for the extreme vulnerability of individuals resulting from the socialization process itself.[14] It excludes, however, questions about the individual's moral motivation and moral character.[15] Thus, in keeping with his proceduralist account of moral validity, Habermas offers a "thin" account of the moral person. He focuses only on her rational accountability—on her capacity for engaging in rational discourses—leaving aside the subjective visions of the good through which she defines herself and shapes her life-history.[16] (This is quite deliberate, and part of Habermas's postmetaphysical strategy that requires of philosophy a "methodological atheism" with regard to metaphysical questions of the good for human beings.[17]) The advantage of such a proceduralist approach is that it avoids moral subjectivism by providing a vantage point for an objective assessment of the moral validity of norms and principles, based on an intersubjectively conducted universalizability test. Its disadvantage is that it lacks the resources for an adequate conceptualization of moral evil. It fails in particular to provide a basis for discrimination between, and ranking of, types of moral evil, and to allow for differences of degree. Moreover, since it disconnects evil from moral character it is unable to make sense of the kind of evil at issue in a case like Eichmann's.

Discourse ethics permits no distinction between types of moral evil. It cannot distinguish between the evil deeds of the Holocaust and the evil of telling lies. Similarly, it places all human agents who exercise their capacity for rationally accountable action in the same moral basket. It does not, for example, permit distinction between persons who are shallow and selfish and those who deliberately seek to dehumanize others. It is thus unable even to raise the question of whether evil is banal, much less to try to make sense of its banality. Nor does it allow any hierarchy of evil actions or agents. From its point of view, all morally invalid norms and principles are equally reprehensible. Habermas's theory does not, for example, allow a moral distinction between norms and principles that fail the universalizability test but have no apparent seriously harmful consequences, and ones that do have such consequences; or again, between morally invalid proposals that express thoughtless selfishness, ones that express ruthless ambition, and ones that express a sadistic delight in injuring others. There is, in addition, a second sense in which discourse ethics fails to permit a moral distinction between degrees of evil. It collapses the distinction between a trespass and systematic transgression of the moral law: it makes no moral distinction between a basically good person who commits single or occasional immoral acts, and one whose identity is fundamentally evil or corrupt. Worse, it appears to see both immoral motivations and immoral actions as irrelevant to moral identity, for what counts is a person's capacity and readiness to engage in rational argumentation—and, perhaps, the achievement of an argumentatively conducted universal consensus on the moral validity of the norms or principles she affirms.[18] For Habermas, neither the fact that Eichmann was shallow and selfish, or that he perpetrated horrendous acts, can have any bearing on his moral identity. Indeed, in presenting himself as rationally accountable, Eichmann meets the main criterion for moral autonomy as specified by Habermas. As Arendt reminds us, one of the perplexing things about Eichmann was that for all his apparent shallowness and thoughtlessness, he was sufficiently skilled at moral argumentation to cite Kant (with reasonable accuracy) at his trial in Jerusalem in justification of his conduct in sending victims to death camps.[19]

This is a good example of the difficulties arising from Habermas's proceduralist account of moral validity with its thin account of moral agency. It is hard to imagine that Habermas himself could be happy with the conclusion that the atrocities perpetrated by Eichmann have no bearing on his moral identity. He is even less likely to welcome the conclusion that Eichmann satisfies the main requirement for morally autonomous agency.

In short, the inadequacies of proceduralist approaches such as Habermas's call for an approach to moral validity that offers a more convincing conceptualization of evil: one that would allow us to discriminate between and rank types of evil; furthermore, to distinguish between a trespass and systematic transgression of the moral law; and, finally, to acknowledge an interrelation between moral motivation, the moral validity of actions, and moral identity as a whole.

Alessandro Ferrara's model of reflective authenticity is interesting for its pursuit of an alternative postmetaphysical strategy.[20] By contrast with discourse ethics, it develops an account of validity in terms of identity. Despite its strengths, however, its radical subjectivism prevents it from developing a convincing conception of evil. This is because its normative account of identity lacks a specifically moral dimension.

Whereas Habermas's discourse ethics is guided by the Kant of the second *Critique,* the *Critique of Practical Reason,* Ferrara draws his inspiration from the Kant of the third *Critique,* the *Critique of Judgment.* Rejecting the Kantian model of determinant judgment as inappropriate for practical reason, Ferrara is inspired by the Kantian principle of aesthetic validity. He argues that the best means of judging the validity of a symbolic formation (for instance, an individual or a collective identity, or a work of art) is in terms of its authenticity. Guided by a commitment to postmetaphysical thinking, he proposes a normative notion of reflective authenticity that brings with it a new ideal of universal validity linked with the Kantian model of the exemplary uniqueness of a well-formed work of art. According to his complex and nuanced account, reflective authenticity comprises four dimensions: coherence, vitality, depth, and maturity; identities that are authentic in this sense display exemplary universality.

Ferrara argues that the exemplary universality of authentic identities is best captured by categories (such as "degree of fit") that modernity has

tended to relegate to the realm of the aesthetic. Moreover, although judgments of authenticity appeal to reasons, such reasons are always context-
bound, concrete, singular reasons that are logically undemonstrable yet
intuitively compelling. They articulate a sense of validity that ultimately rests
on intuitions about what Kant has called the "furtherance of life": the feeling that my life—or anyone else's life—is in some way enhanced through
the authenticity of the given identity. This shows that exemplary universality operates by way of intuitions and feelings: it does not impose itself on us
like a conqueror but attracts us like a seducer.

One good way of showing the advantages—and limitations—of Ferrara's
authenticity approach is through reference to Arendt's question about
Eichmann and the banality of evil.

As we have seen, Habermas's discourse ethics lacks the resources necessary to make sense of Eichmann as an apparently innocuous perpetrator of
evil. Moreover, it leads to the unhappy conclusion that neither the quality of
the immoral acts perpetrated by Eichmann nor his immoral motivations are
relevant to his moral identity. Ferrara's approach, by contrast, can avoid
these problems since it provides a basis for the evaluative judgment of identity that goes beyond mere rational accountability. If we apply Ferrara's
notion of reflective authenticity to Eichmann, we see that he clearly lacks
the exemplary universality displayed by authentic identities. For one thing,
the thoughtlessness underscored by Arendt implies that he lacks the maturity required by authentic identities as characterized by Ferrara. Her emphasis on his "shallowness" further serves to disqualify him as an authentic identity (for which, we will recall, depth is required), and if we accept Arendt's
reports of his ability to swap one set of convictions for another,[21] he also fails
to meet the requirement of coherence.

A further strength of Ferrara's approach is that it may help to cast light
on the *experience* of moral evil. The model of reflective judgment focuses on
the subjective experience of validity (that is, on the subjective experience of
authenticity or the lack of it)—on the feelings that are evoked when we confront an authentic or inauthentic identity. This seems particularly important
in the case of evil which, as indicated earlier, incites passionate reactions.

However, notwithstanding the apparent success of Ferrara's approach in
the case of Eichmann and the potential fruitfulness of an approach that
makes feelings central, his model of reflective authenticity is inadequate for
the purposes of conceptualizing evil. The crux of the problem is that
Ferrara equates an evil character with an inauthentic one. He offers no
account of specifically moral identity. There are at least two difficulties here.
The first is that is it phenomenologically unconvincing. In equating an evil
character with an inauthentic one, the authenticity thesis interprets our
reaction to identities such as Eichmann—or, indeed, Hitler—as a feeling of
distaste rather than moral condemnation. Against this it could be argued

that there is a difference between feeling distaste or displeasure in the face of inauthenticity and feeling moral revulsion or outrage in the face of evil. At the extreme, perhaps, feelings of distaste and moral revulsion blend into each other. It is, for example, arguable that no one could respond with distaste to another person's extreme lack of maturity, depth, and coherence while at the same time deeming him morally irreproachable. However, there are clearly degrees of inauthenticity that do not provoke feelings of moral revulsion at all. More generally, Ferrara's position requires him to deny any difference between distaste and moral revulsion and that, surely, is phenomenologically implausible.

The second difficulty connected with Ferrara's equation of an evil character with an inauthentic one is that he fails to allow for the possibility of "thoughtful" evil—evil that has depth and coherence. As Karl Jaspers observed in a letter to Arendt, evil per se is not banal.[22] Indeed, Ferrara himself seems to be aware of this possibility, for he raises the question of the "authentically evil" individual identity, admitting that it poses a problem for this thesis.[23] Thus, insofar as an authentically evil identity is a meaningful possibility, it too challenges Ferrara's equation of evil with inauthenticity.

In short, Ferrara's approach is simply too subjectivist to allow an adequate account of moral identity. It cannot make sense of the specifically moral dimension in our response to authentic and inauthentic identities. Furthermore, its equation of moral evil with inauthenticity is an unjustifiable reduction.

I have suggested in the foregoing that we need a conceptualization of moral evil that overcomes the weaknesses of Habermas's and Ferrara's approaches to moral validity while retaining some elements of their postmetaphysical orientation. I have argued that such a conceptualization requires a more robust moral theory and a richer account of moral identity than is possible within the proceduralist framework of Habermas's theory, and a more convincing account of the specifically moral dimensions of identity than is possible within Ferrara's radically subjectivist framework.[24]

My proposed account of moral evil aims to retain Habermas's and Ferrara's postmetaphysical emphasis on the contextuality of knowledge while avoiding the deficiencies of their approaches. It presents moral evil as closely connected with moral identity as a whole, more precisely with a loss or perversion of fundamental moral character. It conceives of moral evil as a fundamental disorder of the self, whereby the self loses or abandons its orientation toward the universal moral imperative to treat human beings in a moral way. In doing so, it makes use of Kant's approach to radical evil as developed in his *Religion within the Limits of Reason Alone*.[25] Although there are a number of indisputable difficulties with Kant's discussion of radical evil, it provides a useful basis for an account of evil such as I propose.

In the first book of *Religion within the Limits of Reason Alone*, Kant offers an account of moral evil in terms of individual human identity. He holds that, strictly speaking, it is not action but identity that is evil: "We call a man evil ... not because he performs actions that are evil (contrary to law) but because these actions are of such a nature that we may infer from them the presence in him of evil maxims."[26] His point here is that mere conformity to the law is not evidence of goodness: what matters is whether or not the moral law has been adopted by the will as the overriding incentive or motivation *(Triebfeder).*[27]

Kant's starting point is the assumption that a predisposition *(Anlage)* to want to obey the moral law is an essential component of human personality, and that following the moral law is thus a fundamental human motivation.[28] Although in his view moral personality cannot be corrupted—for the incentive to be moral belongs to the very meaning of being human[29]—human beings have a capacity for evil that Kant refers to as an evil heart.[30] It is not easy to make sense of Kant's use of the term "evil heart" (and the apparently synonymous term "radical evil").[31] This difficulty is connected with Kant's equivocation on the question of whether—and in what sense—a propensity to evil is innate to human beings.[32] I want to argue that there are two possible readings of Kant's terms "radical evil" and "evil heart." There is an official reading, which is well supported by textual evidence, and then an alternative reading, which is less well supported but avoids a central tension in Kant's discussion; moreover, the alternative is more in tune with certain key elements of the interpretations and evaluations that constitute modern self-understandings—in particular, with a commitment to the importance of free will and moral responsibility as expressed by the normative ideal of individual autonomy.

According to the official reading, an "evil heart" refers to the human propensity *(Hang)* for moral evil. Kant refers to it, for instance, as the will's incapacity, arising from a natural propensity to evil, to adopt the moral law as part of its fundamental maxim.[33] Or again, he defines an evil heart as a propensity of the will to reverse the moral order of priority governing incentives guiding a free will *(Willkür).*[34] As has been noted by a number of commentators, this thesis of a propensity to evil is the source of many inconsistencies in Kant's account, for he himself finds it hard to reconcile with his insistence that moral evil is always a matter of human free will.[35]

I prefer an alternative reading of the idea of an evil heart. This reading, which is possible only if one *disregards* some of Kant's explicit formulations, is more in harmony with his insistence that moral good and evil can result only from the exercise of human free will. On this reading, an evil heart is not a propensity for moral evil but a perversion or corruption of the human heart that results from a faulty moral disposition. Corruption of moral disposition occurs when the ethical order of incentives is reversed;[36] that is, when human beings exercise their free will in such a way that the motivation to follow the moral law is subordinated to other, nonmoral motivations.[37]

What does Kant mean by "disposition" *(Gesinnung)*? Like the notion of "propensity," the term *Gesinnung* poses problems of interpretation. One difficulty is that although Kant implies that there is a clear distinction between disposition, predisposition, and propensity, he appears to use the terms interchangeably on occasion. However, I want to leave aside this difficulty here.[38] I take *Gesinnung* to refer to an individual's fundamental moral attitude, to what we can call her disposition or character (this is also its standard German meaning). It is defined by Kant as the ultimate subjective ground for the adoption of maxims[39]—as the internal principle according to which maxims are adopted. (A maxim is a rule made by the human will *[Willkür]* for the use of its freedom.)[40] We can see from this that *Gesinnung* has two central aspects: the aspect of fundamental moral orientation resulting from the exercise of free choice (the English term "disposition" captures this first aspect well), and the aspect of continuity: *Gessinung* also refers to the enduring and organizing aspect of human agency and identity, to that which makes the moral agent more than just a collection of discrete choices and maxims (the English term "character" better captures this second aspect). In short, *Gesinnung* refers to the individual's freely chosen ordering of her maxims over time: to her (historically developed) fundamental moral orientation resulting from the exercise of the free empirical will.[41] *Gesinnung* is corrupted when the individual will *(Willkür)* subordinates its incentive to observe the moral law to other, nonmoral incentives, more precisely, to incentives arising from sensuous nature. Thus, on the proposed alternative reading, an evil heart (radical evil) refers to a fundamentally disordered (or disoriented) moral personality, a disorder (or disorientation) that arises from the exercise of human free will.

At this point it is necessary to comment briefly on the relationship between an evil disposition and evil action. We will recall that Kant asserts a disjunction between the two: the performance of evil actions does not entitle us to deem the agent who performs them evil, for evil is a matter of disposition, a perversion of will *(Willkür)* resulting from subordination of the incentive to follow the moral law to other, nonmoral ones. From the point of view of the modern idea of the inescapable contextuality of knowledge, the thesis of a disjunction between the morality of actions and the disposition of the agent seems problematic. For, given the absence of a privileged vantage point for judging the moral condition of an agent's *Gesinnung,* the basis for such judgment can only be observation and experience of her actions. However, a stronger and a weaker interpretation of the thesis is possible here. On the stronger interpretation, a privileged vantage point is available that permits reliable assessment of the moral condition of a person's disposition independently of her actions. This is clearly out of tune with the idea of the contextuality of knowledge.[42] On the weaker interpretation, which is more in harmony with this view of knowledge, the moral condition of a person's disposition can be judged only through observation and experience of her actions. But how then should we make sense of the thesis of a disjunction? If observation and experience of a person's actions is the sole available basis for judgments regarding her *Gesinnung*, why assert a disjunction between the two in the first place?

Even on the weaker interpretation, however, the thesis of a disjunction between disposition and action is not meaningless. I take it to make three main points. First, that an evil disposition is a matter not of occasional wrongdoing but of systematic transgression: the basis for moral assessment of a person's disposition is never a single action but only a pattern of actions that emerges over time. Second, that the evil manifested in evil actions always in some way refers back to an independently defined evil disposition: that moral evil cannot be accounted for without reference to moral motivation and to moral identity as a whole. Finally, that there is no relation of simple equivalence between disposition and action: although a corrupt disposition must always manifest itself in actions over time (for otherwise we would have no basis for imputing it), the evil of the deeds perpetrated need not be proportionate to the state of corruption of the perpetrator's *Gesinnung*—historical and contingent factors come into play here. For this reason, in certain contexts, a fundamentally selfish *Gesinnung* may give rise to large-scale atrocities while in other contexts, a fundamentally sadistic *Gesinnung* may have more limited effects.

One advantage of the reading of Kant I propose is that it offers a plausible answer to Arendt's question of how an apparently innocuous character such as Eichmann could be the perpetrator of evil actions. I suggested above that Arendt's difficulty arose from her reluctance to relate evil to moral identity. In resisting the view that Eichmann himself was evil, she was faced with the dilemma of how to make sense of the kind of evil at issue in his case. However, if Eichmann himself is seen as evil, Arendt's dilemma evaporates. The perspective on evil outlined in the foregoing allows us to connect the evil deeds performed by Eichmann with a corruption of his *Gesinnung* and to clarify the sense in which he was evil. Eichmann is seen as evil insofar as he subordinates the moral imperative to treat human beings in a moral way to other, nonmoral, incentives. If Arendt's depiction of him is accurate, his fundamental motivation in life was self-interest. This was his *Gesinnung*, or fundamental moral orientation. From the point of view of his fundamental moral disposition, the fact that he professed to observe the categorical imperative is not conclusive evidence that he did indeed do so. Evaluating moral disposition entails far more than subjective self-description. Any adequate assessment has to study it as manifested in patterns of human relationships and actions over time. It is not Eichmann's self-

definitions but careful consideration of his biography as a whole that
decides whether or not he had an evil heart. The biography sketched by
Arendt suggests that he had. To be sure, in other historical contexts and
under different conditions, his evil heart might not have led him to perpe-
trate such atrocities. As I have said, there is no relation of simple equivalence between corruption of character and the evil of the actions produced
by it—history and contingency always play a role. A full account of the kind
of evil at issue in the case of Eichmann would have to consider the specific
historical factors that facilitated his role as perpetrator of evil.[43]
Nonetheless—and this is my main point—only an account of evil that
starts from an analysis of moral identity as a whole will be able to make sense
of a case like Eichmann's.

The ability of this approach to moral evil to make sense of Arendt's question about Eichmann is not, of course, the only reason to prefer it. Some
more general reasons for seeing moral evil as a fundamental disorientation
of moral personality include the following:

- it allows for differences in types of moral evil;
- it allows distinction between degrees of moral evil;
- it makes clear its reliance on a nonsubjectivist reference point for judgments of moral validity;
- it emphasizes free choice and moral responsibility while allowing for
  contingency and the influences of history and cultural context;
- it allows for moral transformation.

In conclusion, let me say a few words about each of these points.

Conceiving moral evil as a fundamental disorientation of moral personality permits differentiation between types of moral evil. We can see this if we
recall the main elements of Kant's account. On the proposed alternative
reading of this, corruption of moral identity occurs when someone subordinates the incentive to observe the moral law to other, nonmoral incentives.
This approach provides a basis for distinguishing between types of moral evil
depending on which kind of nonmoral incentive is given priority over the
moral law. We can distinguish, for example, between the evil dispositions of
those who subordinate the moral incentive to sympathetic feelings for their
fellow human beings,[44] those who subordinate it to selfish ambition
(Eichmann appears to fall into this category), and those who subordinate it
to delight in harming or dehumanizing others. Admittedly, Kant himself fails
to make such distinctions. However, this is clearly a result of his limited moral
psychology, which relegates all nonmoral incentives to the same moral category.[45] I see no obstacle in principle to a typology of evil dispositions that differentiates between types of nonmoral incentives.

The proposed perspective on moral evil also permits distinction between

degrees. It does so in at least two ways. First of all, a typology of evil dispositions of the kind suggested is compatible with a ranking of evil types. There
are a number of possible bases on which this could be done. One possibility would be a ranking based on the consequences of action, another would
be a ranking based on the effects on the individual concerned. The details
are relatively unimportant. The point is that the approach I propose opens
up the possibility of a hierarchy of evil types.

There is, in addition, a second way in which this approach permits distinction between degrees of moral evil. It enables us to discriminate morally
between those who are guilty of occasional moral trespasses and those who
systematically transgress the moral law. Kant can be read as denying this possibility. He defends moral rigorism, a strict mode of thinking that seeks to
avoid anything intermediate, whether in actions or in evil dispositions.[46]
Again, however, more than one reading of Kant can be suggested here. I
take Kant to be making a point about the effect on the individual of moral
corruption—to be reminding the reader that a loss of moral orientation has
disastrous consequences for the moral identity of the individual concerned.
Once she begins systematically to subordinate her fundamental motivation
to observe the moral imperative to other incentives, she is embarked on a
moral trajectory that leads to corruption of her moral character. It is in this
sense that an individual's disposition *(Gesinnung)* is never indifferent with
respect to the moral law; as a fundamental orientation either toward or away
from the moral law, it is never neither good nor evil.[47] This position is not
only compatible with the distinction between trespass and systematic transgression, it actually seems to call for it. We will recall that disposition (character) refers to the enduring and organizing aspect of moral identity. It is a
matter of fundamental orientation as manifested in habits, actions, beliefs,
relationships with others, traits of personality, and so on over time. It is not
a matter of a single act, be this a moral or an immoral one. An individual's
fundamental moral orientation is constituted only by a pattern of acts and
relations—acts and relations with others that share common features or a
common structure. This is why we can say that only a systematic subordination of the moral imperative to nonmoral imperatives makes a person evil.
An occasional trespass is not sufficient for the kind of fundamental moral
disorientation at issue here. Nor, however, is an occasional virtuous act
sufficient to redeem someone with an evil heart.[48]

A major challenge for an approach to evil of the kind proposed is to find
some reference point that, though nonsubjectivist, is sensitive to the influences of history and context on human interpretations and evaluations.
Kant's reference point, as we know, is the moral law: the categorical imperative to act in such a way that the maxim guiding one's action could at all
times also be valid as the principle guiding a general law. The categorical
imperative can be said to express moral intuitions that have gained currency

within the normative horizons of Western modernity and that now irreversibly shape Western self-understandings. At first glance it may look as though this kind of cultural contextualization of the Kantian categorical imperative undermines its capacity to act as a noncontingent reference point for moral critique. Against this it can be argued that the idea of a context-transcendent basis for moral criticism is readily compatible with an approach to knowledge that acknowledges the influences of history and cultural context on moral thinking.[49] Kant stands accused of disregarding such influences by presenting the incentive to observe the moral law as an innate predisposition of human beings in general. Furthermore, in claiming to derive knowledge of this innate predisposition from a priori philosophical insight, he sets up the latter as an authority immune to challenge by empirical evidence of any sort. By contrast, a moral-philosophical approach that takes account of the contextuality of knowledge has to allow for the possibility of rationally querying or refuting the thesis of a universal inclination to obey the moral law. Here, Habermas's fallibilist model of the validity of knowledge may be fruitful. In his most recent work, the fallibilism of knowledge is expressed in the image of "Janus-faced" conceptions of truth and rightness. The "Janus-face" of these conceptions refers to the dynamic interplay between everyday behavioral certainties and moral intuitions on the one hand, and argumentative justification of their validity on the other.[50] On this fallibilist model, everyday behavioral certainties and intuitions (for instance, moral intuitions about human nature) may be subjected to scrutiny in rational discourses whenever they become problematic; the fallible results of such discussions are then fed back as "truths" into the everyday communicative practices of the lifeworld. It should be noted here that this kind of fallibilist approach does not rule out metaphysical hypotheses— it merely "demotes" or "detranscendentalizes" them by subjecting them to ongoing processes of critical deliberation based on evidence drawn from a variety of theoretical and everyday experiential sources. Admittedly, Habermas himself tends to imply a necessary connection between this kind of detranscendentalization and (a weak form of) naturalism; however, the connection is not at all evident: "detranscendentalization" seems just as compatible with metaphysical interpretations of human nature and the world as with naturalistic ones.[51] Thus, the crucial question in my view is not whether historical contextualization undermines the very idea of objective validity but whether a *non-metaphysical* interpretation of the ideas of truth and moral rightness is ultimately sustainable.[52] While this question has serious implications for postmetaphysical projects such as Habermas's and Ferrara's, it is not of immediate concern to us here. For our purposes it is sufficient to note that the moral intuitions expressed in Kant's categorical imperative can be historically contextualized without significant weakening of their critical power.

The proposed perspective on moral evil has yet another advantage. In keeping with our modern Western commitment to the ideal of autonomy, it emphasizes free choice and moral responsibility. It makes moral character ultimately a matter of free will. The subordination of the incentive to observe the moral imperative to nonmoral incentives is in the end always freely chosen. To deny an element of free choice here is to deny a constitutive element of what it is to be an autonomous human being.[53] Again, this claim seems open to the objection that it is culture-specific. The objection in this case is that it privileges a conception of moral identity that is specific to the interpretative horizon of Western modernity (or similar interpretative horizon), that is, that it privileges the ideal of the autonomous moral agent. However, while agreeing that it does so, I regard this as unavoidable. If, for us, as inhabitants of Western modernity, the concept of moral evil is to make any sense at all, it has to be congruent with (or fundamentally reorient[54]) our traditions and values. The ideas of free will and moral responsibility, and normative conceptions of autonomy based on these ideas, are central to such traditions and values. However, as already indicated, even fundamental, formative moral intuitions are subject to the constraints of contextuality and temporality: they always emerge in historically specific contexts and they are always open in principle to reevaluation on the basis of rational arguments that result from a new way of seeing the world.[55] The validity of the ideal of autonomy is not undermined by the constraints of contextuality and temporality, for these are inescapable. Not only must it explicitly acknowledge its own genealogy within specific historical contexts, but it must also "prove" its superiority over competing normative conceptions of human agency in actual historical contexts: both in everyday contexts of interaction and in processes of rational argumentation in which evidence is drawn from a variety of sources—from culturally diverse everyday experiences as well as from religious beliefs, philosophical insights, and empirical theories.

To be congruent with the normative self-understandings of late modernity, therefore, any account of moral evil must conceive moral disposition as something for which the individual subject ultimately has to bear responsibility. Kant, of course, is very clear on this point.[56] This is why he insists that the ultimate subjective ground of the adoption of maxims is inscrutable.[57] However, this by no means rules out the influences of history, culture, and contingency. The view that individuals are ultimately responsible for their moral disposition is readily compatible with the claims, for example, that certain cultural, social, economic, or political conditions are more favorable than others to maintaining a morally good character, or that situations of social crisis are more conducive to corruption of moral character, to developing an evil heart.[58] This sensitivity to the influences of history, culture, and contingency constitutes a further respect in which the proposed account of evil is in tune with the contextualist strand of postmetaphysical thinking.

Finally, the proposed account has the advantage of allowing for moral transformation. This is connected with its emphasis on free choice and responsibility. If moral disorientation is always ultimately a matter of free choice, reorientation is always possible in principle. Following Kant, we can say that what is required from the individual here is both a "revolution in her cast of mind" and a "gradual reform in her sensuous nature," for only in "continuous growth and labor" can one become a good human being.[59] Again, this by no means denies the importance of historical, biological, economic, cultural, social, and purely contingent factors. Although moral transformation is deemed ultimately to be a matter for the free choice of the individual herself, some conditions favor it more than others.

My concern in the foregoing has been to propose an approach to moral evil in terms of moral disposition or character that is congruent with key elements of the normative horizons of modernity, in particular, with the ideas of the contextuality of knowledge and of free will and moral responsibility. Admittedly, my argument has been rudimentary and many questions remain open. By way of conclusion I want to mention one of these.

This question brings us back to the notion of an "evil heart" in the first of the two senses distinguished earlier. Although I have offered an account of moral evil based on the idea of an evil heart in the second of these two senses, the first sense also raises questions that deserve consideration. In its first sense, the idea of an "evil heart" refers to a propensity for evil as an apparently innate—though not transcendental—feature of human nature. This is, of course, central to Christian teaching, but it remains important for any contemporary theory concerned with human beings and their interrelationships.

Kant may be right to suggest that subjectivity has dimensions that are *not* the product of socialization processes. If there is good reason to think that he is, then clarity is needed as to which, if any, elements of nonsocially produced subjectivity are amenable to formation through socialization processes and social practices and institutions and which resist any kind of mediation. If there is good reason to think that some components of nonsocially produced subjectivity can be mediated socially through education processes, social practices, and institutional frameworks, this calls in turn for corresponding normative accounts of such mediating processes, practices, and frameworks. Rather than simply assuming that human nature has certain innate tendencies or that it is entirely socially produced, Kant reminds us of the need to consider arguments about human nature from many disciplines and to draw on empirically based theories as well as on metaphysically oriented inquiries. He reminds us of the need to find a mode of reflection on human nature that is sensitive to history, context, and contingency without ruling out the possibility of universal anthropological hypotheses. For this purpose, philosophy must cooperate with other disciplines such as history, sociology, psychology, anthropology, and theology, and employ a range of methodological strategies.

8

Understanding Evil

Arendt and the Final Solution

Robert Fine

Robert Fine

MAKING SENSE OF THE SENSELESS

The evil Hannah Arendt most immediately confronted was the Holocaust. She saw it as a "rupture with civilisation" that shattered all existing ideas of progress, all feelings of optimism, all previously engraved images of Europe as a civilized community, all notions of the innocence of modern political thought. In the face of this phenomenon she wrote that not only are all our political concepts and definitions insufficient for an understanding of it, but that "all our categories of thought and standards of judgment seem to explode in our hands the instant we try to apply them."[1] Arendt was one of the first to argue that the attempted extermination of Jews—only later to be called the Holocaust or Shoah—was an event that marked, or should mark, a rupture in social and political thought.

The concern of this paper is with the "gap" between past and future which is provoked by the experience of the Holocaust. This question may be seen as a case study of the impact of historical events on social theory and pre-supposes that social theory does not develop in isolation from the political world of which it is part. The focus on the writings of Hannah Arendt is cho-sen not only because she took seriously the question of evil in the modern political world and not only because she was an extraordinarily gifted and radical political thinker; it is chosen also because she offered a "worldly" per-spective on this rupture with civilization which was rather lost in later reflec-tions on the Holocaust which stressed its uniqueness, singularity, nonrepre-sentability, and ineffability, and which treated Auschwitz as an emblem for the breakdown of human history and/or the limit of human understanding. Gillian Rose echoes the voice of Arendt when she writes of our tendency to "mystify something we dare not understand, because we fear that it may be all too understandable, all too continuous with what we are—human, all too

human," and poses the questions, "what is it that we do not want to understand? What is it that Holocaust piety . . . protects us from understanding?"[2]

As the title of her 1954 essay, "Understanding and Politics," indicates,
Arendt emphasized the centrality of both understanding and politics in relation to the Holocaust.[3] The difference between Arendt's way of thinking and
later Holocaust discourse might be illustrated by a passage from the author
and survivor Elie Wiesel, in which he criticizes the television drama called
Holocaust: "The series treats the Holocaust as if it were just another event. . . .
Whether culmination or aberration of history, the Holocaust transcends history. . . . The dead are in possession of a secret that we, the living, are neither
worthy of nor capable of recovering. . . . The Holocaust? The ultimate event,
the ultimate mystery, never to be comprehended or transmitted."[4]

Equally, it may be illustrated by the thought-experiment conducted by
the French philosopher Jean-François Lyotard, where he draws an analogy
between the Holocaust and the image of an earthquake so catastrophic as
to "destroy not only lives, buildings, and objects but also the instruments
used to measure earthquakes directly and indirectly."[5] In Lyotard's thought-
experiment, it is not only Jews who are exterminated in the Holocaust, but
the means to prove that fact are also exterminated. The point Lyotard
makes is that Auschwitz cannot be grasped in thought simply as a *historical
event* subject to normal procedures of historical investigation. Imagine that
there are no indicators of its existence that survive, all documents are
destroyed, there is nothing to preserve memory from oblivion, the victims
are condemned to silence, and the authority of the tribunal supposed to
establish the crime and its quantity is itself discredited on the ground that
the judge is "merely a criminal more fortunate than the defendant in war."
Lyotard offers this thought-experiment to demonstrate that "the name of
Auschwitz marks the confines wherein historical knowledge sees its compe-
tence impugned," and on this basis advances an *ethical relation* to "Auschwitz"
different from one based on *understanding and politics:* "the impossibility of
quantitatively measuring it, does not prohibit but rather inspires in the
minds of the survivors the idea of a very great seismic force."[6]

Arendt also speaks of the "explosion" of our categories of thought and
standards of judgment when confronted by the Holocaust, but the conclusion she draws is not the same as that drawn by Lyotard. Consider one key
example of this "rupture" which she offers: that of the impossibility of
applying a means/ends calculus to the phenomena of totalitarian terror. In
the conventional use of terror, she argues, violence is exercised as a means
either to retain power, intimidate enemies, or force people to work. But in
circumstances where opposition has already become impossible, where it
does not make a jot of difference what I do, for my fate is already sealed, and
where the exploitation of labor is at most only a secondary benefit subordinate to the main goal of extermination, such rationales make little sense. In

the totalitarian use of terror, violence ceases to be a means to an end; it is deprived of that element of rational calculation which governs its exercise even in the worst of states; it becomes instead the very essence of rule and ends up, as it did in the Holocaust, in a "frenzy of destruction" without political, economic, or military utility. [7]

If this characterization of totalitarian terror is correct, then Arendt's point is that categories of thought and standards of judgment, which presuppose an element of rational choice on the part of social actors, are stretched beyond their limit in the attempt to understand such phenomena. In an earlier essay, "Social Science Techniques and the Study of Concentration Camps" (1950), Arendt explores this issue from its other side—that of the appearance of the impossibility of human understanding—when she writes as follows:

> If we assume that most of our actions are of a utilitarian nature and that our evil deeds spring from some "exaggeration" of self-interest, then we are forced to conclude that this particular institution of totalitarianism is *beyond human understanding*. . . . [I]t is not only the non-utilitarian character of the camps themselves—the senselessness of "punishing" completely innocent people, the failure to keep them in a condition so that profitable work might be extorted from them, the superfluousness of frightening a completely subdued population—which gives them their distinctive and disturbing qualities, but their anti-utilitarian function, the fact that not even the supreme emergencies of military activities were allowed to interfere with these "demographic policies." It was as though the Nazis were convinced that it was of greater importance to run extermination factories than to win the war.[8]

Arendt did not suggest that the death camps were "beyond human understanding." Rather, her argument is that it is only because we have a restrictively rationalistic model of human action that the death camps *appear* to be beyond human understanding. The path which Arendt herself took was not to revert to the conventional view that there must be some rational explanation for the Holocaust in terms of economics, politics, or military strategy, but neither was it to conclude that the Holocaust is beyond human understanding. The path she took is indicated by the subtitle of "Understanding and Politics: The Difficulties of Understanding." Neither ease of understanding nor impossibility of understanding but difficulty of understanding.

The conventional view and the radicalism which declares that the Holocaust is beyond human understanding are two sides of the same coin. The former cannot come to terms with what is unprecedented about the Holocaust. Most modern forms of organized violence are comprehensible inasmuch as they have a "definite purpose" and "benefit the ruler in the same way as an ordinary burglary benefits the burglar."[9] Arendt mentions in this context aggressive wars, massacres of enemy populations, extermination of indigenous peoples in the process of colonization, enslavement of subject peoples, and so forth. These modern forms of organized violence doubtless paved the way for totalitarian terror but they were different in kind. In totalitarian terror itself, she saw the absence of any such utilitarian criteria. Thus in respect of the Holocaust Arendt writes:

> The gas chambers did not benefit anybody. The deportations themselves, during a period of acute shortage of rolling stock, the establishment of costly factories, the manpower employed and badly needed for the war effort, the general demoralising effect on the German military forces as well as on the population in the occupied territories—all this interfered disastrously with the war in the East, as the military authorities as well as Nazi officials . . . pointed out repeatedly. . . . And the office of Himmler issued one order after another, warning the military commanders . . . that no economic or military considerations were to interfere with the extermination programme.[10]

It is this absence of instrumental or utilitarian rationality which not only gives to totalitarian terror in general, and to the Holocaust in particular, their "horrible originality," but makes them incomprehensible to a social science fixed within rationalistic ways of thinking. The counterproposition, that the Holocaust is beyond human understanding, has the definite merit of recognizing that "rational choice" models of social science cannot begin to explain the Holocaust nor other phenomena of totalitarian terror, but it refuses to extend human understanding beyond these rationalistic limits. Arendt's message is that in the face of the Holocaust we do not encounter the limits of understanding as such, but rather the limits of a particular understanding which presupposes the rationality of human action.

Arendt defends the activity of understanding as such. It is, in and of itself, a sign of our humanity and of our resistance to the conditions which made the Holocaust possible. It is an activity which totalitarianism suppresses and which conversely is one mark of our struggle against it. It is an activity which "begins where violence ends," which is "profoundly and fundamentally human"; it is a way in which "we come to terms with and reconcile ourselves to reality" and try to be "at home in the world"; it is "the specifically human way of being alive; for every single person needs to be reconciled to a world into which he was born a stranger and in which, to the extent of his distinct uniqueness, he always remains a stranger."[11] To abandon the quest for understanding is to surrender to the totalitarian elements which survive within our own society: if people in the camps who were defenselessly exposed to a seemingly inexplicable power sometimes found the resources to make sense of it (let us think of Primo Levi or Tadeusz Borowski[12]), then there is all the more reason for those of us who are not so exposed to ensure that this absolute betrayal of human values does not rule supreme. In this context the human activity of understanding is itself a reaffirmation of human values.

The perception that our existing categories of thought and standards of judgment are lacking when it comes to the Holocaust, does not invalidate all our categories and standards and does not mean that they must all be abandoned. The notion that Auschwitz represents a *novum* in the exercise of evil implies that we still have the categories and standards which make it possible to recognize how unprecedented and original the Holocaust was in human history. The activity of understanding is not the *imperium* of the modern philosophical subject who represents the Holocaust like a voyeur removed from the terrible events which he or she observes. It is not about imposing abstract concepts onto lived experience and reiterating the false promise of a universal politics. It is not a sign of disrespect for the silence which the suffering of the victims demands nor an appropriation of their experience by the theoretician. It is certainly not about forgiving the perpetrators in the sense that *tout comprendre, c'est tout pardonner,* nor is it about using the Holocaust to indoctrinate people with "final results" that can serve as weapons in ideological warfare. It does not mean engaging in some kind of "dialectical acrobatics" based on the "superstition that something good might come from evil"—a view which can only be justified as long as "the worst that man could inflict upon man was murder."[13] Rather, making sense of the senseless remained for Arendt an essential element in recovering the idea of humanity in the face of determined efforts to obliterate it.

The activity of understanding will not be able to confront the burden of events which weigh down upon the twentieth century if, as Nietzsche put it in *The Will to Power,* it determines to "reduce the unknown to something which is known,"[14] or, as Arendt reformulates it, to "submerge what is unfamiliar in a welter of familiarities."[15] We must resist the presumption that nothing can happen which our categories are not equipped to understand and which cannot be deduced from its precedents. In the case of the Holocaust and of other forms of totalitarian terror, "all parallels create confusion and distract attention from what is essential."[16] If the Holocaust has deprived us of our *traditional tools* of understanding, still we must confront the difficulty of constructing *new tools.*

In *The Origins of Totalitarianism* Arendt acknowledges the "great temptation to explain away the intrinsically incredible by means of liberal rationalisations"—in each one of us, she writes, "there lurks such a liberal wheedling us with the voice of common sense."[17] The failure of liberalism to live up to its own ideals or effectively to oppose those who devalue them seemed to Arendt to be a clear and distinct lesson to be drawn from the origins of totalitarianism. Liberalism, she wrote in "The Eggs Speak Up" (1951), has "demonstrated its inability to resist totalitarianism so often that its failure may already be counted among the historical facts of our century."[18] We might look back on the heyday of the liberal tradition with a certain nostalgic affection but not pretend that "the past is alive in the sense that it is in our power to return to it." The liberal way of thinking allows us only to "take that which was good in the past and simply call it our heritage" and to "discard the bad and simply think of it as a dead load which by itself time will bury in oblivion."[19] Liberalism promises only an eventual restoration of the old world order, but if we are to confront the eventness of the Holocaust, then we cannot remain content with this thin gruel.

If the catastrophe were so consuming as to destroy all our categories of thought and all our standards of judgment, then the task of understanding would indeed be hopeless: "how can we measure length if we do not have a yardstick, how could we count things without the notion of numbers?" The conclusion, however, which Arendt draws from this thought-experiment is not that drawn by Lyotard. Lyotard describes *what might have been* if the voice of resistance had been silenced, if the attempt to exterminate Jews—and the successors of the Jews—had been successfully carried to its conclusion, if the yardsticks which make possible human understanding, including the idea of humanity itself, were destroyed. But Arendt's thought-experiment highlights the fact that "total domination" was fully actualized only within the confines of the concentration and death camps. If it had been extended to the social body as a whole, then the activity of understanding may well have been killed along with the victims, but this hypothetical possibility reveals "the necessary limitations to an experiment which requires global control in order to show conclusive results."[20]

These sealed-off camps were to totalitarianism in power what the "panopticon" was to normal disciplinary power or the factory was to capitalist production: they were the central institution of totalitarian power because it was in these camps alone that the experiment of total domination, impossible to accomplish under normal circumstances, could be actualized. They were the laboratories in which the nihilistic credo that "everything is possible" was reduced to the totalitarian dogma that "everything can be destroyed," including the idea of humanity itself.[21] In the camps destruction was not a by-product of production, in the sense that one cannot make a wooden table without destroying a tree. Destruction was rather the aim of production—an end in itself deprived of any "element of utilitarian calculation." The achievement of the camps lay neither in the making of the "new man" nor in the making a "new order of things." It did not lie in *making* anything but in "robbing man of his nature . . . under the *pretext* of changing it." The camps were the visible proof that human beings can be turned into inanimate things and that murder can be made as impersonal as "the squashing of a gnat."[22]

It was this "peculiar unreality and lack of credibility" of life in the camps which generated the mystery of Auschwitz as the emblem of that which is beyond human understanding. The extreme difficulty that faces victims or eyewitnesses or anyone else, is to make sense of what happened, and for the victims it is even harder to find ways of communicating this which happened to "normal people" in the outside world. Commenting on the reports of survivors that were available at the time of writing *Origins* (first published in 1951), as well as on their reception, Arendt describes the difficulties with great insight:

> There are numerous reports by survivors. The more authentic they are, the less they attempt to communicate things that evade human understanding and human experience—sufferings, that is, that transform men into 'uncomplaining animals'. None of these reports inspires those passions of outrage and sympathy through which men have always been mobilised for justice. On the contrary, anyone speaking or writing about concentration camps is still regarded as suspect; and if the speaker has resolutely returned to the world of the living, he himself is often assailed by doubts with regard to his own truthfulness, as though he had mistaken a nightmare for reality. . . . What common sense and 'normal people' refuse to believe is that everything is possible. We attempt to understand elements in present or recollected experience that simply surpass our powers of understanding. We attempt to classify as criminal a thing which, as we all feel, no such category was ever intended to cover. What meaning has the concept of murder when we are confronted with the mass production of corpses. . . . If it is true that the concentration camps are the most consequential institutions of totalitarian rule, 'dwelling on horrors' would seem to be indispensable for the understanding of totalitarianism. But recollection can no more do this than can the uncommunicative eyewitness report. In both these genres there is an inherent tendency to run away from the experience; instinctively or rationally, both types of writer are so much aware of the terrible abyss that separates the world of the living from that of the living dead that they cannot supply anything more than a series of remembered occurrences that must seem just as incredible to those who relate them as to their audience. . . . Only the fearful imagination of those who have been aroused by such reports but have not actually been smitten in their own flesh, of those who are consequently free from the bestial desperate terror which, when confronted by real, present horror, inexorably paralyses everything that is not mere reaction, can afford to keep thinking about horrors. Such thoughts are useful only for the perception of political contexts and the mobilisation of political passions.[23]

In this passage Arendt expresses the difficulty confronted by survivors of distinguishing nightmare from reality; our own difficulty of understanding when confronted by the lunacy of a process based on the "mass production of corpses"; the difficulty faced by the human imagination in "dwelling upon horrors"; the difficult relation between survivors and people like herself, who are aroused by their reports and have the capacity to draw political conclusions precisely because they were not themselves engulfed by the actuality of "real, present horror." Difficulty compounded upon difficulty. Why should people construct this microworld of senselessness in which "punishment is meted out without connection with crime . . . exploitation is practised without profit, and . . . work is performed without product";[24] why on earth should they make this representation of Hell in which "the whole of life was thoroughly and systematically organized with a view to the greatest possible torment."[25] The only categories which seem to make sense of this world are those of senselessness, madness, unreality, insanity. It has the *appearance*, as Arendt put it in a term drawn from Kant, of "some radical evil previously unknown to us."[26]

The camps seem incomprehensible, mad, insane according to the normal rules of historical knowledge. But the silence with which the questions posed by the camps were met, at the time when Arendt was first writing, was not because of any shortage of documents and testimonies, nor because the perpetrators succeeded in their attempt to abolish all trace of the camps and the killing fields—there survived an abundance of documents, signs, traces, and testimonies precisely because the perpetrators in the end failed to eliminate Jews from the face of the earth. It was because the sources from which such answers should have sprung had themselves dried up. It was loss of "the quest for meaning and need for understanding" that Arendt feared most "after Auschwitz," for to yield to the impossibility of understanding would be an abdication that would grant totalitarian terror, as it were, the last word.[27] But why do we lose the quest for meaning and the need for understanding? What is it that we do not want to understand?

THE JURIDICAL POINT OF VIEW

The "difficulties of understanding" are evident in the attempt to apply juridical categories to some of the perpetrators of the Holocaust. Both in legal prosecutions and in everyday speech, the terms "crime" and "criminal" were regularly used to refer to the acts and agents of the Holocaust. Arendt certainly did not wish to invalidate the use of these categories, but she did problematize their application. In relation to the violence perpetrated by the Nazis against Jews and other victims of the Holocaust, she observed that the category of "crime" and "criminal" is hopelessly inadequate. It neglects the difference between mere criminality and the facts of mass extermination—between "a man who sets out to murder his old aunt" and "people who without considering the economic usefulness of their actions at all . . . built factories to produce corpses."[28] What is distinctive about the latter is that they "explode the limits of the law" and their guilt, in contrast to all criminal guilt, "oversteps and shatters any and all legal systems."[29] There is also the disproportion between the few Nazis who were tried and punished at Nuremberg and the mass of perpetrators who committed the deeds in question. When the machinery of mass murder forces practically everyone in a society to participate in one way or another, "the human need for justice can find no satisfactory reply to the total mobilisation of a people to that purpose. Where all are guilty, nobody in the last analysis can be judged."[30] The effacement of visible signs of distinction between the guilty and the innocent—through a policy of making each individual dependent upon committing crimes or being complicit in them or at least appearing to be complicit in them—marks the limit of criminal law.

The inadequacy of legal categories is apparent in the language of "personal responsibility" which criminal law presupposes. The perpetrators typically saw themselves as "cogs in the mass murder machine" who did the job of killing "only in a professional capacity, without passion or ill will," and no longer recognized any contradiction between being a good father, husband, and dog-owner at home and killing Jews if that was his public duty and legal obligation. Between this "modern type of man" and conventional notions of responsibility, a new kind of gap opens up: "if we tell a member of this new occupational class which our time has produced that he is being held to account for what he did, he will feel nothing except that he has been betrayed."[31] This new type of "bourgeois" is no longer the citizen who combines the public virtue of civic patriotism with the private virtue of personal responsibility, but the "man of the masses" who does his or her duty, even at the expense of his own inclinations, and cannot think otherwise.

Such perpetrators are in fact human beings, not cogs in a machine, yet they conceive of themselves *as if* they were cogs in a machine. It is this "as if" quality that is so difficult to comprehend. On the one hand, the positivistic social sciences which declare that the perpetrators were *in fact* merely cogs in a killing machine and were incapable of moral awareness, merely mirror the illusions of the world they purport to explain. Against this it was a definite achievement of the trials that "all the cogs in the machinery, no matter how insignificant, are *in court* forthwith transformed back into perpetrators, that is to say, into human beings."[32] However, the juridical conception of personal responsibility would be a mere legal fiction if it were imposed upon a social reality in which responsibility had no factual existence (like holding peasants dispossessed of their land responsible for becoming vagrants).[33]

If the question of responsibility cannot be adequately handled either by a positivism which denies its existence or by a juridical consciousness which turns it into an absolute presupposition, Arendt's writings inaugurate an approach which foregoes all a priori, metaphysical conceptions of responsibility in order to explore the actuality of moral responsibility within the killing machines. The subtext of her argument is that, if totalitarianism indicates the collapse of all existing moral standards, it is accompanied by a restructured moral point of view in which personal responsibility is not simply annulled but reconfigured. Arendt demonstrates that the totalitarian form of organization is based on "authority" rather than naked force and as such depends on "the unquestioning recognition of orders" by those who are asked to obey, so that neither coercion nor persuasion is needed.[34] The perpetrators of the Holocaust did not generally question orders, let alone disobey them, membership of murder-squads was not on the whole compulsory and individuals were not generally forced to kill under pain of death themselves.[35] It was not a case of "kill or be killed," and if it had been, this would have been a legitimate defense or at least plea of mitigation at Nuremberg. As Adolf Eichmann put it in his trial, he acted according to his conscience and his conscience would have troubled him only if he had questioned orders—a thought which seems never to have occurred to him.

Max Weber long ago demonstrated that in a rational bureaucracy officials are not simply cogs in a machine, for the very act of "following a rule" requires for its fulfillment all manner of interpretative endeavour and moral evaluation.[36] In the organization of the Holocaust some use was made of some elements of rational bureaucracy, but these elements were subordinated to the Nazi movement and its secret police forces, and radically reconfigured according to the so-called *Führerprinzip*, or leader principle. In place of hierarchical order, the leader principle demanded that every member of the killing machine think and act in accordance with the will of the leader and owe allegiance to the leader himself. As Hans Frank famously formulated it, in mockery of Kant, the categorical imperative of the Third Reich was: "Act in such a way as the Führer, if he knew your action, would approve it."[37] Wide latitude was given to officials in the execution of general policies and all holders of position were responsible not only for their own actions but also for the actions of their subordinates— even when they disobeyed or failed to fulfill orders. To grasp the "will of the Führer" in this context demanded zeal and creativity far in excess of the old-fashioned plodding bureaucrat.

If this, or something like this, was the actuality of "personal responsibility" in the Nazi killing machines, the question raised by Arendt (in reference to Kierkegaard and Jaspers[38]) is how to create a new sense of "universal responsibility" in which

> human beings . . . assume responsibility for all crimes committed by human beings, in which no one people are assigned a monopoly of guilt and none considers itself superior, in which good citizens would not shrink back in horror at German crimes and declare "Thank God, I am not like that," but rather recognise in fear and trembling the incalculable evil which humanity is capable of and fight fearlessly, uncompromisingly, everywhere against it.[39]

One way is through the establishment of what Kant called "cosmopolitan law" which would hold to account the perpetrators of such atrocities as were committed in the Holocaust. In spite of her reservations, Arendt saw the glimmer of this new dawn in the Nuremberg prosecution of top Nazis. It was an event that announced that individuals, rather than states, can be held responsible for crimes under international law; that individuals acting within the legality of their own state can be tried as criminals; that service to the state does not (as Alain Finkielkraut put it) exonerate any official in any bureaucracy or any scientist in any laboratory from his or her responsibilities as a thinking individual; that no one can hide behind the excuse of "only obeying orders" and that those who sit behind desks planning atrocities are as guilty as those who participate directly in their execution. Not least, it announced that atrocities committed against one set of people, be it Jews or Poles or Rom, are an affront not only to these particular people but also to humanity as a whole, and that humanity would find means of bringing the perpetrators to justice.[40]

To be sure, the promise of a new cosmopolitan order was precarious and almost stillborn. At Nuremberg it excluded in principle crimes committed by the Allied powers (including Stalin's terror), and in respect of the Germans it focused mainly on traditional "war crimes" and "crimes against peace" rather than on the "crimes against humanity" committed in the camps and killing fields. After Nuremberg, the cosmopolitan precedent set by the Charter and these trials quickly evaporated as international consensus collapsed and rival cold war interests prevailed. The few cases that were held for crimes against humanity were almost exclusively concerned with the wartime activities of Nazis rather than later atrocities like those committed by colonial powers or sometimes by anticolonial movements after the war.

This was the nub of Arendt's criticisms of the Eichmann trial. She upheld the legitimacy of the trial. The fact that Eichmann had been illegally kidnapped from Argentina was justified given that he had been indicted at Nuremberg, charged with crimes against humanity, and was hiding in a country with a bad record of extradition. The use of an Israeli national court was justified in the absence of an international court or a successor court to Nuremberg, and in light of the fact that Eichmann's job was to organize the transportation and killing of Jews. The contention that there were more important issues at stake than the trial of a single individual—for example, the political character of modern anti-Semitism, the origins of totalitarianism, the nature of evil, the question of why the Germans?—was no reason not to seek justice in this particular case.[41] For Arendt, the trial of Eichmann was one means by which the abstract conception of universal responsibility could be made actual.

On the other hand, Arendt criticized the Eichmann trial for its misuse in the service of Israeli nationalist aims: the contention that only in Israel could a Jew be safe, the attempt to camouflage the existence of ethnic distinctions in Israeli society, the concealment of the cooperation of certain Jewish leaders in the administration of the Holocaust, and so forth.[42] What Arendt expressed was a growing sense of lost opportunity: that the precedent set by Nuremberg was being ignored in the era of cold war, that the

universalistic import of crimes against humanity was being corralled back
into a nationalist frame of reference, that the ethical significance of the
Holocaust was being lost to a moral division of the world between them and
us, good and evil, which served only as an index of a world purged of all
political profundity. To those who thought that the institution of "crimes
against humanity" could achieve some sort of release from the elements of
totalitarian thought which inhere within the modern world, the fear that
Arendt expressed was that it was being used to reinforce the very situation
it had sought to correct—the breaking up of the human race into a multitude of competing states and nations.[43]

Far from condemning all juridical categories, Arendt argued that the category of "crimes against humanity" was well chosen since in the most literal
sense such crimes as the perpetrators of the Holocaust committed were
"against humanity." In the Holocaust "individual human beings did not kill
other individual human beings for human reasons"; rather an organized
attempt was made to "eradicate the concept of the human being."[44] If the
camps were an attempt not only to eradicate human beings but the idea of
humanity, the legal category of "crimes against humanity" expresses this aim
very well:

> Something seems to be involved in modern politics that actually should never
> be involved in politics as we used to understand it, namely all or nothing—all,
> and that is an undetermined infinity of forms of human living together, or
> nothing, for a victory of the concentration camp system would mean the same
> inexorable doom for human beings as the use of the hydrogen bomb would
> mean the doom of the human race.[45]

The legal concept of crimes against humanity expresses the rise of a politics which strives for "total domination" by "eliminating under scientifically
controlled conditions spontaneity itself as an expression of human behav-
iour and of transforming the human personality into a mere thing"; a politics whose aim is the destruction of all human spontaneity, plurality, and differentiation; a politics based on the notion that "all men have become
equally superfluous."[46] The international lawyers were more right than they
probably knew when they said that the intent of such politics was to destroy
"humanity." For Arendt, the point was not to declare prematurely the death
of humanity, but to try to understand why the idea of humanity may appear
as something so offensive that it has to be destroyed and how it can be
restored as something more than an empty slogan.

THE RADICALISM AND BANALITY OF EVIL

When Arendt wrote of the "*appearance* of some radical evil," it was doubtless
to distinguish her use of the concept from any ontological conception of

radical evil. This appearance was due to the intent behind the Final Solution: to get rid of not just Jews and other "undesirables" but the idea of humanity. If the idea of humanity is the achievement of the modern age, the Holocaust may be understood as an attempt to undo this achievement. But to declare that the "idea of humanity" is dead is to grant the Nazis a posthumous victory.

Implicit in the use of the term *radical* evil is an opposition to any relativizing of the evil of the Holocaust. The collapse of moral standards that was encountered in totalitarian terror, and the equally rapid adaptation of former Nazis to the "democratic way of life" after the war, gives the impression that what we call morality consists merely of "our habits" and is no more than "a set of *mores*, customs and manners which could be exchanged for another set with hardly more trouble than it would take to change the table manners of an individual or a people."[47] The concept of "radical evil" may be read as opposing any tendency in social theory to relativize morals in relation to contingent and transitory social norms. The Holocaust is visible proof, if any were needed, that the reduction of what is right to mere opinions about what is right is the mark of a subjectivism which omits all question of substance.

Karl Jaspers highlighted certain risks involved in the use of the term "radical evil" in his correspondence with Arendt after the war. Jaspers argued that it might endow the perpetrators with what he called a "streak of satanic greatness" and mystify them and their deeds in "myth and legend." It was against this danger that Jaspers emphasized the "prosaic triviality" of the perpetrators and coined the phrase "the banality of evil" to bring this to the surface. He argued, for instance, that the great advantage of treating the perpetrators as "mere criminals" was to present them "in their total banality."[48] Arendt expressed her agreement in principle and acknowledged that in her use of the term she was coming close to "mythologising the horrible."[49] No longer mindful of its original source she introduced the term "banality of evil" in her writings at the time of the Eichmann trial to face up to the fact that the perpetrators were "men like ourselves" who demonstrated what terrible deeds "ordinary men" are capable of. It was a rejoinder to conventional images of the "Nazi monster" that had nothing to do with people like ourselves and which painted the world in terms of a dichotomy between our own absolute innocence and the unspeakable Nazi beast. What she took from the Eichmann case was that the perpetrators of the most radical evil could be pedestrian, bourgeois individuals, rooted in an everydayness that made them incapable of critical reflection or serious moral judgment, marked more by "thoughtlessness" and "remoteness from reality" than by any streak of Satanic greatness. She thought that nothing was further from Eichmann's mind than "to prove a villain," nor was he even a convinced anti-Semite; in fact, he had few motives beyond his diligence in looking out for his own career advancement. The mark of his character was sheer thoughtlessness and it was this which predisposed him to become one of the greatest criminals of the modern age. The lesson Arendt took from Jerusalem was that "such remoteness from reality and such thoughtlessness can wreak more havoc than all the evil instincts taken together,"[50] and that we have to come to terms with the fact that the man responsible for the execution of the Holocaust was terrifyingly normal: "the deeds were monstrous but the doer . . . was quite ordinary, commonplace, and neither demonic nor monstrous."[51]

Richard Bernstein has convincingly argued that between the "monstrous deed" (the appearance of radical evil) and the "commonplace doer" (the banality of evil) there is no contradiction.[52] The subtext of this terminological turn, however, may be understood in relation to the new ways of mythologizing the horrible that were emerging in the 1960s. The experience of watching and hearing Eichmann was the trigger for Arendt's reaffirmation of a humanist tradition according to which only good is radical and evil is merely the deprivation of good with no independent reality of its own. Evil is never radical, she argued, "it is only extreme, and . . . it possesses neither depths nor any demonic dimension. . . . Only the good has depths and can be radical."[53] With the Eichmann trial, the wall of silence which so often surrounded victims of the Holocaust during the 1950s was increasingly broken. Arendt welcomed, of course, this development but what was at issue was the form in which the silence is broken.

When the new discourse makes use of theological terms like the "Holocaust" and "Shoah" to name the unnameable event, it insists upon its uniqueness and singularity. It uses "Auschwitz" synecdochically for the Holocaust and isolates the Jewish catastrophe from the wider catastrophe embodied in the rise of totalitarianism. Auschwitz is treated as irrefutable proof that, as Adorno put it, "culture had failed":

> All post-Auschwitz culture, including its urgent critique, is garbage. . . . Whoever pleads for the maintenance of this radically culpable and shabby culture becomes its accomplice, while the man who says no to culture is directly furthering the barbarism which our culture showed itself to be. . . . Not even silence gets us out of the circle. In silence we simply use the state of objective truth to rationalise our subjective incapacity, once more degrading truth into a lie.[54]

What I think worried Arendt was that the concept of radical evil was implicated in a discourse which denied the possibility of understanding. The idea of the banality of evil was challenged by certain Jewish critics on the ground that it diminished the significance of the Holocaust. Gershom Scholem, for example, was by no means alone in reading the phrase as trivializing the Holocaust and diminishing the *novum* of this event.[55] For both

Scholem and Arendt, however, the Holocaust was the pivotal event in the definition of political modernity. The *real* difference between them concerned Arendt's refusal to singularize the Holocaust, to extract it from the wider phenomena of totalitarian terror, or to rule out an essentially political response. In this context, the use of the term "banality of evil" was, I think, her way of saying that the Holocaust was "human, all too human."

In his memoir *At the Mind's Limits: Contemplations by a Survivor on Auschwitz and Its Realities* (1966) Jean Améry argues that Arendt was unable to come face to face with the event because she saw only "codified abstractions." Her use of the concept of totalitarianism is a case in point. Améry writes with unconcealed impatience:

> I hear indignant objection being raised, hear it said that not Hitler embodied torture but rather something unclear, "totalitarianism." I hear especially the example of Communism being shouted at me. And didn't I myself just say that in the Soviet Union torture was practised for 34 years? And did not already Arthur Koestler . . . ? Oh yes, I know, I know.[56]

Améry goes on to write that Stalin and Hitler were different in principle: the one "still symbolises an idea of man," the other "hated the word 'humanity' like the pious man hates sin" (p.180). Yet this contrast, between one who symbolized the idea of man and the one who hated the word humanity, takes Stalin at his word and lets him off the hook on which Arendt hung him. Be that as it may, the crucial point for Améry takes off from a discussion of Proust:

> Proust writes somewhere: Nothing really happens as we hope it will, nor as we fear it will. But not because the occurrence, as one says, perhaps "goes beyond the imagination" . . . but because it is reality and not fantasy. . . . What one tends to call "normal life" may coincide with anticipatory imagination and trivial statement. I buy a newspaper and am "a man who buys a newspaper." The act does not differ from the image through which I anticipated it, and I hardly differentiate myself personally from the millions who performed it before me. Because my imagination did not suffice to entirely capture such an event? No, rather because even in direct experience everyday life is nothing but codified abstraction. Only in rare moments of life do we truly stand face to face with the event and, with it, reality.[57]

One such rare moment of life for Améry is when he faced torture by the Gestapo.

> Gestapo men in leather coats, pistol pointed at their victim—that is correct, all right. But, then, almost amazingly it dawns on one that the fellows not only have leather coats and pistols, but also faces . . . like anyone else's. Plain, ordinary faces. And the enormous perception at a later stage, one that destroys all abstractive imagination, makes clear to us how the plain, ordinary faces finally become Gestapo faces after all, and how evil overlays and exceeds banality. For

there is no "banality of evil" and Hannah Arendt . . . knew the enemy of mankind only from hearsay, saw him only through the glass cage.[58]

The "codified abstraction" of totalitarianism offends Améry because it draws the reader away from the sheer corporeality and sadism of that reality:

> National Socialism in its totality was stamped less with the seal of a hardly definable "totalitarianism" than with that of sadism. Sadism as radical negation of the other, as the denial of the social principle as well as the reality principle. The sadist wants to nullify this world, and by negating his fellow man, who also in an entirely specific sense is "hell" for him, he wants to realise his own total sovereignty.[59]
>
> "I have experienced the ineffable," Améry writes, "I am filled with it entirely."[60] In this context "thinking is almost nothing else but a great astonishment."

According to Améry, when Arendt dissolves the experience of the Holocaust into an abstract codification like "totalitarianism," she not only identifies Hitler and Stalin as one and same thing, but also views the perpetrators through a glass cage and diminishes the sheer sadism of their practices. This is not the place to defend in detail Arendt's account, except to say that she saw it necessary to distinguish between the memoir of the survivor and the understanding of one moved by the survivor's account, and to find new words and new uses of words to capture new phenomena. Thus Arendt had to extract the term "totalitarianism"—which had been coined by the Italian fascist Giovanni Gentile in the 1920s to express the actuality of "total freedom" when the self-realization of the individual is absolutely identified with the universality of the state and when the state itself is "comprehensive, all embracing, pervasive . . . total"—from the megalomaniac ambitions of this fascist ideologue if she was not to be accused of turning the *fantasy* of the "total" state into the *actuality* of a political formation.[61] But this was precisely Arendt's point: it was not the realization of the dream of total domination, but its collapse, that led to the escalating orgies of destruction. In this usage, the concept of totalitarianism is not in my opinion, as Dana Villa argues, the "terrible revelation" of the essence of the West to itself. It is not the case that "The presencing of everything as orderable and controllable is the *conditio sine qua non* for everything appearing to be possible—for the totalitarian project as such."[62] Rather the concept of totalitarianism helps us to make sense of the senseless by revealing the dynamics of madness that lie at the core of this conception.

THE WILL TO DESTROY

Why did the idea of humanity cause such offense and why did movements arise which tried so hard to destroy it? Arendt's answer draws on Nietzsche's *The Will to Power* where he defines nihilism thus: "what does nihilism mean? That the highest values devaluate themselves. The aim is lacking; 'why?' finds no answer."[63] Nietzsche prefigured the fin de siècle mood of irredeemable decline when the values and beliefs that were taken as the highest manifestation of the spirit of the West lost their validity. He believed that this loss of values bred a destructive and spiritless radicalism, full of hostility to culture and images of destruction, [64] and the specter of barbarism which he anticipated turned out to be a pale image of the barbarism of later totalitarian movements.

Following Nietzsche, Arendt views European nihilism not so much as a pathological state of mind but as a valid expression of a disenchanted world. Nihilism became the specter haunting Europe because it was well grounded and because all thinking beings shared the sense of revulsion felt by those who confronted the gulf between established values and the experience of extreme violence in World War I: "Simply to brand as outbursts of nihilism this violent dissatisfaction with the pre-war age . . . is to overlook how justified disgust can be in a society wholly permeated with the ideological outlook and moral standards of the bourgeoisie."[65]

> Disillusionment fed the "anti-humanist, anti-liberal, anti-individualist and anti-cultural instincts" of a front generation which elevated violence, power and cruelty as the "supreme capacities of humankind" and became "completely absorbed by their desire to see the ruin of this whole world of fake security, fake culture and fake life." What emerged in the place of conventional values was disgust with all existing standards and with every power that be; the hope that the whole culture and texture of life might go down in "storms of steel" (Jünger); "destruction without mitigation, chaos and ruin as such assumed the dignity of supreme values." For the front generation, war was not just the offspring of the old world but the progenitor of the new: a means of "chastisement" and "purification" in a corrupt age (Thomas Mann), the "great equaliser" in class-ridden societies (Lenin), the arena where "selflessness" obliterates bourgeois egoism (Bakunin), the site of the "doomed man" with "no personal interest, no affairs, no sentiments, attachments, property, not even a name of his own" (Nechaev), the ruined ground on which philosophies of action dream of escape from society into the world of doing something, heroic or criminal, that is undetermined. The double standards of bourgeois civil society incited a politics of unmasking. . . . Since the bourgeoisie claimed to be the guardian of Western traditions and confounded all moral issues by parading publicly virtues which it not only did not possess in private and business life, but actually held in contempt, it seemed revolutionary to admit cruelty, disregard of human values, and general amorality, because this at least destroyed the duplicity upon which the existing society seemed to rest.[66]

In the twilight of double moral standards, it seemed radical to flaunt extreme attitudes: "to wear publicly the mask of cruelty if everybody . . . pretended to be gentle." Arendt cited the case of Celine's *Bagatelles pour un Massacre* in which he proposed the massacre of all Jews, and the welcome which André Gide gave to it, "not of course because he wanted to kill the Jews . . . but because he rejoiced in the blunt admission of such a desire and in the fascinating contradiction between Celine's bluntness and the hypocritical politeness which surrounded the Jewish question in all respectable quarters."[67] Such spiritless radicalism exposed the double standards endemic in the separation of *citoyen* and *bourgeois* only to attack the very separation of public and private life in the name of the "wholeness of man." It revealed the false trust on which representative institutions were based, only to promote a philosophy of universal distrust. It turned the untruths of the bourgeois system of rule into a repudiation of the very distinction between truth and falsehood. Its contempt for facts preceded the determinate lies of totalitarian movements. Its contempt for political parties was channeled into a doctrine of "movements" that suppressed all forms of representation except the totalitarian movement itself. The devaluation of the idea of humanity impelled many thinking beings into totalitarian movements, even if they later discovered that these movements were basically anti-intellectual and either devoured or expelled their intellectuals.

The desire for blunt admission and the blunt admission of desire were often welcome to a bourgeoisie tired of managing the tension between words and deeds and ready to take off their masks and reveal a more naked brutality. Drawing on Marx as well as Nietzsche, Arendt argued that it was under imperialism, when the political rule of the bourgeoisie was finally consolidated, that power was freed from all restraint and expansion for expansion's sake became the credo of the age: "Expansion as a permanent and supreme aim of politics is the central political idea of imperialism . . . it is an entirely new concept in the long history of political thought and action . . . this concept is not really political at all, but has its origin in the realm of business speculation."[68]

The bourgeois principle of power came to mirror that of economics: unlimited accumulation of power accompanying unlimited accumulation of capital. What was new was not, of course, violence as such, but the fact that violence now became the aim of the body politic and would not rest until there was "nothing left to violate."[69] In the age of imperialism the "will to power" was increasingly emancipated from moral constraints and the ground laid for a power which "left to itself can achieve nothing but more power." Nihilism in this sense became the spirit of the age. If the practical nihilism of bourgeois society came up against political limitations— imposed by the proletariat and the nation-state at home and by the growth of national consciousness among conquered peoples abroad—the idea of a common humanity was further imperiled to the extent that proletariats, nation-states, and national movements were themselves invested with the standards of violence and racism which they most opposed. It is in this context that the attempt to destroy the idea of humanity begins to become understandable as a political/philosophical end.

THE PERSISTENCE AND RESISTANCE OF THE IDEA OF HUMANITY

If totalitarianism shows that traditional moral values are no longer sufficient to prevent evil, not least because society reduces morals to the relativity of this or that normative order and can change them at the drop of a hat, we may want to believe that there is something about the human condition—some capacity for "beginning," some individual particularity, some voice of conscience, some sense of judgment—that cannot be transformed according to plan: some relation that resists all reworking. The text of *Origins* is punctuated by Arendt's attempts to find this "something" that resists all transformation. In a world where lives are superfluous and the notion "I want you not to be" prevails, she looked primarily among the victims, pariah peoples, stateless refugees to find those who affirm what she called that "grace of love which says with Augustine . . . 'I want you to be' without being able to give any particular reason for such supreme and unsurpassable affirmation."[70] In a world which suppresses uniqueness and portrays difference as alien, she looked to those who recognize "the fact of difference as such and the disturbing miracle contained in the fact that each of us is made as he is—single, unique, unchangeable."[71] In a world of the camps, where all spontaneity is denied, she looked to the capacity of human beings for creative action: "'That a beginning be made, man was created,' said Augustine."[72] In a world in which friendship was subordinated to party loyalty and the duty to denounce disloyalty, she looked to a conception of friendship which is not only personal but makes its own political demands.[73] In a world where politics was equated with total domination, she looked to a conception of politics whose raison d'être is total freedom.

Arendt does not idealize the pariah as the cradle of a new universal class. When civilization forces millions of people into the "conditions of savages," it may equally well produce new barbarians.[74] People who have lost the rights and protection that nationality once gave them may resort all the more desperately to nationalism; communal relationships built in the hope of preserving some "minimum of humanity in a world grown inhuman" may generate a "worldlessness" vulnerable to its own forms of barbarism.[75] The capacity to judge what is right and wrong and act according to conscience are not the exclusive property of the oppressed minorities—witness the case of the German sergeant, Anton Schmidt, executed for helping Jews—and what makes this planet "a place fit for human habitation," as Arendt saw it, is simply that there are always *some* people who will not comply with power even under conditions of terror.[76] Richard Bernstein points out that Arendt finds no consolation in the claim that there is "something deep down in human beings that will resist the totalitarian impulse to prove that 'everything is possible.'"[77] Indeed, the fear that haunts her work is that the organized attempt to "eradicate the concept of the human being" might succeed. But her work also expresses a sense of hope which derives from the fact that the idea of humanity stood up to the supreme example of destructive will.

PART THREE

Postmetaphysical Approaches for a Theory of Evil

9

Toward a Sociology of Evil

Getting beyond Modernist Common Sense about the Alternative to "the Good"

Jeffrey C. Alexander

> *Evil . . . has a sovereign value for us. But this concept does not exclude morality: on the contrary, it demands a "hypermorality." ". . . A rigorous morality results from complicity in the knowledge of Evil, which is the basis of intense communication.*
> GEORGES BATAILLE, "LITERATURE AND EVIL"

The social sciences have not given evil its due. Social evil has not been sufficiently respected; it has been deprived of the intellectual attention it deserves. Evil is a powerful and sui generis social force. It must be studied in a direct and systematic way.[1]

MODERNIST COMMON SENSE

This is not to suggest that the deficiencies of our societies—our "social problems," in the jargon of sociology—have not been of great concern to social scientists. Nothing could be further from the truth.[2] From its beginning, sociology in particular has been motivated by a reforming zeal for uplift and purification. Its practitioners, great and small, have conscientiously directed their studies to what they have taken to be the sources of social evil: oppression, domination, inequality, racism, sexism, xenophobia, and corruption.

What these studies have not demonstrated is theoretical reflexivity about what might be called the existence of evil as such,[3] for social scientists have conducted their studies in the framework of common sense. Within this framework, what is evil and what is good "go without saying." The orientation to good and evil is informed by an implicit assumption of objective transparency, of "obviousness." Rather than problematizing the categorical distinctions themselves, the existence of the good and the evil is assumed to be natural, and social scientific effort is devoted not to explaining how the categories came to be established, but rather to explaining how particular manifestations of these categories come into being. Thus, earlier social scientists asked: How is the "criminal mind" or the "sociopath" formed? What makes underdeveloped societies primitive? Later studies asked: How is crime created by poverty, homophobia by prejudice or lack of education, political extremism by endemic racism? How does globalization distort local economic development? In each of these cases, the dependent variable is taken as an obvious representation of some form of social evil. The point has been to find the independent variable that explains it, not to question how it is that such a highly evaluative, highly negative dependent variable ever came into being.

The implication of the common sense approach to evil is that when and if these social causes and effects are altered, social problems will be banished from the world and good will reign.[4] But what if evil can never be eliminated from the social world, no matter how well motivated or effective the social reform? What if the point of sociology and, indeed, the other ameliorating social sciences is not to do away with evil but actually to establish the fundamental reality of its existence?[5]

This is not to suggest moral relativism or political resignation, but rather the necessity to make a fundamental break with the framework of modernist common sense.

THE CULTURAL TURN AND THE PROBLEM OF EVIL

To break from the path of common sense, we must follow the cultural turn more faithfully and persistently than naturalistically minded social scientists are usually inclined. Perhaps good and evil should be seen, in the first instance, as products of cultural understanding, not as the results of social arrangements in and of themselves? Perhaps evil is an effect, an inevitable and necessary result, of the act of social interpretation, of the categorical system human beings employ to make sense of the societies in which they live?

It seems likely, in fact, that the objects of sociological investigations of evil are relative and historically various. There is less a naturalistic, objectively given conflict between good and evil—between "positive" and "healthy" social forms, such as law, equality, or religion, and "negative" or "sick" forms, such as criminality, domination, or alienation—than a culturally constructed division that has taken the widest possible variety of organizational, material forms. From this perspective, reformist social analysis is more, and less, than either a scientific effort to sketch cause or a hermeneutical effort to understand meaning. It is, in addition, a morally inspired symbolic effort to establish the ontological reality of evil and to organize appropriate indignation in response to it.

These observations underscore the need for a cultural rather than simply an organizational, institutional, or interactional social science. Functional patterning is one thing, the symbolic construction of the meaning of this patterning, and of actors' orientations to it, quite another. At the beginning of the twenty-first century, after Wittgenstein, Saussure, and Geertz, it seems possible finally to entertain this proposition in a serious way. Yet, it has been and still remains an idea that has been difficult for social scientists to accept. It has seemed, for many, to undermine the point of a social science, and its very suggestion has aroused controversy. Lévi-Strauss was forced to make a radical break with the entire history of social anthropology when he insisted that kinship was a linguistic structure, not just a set of institutionally determined social roles: "Exist[ing] only in human consciousness[,] it is an arbitrary system of representations, not the spontaneous development of a real situation."[6] In much the same way and at about the same time, Parsons seemed to be denying all things sociological when he proclaimed the fundamental analytical distinction between cultural and social systems.[7] Yet, in making these controversial claims, Lévi-Strauss and Parsons were drawing on arguments that were already fifty years old, on semiotics and hermeneutics, respectively.[8] And it would take another fifty years before their disciplinary arguments would be taken seriously enough for culture to begin to be given its rightful place.

In the course of the last two decades, there has emerged a new recognition of the independent structuring power of culture. Yet it turns out that this new disciplinary self-consciousness has not been any more successful in addressing evil than its reductionist predecessor. In thinking about culture—values and norms, codes and narratives, rituals and symbols—"negativity" has been set off to one side and treated as a residual category. While it has not been treated naturalistically, it has been presented merely as a deviation from cultural constructions of the good. Thus, in social scientific formulations of culture, a society's "values" are studied primarily as orientations to the good, as efforts to embody ideals.[9] Social notions of evil, badness, and negativity are explored only as patterned departures from normatively regulated conduct. If only this were the case! It seems to me that this cultural displacement of evil involves more moralizing wish-fulfillment than empirical realism. Not only does it detract from our general understanding of evil, but it makes the relation of evil to modernity much more difficult to comprehend. Thinking of evil as a residual category camouflages the destruction and cruelty that has accompanied enlightened efforts to institutionalize the good and the right. The definition of social evil and the systematic effort to combat it have everywhere accompanied the modern pursuit of reason and moral right. That is the central and most legitimate meaning of Michel Foucault's lifework, despite its simplifications, one-sidedness, and undermining relativism. It is the salvageable, saving remnant of the postmodern critique of modernity.

Culture cannot be understood only as value and norm, which can be defined as conceptual glosses on social efforts to symbolize, narrate, code, and ritualize the good. Culturalizing evil is, in sociological terms, every bit as important as such efforts to define and institutionalize the good. In semiotic terms, evil is the necessary cognitive contrast for "good."[10] In moral terms, exploring heinous evil is the only way to understand and experience the pure and the upright.[11] In terms of narrative dynamics, only by creating antiheroes can we implot the dramatic tension between protagonist and antagonist that is transformed by *Bildung* or resolved by catharsis.[12] In ritual terms, it is only the crystallization of evil, with all its stigmatizing and polluting potential, that makes rites of purification culturally necessary and sociologically possible.[13] Religiously, the sacred is incomprehensible without the profane, the promise of salvation meaningless without the threat of damnation.[14] What I am suggesting here, in other words, is that for every value there is an equal and opposite antivalue, for every norm, an antinorm. For every effort to institutionalize comforting and inspiring images of the socially good and right, there is an interlinked and equally determined effort to construct social evil in a horrendous, frightening, and equally realistic way. Drawing Durkheim back to Nietzsche, and writing under the impact of the trauma of early twentieth-century modernity, Bataille articulated this point in a typically pungent and literary way.

> Evil seems to be understandable, but only to the extent to which Good is the key to it. If the luminous intensity of Good did not give the night of Evil its blackness, Evil would lose its appeal. This is a diffcult point to understand. Something flinches in him who faces up to it. And yet we know that the strongest effects on the sense are caused by contrasts. . . . Without misfortune, bound to it as shade is to light, indifferences would correspond to happiness. Novels describe suffering, hardly ever satisfaction. The virtue of happiness is ultimately its rarity. Were it easily accessible it would be despised and associated with boredom. . . . Would truth be what it is if it did not assert itself generously against falsehood?[15]

Actors, institutions, and societies systematically crystallize and elaborate evil. They do so, ironically, in pursuit of the good. To these paradoxical and immensely depressing facts attention must be paid.

THE INTELLECTUAL ROOTS OF THE DISPLACEMENT OF EVIL

To appreciate the pervasiveness of this truncated conception of culture, it is important to recognize that, while deeply affecting contemporary social science, it is rooted in earlier forms of secular and religious thought.[16] From the Greeks onward, moral philosophy has been oriented to justifying and sustaining the good and to elaborating the requirements of the just society.

Plato associated his ideal forms with goodness. To be able to see these forms, he believed, was to be able to act in accordance with morality. In dramatizing Socrates' teachings in the *Republic,* Plato made use of the figure of Thrasymachus to articulate the evil forces that threatened ethical life. Rather than suggesting that Thrasymachus embodied bad values, Plato presented Thrasymachus as denying the existence of values as such: "In all states alike, 'right' has the same meaning, namely what is for the interest of the party established in power, and that is the strongest." Thrasymachus is an egoist who calculates every action with an eye, not to values, but to the interests of his own person. Plato makes a homology between self/collectivity, interest/value, and evil/good. In doing so, he establishes the following analogical relationship:

Self:collectivity::interest:value::evil:good
Self is to collectivity, as interest is to value, as evil is to good.

The commitment to values is the same as the commitment to collective beliefs; beliefs and values are the path to the good. Evil should be understood not as the product of bad or negatively oriented values, but as the failure to connect to collective values. Evil comes from being self-interested.

In elaborating what came to be called the republican tradition in political theory, Aristotle followed this syllogism, equating a society organized around values with an ethical order: "the best way of life, for individuals severally, as well as for states collectively, is the life of goodness duly equipped with such a store of requisites as makes it possible to share in the activities of goodness."[17] Republics contained virtuous citizens, who were defined as actors capable of orienting to values outside of themselves. As individuals become oriented to the self rather than the collectivity, republics are endangered; desensitized to values, citizens become hedonistic and materialistic. According to this stark and binary contrast between morality and egoism, value commitments *in themselves* contribute to the good; evil occurs, not because there are commitments to bad values, but because of a failure to orient to values per se. While it is well known that Hegel continued the Aristotelian contrast between what he called the system of needs and the world of ethical regulation, it is less widely appreciated that pragmatism endorsed the same dichotomy in its own way. For Dewey, to value is to value the good. Interpersonal communication is bound to produce altruistic normative orientation. Crass materialism and selfishness occur when social structures prevent communication.[18]

This philosophical equation of values with goodness and the lack of values with evil informs contemporary communitarianism, which might be described as a marriage between republican and pragmatic thought. Identifying contemporary social problems with egoism and valuelessness, communitarians ignore the possibility that communal values are defined by making pejorative contrasts with other values, with others' values, and, in fact, often with the values of "the other."[19] Empirically, I want to suggest that the issue is not values versus interests or having values as compared with not having them. There are always "good" values and "bad." In sociological terms, good values can be crystallized only in relation to values that are feared or considered repugnant. This is not to recommend that values should be relativized in a moral sense, to suggest that they can or should be "transvalued" or inverted in Nietzschean terms. It is, rather, to insist that social thinkers recognize how the social construction of evil has been, and remains, empirically and symbolically necessary for the social construction of good.[20]

In the Enlightenment tradition, most forcefully articulated by Kant, concern about the parochial (we would today say communitarian) dangers of an Aristotelian "ethics" led to a more abstract and universalistic model of a "moral" as compared to a good society.[21] Nonetheless, one finds in this Kantian tradition the same problem of equating value commitments in themselves with positivity in the normative sense.[22] To be moral is to move from selfishness to the categorical imperative, from self-reference to a collective orientation resting on the ability to put yourself in the place of another. What has changed in Kantianism is, not the binary of value-versus-no-value, but the contents of the collective alternative; it has shifted from the ethical to the moral, from the particular and local to the universal and transcendent. The range of value-culture has been expanded and generalized because more substantive and more metaphysical versions came to be seen as particularist, antimodern, and antidemocratic.

If communitarianism is the contemporary representation of the republican and pragmatic traditions, Habermas's "theory of communicative action" represents—for social theory at least—the most influential contemporary articulation of this Kantian approach. Underlying much of Habermas's empirical theory one can find a philosophical anthropology that reproduces the simplistic splitting of good and evil. Instrumental, materialistic, and exploitative "labor," for example, is contrasted with altruistic, cooperative, ideal-oriented "communication." These anthropological dichotomies in the early writings are linked in Habermas's later work with the sociological contrast between system and lifeworld, the former producing instrumental efficiency, domination, and materialism, the latter producing ideals and, therefore, making possible equality, community, and morality. According to Habermas's developmental theory, the capacity for communication and moral self-regulation is enhanced with modernity, which produces such distinctive values as autonomy, solidarity, rationality, and criticism. The possibility of connecting to such values, indeed of maintaining value commitments per se, is impeded by the systems-rationality of modern economic and political life, the materialism of which "colonizes" and undermines the culture-creating, solidarizing possibilities of the lifeworld.[23] In arguing that it is recognition, not communication, that creates value commitments and mutual respect, Axel Honneth similarly ignores the possibility that pleasurable and cooperative interaction can be promoted by immoral and particularistic values that are destructive of ethical communities.[24]

This deracinated approach to culture-as-the-good can also be linked, in my view, to the Western religious tradition of Judaism and Christianity. In order to achieve salvation, the believer must overcome the temptations of the earthly, the material, and the practical in order to establish transcendental relations with an otherworldly source of goodness. According to this dualistic consciousness, evil is presented as an alternative to the transcendental commitments that establish value. As Augustine put it, "evil is the absence of the good."[25] The "original sin" that has marked humanity since the Fall was stimulated by the earthly appetites, by lust rather than idealism and value commitment. This sin can be redeemed only via a religious consciousness that connects human beings to higher values, either those of an ethical, law-governed community (Judaism) or the moral universalism of a church (Christianity). In this religious universe, in other words, evil is connected to nonculture, to passions and figures associated with the earth in contrast with the heavens. According to recent historical discussions, in fact, devil symbolism first emerged as a kind of iconographic residual category.[26] Radical Jewish sects created it as a deus ex machina to explain the downward spiral of Jewish society, allowing these negative developments to be attributed to forces outside the "authentic" Jewish cultural tradition. This nascent iconography of evil was energetically elaborated by early Christian sects who were similarly attracted to the possibility of attributing evil to forces outside their own cultural system. The Christian devil was a means of separating the "good religion" of Jesus from the evil (primarily Jewish) forces from which it had emerged.

THE DISPLACEMENT OF EVIL IN CONTEMPORARY SOCIAL SCIENCE

Given these philosophical and religious roots,[27] it is hardly surprising that, as I have indicated above, contemporary social science has conceived culture as composed of values that establish highly esteemed general commitments and norms as establishing specific moral obligations to pursue the good. This is as true for social scientists, such as Bellah and Lasch, who engage in cultural criticism, as it is in more mainstream work.[28] While issuing withering attacks on contemporary values as degenerate, narcissistic, and violent, such culture critics conceive these values as misguided formulations of the good—stupid, offensive, and pitiable but at the same time fundamentally revealing of how "the desirable" is formulated in the most debased modern societies.

On the basis of the identification of values with the good, mainstream social scientists and culture critics alike assume that a shared commitment to values is positive and beneficial to society. Functionalism is the most striking example of this tendency, and Talcott Parsons its classic representative. According to Parsons, value internalization leads not only to social equilibrium but to mutual respect, solidarity, and cooperation. If common values are not internalized, then the social system is not regulated by value, and social conflict, coercion, and even violence are the probable results.[29] In this sociological version of republicanism, Parsons follows the early- and middle-period Durkheim, who believed that shared values are essential to solidarity and social health. The lack of attachment to values marks the condition Durkheim defined as egoism, and it is by this standard that he defined social pathology. Durkheim emphasized education because he regarded it as the central means for attaching individuals to values. Since the simple attachment to culture is valued so highly, it is clear that neither Durkheim nor Parsons seriously considered the theoretical or empirical possibility that evil might be valued as energetically as the good.[30]

Because sociological folklore has so often pitted the functionalist "equilibrium" theory against the more critical "conflict" theory, it is well to ask whether, in fact, Parsonian functionalism is the only guilty party here. Have the theoretical alternatives to functionalism provided a truly different approach to the problem of evil? Let us consider, as a case in point, how Marx conceptualized the depravity of capitalism. Rather than pointing to the social effects of bad values, Marx argued that capitalism destroyed their very possibility. As he put it so eloquently in *The Communist Manifesto:* "All that is holy is profaned, all that is solid melts into air." The structural pressures of capitalism create alienation and egoism; they necessitate an instrumental and strategic action orientation that suppresses values and destroys ideals. Because materialism destroys normativity, there is no possibility for shared understanding, solidarity, or community. Only after socialism removes the devasting forces of capitalist competition and greed does value commitment become possible and solidarity flourish.

The notion that it is not evil values but the absence of values that creates a bad society continues to inform the neo-Marxism of the early Frankfurt school. For Horkheimer and Adorno, late capitalism eliminates authentic values.[31] Culture exists only as an industry; it is a completely contingent set of expressive symbols, subject to continuous manipulation according to materialistic exigencies. While Habermas's later theory of discourse ethics avoids this kind of mechanism and reduction, it continues to be organized around the pragmatic notion that communicatively generated value commitment leads to mutual understanding, toleration, and solidarity.

The apotheosis of this "critical" approach to evil-as-the-absence-of-value—evil as the displacement of culture by power—is Zygmunt Bauman's explanation of the Holocaust in his highly praised book, *Modernity and the Holocaust*.[32] Bauman writes that Nazi genocide has largely been ignored by social theory, suggesting that it has troubling implications for any positive evaluation of modernity. Bauman is right about this, but for the wrong reasons. He attributes the social evil of the Holocaust not to motivated cultural action but to the efficiency of the Nazis' bureaucratic killing machine. There is no indication in his explanation that this genocide was also caused by valuations of evil, by general representations of the polluted other that were culturally fundamental to Germany and its folkish, romantic traditions, and more specifically by representations of the Jewish other that were endemic not just to German but to Christian society. Yet only if this possibility is seriously entertained can the Holocaust be seen as an intended action, as something that was desired rather than merely imposed, as an event that did indeed grow out of systematic tendencies in the culture of modernity. It seems important, both morally and empirically, to emphasize, along with Goldhagen, that the Nazis and their German supporters wanted to kill Jews.[33] They worked hard to establish Judaism as a symbol of evil and in turn they annihilated Jews to purge themselves of this evil. The act of murdering millions of Jewish and non-Jewish people during the Holocaust must be seen as something valued, as something desired. It was an evil event motivated not by the absence of values—an absence created by the destructive colonization of lifeworld by economic and bureaucratic systems—but by the presence of heinous values. These polluted cultural representations were as integral as the positive idealizations upon which it pretended exclusively to rest.

GIVING EVIL ITS DUE: TOWARD A NEW (POSTMODERN)
CULTURAL AND SOCIOLOGICAL MODEL

We need to elaborate a model of social good and evil that is more complex, more sober, and more realistic than the naturalistic or idealistic models. Symbolically, evil is not a residual category, even if those who are categorized by it are marginalized socially. From the merely distasteful and sickening to the truly heinous, evil is deeply implicated in the symbolic formulation and institutional maintenance of the good.[34] Because of this, the institutional and cultural vitality of evil must be continually sustained. The line dividing the sacred from profane must be drawn and redrawn time and time again; this demarcation must retain its vitality, or all is lost.[35] Evil is not only symbolized cognitively, but experienced in a vivid and emotional way. Through such phenomena as scandals, moral panics, public punishments, and wars, societies provide occasions to reexperience and recrystallize the enemies of the good.[36] Wrenching experiences of horror, revulsion, and fear create opportunities for purification that keep what Plato called "the memory of justice" alive. Only through such direct experiences—provided via interaction or symbolic communication—do members of society come to know evil and to fear it. The emotional-cum-moral catharsis that Aristotle described as the basis for tragic experience and knowledge is also at the core of such experiences of knowing and fearing evil.[37] Such knowledge and fear triggers denunciation of evil in others and confession about evil intentions in oneself, and rituals of punishment and purification in collectivities. In turn, these renew the sacred, the free, the moral, and the good.

Evil is produced, in other words, not simply to maintain domination and power, as Foucault and Marx would argue, but in order to maintain the possibility of making positive valuations. Evil must be coded, narrated, and embodied in every social sphere—in the intimate sphere of the family, in the world of science, in religion, in the economy, in government, in primary communities. In each sphere, and in every national society considered as a totality, there are deeply elaborated narratives about how evil develops and where it is likely to appear, about epochal struggles that have taken place between evil and the good, and about how good can triumph over evil once again.

This perspective has profound implications for the way we look at both cultural and institutional processes in contemporary societies. I will discuss the former in terms of "binary representations," drawing in some detail from my ongoing research on the discourse of civil society. I will discuss the latter in terms of "punishments." While space limitations preclude a detailed discussion of such institutional processes, their central elements will be laid out.[38]

Binary Representations: The Discourse of Civil Society

In the last two decades, the rush of real historical events has brought the concept "civil society" back into social theory and empirical social science.[39] Civil society refers to the social and cultural bases for political democracy, to the capacity for autonomy and self-regulation that allows independence from coercive political authority. Beyond this broad understanding, of course, civil society is a highly contested concept. It is used both to justify capitalist market relations and to legitimate social movements that oppose and regulate them; some think it refers to everything outside the state, others that it demarcates only the differentiated and univeralistic sphere of the "public" life. Despite their variation, these approaches agree that civil society indicates a democratic manner of demarcating the good, the moral, the right. When the values of civil society are discussed, and they often are, they are conceived as referring to qualities and relationships that allow self-regulation and equality. At the basis of this universalistic community, it is argued, there exists an idealization of the "free and autonomous" individual that sustains strongly normative commitments to rationality, honesty, responsibility, openness, cooperation, inclusion, and transparency. Action according to these values, it is argued, allows individuals and groups to become members of civil society, to be included in its privileges and collective obligations. Whether in the hands of Habermas or Putnam, Cohen or Keane, Fraser or Arato, civil society is conceptualized in this highly idealistic way.

In my own studies of civil society, by contrast, I have suggested that insofar as it can be understood as a sign system its signifiers identify not only the qualities that allow individuals to become members of civil society but the qualities that legitimate their exclusion. The cultural core of civil society is composed not only of codes but of countercodes, antitheses that create meaningful representations for "universalism" and "particularism." On the one side, there is an expansive code that identifies the actors and structures of civil society in terms that promote wider inclusion and increasing respect for individual rights; on the other, there is a restrictive code that identifies actors and structures in terms that focus on ascriptively grounded group identities and promote the exclusion that follows therefrom. The discourse of civil society is constituted by a continuous struggle between these binary codes and between the actors who invoke them, each of whom seeks hegemony over the political field by gaining definitional control over unfolding events.

The binary character of "civil culture" is demonstrated not simply by the fact that code and countercode are present in every society that aspires to be a civil one, but also by the striking circumstance that each code can be defined only in terms of the alternate perspective the other provides. The discourse of civil society can be seen, in a certain sense, as revolving around secular salvation. To know how to be part of civil society is to know how one can be "socially saved." Members of a society can understand the requirements of social salvation, however, only if they know the criteria for social damnation, for exclusion on the basis of lack of deserts. In fact, just as monotheistic religion divides the world into the saved and the damned, civil discourse divides the world into those who deserve inclusion and those who do not. Members of national communities firmly believe that "the world," and this notably includes their own nation, is filled with people who either do not deserve freedom and communal support or are not capable of sustaining them. Members of national communities do not want to "save" such persons. They do not wish to include them, protect them, or offer them rights, because they conceive them as being unworthy, as in some sense "uncivilized."

When citizens make judgments about who should be included in civil society and who should not, about who is a friend and who is an enemy, they draw upon a highly generalized culture structure, a symbolic code that has been in place since the emergence of democratic communities. The basic elements of this structure are sets of homologies, which create likenesses between various terms of social description and prescription, and antipathies, which establish antagonisms between these terms and other sets of symbols. Those who consider themselves worthy members of a national community—as most people do, of course—define themselves in terms of the positive side of this symbolic set; they define those who are not deemed worthy in terms that are established by the negative side. In this sense it is fair to say that members of the community "believe in" both the positive and negative sides, that they employ both as viable normative evaluations of political communities. The members of every democratic society consider both the positive and the negative symbolic sets realistic descriptions of individual and social life.

The discourse of civil society rests upon relatively unreflexive assumptions about human nature, which allow the motives of political actors to be clearly conceptualized along with the kind of society they are capable of sustaining. Code and countercode posit human nature in diametrically opposed ways. Because democracy allows self-motivated action, the people who compose it must be described as being capable of activism and autonomy rather than as being passive and dependent. They must be seen as rational and reasonable rather than irrational and hysterical; calm rather than excited; controlled rather than passionate; sane and realistic, not mad or given to fantasy. Democratic discourse, then, posits the following qualities as axiomatic: activism, autonomy, rationality, reasonableness, calm, control, realism, and sanity. The nature of the countercode, the discourse that justifies the restriction of civil society, is already clearly implied. If actors are passive and dependent, irrational and hysterical, excitable, passionate, unrealistic, or mad, they cannot be allowed the freedom that democracy allows. On the contrary, it is believed these persons deserve to be repressed, not only for the sake of civil society but for their own sakes as well.

The Discursive Structure of Social Motives

Democratic Code	Counterdemocratic Code
activism	passivity
autonomy	dependence
rationality	irrationality
reasonableness	hysteria
calm	excitability
self-control	passion
realism	unreality
sanity	madness

Upon the basis of such contradictory codes about human motives, distinctive representations of social relationships can be built. Democratically motivated persons will be capable of forming open social relationships rather than secretive ones; they will be trusting rather than suspicious, straightforward rather than calculating, truthful rather than deceitful; their decisions will be based on open deliberation rather than conspiracy and their attitude toward authority will be critical rather than deferential; in their behavior toward other community members they will be bound by conscience and honor rather than by greed and self-interest, and they will treat their fellows as friends rather than enemies.

If actors are conceived of as counterdemocratic, on the other hand, the social relationships they form will be represented by the second side of these fateful dichotomies. Rather than open and trusting relationships, they will be said to form secret societies that are premised on their suspicion of other human beings. To the authority within these secret societies they will be deferential, but to those outside their tiny group they will behave in a greedy and self-interested way. They will be conspiratorial, deceitful toward others, and calculating in their behavior, conceiving of those outside their group as enemies. If the positive side of this second discourse set describes the symbolic qualities necessary to sustain civil society, the negative side describes a solidary structure in which mutual respect and expansive social integration has broken down.

The Discursive Structure of Social Relationships

Democratic Code	Counterdemocratic Code
open	secret
trusting	suspicious
critical	deferential
honorable	self-interested
conscience	greed
truthful	deceitful
straightforward	calculating
deliberative	conspiratorial
friend	enemy

Given the discursive structure of motives and civic relationships, it should not be surprising that this set of of homologies and antipathies extends to the social understanding of political and legal institutions themselves. If members of a national community are depicted as irrational in motive and distrusting in social relationships, they will naturally be represented as creating institutions that are arbitrary rather than regulated by rules; that emphasize brute power rather than law and hierarchy rather than equality; that are exclusive rather than inclusive and promote personal loyalty over impersonal and contractual obligation; that are regulated by personalities rather than by office obligations and that are organized by faction rather than by groups that are responsive to the needs of the community as a whole.

The Discursive Structure of Institutions

Democratic Code	Counterdemocratic Code
rule regulated	arbitrary
law	power
equality	hierarchy
inclusive	exclusive
impersonal	personal
contractual	ascriptive loyalty
social groups	factions
office	personality

When they are presented in their simple binary forms, these cultural codes appear merely schematic. In fact, however, they reveal the skeletal structures upon which social communities build the familiar stories that guide their everyday taken-for-granted political life. The positive side of these structured sets provides the elements for the comforting and inspiring story of a democratic, free, and spontaneously integrated social order, a civil society in an ideal sense. The structure and narrative of political virtue form the "discourse of liberty." The discourse is embodied in the great and the little stories that democratic nations tell about themselves, for example, the American story about George Washington and the cherry tree highlights honesty and virtue; English accounts of the "Battle of Britain" reveal the courage, self-sufficiency, and spontaneous cooperative of the British in contrast to the villainous forces of Hitlerian Germany; no matter how apocryphal, French legends about the honorable, trusting, and independent patriots who resisted the Nazi occupation underlay the construction of the Fourth Republic after World War II.

The elements on the negative side of these symbolic sets are also tightly intertwined. They provide the categories for the plethora of stories that permeate democratic understanding of the negative and repugnant sides of community life. Taken together, these form the "discourse of repression." If people are not represented as having the capacity for reason, if they cannot rationally process information and cannot tell truth from falseness, then they will be loyal to leaders for purely personal reasons and in turn be easily manipulated by those leaders. Similarly, because such persons are ruled by calculation rather than by conscience, they are without the honor that is critical in democratic affairs. Constructing people in terms of such anticivil qualities makes it necessary that they be denied access to rights and the protection of law. Indeed, because they have the capacity for neither voluntary nor responsible behavior, these marginal members of the community—those who are unfortunate enough to be constructed under the counterdemocratic code—must ultimately be repressed. They cannot be regulated by law, nor will they accept the discipline of office. Their loyalties can be only familial and particularistic. The institutional and legal boundaries of civil society, it is widely believed, can provide no bulwark against their lust for personal power.

The positive side of this discursive formation is viewed by the members of democratic communities as a source not only of purity but of purification. The discourse of liberty is taken to sum up "the best" in a civil community, and its tenets are considered sacred. The objects that the discourse creates seem to possess an awesome power that places them at the "center" of society, a location—sometimes geographical, often stratificational, always symbolic—that compels their defense at almost any cost. The negative side of this symbolic formation is viewed as profane. Representing the "worst" in the national community, it embodies evil. The objects it identifies threaten the core community from somewhere outside of it. From this marginal position, they present a powerful source of pollution. To be close to these polluted objects is dangerous. Not only can one's reputation be sullied and one's status endangered, but one's security as well. To have one's self or movement be identified in terms of these objects causes anguish, disgust, and alarm. This code is taken to be a threat to the center of civil society itself.

For contemporary Americans, the categories of the pure and polluted discourses seem natural and fully historical. Democratic law and procedures are seen as having been won by the founding fathers and guaranteed by documents like the Bill of Rights and Constitution. The qualities of the repressive code are embodied, with equal versimilitude, in the dark visions of tyranny and lawlessness, whether embodied by eighteenth-century British monarchs or twentieth-century Soviet communists. Pulp fiction and highbrow drama seek to counterpose these dangers with compelling images of the good. When works of the imagination seem to represent the discursive formation in a paradigmatic way, they become contemporary classics. For the generation that matured during World War II, for example, George Orwell's *1984* made the discourse of repression emblematic of the struggles of their time.

Of course, some events are so gross or so sublime that they generate almost immediate consensus about how the symbolic sets should be applied. For most members of a national community, great national wars clearly demarcate the good and the bad. The nation's soldiers are the embodiments of the discourse of liberty; the foreign nations and soldiers who oppose them represent some potent combination of the counterdemocratic code. In the course of American history, this negative code has been extended to a vast and variegated group, to the British, native peoples, pirates, the South and the North, Africans, old European nations, fascists, Communists, Germans, and Japanese. Identification in terms of the discourse of repression is essential if vengeful combat is to be pursued. Once this polluting discourse is applied, it becomes impossible for good people to reason with those on the other side. If one's opponents are beyond reason, deceived by leaders who operate in secret, the only option is to read them out of the human race. When great wars are successful, they provide powerful narratives that dominate the nation's postwar life. Hitler and Nazism formed the backbone of a huge array of Western myths and stories, providing master metaphors for everything from profound discussions about the Final Solution to many of the good guy/bad guy plots of television dramas and situation comedies.

For most events, however, discursive identity is contested. Political fights are, in part, about how to distribute actors across the structure of discourse, for there is no determined relationship between any event or group and either side of the cultural scheme. Actors struggle to taint one another with the repressive brush and to wrap themselves in the rhetoric of liberty. In periods of tension and crisis, political struggle becomes a matter of how far and to whom the discourses of liberty and repression apply. The cause of victory and defeat, imprisonment and freedom, and sometimes even of life and death, is often discursive domination, which depends upon how popular narratives about good and evil are extended. Is it protesting students who are like Nazis, or the conservatives who are pursuing them? Are the members of the Communist Party or the members of the House Un-American Activities Committee to be understood as fascistic? When Watergate began, only the actual burglars were called conspirators and polluted by the discourse of repression. George McGovern and his fellow Democrats were unsuccessful in their efforts to apply this discourse to the White House, the executive staff, and the Republican Party, elements of civil society that succeeded in maintaining their identity in liberal terms. At a later point in the crisis, such a reassuring relationship to the culture structure no longer held. The general discursive structure, in other words, is used to legitimate friends and delegitimate opponents in the course of real historical time.

Punishment: Social Process and Institutions

If it is vital to understand the cultural dimension of society as organized around evil as much as around good, this by no means suggests that the problem of social evil can be understood simply in discursive terms. On the contrary, organizations, power, and face-to-face confrontations are critical in determining how and to whom binary representations of good and evil are applied. While these social processes and institutional forces do not invent the categories of evil and good—that they are not responsive purely to interest, power, and need has been one of my central points—they do have a strong influence upon how they are understood. Most importantly, however, they determine what the "real" social effects of evil will be in time and space.

The social processes and institutional forces that specify and apply representations about the reality of evil can be termed "punishment." In the *Division of Labor in Society* (1893), Durkheim first suggested that crime is "normal" and necessary because it is only punishment that allows society to separate normative behavior from that which is considered deviant. In our terms, we can suggest that punishment is the social medium through which the practices of actors, groups, and institutions are meaningfully and effectively related to the category of evil. It is through punishment that evil is naturalized. Punishment "essentializes" evil, making it appear to emerge from actual behaviors and identities, rather than being culturally and socially imposed upon them.[40]

Punishment takes both routine and more spontaneous forms. The bureaucratic iterations of evil are called "crimes." In organizational terms, the situational references of criminal acts are precisely defined by civil and criminal law, whose relevance to particular situations is firmly decided by courts and police. Polluting contact with civil law brings monetary sanctions; stigmatization by contact with criminal law brings incarceration, radical social isolation, and sometimes even death.

The nonroutine iterations of evil are less widely understood and appreciated. They refer to processes of "stigmatization" rather than to crimes.[41] What Cohen first identified as *moral panics* represent fluid, rapidly formed crystallizations of evil in relation to unexpected events, actors, and institutions. Historical witch trials and more contemporary anticommunist witch hunts, for example, are stimulated by the sudden experience of weakness in group boundaries. Panics over "crime waves," by contrast, develop in response to the chaotic and disorganizing entrance of new, formerly disreputable social actors into civil society.[42] Whatever their specific cause, and despite their evident irrationality, moral panics do have a clear effect, both in a cultural and a social sense. By focusing on new sources of evil, they draw an exaggerated line between social pollution and the good. This cultural clarification prepares the path for a purging organizational response, for trials of transgressors, for expulsion, and incarceration.

Scandals represent a less ephemeral but still nonroutine form of social punishment. Scandals are public degradations of individuals and groups for behavior that is considered polluting to their status or office. In order to maintain the separation between good and evil, the behavior of an individual or group is "clarified" by symbolizing it as a movement from purity to danger. The religious background of Western civil society makes such declension typically appear as a "fall from grace," as a personal sin, a lapse created by individual corruption and the loss of individual responsibility. In the discourse of civil society, the greatest "sin" is the inability to attain and maintain one's autonomy and independence.[43] In terms of the present discussion, scandal is created because civil society demands more or less continuous "revivifications" of social evil. These rituals of degradation range from the apparently trivial—the gossip sheets which, nonetheless, demand systematic sociological consideration—to the kinds of deeply serious, civil-religious events that create national convulsions. The Dreyfus affair that threatened to undermine the Third Republic in France and the Watergate affair that toppled the Nixon regime in the United States represented efforts to crystallize and punish social evil on this systematic level. Once again, scandals, like moral panics, have not only cultural but fundamental institutional effects, repercussions that range from the removal of specific persons from status or office to deep and systematic changes in organizational structure and regime.

There is nothing fixed or determined about scandals and moral panics. Lines of cultural demarcation are necessary but not sufficient to their creation. Whether or not this or that individual or group becomes punished is the outcome of struggles for cultural power, struggles that depend on shifting coalitions and the mobilization of resources of a material and not only ideal kind. This applies not only to the creation of panics and scandals but to their denouements. They are terminated by purification rituals reestablishing the sharp line between evil and good, a transition made possible by the act of punishmment.

Transgression and the Affirmation of Evil and Good

This essay has been an effort to establish the theoretical framework for a new field of investigation, one which might be called "the sociology of evil."[44] Considerations of time and space have limited this initial effort to the most elementary concerns. Not only have I been able to consider central issues only in a schematic way, but I have not been able even to take up areas of real theoretical and empirical import.

One critical area concerns the manner in which the "autonomy" of evil, culturally and institutionally, allows the experience and practice of evil to become, not simply frightening and repulsive, but also desirable. For the sociological creation of evil results not only in the avoidance of evil but also in the pursuit of it. Rather than a negative that directs people toward the good, in other words, social evil can be and often is sought as an end in itself. As Bataille observed, "evil is always the object of an ambiguous condemnation"; it is "not only the dream of the wicked" but "to some extent the dream of [the] Good."[45]

Attraction to the idea and experience of evil motivates the widespread practice that Bataille called transgression, and that Foucault, following Bataille, termed the "limit experience."[46]

> *Sacred* simultaneously has two contradictory meanings. . . . The taboo gives a negative definition of the sacred object and inspires us with awe. . . . Men are swayed by two simultaneous emotions: they are driven away by terror and drawn by an awed fascination. Taboo and transgression reflect these two contradictory urges. The taboo would forbid the transgression but the fascination compels it. . . . The sacred aspect of the taboo is what draws men towards it and transfigures the original interdiction.[47]

In particular situations, evil becomes positively evaluated, creating a kind of inverted liminality. Transgression takes place when actions, associations, and rhetoric—practices that would typically be defined and sanctioned as serious threats to the good—become objects of desire and sometimes even social legitimation. Bataille believed that transgression occurred mainly in the cultural imagination, that is, in literature, although he also wrote extensively about "eroticism" and was personally motivated by a desire to comprehend the dark social developments of the early and midcentury period—Nazism, war, and Stalinism.[48] Transgression, however, also takes a decidedly social-structural form. In criminal activity and popular culture, evil provides the basis of complex social institutions that provide highly sought after social roles, careers, and personal identities. Without evoking the term, Jack Katz certainly was investigating transgression in his profound phenomenological reconstruction of the "badass syndrome," as was Richard Strivers in his earlier essay on the apocalyptic dimension of 1960s rock and roll concerts. The latter embodied the long-standing "noir" strain of popular culture that has transmogrified into the "bad rapper" phenomenon of today.[49]

It seems that every social thinker and artist who sets out to explore the attractions of this dark side, whether in the moral imagination or in social action and structure, risks being tarred by self-proclaimed representatives of social morality with a polluting brush. This tendency is fuelled by the apparent fact that those who are personally attracted to transgressive practices are those who are most drawn to exploring them in art and social thought. The analysis set forth in this essay suggests, however, that those who are seriously interested in maintaining moral standards should refrain from this kind of knee-jerk response. It confuses causes with effects. Societies construct evil so that there can be punishment, for it is the construction of, and the response to, evil that defines and revivifies the good. One should not, then, confuse the aesthetic imagining of evil, the vicarious experiencing of evil, much less the intellectual exploration of evil with the actual practice of evil itself.

Modern and postmodern societies have always been beset by a socially righteous fundamentalism, both religious and secular. These moralists wish to purge the cultural imagination of references to eros and violence; they condemn frank discussions of transgressive desires and actions in schools and other public places; they seek to punish and sometimes even to incarcerate those who practice "victimless" crimes on the grounds that they violate the collective moral conscience. The irony is that, without the imagination and the social identification of evil, there would be no possibility for the attachment to the good that these moralists so vehemently uphold. Rather than undermining conventional morality, trangression underlines and vitalizes it. Bataille, whom James Miller pejoratively called the *philosophe maudit* of French intellectual life,[50] never ceased to insist upon this point. "Transgression has nothing to do with the primal liberty of animal life. It opens the door into what lies beyond the limits usually observed, but it maintains these limits just the same. Transgression is complementary to the profane [i.e., the mundane] world, exceeding its limits but not destroying it."[51]

Amnesty International, winner of the Nobel Peace Prize, has been one of the world's most effective nongovernmental democratic organizations, exposing and mobilizing opposition against torture and other heinous practices of authoritarian and even democratic governments. It is all the more relevant to note, therefore, that at the heart of the internal and external discourse of this prototypically "do-gooder" organization one finds an obsessive concern with defining, exploring, and graphically presenting evil, the success of which efforts allows members and outsiders vicariously to experience evil's physical and emotional effects.[52] In the Amnesty logo, good and evil are tensely intertwined. At the core is a candle, representing fervent attention, patience, and sacrality of Amnesty's commitment to life. Surrounding the candle is barbed wire, indicating concentration camps and torture. This binary structure is iterated throughout the persuasive documents that Amnesty distributes to the public and also in the talk of Amnesty activists themselves. They revolve around narratives that portray, often in graphic and gothic detail, the terrible things that are done to innocent people, and, in a tone of almost uncomprehending awe, the heroism of the prisoner to endure unspeakable suffering and remain in life and at the point of death a caring, dignified human being. Amnesty's attention to evil, to constructing the oppressor and graphically detailing its actions, in this way contributes to maintaining the the ideals of moral justice and sacralizing the human spirit, not only in thought but in practice.

It is in order to explain and illuminate such a paradox that a sociology of evil must be born.

10

The Evil That Men Do

A Meditation on Radical Evil from a Postmetaphysical Point of View

Alessandro Ferrara

After the linguistic turn, we live in times when the foundationalist notions of a rationality inherent in the human subject or in history have yielded to a more sober appreciation of the context-boundness, culture-boundness, time-boundness of our basic notions. Among the problems generated by this transformation is an increasing difficulty that we experience in conceiving of radical evil without resorting to "prepostmetaphysical" ways of thinking. Has the death of God as a publicly invocable figure—the fading away of Yahweh mentioned by Jaspers—led to the disappearance of a publicly invocable notion of evil with capital *E*, of the kind of notion that we would apply to events such as Auschwitz, the Gulag, ethnic cleansing, the Cambodian "killing fields," or the massacre of the Tutsi, as opposed to instances of "ordinary evil"? Can evil on such a scale be conceived at all within a postmetaphysical horizon? Or does it call for some transcendent, even religious, notion of an absolute which functions as a normative background against which evil would then be defined as transgression?

At first sight, two problems seem to stand in the way of reformulating some kind of notion of radical evil along thoroughly postmetaphysical or nonfoundationalist lines. First, most of us are pluralists when we think of the good. Few would envisage the possibility of conclusive arguments on the superiority of one conception of the good (say, *bios theoretikos,* or the life of contemplation) over another (say, *vita activa,* or the life of active involvement in public affairs). Yet, when it comes to radical evil, we feel very uneasy with the idea that what appears to us as an instance of radical evil—Auschwitz or the Gulag—may become more acceptable or less of an evil when considered from a different perspective. Are we contradicting ourselves? Can we reconcile these two seemingly contrasting intuitions?

Second, we intuitively perceive a gap between "ordinary" evil and "radical" evil. Ordinary evil can enter a relation of "definition by opposition" with the good. Lying is the negative counterpart of "telling the truth," being loyal is the good to which being disloyal corresponds as an evil thing. Evil on the scale of Auschwitz, instead, cannot be brought into any such relation: there is no good that can be defined as "not doing what was done at Auschwitz." Simply, we feel that evil of such magnitude ought to be eradicated from the world—this sort of evil is too much even to function as "the opposite of the good." The difficulty is that radical evil cannot be brought into a meaningful relation with the shared basis of human action.

Despite these two problematic aspects, I would like to defend the idea that a postmetaphysical notion of radical evil can be conceived of, and in the rest of this paper I will try to highlight some thoughts that could work as building blocks for such a conception of radical evil.

I. RADICAL EVIL AND THE HUMAN WILL

I will start from the assumption that radical evil—provisionally defined as that which is repugnant to our conscience to bring into any kind of relation to the good, *even into an opposition to the good*—is never pursued *directly* by human beings. As Plato reminds us in *Protagoras,* no one commits evil actions while thinking that they are evil.[1] People commit evil actions while carried away by their misconceived views of the good. A similar point is made by Kant. In the section called "Man is Evil by Nature" of book 1 of *Religion within the Limits of Reason Alone,* Kant points out that "man (even the most wicked one) does not, under any maxim whatsoever, repudiate the moral law in the manner of a rebel (renouncing obedience to it)."[2] In fact, a "reason exempt from the moral law" or a "malignant reason" or a "thoroughly evil will" cannot, according to Kant, be a *human* form of reason. It can only be a form of reason of a *devilish* being. The evil person, instead, is distinct from the morally good one neither by the absence of the moral law in her heart (for Kant, the moral law is innate to our inner consitution qua moral subjects) nor simply by her receptiveness to incentives of a sensuous nature (for also that receptiveness is equally part of every human subject), but rather is set apart from the good person on the basis of the priority she accords to sensuous incentives, over the moral law, in shaping the maxims of her conduct: "man is evil only in that he reverses the moral order of the incentives when he adopts them into his maxim."[3] Thus, concludes Kant, we cannot locate the source of evil in a "*corruption* of the morally legislative reason—as if reason could destroy the authority of the very law which is its own, or deny the obligation arising therefrom."[4]

If we try to apply Kant's line of reasoning to our own philosophical context, we immediately run up against a major obstacle. After the linguistic turn we live in a philosophical world where even partisans of moral universalism like Habermas and Rawls do find the notion of "one transcendentally anchored moral law" problematic in various ways. For instance, we would not understand the distinction, drawn by Rawls, between classical liberalism and *political* liberalism, if we did not understand how deeply problematic the notion of one moral law objectively directing the conduct of the moral subjects has become. This predicament raises new challenges, but also opens up new possibilities. For instance, where Kant could not think of an evil will as devoted to the deliberate subversion of the moral law because he conceived of the law in objectivistic terms, we, on the contrary, are in a position to make sense of a moral will that orients itself to a reconstruction of the moral point of view which happens to be misguided or flawed *in its own terms*.

II. THE NAZI CONCEPTION OF THE GOOD

It is perhaps more fruitful to discuss the issue with reference to a concrete example. In the twentieth century, people of my generation, born after World War II and already grown into adulthood when the Berlin Wall fell, are experiencing with disconcert the rapid evaporation of the hope that the post–cold war world would be a peaceful march toward global democratization. And in recent times the events occurring in former Yugoslavia have given rise to horror at the radically evil practices of ethnic cleansing, mass ethnic rape, forced deportation—in one word, genocide. I will not address these practices, however. I would rather go back to the paradigmatic example of radical evil in our century: the Holocaust.

If we can reconstruct our intuitions concerning radical evil with respect to Nazism and bring them into one coherent moral picture, we will have moved one important step toward a postmetaphysical conception of radical evil and we will have acquired a compass that can orient us in the moral intricacies of the new tribal, ethnic, and regional wars of the post–cold war era. The first point to understand in this respect is that a demonic view of what happened at Auschwitz and other such places as the embodiment of evil would amount to a posthumous vindication of a Hitlerian understanding of the moral world as the theater of a deadly confrontation between good and evil. We should not help Hitler to win posthumously the battle he lost on the battlefield. James Bernauer has to be credited for having dedicated great energies to a thorough reconstruction of what sounds blasphemous: a reconstruction of Nazi ethics, of the Nazi conception of the good.[5] For what was done at Auschwitz was done in the name of the good—a certain conception of the good for a certain community. It was not done as a deliberate denial of the moral law, but as an intended affirmation of it. As Hitler put it, "only the German people has turned the moral law into a reigning principle of action."[6] We should never overlook this fact, but should rather concentrate on grasping where the mistake was made.

At the core of the Nazi moral vision was a biological understanding of the good as the furthering of the racial purity of a people. Racial purity, in turn, was deemed valuable as a way of increasing the chances of survival in a Darwinistically conceived process of evolution in which the human species, and the peoples or races that compose it, are always immersed. The life of humanity was conceived as an evolutionary process of an eminently biological, as opposed to cultural, nature. Culture mattered insofar as its processes impinged on biology. For example, the cultural anomie, individualization, differentiation, and rapid cultural change associated with the processes of modernization (to a certain extent symbolized by the independence, secularized and kaleidoscopic spiritedness of Jewish high culture, together with the lightness of the *Zivilization* typical of French culture) were understood as the vehicles of an enfeebling of the temper of the German people. The chances for a people's evolutionary success or failure within this larger process were thought to be primarily affected by that people's capacity to prevent contamination by foreign genes—interracial promiscuity being obviously the chief vehicle of exogenous diseases. Hitler and the other Nazi leaders presented themselves not simply as military leaders, but also as "collective physicians" who would take the adequate measures for eradicating what they had discovered—namely, the ominous consequences of a racial virus called "internationale Judentum," which had begun to spread its effects everywhere, but with particular virulence in Germany. World history was recast as a biological lab—where *Rassenhygiene*, racial hygiene, became the main imperative.

This bioevolutionary, consequentialist morality generated its own *Tugendlehre* or "catalogue of virtues." As Goebbels summed it up, this catalogue included: "generosity" *(Großmütigkeit)*, "heroism" *(Heldentum)*, "masculine courage" *(Männlichkeit)*, "readiness to sacrifice" *(Bereitschaft zum Opfer)*, and "discipline" *(Zucht)*.[7] It was a kind of disciplinary asceticism in which individuals were required to adhere to a regimen of strict bodily and moral training in order to eradicate the seeds of depravity within themselves, and were asked to subordinate their own private interests to the advancement of the common good. Himmler summed up these virtues in the SS ideal of "severity" or "hard-heartedness" *(Härte)* as a combination of personal honesty, of the capacity to overcome feelings of compassion, and of the capacity to feel permanently at war. That "life" and "death," evolutionary triumph or defeat, were the leading moral metaphors is also signalled, among other things, by Hitler's understanding of politics as "the art of leading the struggle of a people for its earthly survival."[8] In this kind of naturalized moral world, there was no place for the modern notions of *equal respect* and of *human dignity*. Again, in *Mein Kampf*, Hitler connects the right to life to the factual capacity to defend it, or in fact empties it of all normative substance: "When a people no longer possesses enough strength to fight for its own health, then its right to survive in this world of struggle comes to cease."[9]

Bernauer points out the elements of continuity that connect this moral vocabulary with other moral vocabularies that are very respectable. On the one hand, Hitler and the Nazis failed to grasp the extent to which their moral conception resembled the central idea of an eternal struggle between Life and Death, Eros and Thanatos expounded in Freud's books, which were publicly burned. The biological was at the center of Freud's moral world and life was understood also by him as a primarily *natural* force, a natural force which naturally opposes death. On the other hand, the use of Christian symbols alongside the more well-known neopagan and post-Christian ones, as well as the existence of pro-Nazi Christian movements testify to the possibility of tracing continuities between the traditional paleo-Christian anti-Judaism and the new post-Christian Nazi anti-Semitism. More than external symbols, however, Nazi ethics seems to have appropriated and radicalized a certain Christian ideal of *purity*—not so much the "purity of blood" that was the object of Counter Reformation discussion in sixteenth-century Spain, as a kind of "spiritual purity" which under the heading of "simpleness of spirit" stood in opposition to the classical Greek ideal of "megalopsyche" or "magnanimitas" and provided the ground for a kind of anti-intellectual populism tinged with authoritarian propensities. But through its ideal of "purity" Nazism appropriated also another cultural source—the Catholic ethics of sexual purity—and gave it a peculiarly racist twist. Purity became an ideal not just of private conduct but an ideal binding for entire races. Purity of race came to constitute a projection of sexual purity on a collective plane.

So underneath the Holocaust was not just a misguided reconstruction of the good for a single historical community (the German *Volk,* as construed by the Nazi leaders), but also a misguided reconstruction of the moral point of view. Misguided in what sense? Not in the sense that formally one could not generalize the maxim of practicing *Rassenhygiene* into the imperative of maximizing racial purity within each nation—an idea that, couched in cultural and religious more than biological terms, has dramatically come back to centerstage under the heading of "ethnic cleansing." The Nazi conception of the moral point of view was misguided rather in the sense that the background assumptions against which a "generalization" of *Rassenhygiene* was supposed to make sense were untenable. Among these assumptions were three propositions: *(a)* the moral life is a struggle of nations for survival, *(b)* racial purity is the best means to ensure survival and evolutionary success to a nation understood as a race, *(c)* human races incapable of raising themselves up to purity or who live to corrupt other races do not have a right to survive.

This distinction between, on the one hand, the conception of the moral point of view as bound up with the universalizability of maxims and, on the other hand, the substantive assumptions in the light of which the universalization test is carried out is important to our assessment of evil. As Hegel has shown in his critique of Kant's moral philosophy, the formal process of generalization of which the categorical imperative consists only works in conjunction with substantive assumptions about the desirability of ends.[10] I cannot appropriate a deposit entrusted to me because if everybody did so under comparable conditions then the institution of promising—which independently we prize as a valuable one—would be undermined. On the other hand, if a beggar asks me for some spare change, the obvious fact that if everybody gave liberally poverty and with it begging would be undermined does not make my act immoral, for the generalization-independent reason that we do not prize poverty as a valuable thing to be preserved. Applying this distinction to our example of radical evil, we could say that the Nazi conception of the moral point of view is vitiated, indeed perversely corrupted, by the very background assumptions concerning the nature of the moral life—to repeat: the idea that the moral life amounts to a struggle for survival and the idea that the right to life is contingent on the possession of the power to assert it—on the basis of which it is put to work.

III. BRIEF EXCURSUS ON THE "BANALITY" OF EVIL

This distinction between the universalization test as such and the background assumptions against which it is carried out somehow also explains how evil could appear "banal." When these questionable assumptions are accepted—and we have seen that in certain respects bits and pieces of them can be found in several other moral conceptions which as a whole have nothing to share with Nazism—they can congeal into a shared lifeworld and sustain a sense of "normality" in perpetrating the horror. If the source of evil cannot be located in the transgression of a moral point of view which cannot be grasped from outside a conceptual scheme, but must—if we want to be coherent with the linguistic turn—be traced to the inner normativity of a moral culture called "evil" only from the outside, from the observer's point of view, one of the consequences is that evil is no less intersubjectively constituted than the good. This intersubjective character—shared assumptions, shared values, a common vocabulary of moral relevance—in turn accounts for its "banality," for the "everyday" and "low-key" as opposed to "grandiose" and "heroic" quality of evil in our times. And in fact, under different substantive presuppositions, we have witnessed the resurgence of the "banality of evil" again and again, in Cambodia, Rwanda, and the former Yugoslavia—meaning by the phrase "banal evil" not evil that is any less horrible, but evil that becomes entwined with everyday life, *evil as a temporarily shared form of life* rather than as the dramatic rupture of a form of life or, using yet another formulation, evil that has lost the quality of being a temptation and has turned into a habit.

So the problem of radical evil raises a challenge for us in the sense that even evil of the magnitude of the Holocaust does not take the appearance of an *intentional* violation of the moral point of view but merely comes to us as a perverted application of it in the light of assumptions that amount to a misguided view of the moral life. Yet, here is the rub. Within the horizon of his *Subjektsphilosophie*, Kant could believe that his own reconstruction of the moral point of view and his way of applying it in light of the assumptions typical of his philosophical horizon—assumptions which allowed him to conclude, among other things, that the death penalty is the appropriate punishment for murder, that a child born outside of marriage, being born "outside the social contract," could be suppressed, and that women should be barred from suffrage—was neutral with respect to all diversity of opinion and a direct reflection of normative structures and intuitions deep-seated in the moral constitution of all human beings. We cannot. We live within a philosophical horizon based on the assumption of a plurality of language games or conceptual schemes and for this reason our condemnation of the Nazi view of the good as conducive to evil cannot proceed from the idea of its constituting a transgression of a moral point of view located outside all language games and conceptual schemes. Hence the difficulty: if, perverted though it appears to us, the Nazi view of the good constitutes a "comprehensive conception of the good," on what ground can we condemn it as "evil," as opposed to merely limiting ourselves to the sober realization that its basic evaluative orientations just happen to lie beyond all possibility of an "overlapping consensus" with our own, without violating the pluralistic premises of the linguistic turn?

It is at this point that an understanding of normative validity based on authenticity and judgment can be helpful. First, the horizon inaugurated by the linguistic turn does not just create difficulties but also contains conceptual resources that can help us draw the line between ordinary and radical evil on a new and thoroughly postmetaphysical basis. Ordinary evil (the bank robbery taking place around the corner, the episode of political corruption reported in the local newspaper, the marital violence occurring next door) can be conceived as "intra-paradigmatic" evil—evil as the failure to live up to a set of shared normative assumptions amounting to one moral culture. When Himmler deplores the stealing of even a cigarette from the body of an exterminated Jew, he points to an instance of ordinary evil from within a Nazi conception of morality. *Radical* evil, instead, is the name that we give to "paradigmatic" evil, namely to a moral culture taken as a whole and to those acts which we take as representative of this moral culture. Before Nazism came to constitute the ultimate term of comparison for evil, "Oriental despotism" played pretty much an analogous role in the social philosophy of Montesquieu, Hegel, and Marx. It constituted a *radically evil* moral culture. The culture of the plantation in the South of the United States represented another case in the eyes of many Northerners. For that matter, the individualist way of life of the postindustrial societies of the West represented a devilish embodiment of ultimate evil in the eyes of Ayatollah Khomeini. Thus we are now faced with the issue: what does it mean for a moral culture as a whole to constitute an instance of radical evil? Or, better said, what does it mean for a moral culture to constitute an instance of radical evil "in the eyes of everyone" and not just to our own, or Khomeini's, eyes?

IV. HOW CAN A CONCEPTION OF THE GOOD BE EVIL?

According to a judgment view of justice, evil, no less than the good, is always *evil for someone*. We call the Nazi view of the good as racial purity evil in that it systematically violates the principle of equal respect for all human beings regardless of their ethnic ancestry. The grounding of such principle rests on nothing else than the fact that we could not regard us as ourselves anymore, as Western moderns of the twentieth and twenty-first centuries, if we embraced a view of the moral life that did not include it. The Nazis were, after all, Western moderns of the twentieth century as well, and we can legitimately challenge their interpretation of the moral point of view as the ultimate betrayal of the values that constitute us as the kind of human beings that *we* would want to be. We can claim that their "evil view of the good," if successfully institutionalized, would turn our history—the history of the West—into a tale of moral horror where human dignity, the idea of equal respect for all human beings, and the critical spirit ("Hier ist kein Warum" was the standard answer given by the Lager supervisors) would all fade away to leave us in a Darwinized moral world.

At the same time, when we claim that the Nazi view of morality is evil we claim something more than that. We claim that *no one,* not just we the Westerners of the twentieth or twenty-first centuries, could embrace it and still remain faithful to herself. How is this possible without invoking some Archimedean point and falling back into some kind of fundamentalism of equal respect or of human rights? It *is* possible, if we rethink the point of view of justice violated by the Nazi understanding of the good as the point of view of the good for humanity as such. I cannot develop here the argument in support of a judgment view of justice, but will mention only one aspect of it. There is no human political community whose members are not part of humanity as well and, for this reason, a political conception of normative validity which failed to include some reflection, however minimal or implicit, of an understanding of the good for humanity would thereby also fail to be true to that part of the people's collective identity which overlaps, however minimally or implicitly, with the identity of humanity in its entirety. It does not matter how thinly anticipatory this notion of the realization of humanity in its entirety is at present. There is little doubt of the fact that the Jewish people's survival would be jeopardized by the affirmation of a Nazi ethical conception. A Nazi, however, could reply by questioning the moral import of the survival of an inferior race: he could claim that the lot of humanity would in fact be improved by that disappearance.

We have two options open at this juncture if we want to challenge this claim while avoiding a fundamentalizing of egalitarian intuitions that might put us in the same position Khomeini and the Ayatollahs found themselves when indicting the Western way of life from the standpoint of their own comprehensive conception of the good. We could answer that a view of the good for humanity that did not include the equal dignity of all human beings and all peoples would be a view that ultimately betrays all that *we* think should be part of the notion of realizing the good for humanity. In so arguing, however, we could not appeal to a superordinate standpoint that adjudicates the case between us and the Nazi, but would simply have to be ready to fight for preventing the narrative of the identity of that humanity of which we are a part to become tainted by the horror of a Nazi view. While I think that politically there might have been, and in the future there might be, no alternative, I am philosophically uneasy with this line of response. Let us assume counterfactually that the Nazi regime had not been imperialistically aggressive, but had tried to carry out its program of exterminating the Jews just within the boundaries of post–World War I Germany. While I still believe that war should have been waged in order to prevent genocide even in the absence of expansionistic aggression, our justifying war on that basis would not put us in a significantly different position than a theocratic state (say, Iran) which claims to be justified in waging war against the West in order to prevent our secularized, plural understanding of the good from leading to what from its point of view looks like the ultimate corruption of humanity's identity.

The other line of response, instead, deconstructs the Nazi's view immanently, so to speak, by pointing to the inconsistency of claiming that the right to life exists only for those who are in position to assert it and at the same time calling this a *moral* vision. In fact, only in the "state of nature," as opposed to the moral world, one could say that the right to life is subordinated to the factual power to assert it. It appears to be self-contradictory to state that one people deserves to survive only if it is able to physically defend its existence with military force and that this evaluative statement is a moral one as opposed to one that belongs in the state of nature. This is the basis on which it could be claimed—without invoking controversial values and standards—that a Nazi view of ethics would fail the test of constituting a viable reconstruction of the point of view of the good for humanity.

But why should the idea of the "good for humanity" represent a cogent normative standpoint for all locally shared moral cultures? Why could we not in principle conceive of a moral culture shared by a community which on the whole refuses to care for the good of humanity? Here the judgment view of justice mentioned above comes into play. Given an intersubjective understanding of the nature of identity, as always bound up with mutual recognition on the part of other identities—a recognition that, in turn, is made possible by the existence of some, however minimal, intersection of shared values and beliefs—for a collective identity to seek its own good or fulfillment at the expense of, or even simply overlooking, the fulfillment of the larger identity of humanity means to reduce the degree of fulfillment attainable by that identity. More precisely, it means to reduce the scope of that fulfillment by comparison with the degree of fulfillment attainable by the same identity if it were to take into full account all of its constitutive interconnections with the other identities with which it entertains relations of recognition.

To conclude this section, because no political community exists whose members are *not* part of humanity, any community which in its conception of normative validity failed to include some understanding, however minimal or implicit, of the good for humanity would thereby also fail to be true to the part of its own collective identity which overlaps, however minimally or implicity, with the (as yet virtual) identity of humanity in its entirety. Only the "race of devils" hypothesized by Kant could set a radical opposition of justice as the anticipated good for their race as a whole and the affirmation of the political identity of one specific subcommunity of devils—provided that such a race decided to live in a political community. Only those devils, in fact, could conceive of the pursuit of their own communal but local good as the undermining of the good for the race of devils as a whole. But even the Nazis were not devils. They were all-too-human humans. Thus authentic evil is not a human, but a devilish possibility. More modestly, humans pursue what they believe to be the good and only subsequently learn that it is evil, and evil, including radical evil, thus always fails to be authentic in that it always includes a moment of self-deception—at the very least in the form of misconstruing the relevance of certain constitutive relations with other identities.

V. THE RADICALITY OF RADICAL EVIL

Obviously there exist thousands of ways of violating the moral point of view, reconstructed as the point of view of the good for humanity, that nonetheless cannot be put on a par with Auschwitz. Sexist talk in everyday informal conversation violates the ideal of equal respect, yet we do not call that *radical* evil. We are still in need of a postmetaphysical definition of what radical evil on a human, as opposed to a devilish, scale could possibly mean. Where, and above all how, are we to locate the threshold between ordinary and extraordinary or radical evil? Intuitively, genocide seems to always fall under the category of radical evil, while the death penalty—which to the public culture of certain, though not all, democratic societies is morally repulsive—does not.

The distinction between ordinary and radical evil is of the greatest importance because in the world of the twenty-first century the line that separates legitimate and illegitimate interference in the "internal affairs" of a sovereign state could very well rest on it. Notice first of all that the line that separates ordinary and radical evil cannot be equated with the line that separates the violation of human rights from the violation of other rights. For there are countless violations of human rights in many countries which, unfortunate and morally condemnable as they are, would not justify the waging of the kind of military action that we have seen taking place hopefully as the forerunner of a future United Nations–led police operation aimed at states that repeatedly make themselves guilty of crimes against humanity. In fact, the legal notion of human rights—if we take the Universal Declaration of Human Rights as our source—is very broad. It contains both reference to rights (e.g. the "right to life" mentioned in Article 3) whose systematic violation would amount to an instance of radical evil justifying humanitarian interference as well as reference to rights (e.g. the "right to rest and leisure" mentioned in Article 24) whose violation would certainly fall short of justifying any such military action, and nothing in the text of the Declaration suggests that there is a *legally grounded* way of ranking human rights. We are left to the resources of *moral* argument.

If we survey the cases which most univocally would fit the category of radical evil, besides the Holocaust we perhaps can think of the killing fields in Cambodia, the events in Rwanda, mass rape in Bosnia, ethnic cleansing, the Gulag. The decisive trait seems to be not so much the event's violent quality per se (because many instances of political conflict or civil wars also exhibit the characteristic of being extremely violent) as the deliberate quality of the attempted annihilation of a collective, of a group of people singled out on account of some shared characteristic of theirs—being born in the wrong ethnicity, religion, or ideology. Constitutive of radical evil seems to be the unleashing of violence on a victimized group unable to adequately react—targeting the individual only insofar as she is part of that group. Radical evil also seems to have to possess a characteristically systematic quality which episodic violence—for example, lynchings and pogroms—does not possess. It is violence exerted by a majority on a minority by means of using state power. But here as well conceptual difficulties await us. The Night of St. Bartholomew and the killing of the Huguenots in France, as well as countless episodes of ancient, medieval, and early modern history do exhibit ferocious attacks against a scapegoated and defenseless minority on the part of a religious or ethnic majority. Yet somehow we realize that those episodes horrify us less, not because on some objective scale less evil occurred, but rather because the actors involved are further removed from our own moral world. The closer to home, the more radical evil arouses moral horror. Nazism horrifies us because it occurred in the very midst of one of the most developed and civilized parts of Europe. Ethnic cleansing in the former Yugoslavia elicits moral sentiments of horror also because it is taking place *after* we all thought that the lesson of Auschwitz had been thoroughly metabolized in Europe. These moral feelings suggest that perhaps our perspective ought to change. The criterion for the radicality of radical evil ought perhaps to be internal to us, the moral community, rather than external, objective. Evil then is perhaps best conceived as a *horizon* that moves with us, rather than as something that stands over against us.

In order to further articulate this way of conceiving of radical evil, we can go back to Durkheim. An inspiring perspective can be found in his discussion of the sacred. In his writings on religion—the 1898 essay "On the Definition of Religious Phenomena"[11] as well as in his 1912 book *The Elementary Forms of Religious Life*[12]—Durkheim always stressed the difficulty of pinpointing the sacred to some kind of essential, objective dimension. All human collectivities share some sense of the sacred, but what is deemed sacred varies in the broadest imaginable way. Yet the sacred cannot be defined with reference to some general principle. For example, it cannot be associated with the supernatural, because cultures exist that do not incorporate the distinction between what is natural and what goes beyond the natural. The sacred cannot be associated with the idea of divinity, because there exist religions that do not presuppose the notion of an individuated divine figure. Nor can it be associated with a hierarchy of what is "high" and what is "low" on a scale of value. For many conceptual dichotomies exist— rich and poor, master and slave, rulers and ruled—which we associate with the idea of a distribution in terms of high and low, but where the superordinate category by no means appears closer to the sacred than the lower. The innovative conceptual shift introduced by Durkheim was to conceive of the sacred in a thoroughly relational or oppositional way and to give that relational definition a certain expressivist twist. The sacred is defined as that which is radically opposed to the profane. But also health is radically opposed to disease, and so is progress with respect to decadence. Thus the sacred is on one hand anything that we are repelled at the idea of seeing indiscriminately mixed up with the profane—anything that we think should ideally be kept insulated and protected from the profane—but also something which somehow expresses crucial aspects of ourselves.

For something to count as sacred, it is not enough that it be perceived as endowed with value in the moral sense and that such perception be shared across a community. What is needed in order to turn something collectively prized into something sacred is a certain *exemplariness* of the sacred thing, namely its capacity to bring to expression some dimension of the group which at the same time is unique and is located at the symbolic center of the group's identity. No phrase captures better the spirit of Durkheim's understanding of the sacred as the experience of collective authenticity than Giorgio Agamben's aphorism: "That the world does not reveal any divine plan, that is truly divine."[13] Just as authenticity—now understood as the specific dimension of modern individuation discovered by Diderot and Rousseau—is somehow the equivalent of the sacred on the scale of individual identities, so the sacred is anchored to the authenticity of a collective identity. It captures the uniqueness of that collectivity and objectifies that uniqueness in shared symbols that—becoming religion, liturgy, tradition— then are always exposed to the wear and tear of shared symbolism and sometimes lose the power to evoke such uniqueness. From another perspective, the Durkheimian notion of the sacred can be said to represent the non-negotiable normative core of a collective identity, the symbolic locus of commitments that cannot be disattended without the members of the collectivity perceiving that their identity is being betrayed, that their integrity as a collective in thrown into question, and that their collectivity is in the process of becoming another.

Pushing this reconstruction of Durkheim's notion of the sacred one step further, we could ask: What society is being represented in the sacred symbols that religious rituals always try to pin down and systematize into materials for theological speculation and ritual practice? If what Durkheim calls the sacred is somehow an objectification of the "individual law" of an entire society, a representation of that which in the eyes of its participants constitutes that society's unique identity, what is really meant by "society"? Certainly not society as it really is, meaning the society we encounter every day. But neither is it an ideal or perfect society in the sense of being a product of the mind of a philosopher. For Durkheim the society which we presuppose in our experience of the sacred is the *actual society idealized*— namely a society which neither is taken "as is" nor gets transfigured into some transcendent ideal no longer connected with who we are. It is our actual society as it *could* be if all of its positive potentials were to unfold, thus a society that does not exist here and now, and yet maintains all those characteristics that make of it *the good society for us*, namely *our own* ideal society, different from other people's ideal societies. The society idealized in the symbols of the sacred is a "concrete universal," which exerts an orienting function similar to that of the aesthetic idea which an artist follows in giving shape to his or her materials, or as a concrete ideal self that an individual tries to shape his or her life by. In the sacred we can always discern the contour of what we collectively want to be, and that image is as individuated as we are.

Finally, the production of these symbols is not something that happens to society or its members. "A society can neither create itself nor recreate itself without at the same time creating an ideal. This creation is not a sort of work of supererogation, by which it would complete itself, being already formed; it is the act by which it is periodically made and remade."[14]

Durkheim's understanding of the sacred can be put to use in our discussion of evil. First, just as the production of the sacred is part and parcel of social life and cannot be eradicated from it—secularization, in other words, affects the religious sedimentation of collective experiences of the sacred and the role of religion in social life, but not the production of the sacred—so radical evil is best understood as the polar opposite of the sacred. If the sacred is a projection of us *at our best*, and the world of the profane a representation of us *as we actually are*, including the manifestations of ordinary evil that we experience, radical evil can be conceptualized as a projection of us *at our worst*, the worst that we can prove to be while still maintaining those characteristics that make us—us as a community, a society, or humanity—what we are.

In that sense evil, even radical evil, cannot be overcome. Concrete manifestations of it can be overcome—Auschwitz can be driven out of this world, ethnic cleansing hopefully can too—but if evil is a horizon that moves with us, then there will always be a collectively shared symbolic representation of what we, we as a single moral community or we as humans, can be at our worst. The idea of a good society where evil has been eradicated is, from a postmetaphysical standpoint, as meaningless as the idea of a pacified moral world where no conflict of values exists any longer or as meaningless as the dove's wish, mentioned by Kant, that no air existed to obstruct its flight. Just as Kant's dove failed to realize that the same air that obstructs its flight also sustains it, so those who think that idealized conditions could in principle exist under which no evil affected the human world fail to understand the extent to which the constitution of ourselves as moral subjects requires that we distance ourselves from shared images of radical evil.

I would like now to build on this notion of radical evil as a symbolic horizon constituted by what we take to be the image of "us at our worst" and go back to the question "What distinguishes ordinary and radical evil?" Ordinary evil is somehow evil whose existence is understood as part of the normal fabric of social life. Radical evil is evil that we think should have never occurred—evil that changes the relation of the moral subject to itself. Ordinary evil exemplifies what ought not to be done and by contrast points to what should be done, radical evil is what should have never happened and is repugnant for us to think that it should be connected in any way—even by exemplifying what ought not to be done—with a worthy human life. Auschwitz marks a discontinuity that ought to be thought of perhaps in terms of identity. Ordinary evil is like the countless events that affect our lives peripherally. Auschwitz is one of those events that does not allow an identity, individual or collective, to remain impassive. The radicality of the evil that took place at Auschwitz vis-à-vis the ordinary quality of, say, the evil embedded in an episode of robbery or political corruption is reflected in our perception that the relation of humanity to itself and its own history and future has been changed in the former case, but not in the latter.

But what can explain the horror aroused by radical evil, if we do not want to link that horror with the transcendent nature of that which is violated by radical evil? If we accept Plato's and Kant's idea that no human being acts in a deliberately immoral way, following a principle aimed at destroying the moral point of view, then the horror aroused by radical evil comes from among other things the realization of the extreme extent to which our representations and moral judgments may, when wrong, lead us to lose touch with reality. Moral communities always discover *afterwards—ex post facto—* that what was done by their members in pursuit of shared views of the good was radically evil. The horror we experience when thinking of the Holocaust or of other episodes of radical evil is linked with the horror that the abyss of psychosis arouses—the horror at the idea of total loss of touch with the reality as seen by other human beings, or total encapsulation into a world no one understands, of total unrelatedness between the meaning we assign to our actions and the meaning they acquire in the world of all other human beings. When we look at radical evil from the perspective of the victims, the horror is aroused by the abyss that separates their innocence from their fate, again, the meaninglessness for them of the destruction they suffered or the total unrelatedness of their deeds and their fate. That is why Habermas speaks of a "reflection on the incomprehensible" in relation to Auschwitz.

This brings me, in closing, to the issue of the moral sentiment of compassion for the victims of radical evil. It has been said that somehow a theological framework is called for, whenever we think of radical evil in history, if anything because it allows some kind of hope that the victims of evil will at some point be compensated for what they suffered. What seems lacking in a postmetaphysical understanding of radical evil is the possibility of thinking of "undoing" the past injustices. The suspicion remains that "the result of this avoidance of the theological dimension is a tendency for the notion of anamnestic solidarity to become instrumentalized."[15] Once again, I believe that Durkheim's approach to religious life and in particular to the significance of mourning could be of help. We could say that the "instrumentalization of memory" to the interests of the survivors could be avoided if we think that the sacrifice undergone by victims of radical evil, though not voluntary, has not been in vain insofar as they somehow continue to live, implanted in the moral fiber of a democratic community that remembers them, honors them, and feels indebted to them for its existence. When the

Italian Constitution was framed in 1947, after the fall of fascism, there was a proposal to dedicate it, via a preamble, to the memory of all those who paid their resistance to fascism with their lives and whose sacrifice had contributed to making today's democratic Italy possible. The proposal was not adopted (because some Catholics wanted a reference to God instead), but had that preamble ever materialized in the form of positive law, it would have embodied a kind of noninstrumental and secular anamnestic solidarity with the victims of fascism.

As Shakespeare's Mark Anthony puts it, indeed the evil that men do lives after them, but the relation that successors form to the evil passed onto them by previous generations is quite peculiar. Evil does not really survive as such unless in disguise. Because, as Plato and Kant have taught us, a deliberate and authentic pursuit of radical evil is not a human possibility, when something is recognized as evil, it means that we are already distancing ourselves from it, that the darkness of the night is over and a new dawn is beginning.

Major Offenders, Minor Offenders

Sergio Pérez

Evil, its actions, its very name, inspires awe. This is quite normal since each offense depicts the limit between the human and the inhuman. Nonetheless, beyond the paralyzing presence of horror, it is possible to differentiate between two patterns: major offenders and minor offenders. Naturally, both groups commit abhorrent crimes, and it is not our intention to be lenient about their relative culpability. But perhaps, if we examine both cases thoroughly, we can stress certain characteristics of the presence of evil. At least, this is the hypothesis we wish to show in this paper. On the one hand there is an aspect of evil which is magnificent, supreme, breaking all taboos. On the other hand there is a more treacherous aspect, displaying itself in our daily lives. The first type is the pompous aspect of evil which loves to shake everyone, show off, to be on stage, when persecuted with firmness. There is no doubt that many times this aspect lurks in the shadows, but even in those cases it secretly hopes to be discovered one day and to dazzle everyone with its atrocities. The second type refers to the evil actions perpetrated by souls of less sublime disposition, by obscure offenders whose behavior barely deserves a place in the crime section of the newspapers. Their evil behavior does not make for a glamorous story. They only remind us that evil does not contradict but complements human life.

Among the many possible definitions, let us choose one that narrows down our objectives—evil is noncontrolled inhumanity manifesting itself individually, socially, or politically. By defining it as noncontrolled inhumanity, we want to stress the fact that we do not consider evil as a theological issue, neither do we refer to the disasters caused by certain acts of God. We are talking about evil caused by human beings, guided by decisions, and carried out against human beings or against something meaningful to human beings. Consequently, evil is an act which involves human beings as subjects and objects. From this viewpoint—indeed limited—evil has nothing to do with the negation of the divine or of nature, but the negation of what is specifically human caused by the behavior of human beings themselves.

EVIL AS A LIFE CHOICE

For some major offenders, being evil, being a monster, an unchained force foreign to human beings, is a life choice. This fact might be morally unacceptable, but it does exist. Under this category we can include those who like evil for evil itself, those who act wrongly because they like to be wicked. In other words, these are inner dispositions seeking evil in the same way that others seek good. In the face of this (im)moral choice, we are forced to reflect—above all, because evil as a life choice is nothing that can be attained by just deciding to do so, as if it were a radiant moment when every single issue would seem to be clarified. On the contrary, one gets immersed in evil progressively, as with a lifelong task, step-by-step, through a gradual absorption that separates the individual from his fellow men. A long list of offenders' biographies, from Sade to Genet, seems to make it clear that, in a human being's journey, evil perfects itself.

This gradual immersion can be explained by the very possibility of evil. Indeed, humanity is the result of the observance of specific prohibitions, which in certain cases are universal. To protect itself from the threat of dissolution, human life requires rules, laws, and the continuity provided by individuals and institutions preserving and supporting it. We could call that continuity, as well as law and order, "the good." Laws and rules are the good in itself, and good is the instrument through which continuity achieves permanence. Certainly, such continuity carries with it a set of prohibitions which are inherent to the human personality, but which might also be considered as restrictions to individual sovereignty. We can define various ways of conceiving human nature by taking these prohibitions into account. Evil as a life choice is one of them—that which is associated to the freedom of violating those prohibitions. It is evil—and not good—which immediately brings up the issue of the origin of law. Evil starts its course simultaneously with the beginning of human freedom (this is what the Judeo-Christian myth states in Genesis), because a perverse act only arises from our own actions.

The choice of evil is a sort of rebelliousness (sometimes defined against God, sometimes against reason), but a rebelliousness that needs the good in order to make sense. There are various reasons for this—first, the preservation of life indicates that human nature tends toward the good; second, in order for rebelliousness to be authentic and to entail a risk, something must exist against which one can rebel—this something is the existence of rules. For evil to exist, good has to exist, and it is also necessary that rules and reason exist. But the opposite is true as well. For the human possibility to exist, the effective presence of the norm is necessary. Yet for that continuity to work effectively, the threat of transgression is indispensable, because this menace allows the continuity to work as a fine line between what is considered normal and what is considered abnormal, a distinction intended to be established by every culture again and again: ". . . everything would perish at once if there were just virtues on earth . . . you do not want to understand that, provided that vices ought to exist, it is as unfair to punish them as it would be to make fun of a one-eyed person."[1] The usual definition of evil as a parasite's existence, as a fragile, weak entity without any self-support, comes from this unshakable unity and the preeminence of the good. But from this same concept comes also one of the more disheartening conclusions about evil—its presence is a part of life which, although repressed and denied, manages to remain latent, pressing from the shadows and fighting to exist.

Inhuman behavior as a life choice, therefore, creates a number of paradoxes and antinomies. Firstly, because choosing evil is a lifestyle decision that is either obstinate or becomes a farce, and it must be permanent; otherwise it may become a ridiculous situation. A bad action does not make a wicked man. That is why, when we talk about major offenders, we mean to emphasize the existence of a vertiginous propensity toward abjection, even at the risk of causing suffering to oneself and others. The magnificent and supreme form of evil then consists of the widespread denial of prohibitions, of a continuing search for nothingness, without limitations, which stands for the "awareness of evil," recognized by Baudelaire as the supreme evil.[2] The disgust aroused by this choice creates the conviction that the worst of evils is knowing what good is and then rejecting it to sink into darkness. It is sad to conclude that every prohibition and even good in general signifies a slight, fragile, insufficient obstacle against the will toward evil. Even more so, since in making this decision one can see the same intellectual mechanisms at work as in any other decision—responsibility, inner dialogue, and reflection. The awe in the face of these deserters comes from the fact that they willingly oppose the effort to preserve the conditions of life, as we all attempt in a more or less indirect way. Due to the intellectual faculties at play, they respond to a type, to a specific category—they are adults, fully responsible for the evil they cause (or at least they are competent enough to be held responsible).

Anchored in freedom, the criminal perceives the choice of evil as an act of sovereignty. By "sovereignty" we mean the capacity to overlook the laws preserving the continuity of life, in a state of complete indifference toward death. In this attitude, one can acknowledge the existence of a sort of drunken frenzy which is unbearable for rational human purposes. Consequently, even though there is no logical ground for what could be the origin of evil, we assume that there must exist a source of pleasure associated to it. Of course, the offender's freedom is purely negative, it is the independence of a conscience in itself lacking any type of restraint. It is a false state of freedom because the aspired sovereignty can only be achieved by actions which, if actually carried out, would threaten life itself.

The nature of the major offenders can be deviated, but it is far from stupid. This is because evil, in order to be carried out, requires a certain intelligence. One must be especially tactful in order to identify evil and to eventually carry it out. In order to accomplish all this, experience, a deep insight, and a refined knowledge of the human heart are required. One must know the other person very well in order to make him suffer, in order to figure out the verbal or physical abuse which might deeply wound the victim's nature. Certainly, passion might also lead to a lack of humanity. However, evil is worse when dispassionate, and the criminal is more hateful when he carries out his offenses without the alibi of passion. This knowledge of human suffering can reach extreme gradations, and it is perfectly understandable because the sublime really matters when it comes to evil. In fact, this is one of the reasons for our disgust in the face of evil—we associate it with suffering and we fear suffering or the sight of someone else's suffering. The existence of major offenders causes indignation because we understand that evil also has its peaks, and because those natures show us something that we do not like—that human beings are our own worst enemies.

If the mechanism of goodness functions on its own, massively and globally, evil is bound by detail, interruption, and a total cessation of life. Evil is not like goodness, all-encompassing. Evil is more meticulous, careful about details. Taking into account that evil is opposite to the norm, the evil nature should be as the perfectionist's, and his hate should build up step-by-step, should gradually construe the abyss of nothingness which it pursues, should demolish the aspects of life one by one. It is obliged to detect its corresponding opposite for every virtue, graduate the scale of suffering, maintain total destruction in suspense as long as possible, invent a sublime example each time more refined and exciting. When they have left traces, the reflections of evil people are mathematical nightmares. Good can afford to be colossal because it is organic and structured, but those who wish to dissolve it should look for its peculiar independent circumstances, should imagine its slow demolition, committing themselves to detail. The evil nature not only hates its victim, it also hates goodness in its most ample form. The essence of its acts is to destroy not only the objects or the victims that come their way, which sometimes are only there to respond to its fury to deny, but to destroy everything that exists, including the author of evil. Only a universal hate bordering on perfection can maintain such an iron will capable of opposing an insurmountable barrier against the weak voice of remorse.

Even though it is an exercise of liberty, the fact cannot be ignored that evil will also require objective conditions for its independence. That is why major offenders, those who could liberate the beast inside themselves, were more prevalent (or at least more visible) when an enormous difference of power separated the classes of society. The independence of the powerful tends to be the threshold for future immolations. The major offender emerges when men have sufficient power to transgress the prohibitions of society and to tear down the doors of the kingdom of reason.

In spite of evil aspiring to the absolute, it cannot avoid being a dependent being, whose life is subordinated to the loan conceded by the existence of the goodness it denies. Evil is the being of the nonbeing, and it is the nonbeing of being, as Sartre wrote.[3] Symbolically, its eternal dependence manifests itself in its association with darkness, emptiness, blindness, and the night as opposed to light, brightness, and the clarity of the good. It is precisely the functioning of the principle that psychologists call "synesthesia" that permits the association, in opposite signs within a sole human symbolism, of the moral judgment (good or bad), the potentiality (strong or weak), the activity (active or passive), and moral values in general with colors, sounds, and gravity. Due to all this, we can conclude that evil, like all its accomplices, is associated with nothingness. Furthermore, this persistence, as disgusting as you find it, shows that human beings are permanently torn between the will to endure and the desire to live their freedom destructively. In self-interest the individual has to accept a series of prohibitions, but at the same time he recognizes through his violence, in his nihilism, that indestructible part of himself that leads him to deny them.

Not all philosophical systems have accepted facing this negativity. It is not that they ignore its presence, but many of them tend to think that nonbeing cannot be an object of thought. And even those who, like Leibniz or Hegel, grant negativity efficacy and existence, finally assimilate it as a positive result. This is the case, for example, of "negativity" in Hegelian philosophy, which is without doubt the only acceptable anthropological foundation in the system. But this negativity transforms, through practical or intellectual work, the immediateness of the sensitive world until it achieves a more finite form. Concerning evil, the issue is different: in it, the denial consists of taking toward nothingness as great a quantity as possible of being, annihilating it, eradicating it from the catalogue of created things. Even in Hegel's philosophy of history, where it has a recognized presence, evil is only explained if it is admitted that a rational plan to be fulfilled should exist in spite of evil, or better still, despite putting it to practice. Unlike work, evil is dilapidation. Evil is in the order of excesses, sterile, free, one of those tumultuous and excessive movements which oppose the reasonableness of calculus and productive activity. For the same reason, evil cannot be the first impulse in human life, because its destructive nature would not take place if it did not have something to destroy.

From this parasite's condition some characteristics are derived which deserve to be pointed out—the first is that evil is always personified in the offender. This means that the weakness of its being is such that the evil is obliged to depend on the wicked. In this aspect, it also opposes goodness. Goodness happens somehow spontaneously. It is that which happens when rules are followed. It is therefore something within itself, that which everyone, or the great majority, would do if they found themselves in the same situation. Good has that anonymous character. Evil is the complete opposite: it is correlative to the attitude of the offender; in order to exist, it is necessary that the offender continuously maintains evil from the very moment he first thinks of it: he first draws it in his will, and he fulfills it by his actions. If the offender's attention is distracted, the harm vanishes. Evil does not depend only on one momentary decision, but on an exemplary perseverance of will.

Secondly, evil is an instantaneous act. This means to say that, although the evil situation is prolonged in time, in reality, it is made up of a series (which could be very long) of evil acts, each one with its own objective. This is for various reasons, above all because evil is a violation of a moral rule, and while a rule is an imperative to preserve life, evil is only its interruption. This is what prevents the universalization of evil. This is not due to the impossibility of following a maxim such as "you will commit all the atrocities within your reach," but because the interruption of life only exists as this or that kind of rupture. In this way, the utterance "do evil" does not say nearly enough. It is necessary to add "such and such evil has been done; as such and such harm has been done." Apart from instantaneous, evil is, after all, temporary. The will to do evil should, therefore, renovate itself continuously. That which attracted it like a magnet, in its eagerness to destroy, is no longer anything once the destruction has been fulfilled. The offender is thus obliged to start reinventing the process. It is a remarkable feat that its instantaneity and temporary character be transmitted to the offender. It could be that the criminal aspires to reach immortality through his monstrous acts. In reality, as Sartre wrote, the criminal writes his name in the water.[4] Everyone tries to erase his cursed inheritance, and even sometimes himself expresses his desire to disappear, to eclipse himself without leaving human prints, because he finds that nothing of value has been enough for him to measure up to. Perhaps, because of this, for a long time in the West, the most abhorrent acts were punished by dismembering and throwing away the small pieces of body that were left after the torture.

MINOR OFFENDERS

Just as evil can be a life choice brought to the most exquisite form of horror, there also exist those who violate the continuity of good with no such heroics, on one impulse, in only one dazzling moment. This refers to more or less strange natures who during their lifetime have lived beneath the laws of society, with minor predicaments, but that one day commit atrocious acts for which they owe a passing fame. These people are those minor beings that were useful to Foucault to show one the most significant changes of modernity. Foucault used the term "infamous lives,"[5] not only because they incurred the infamy, but above all because they do not enjoy the grandeur of those who, due to the abominable memories left behind, are awarded a respectful terror by others. These are "infamous" because they lack "fame," even that dubious fame constructed by all the reasons opposed to human greatness. When we call them "minor offenders" we do not wish to suggest that their crimes are less inhuman, because one crime also destroys good and promotes chaos. Yet they are minor because the short-lived light that rescued them from anonymity corresponds to the moment in which they stumbled against a way to exercise power. Their infamy is therefore momentary, partial; and they are small for the very reason that there is no memory of them, other than those words destined to convert them into undignified beings in the memory of men.

If it is worth talking about them at all, it is because they show, perhaps with greater transparency, the type of presence and reflection that the modern world devotes to the problem of evil. Put in another way, they clearly show in what measure the process which associates evil with individuality has been aggravated. In spite of its deformed countenance, evil has been unable to escape the general movement in which the modern individual finds himself trapped. Indeed, evil could not escape the "objectiveness" which has embedded it, as an "object" of reflection, in a web of knowledge and techniques, and which has focused on it by its individualization in a permanent and generalized vigil. Evil has not been able to escape the link with power in daily life. What M. Proust wrote about homosexuality in an ironic fashion has become true concerning evil: it is on the verge of becoming an exact science.[6]

In the process that lead to modernity and to the moral autonomy of a person, which found in Kant its philosophical expression, evil ceased to be ascribed to the extrahuman nature and to the biologically immutable nature of human beings, and was eventually established in the reflection and motivations of the individual; especially in the use of liberty and reason. Philosophy only detected part of the process, which went to the point of involving, in the case of minor offenders, the whole personality of the individual: his interests and calculations, his character, inclinations, and habits. Hence in modern times the attempt was made to ascribe certain evil acts to the personality and the overall conduct of the subject. It was in those acts where they hoped to find the hidden mechanisms of evil. Therefore, reflection about evil ceased to be exclusively moral or philosophical, but conceded its place to medical, physiological, and criminological discourses. As a matter of fact, they became so outstanding that the modern criminal, when he takes the floor, no longer offers a verbal spectacle of regret but expresses himself in the same discourse that condemns him. Previously things were easier: once the limits of goodness had been crossed, prohibitions broken, the offense discovered, the corresponding punishment was awaited. The well-deserved punishment was the culmination of evil, because evil never is more certain than when it is punished. All this time, the criminal had never had to face a question like, "Who are you?" The particularization characteristic of our times can be perceived in the change of the question, "What is the crime?" which nobody mentions, to the new question, "Who is the criminal?" From the act to the motive, and from the motive to the individual's character: this is the chain they are looking to pursue. If for some reason this chain of deduction is interrupted, so surges the sentiment that the crime has not been completely understood. The tendency of "finding the criminal responsible" once again culminates in punishment, because modern societies feel more alleviated when they judge and condemn a man, not because of the metaphysical side of evil, but just as he is, and for what he is.

Of course, we are not suggesting that we have come across this type of criminal for the first time in history. Without doubt, there have been innumerable acts of inhumanity committed by ordinary people that have not been registered in human memory. But the acts of modern criminals have come to light when a certain form of extensive, permanent vigilance practiced on each human being has been generalized. They were brought out of anonymity in the moment in which everyday life permitted records to be kept of those infamous acts committed throughout trivial lives. For a long time, only exceptional evil could stand out. That is why we only remember the major offenders: to be in the limelight it was indispensable to be outstandingly evil. Modern times, by contrast, have brought out a barrage of hates, resentments, conflicts, and vengeance which otherwise would have passed unnoticed because they were situated at the lowest and most persistent levels of reality.

We can draw two consequences from the close relation between the individual and the evil. On one hand, it is the offender who can offer the key to the understanding of the evil act. It is he, throughout the questioning and the exam, who offers the secret of the act, although he himself does not know it. Evil has been made visible by his conduct and, admitting that his behavior can be molded, the general idea is that there might be certain correctives applicable to evil. It is true that the origin, the primary source of evil, continues to be an enigma. Could anyone say that he knows the origin of the human being's inhumanity? However, by associating the act to the character, one comes to the conclusion that the corrective consists of molding the offender's conduct. This approach has contributed to the possible association of violence, which is the nucleus of evil, with social and cultural factors. Moreover, one could even say that the modern individual is at liberty to have any evil nightmares he desires, as long as he does not turn them into actual violence. If evil is difficult to understand, violence, on the other hand, appears to be controllable, and above all is a participant in that deep historic movement, discovered by N. Elias, which has led to the individual's permanent demand of self-control.[7] The even-tempered individual, who has gradually seen direct violence disappear from his life (shunning it in electronic spectacles), has been embedded in a close net of self-subjection principles: responsibility, daily vigilance, and the dominance of his impulses.

Secondly, since evil has been linked to character and conduct, and these are in turn modeled in the social order, the disruption of evil has become a failure for everyone, a disarray of the collective order. The criminal is a sign of the failure of our educational system, of our way of vigilance, and of the information we permit him to receive. It is possible that during no other historical moment has society felt so collectively guilty for the evil caused by so few. Containing evil has become a collective responsibility. That is why its presence is indicative of the lack of adequate control; and this is true because evil and violence are something that individual reason and the rules of society have committed themselves to amputate. As far as the conscience of our societies is concerned, evil inhabits not only grandiose personalities, and it is no longer a patrimony of the more educated that were above the multitude. The evil most feared at present comes from those marginal and wandering personalities, recognizable in the innermost fissures of our cities. For that reason, two characteristic patterns have appeared which show the way in which our societies stand up to the threat of evil. First of all, there are those who make an effort to create the social conditions which prevent the presence of evil: social workers, educators, and experts in family affairs. Secondly, there are the "specialists in motive," namely, those who decipher, among the personal secrets of the evildoers, the mechanisms of their actions: physicians, psychologists, criminologists, and lawyers.

Evil is a lack of humanity. But it is remarkable that, despite being the dark and evasive part it is, evil is also unable to escape the historical transformations imposed on the individual. However, beneath these transformations, evil persists and there seems no solution for it. We are left alone with its presence. In fact, unlike other beings, evil does not need to lay the foundations of its presence: I exist, therefore I suffer. In the face of evil, societies adopt a purely defensive, self-restrictive, and limitative attitude. This has determined the present perspective which is not entirely pessimistic because it refuses to grant legitimacy to the corruption of man. Neither is it entirely optimistic, because it refuses to consider inoffensive the constant threat which inhumanity is. Medieval wisdom was correct when it situated human beings somewhere between angels and beasts.

On Pain, the Suffering of Wrong, and Other Grievances

Responsibility

Manuel Cruz

This essay deals with my belief that responsibility is a problem that concerns us all. It is, I admit, an apparently simple conviction, yet it has left me quite convinced that the question of responsibility, which I address here, is a matter of the greatest importance, affecting us directly and in a manner that cannot be ignored.

A conviction, however, is neither a basic metaphysical principle nor a valuation that can be postulated without further ado and which, as such, is deemed safe from any theoretical challenge. Still less can it be considered mere methodological protocol, a Wittgensteinian ladder that can be dispensed with once the top rung has been reached. Any conviction worth its salt must be open to discussion. If not, it would run the (serious) risk that the belief to which it gave rise, far from being associated with critical enthusiasm—which is the way it should be—would have more in common with a blind, unshakable faith or with any other sinister variant of dogmatism or the absurd.

The conviction that interests us here lies on the borders with reality, not with silence. Put another way: the test of its truth is that it can function to some extent as a diagnosis, allowing us to see things differently than we did before we came to hold this conviction, in short, that we cannot continue to think in the same way. A conviction is therefore neither evidence nor an obvious manifestation. The expression to feel convinced that one is right—incidentally, somewhat contradictory—ought not to be applicable here.[1] (On another occasion I have suggested that perhaps the best definition of dogmatic is: the person who, in response to any objection raised against him, retorts "that only goes to strengthen my position.") On the contrary, we would on principle have to be suspicious of any reason that provided us with the exaggerated feeling of being safe from criticism. If I were to be pressed, there is nothing more desirable than the opposing point of view. Because the strength of a conviction is based on its capacity to shake up commonplaces and established truths, that is, it is based on its effectiveness at upsetting the edifice of commonly shared opinions (those that are worthy of no more consideration than a limp and weak "as we already know").

To what extent do these exceptional characteristics apply to my belief that responsibility is a common problem? Let us take a brief look at recent events. We have become aware of the importance of responsibility to all of us, for our daily life forces us to confront it in the most varied of contexts, ranging from what we expect from politicians to the creating, transforming, and issuing of labor reforms, educational problems, and many issues affecting the family. There are other major historical episodes where the idea of responsibility becomes an even greater problem—for example, the historical role played by the Catholic Church during World War II. It is only recently that the Pope acknowledged the Catholic Church's responsibility in the moral debacle of the Holocaust.

But what I would like to bring to our discussion is how the nature of responsibility is itself misunderstood and the difficulties that we have when we are confronted with its relation to our historical past and to our present. We appear to be witnessing the defense of responsibility from a range of angles, which in most cases only hinders our task of interpretation. If we take the case of politics, this point can perhaps be illustrated more clearly. Beyond question, conservative sectors are using the notion of individual responsibility with the thinly disguised aim of draining all content from the notion of collective responsibility—a notion which makes them uncomfortable, as it means a costly commitment to the most disadvantaged sections of society. These sectors prefer not to speak of society's responsibility to the unemployed, the sick, refugees, and, in general, all those who are marginalized; rather, they propose making it the individual responsibility of the unemployed to obtain a job, of the sick to take their medicine, of the active workforce to provide for their own pensions, and so on.

There is no need to resort to Manichaeanism nor demagogy: those who adopt this line can call on a long tradition that provides them with sound arguments to defend their position. If anyone were to reproach them for an attitude that means the neglect of the collective, the global or social dimension, they would probably reply that these are excessively large concepts and therefore unmanageable, and that to speak of them in terms of human action is not viable. Society and historical events are not thought to have protagonists. Neither does anything for which it could be held responsible: in them all we find is anonymous, autonomous movement. It is, therefore, useless to think that we can preach any variation of responsibility in these areas. Following this logic, the argument goes that responsibility only applies to those human actions undertaken by identifiable private individuals. Responsibility, they conclude, moves on a smaller stage among the bit parts assigned to individual human actions. This, clearly, constitutes a generalized program of withdrawal, the abandonment of any area linked to the public, the common, or the political domain. The world remains in this framework cut adrift, at the mercy of forces, tendencies, and even laws that are completely beyond our control.[2] In short, the world is abandoned to its fate.

Now, if we shift the discussion from political philosophy to moral philosophy, we see that here also the idea of responsibility frequently gives rise to confusion. For example, that which arises when responsibility is automatically bracketed with guilt—a concept about which, according to its critics, nothing need be said as it is disqualified from the start, due to its definition within a Judeo-Christian framework. As in the case described earlier, a large part of the explanation is to be found in the past, specifically and most importantly in the Nietzschean proposals regarding freedom, which have contributed enormously to the antipathy to this concept.

This is not the place to enter into a discussion of these views,[3] nor to seek refuge in the simple consequentialist argument of disqualifying a thesis because of the negative effects to which it might give rise. But it is necessary to clarify a few points. First, when considering—albeit cursorily—the differences between guilt and responsibility, the positive elements of the latter become apparent, perhaps more clearly so than by applying any other method. The fact that responsibility can be delegated, agreed upon, even contracted is indicative of what I wish to demonstrate. To the extent that responsibility lies with the person or institution that undertakes the reparation of the damages caused, the generalization of this mechanism advertises a change in the collective attitude. This change can be summarized as follows: after a certain point in the development of a modern society,[4] it is assumed that, independently of who the guilty party might be, any wrong must be redressed.

This new attitude is neither obvious nor trivial. Throughout history, human beings have tended to resign themselves to pain, catastrophe, and injustice in a fatalistic way, postponing, in the best of cases, the reparation of the suffering undergone in this life to the next. Today we have built into our mentality, our common sense, something perhaps even more important than the principle that the crime should not go unpunished, and this is the idea that the wrong (even if this be a natural wrong, something for which no personal responsibility can be attached) should be rectified.[5] The best evidence of just how widespread this idea has become is the rumpus caused by complaints, claims, and demands for compensation—both material and moral, which according to some is so characteristic of our society (to the point that on occasions we speak of the capacity shown by the citizens of certain countries to apportion responsibility for any matter as an indicator of their development).

Seen in this light, there are sufficient grounds to subject to careful scrutiny the positions of those who defend the need to deactivate responsibility in the collective sphere, which we referred to above: with this in mind, it could be said that what they are defending in reality is, to a certain point, a return to the state of nature in society. And we could go further: on the basis of this discussion it would even be worth reconsidering the outright disqualification of the concept of guilt which today seems to be so widespread. Because, if you will excuse these hastily drawn conclusions, what is wrong with our society is not that there is a proliferation of persons willing to apportion the blame, but rather the absence in equal proportions of those prepared to accept the slightest share of this blame. Continuing with the overly categorical statements: much worse than a general tendency toward self-accusation is that widespread temptation of innocence, to which Pascal Bruckner refers in his book of the same title.[6]

Lest it not be clear: we say that it is worse because it places those who incur it in a limbo in which they remain permanently in their minority, in a kind of original virgin state in which nothing, absolutely nothing, can be expected of them. For one reason or another such people are always—one might think on principle—on the side of the claimant. This is an impossible position—metaphysically impossible if I were to be pushed—given that if responsibility is fundamentally only applicable to your own acts, then the only ones who can escape the demands of others are those who never err, those who never carry out any act whatsoever or, the most unacceptable of the hypotheses, those whose acts, like those of the child or the madman, are not taken into account by anyone. Notwithstanding, it could be said that being safe from all reproach has ended up becoming one of the predominant fantasies in our society, whose cruel caricature is the unabashed cynicism with which most criminals, the world's greatest swindlers, and the perpetrators of the most monstrous acts of genocide are in the habit of declaring that they do not consider themselves to be guilty of anything. It is for this reason, perhaps, that the desire to be considered guilty has come to form the plot of novels of science fiction (I am thinking of the Danish writer Henrik Stangerup's *The Man Who Wanted to Be Guilty*).

Whatever the case, we need to proceed with caution so that this distinction in the argument does not give rise to fresh confusion. What I sought to make clear above was that perhaps guilt is not so terrible as it is often made out to be, not that it should be associated with responsibility. They are clearly different and this difference might take a variety of forms. Were we to incorporate the various features that distinguish the two concepts in one picture—of broad brushstrokes, it goes without saying—we would have to refer to the verticality of one as opposed to the horizontal nature of the other, to the necessarily intersubjective, dialogical character of responsibility, as opposed to the possible solipsism favored by guilt—which in this sense is more inclined to intrasubjectivity. Because while guilt in certain contexts is an issue that is solely concerned with the subject, and with the interiorization that that person makes of the norm (which allows the phenomenon to which we referred a moment ago, by which the cruelest of criminals might declare, without lying or any interior violence at all, that he does not feel guilty on any count), responsibility cannot be considered in terms of a private hermeneutic; it is not a business in which the subject deals alone with the norm. Responsibility, as its etymology reminds us, is structurally intersubjective. Without there being somebody to whom we are answerable, that is, without there being someone demanding that we give a response, there is no possible responsibility.

To speak of intersubjectivity might appear to amount to little, but at least it is something. Intersubjectivity can take many forms, from the most personal to the most public. In any case, this gradation, far from clouding the discussion, should allow us to be more precise. Because if the responsibility demanded by somebody is always in the name of something—be it a code, norm, or custom—the appeal will be that much more effective the more clearly established this point of reference is by all parties. In modern societies, for example, the relationship between a couple who choose to live together, beyond certain clearly specified circumstances (that they do so in certain conditions of equality, that they do not cause harm to any third party, that the relationship is not based on deceit, and so forth), belongs to the private domain, where it apparently escapes public control. It could be said that they are not subject to any general normative code in such a way that beyond any rhetorical formulation, it would make little sense if one member of the relationship should hold the other responsible for the suffering caused by the break up of the relationship. However, as self-apparent as this might be, the moment in which the initial situation is changed and children appear, marriage contracts are entered into (or, in their absence, the registering of common-law marriages), joint assets and properties are acquired, and so forth, a complex structure of laws, rules, and regulations that cannot be eluded entraps the individuals—that is, a public normative code that legitimizes demands for responsibility from the other party.

In this sense, it might well be said that it is responsibility that determines the intersubjectivity of the action, making this feature operative, virtually instrumental—albeit redundant in appearance—and which is used to designate the action as a human action. The emphasis should have significant theoretical consequences. Because if up to this point we have tried to warn against the negative effects that the systematic omission of the concept of responsibility might have, as well as the dangers of confusing it with other analogous though distinct concepts, it is important at this point to highlight the extent to which the connection with the idea of action is not worn away in the simple verification of the external matching up—a simple what corresponds to whom—but rather it affects the content of both categories.

To illustrate this last statement, one example should be sufficient. In recent years—in part due to the great impact of the thesis propounded by Hans Jonas[7]—the claim that man's responsibility today has expanded to such an extent that it has caught up with future generations has become commonplace. There has arisen, if we maintain the same terms used up to now, a new *to whom* our present actions must be accountable: those who have not yet been born. Yet this situation is not primarily the consequence of the introduction of a new theoretical criterion for understanding responsibility—why should we have expanded our idea of moral universality so much that it now includes those who are yet to come—rather it is the result of the fact that our present power has reached an unprecedented magnitude and our capacity to undertake actions that have long-term effects has developed to such an extraordinary degree[8] that we have caught up with the future inhabitants of planet Earth. In other words: this new *to whom* (we must account) is the necessary effect of a new *for what* (we are responsible).

Having established the connection between the categories, I can now return to some of my initial statements—which at the time could only be made in a purely programmatic way—in the hope that they can now be adequately justified. It is because there is such a strong connection between the ideas of responsibility and action that a reconsideration of the former inevitably has a great impact on the latter and vice versa. Hence, from the finding—in the main correct—that our behavior affects the lives of others and that we are constantly impinging on the feelings, impulses, resentments, and sympathies of others, we can draw the conclusion that, given that we are able to have such an influence on others, nothing is gratuitous and we have to shoulder many responsibilities. But we can also conclude this from the other side of the argument, to evoke Arendt,[9] to paraphrase Wittgenstein, and state that in the same way that there cannot be a strictly private language we should not speak too loudly of private human action. Among other reasons because this would mean exclusively identifying the human condition of this action in the agent, and that, with the possibility of being correct in some regard, leaves the idea totally depleted.

Were we to discuss the arguments in favor of a privatizing conception of the action, this would distract us from our stated aims. It is worth mentioning, however, that the defense of this position has specific theoretical costs, that is, it requires adopting certain premises from the outset. Those who hold this position are more or less required to begin their argument by postulating a rigid separation between an action and its effects or results—which should be considered distinct from the action and, therefore, not imputable to the agent. The problem is that this premise is far from indisputable. Many authors adopting different theoretical positions have underlined the impossibility of supporting this division.[10]

Nor would it be appropriate to reopen the debate regarding which is the most suitable perspective for establishing the content and the limits of the human action, or, to express the case in the terms that characterize analytical literature, the debate between those who defend the primacy of the point of view of the first person and those who support the primacy of the third person. The matter, as is evident, is directly concerned with the subject in hand, but it is preferable, given its enormous complexity, to put it to one side. Though I will point out, as I began to do elsewhere,[11] that there is no unilateral alternative that proves satisfactory. Leaving aside the fact that the balance between perspectives is not dealt with identically in all discourses (consider, for example, the contrast between the approach in moral philosophy, where we can only speak of responsibility for the action as it is assumed by the agent, and that in legal philosophy, where the principle applies that ignorance of the law does not excuse the failure to abide by this law), perhaps it might be proposed, in a general sense, that it is advisable to tend toward some form of equilibrium between the point of view of the first and third person: if not, we run the risk that, rather than contributing to configure the intersubjectivity that we mentioned earlier, what we find ourselves shoring up is some variant of either extrasubjectivity (objectivist) or intrasubjectivity (solipsist).

Yet the earlier observation that the action does not belong solely to the agent prompts the inevitable question: "in that case, to whom does it most belong?" Considering everything that has been discussed up to this point, a response could be: the action also belongs to all those who demand responsibility for it. I should emphasize that this statement is not free of its own consequences. It implies the questioning of widely spread clichés, but perhaps this constitutes the most encouraging of its aspects. Not in vain did I state at the outset of this article that the strength of a conviction is measured by its capacity to shake up commonplaces and accepted truths in our society. If this were what was occurring now, we would have the best evidence to show that we are not entirely on the wrong track if we plump for that initial conviction as regards responsibility.

Seen from this perspective, it would be difficult to find actions that might still claim to be private. Of course many of those that before formed the paradigmatic examples of this group would have lost this condition. Thus, there was a time not so long ago in which—probably as a result of the notoriety attained by existential philosophies—certain clichés regarding the unrestricted sovereignty of individuals over their own lives held sway, including the indisputable right to take one's own life. The latter was usually considered a strictly private matter, in which it was believed that it was the business of each and every one of us to weigh up whether the benefits of existence were sufficient to persist in the endeavor, whether sufficient doses of courage had been stockpiled to abandon the world of the living, and so forth.[12]

Let us not create unnecessary misunderstandings: public authorities often do not know how to confront difficult problems with regard to responsibility in cases such as suicide or euthanasia. But an immediate warning should be issued concerning two aspects. The first, and perhaps less important because of its obvious nature, is that such behavior loses its condition of being incommunicado with consummate ease. It seems clear that as soon as we use the argument of the absence of damage to third parties to demand, for example, specially designated areas (for prostitution, for the trade and consumption of illegal substances, etc.), to demand free detoxification treatment and/or the provision of the means whereby addicts can satisfy their need in appropriate sanitary conditions, such actions abandon the realm of the strictly private and enter fully into the public sphere.

The second aspect, intimately connected to the first, serves in fact as a reminder. Responsibility—and we should never lose sight of this—can take many forms; just one of which, though not the main one, is legal responsibility. There is, therefore, not the slightest contradiction in supporting the decriminalization (and in this sense, the "deresponsibilization") of a given behavior, while at the same time holding the agent responsible for the act, only that the responsibility demanded is of a different type. One can, for instance, reproach a friend for betraying one's trust without this meaning that such behavior should be legislated against. In the same way, although adultery has been removed from the criminal code, this does not mean that it should be considered irrelevant but rather that it has been returned to the realm of personal intersubjectivity.

Both clarifications, which might be considered excessively scrupulous, are in reality directed at clearing the path for what follows. Having called into question the idea of private action as such, taken to its most absurd point (What would such an action be? Perhaps only that which has absolutely no effect on others, but can such an act be said to exist?), we will now examine what perhaps constitutes the most significant theoretical difficulty, that is, establishing the procedure by which we institute somebody as the legitimate claimant (and, in the same way, coproprietor of the action). It might be thought that it is the fact of having suffered damages caused by a human action that grants the injured party the right to make a claim. But this situation is too simple, in that it has an objective basis that seems to offer us the perspective as to how it should be solved. The problem arises in other cases. For example, when the damage caused is suffering and, therefore, it is not evident how this pain can be redressed.

At times we come across statements such as, "any victim is innocent," and "those who suffer are always right." Perhaps these are far from obvious assertions, but we know they ease our consciences in light of the virtual unanimity with which they are accepted. Yet, solidarity—though perhaps in this context it would be better to speak of compassion—with those who suffer should not prevent us from explicitly asking, "Can we bring a claim for having suffered?" which means, "What is the specific content of a claim of this type?" It is best to approach it in an open manner, not out of any desire to be provocative or iconoclastic, but rather because on many occasions it seems to be a requirement of a conviction that it should be called into question. I refer to all those cases in which it is taken for granted that there is a preexisting, tangible asset—to which it would seem we have a right—which we could call well-being or happiness, an asset that was destroyed as a result of the suffering caused by somebody's behavior and that now should be redressed, restoring the initial calm.

It is not a matter of opposing an ingenuous optimism, of a slight Rousseauan inspiration, against a pessimism of neat conservative cut—of the form "we were brought into this world to suffer," "we are in the valley of tears," or such—but rather of calling attention to the effects of maintaining given premises. And what is the significance of the fact that the claim for responsibility is usually presented as the mere demand to reestablish the state of things as they were before the damages were inflicted? Very simply: that the claimant gives the appearance of somebody who is doing nothing, remaining almost completely passive. Someone who restricts himself or herself to claiming that everything be put back to how it was before.

Yet it is clear that anyone, for example, who was unable to be happy as a child has forfeited this opportunity forever. Similarly, an eventual claim cannot seek to reestablish a situation that cannot be reestablished, but rather, perhaps, it can seek reparation (which is quite a different matter) or even revenge (sometimes hidden in the type of punishment). In this context there is nothing to object to in either,[13] as long as they do not conceal their real nature. Since both constitute different forms of action they could be termed reaction, but perhaps it would be better to incorporate them in a wider context of interaction in order to understand them better: An interaction that does not recognize itself as such, but for all intents and purposes is an interaction. The demands for punishment which we alluded to above might serve to illustrate the real nature of this conceptual operation. Since the punishment by which someone pays off a debt to the claimant, to put it in Nietzschean terms, does not allow anything to be restored, or for things to be returned to the way they were before (it should at least serve to rid the person responsible of the temptation to rescind, or to dissuade third parties from carrying out similar acts). The punishment is clearly a form of acting against the person who acted first. It does not limit itself to demand a response from the other but rather that he respond to the action that caused the damage.

My intention is not to engage in what is merely an academic discussion of terminology. Depending on which way we approach the matter we are left open to very different theoretical and practical consequences. In any case, if it is necessary to account for the idea of responsibility it is precisely because we have to put it to an undesirable use. The superiority of the category of responsibility over that of guilt, which we commented on earlier, is not a guarantee of the validity of the former in any context. And not only because positive aspects of guilt might be identified—rest assured, a question I shall not go into now—but because, on the contrary, responsibility gives rise to its own dangers, the main one being that of obscuring the nature of our undertakings.

This obscuring effect is not simply the fact that the action itself, when presented as a claim, is not perceived as the said action: we can go further than this and speak of the production of a genuine mechanism of ignorance. The most negative aspect of this "victimism," of the widespread willingness to put oneself ontologically in the place of the claimant, is its tendency to give rise to a derationalized way of thinking, since what makes someone a victim is not the reasons that protect him, but rather the insults to which he has been exposed.

This tendency is probably best illustrated as it functions in the political debate. What does the political debate become when we give way to this temptation? The question is somewhat rhetorical, in that we know at least one of the answers: we convert the political debate into a self-assertive (irrational) litany of insults. And of the consequences of injecting irrationality into politics, we should have learnt something from history by now. Thus, changing the scale and taking the bloodiest example of the twentieth century, the victimist ideology of fascism did not only consist in the doctrine of the superior race, but more accurately in that of the humiliated superior race. From this premise, duly shielded by renouncing the demands to justify rationally the positions adopted, the rest fits automatically into place and the discourse/excuse of the redress can be used at will: we have to reestablish an original (mythical) order that others altered. Nothing new is being sought, simply the reestablishment of what there was before.

Where does this degree of warning lead us? Well, to attempt to clarify a little the content of our defense—if such an emphatic term can be used in this case—it is not a question of postulating or proposing a return to responsibility at any price. But the fact that we have been so measured in our discussion up to this point should help us to be discretely categorical at the outcome. The appeal to responsibility should not become a systematic occasion for producing a paralyzing resentment. Rather on the contrary, it should serve to launch us into the action, fully aware that there is something in it that is ours, that belongs to us—although not in terms of private property. It is evident that, in the first instance, it will sound strange to talk of ownership as regards an action, but it would sound even stranger to talk of ownership in relation to persons, and yet we are bombarded everywhere with the message that we belong to a community. In reality, in this discussion what I have sought to do has been to emphasize that the action is not a territory occasionally crossed by subjects, but rather one of the constituent dimensions of its identity. This is the element of profound truth that is contained within such statements as "we are what we do." Whatever the case, responsibility, if I might borrow for a moment a play on words from Kant, should be the test of our coming of age, not the excuse to remain in a Peter Pan state.

Having cleared away the thorny undergrowth of the discussion, a theoretical landscape, quite distinct to that at the outset, should rise up before our eyes. The concept of responsibility has served, at last, to restore to the subjects (note the plural) what is theirs, what should never have been allowed to escape them. What has been done by the agents does not have the same status as the acts of nature, for the obvious reason that there are no actors in nature. But it is to naturalize, in the worst sense of the word, human life if we become embroiled in the size or limits of the actions as such, as if they had become autonomous, as if they had attained a status that allowed us to develop a discourse of the actions without mentioning the agents.

An ontological reduction of the world should not be accepted uncritically, as if the actions were served up to us in this condition—ready-cut, prepacked, defined—in such a way that these actions are marched in procession before the subject, who does no more than declare himself responsible (or otherwise). From such an image we come away with a picture of responsibility à la carte, which gives no consideration to what is really important. We are not debating whether we should accept responsibility for that which falls within our jurisdiction: we have heard sufficient arguments supporting this. But we should go further than this and introduce the idea of a responsibility that is much more generic, a responsibility that goes beyond this. The idea would allow us, at the extreme, to speak of responsibility for life itself. This could be the appropriate content[14] for the expression "be responsible." Responsibility would lie with that person who would take charge of life itself in its entirety in the same way that someone assumes their destiny.

The conviction we began this discussion with has in the course of this essay been filled out, acquiring strength and complexity along the way. We began by arguing that responsibility is a matter of the greatest importance, affecting us directly and in a manner that cannot be ignored, and I should like to think that this proposal has led to the unfolding of most of its virtues. Responsibility is not only of interest to us because it forms one of the "issues of our age," or something similar, but rather because it goes right to the crux of our existence. It means that reality is seen in another light: that actions reveal their dark, hidden underside. We can therefore conclude, as in the paragraph above, by calling for a change of scale, an exhortation to take responsibility for life itself.

Having come this far, the reader will probably have realized that what we set out to answer apparently remains unanswered, that is a question of "great significance": the procedure by which someone acquires the right to make a claim. By changing scale we have not tried to diffuse the question, but rather to set it in its rightful place. This implies, among other things, rescuing the appeal to the suffering of others from the pharisaic moralistic use to which it is usually subjected. In short, it implies we take this appeal seriously. We know that suffering does not convert the sufferer into a better person, nor does it free them from having to respond to the damage they might have caused on another occasion. That is why it is useless to harp on the sufferings of a fellow human being, as if the mere fact of expressing opposition will place the person presenting the formulation in a theoretically unassailable position.

In general, what the call to be responsible does is raise the stakes, elevating responsibility to the rank of a major commitment, with an almost universal nature. Hans Jonas would probably have spoken of a commitment with the human genre, with the species itself. A commitment which, in any case, forces us to confront one last question: Who would have the right to make such a claim? This amounts to asking: To whom must we hold ourselves responsible when faced by this global responsibility? Probably the question answers itself: we are responsible to those who need us.

13

Forgiveness and Oblivion

A New Form of Banality of Evil?

Carlos Pereda

This essay is divided into four distinct parts. First, I propose some argument strategies for dealing with violators of human rights, taking into account recent situations in Latin America. In the second part I seek to explore to what kinds of disputes these considerations belong. In the third part, which can almost be regarded as a shift of scenery, I connect my discussion—perhaps in a problematic and risky way—with the arguments triggered by Hannah Arendt in her valuable work on the "banality of evil." My suspicion is that, again and again, we will come up against "abstract hate" and "abstract love" while searching for a justification for such "banality." In the fourth part I attempt an approach to the problem of responsibility. These parts are relatively independent and very different as to their tone, level of generality, and length. I hope they contain convergent and worthy points to begin a debate.

I

I shall begin by considering an example which, in a sense overflowing with consequences, brings again into play the difficult relationship between memory and evil, and particularly between social memory and some social ills. I am referring here to the serious problem of the impunity that those who have violated human rights have occasionally enjoyed. At the end of World War II, the message of the Allies in the case of criminals who held high military ranks was intended to be categorical: it was necessary to judge and punish them. This was a way to enforce strictly the moral point of view, while relying on the full force of the law. During the 1980s, this attitude changed in several countries of Latin America. By invoking—with good reason—the Spanish transition to democracy (the process by which Spain overthrew Franco's regime), the change was justified as imposed by political requirements, although—as it is often indicated without hesitation—it overtly opposed the dictates of morality. Thus, the following deliberation was common in many of those countries: after the dictatorships, which have terrorized and divided large sectors of our population, the social function of the memory of evil must be the reconciliation and stabilization of our poor republics. Instead of the moral, "trial-and-punishment" strategy, we are urged to adopt the political, "forgiveness-and-oblivion" strategy. Thus, in Brazil the military regime ended with a wide-ranging amnesty in 1985. In Uruguay the Law for the Expiration of the Punitive Plans of the State of 1989 represented an amnesty law as well. In Argentina the *obediencia debida* (due obedience) laws and the *punto final* (full stop) decrees brought to a close the trials of 1986 and 1987. In 1978 an amnesty decree in Chile withdrew accusations against police agents and members of the military who had been charged with human rights violations. Since 1981 many pardons and amnesties have been granted in Colombia.

What sense should we make of this political strategy designed to cope with the social ills of a recent past? It is not, of course, a new option. One can remember in this respect Cicero, one of the masters of the tradition of prudence, speaking before the senate after the death of Julius Caesar, amidst intrigues and rumors, and while legions were threatening to stage a coup in the streets:

> Such was not long ago the condition of the Republic, bowing to the yoke of those who with weapons in their hands dictated our decisions, instead of allowing us to prescribe what should be done. Today things have changed. . . . And being so, I think it absolutely necessary to banish all kinds of discord, to forget all resentments, and to abjure all enmities in order to bring back peace.

We can pick up Cicero's argument and proceed as follows. In situations such as those found in Latin America during the last decades, the moral, trial-and-punishment strategy puts at risk the most important efforts in these nations, intended to attain a transition to democratic, peaceful, and stable regimes, and the reconstruction of their institutions. And can one exclude the armed forces from a national reconciliation? If they are not fully incorporated into the life of the republic, is there any chance for peace and tranquility? Moreover, the moral strategy seems to be concerned only with the past; its aim is the punishment of certain individuals and, by realizing that all the wrong these individuals have done cannot be modified, it tries to provide symbolic compensations. Unfortunately, there is no redemption for the dead: nothing human can comfort them, save them, or compensate for their suffering and their loss. The dead are dead.

Furthermore, the trial-and-punishment strategy, insofar as it represents a requirement of good conscience, tends to polarize society, dividing it into the innocent and the guilty—the good guys and the bad guys. This destabilizes the life of the community by bringing back all the dangers it was try-ing to expel: since every transition contains many of the tensions and con-flicts of the past, at each step we run the risk of reproducing those tensions and conflicts. (The four attempted coups in Argentina during the trials, the fact that in Uruguay the Law for the Expiration was ratified in 1989 by ref-erendum, the prestige enjoyed by a former dictator—now "life senator"—in important sectors of his country, and the electoral successes achieved by well-known violators of human rights, confirm thought-provoking data and surely support this argument to some degree.) On the contrary, the politi-cal, forgiveness-and-oblivion strategy does not focus on individuals. Nor is it symbolic: it is concerned with the present and above all with the future, with the construction of democratic and just institutions. For, is it not true that what really matters in life are the present goods and their continuation—future goods?

Now it is time for an unpleasant, nervous worry: Are we urged to suppress the demands of memory and morality in order to adopt slogans such as "the past doesn't matter," or "moral considerations are out of place in political issues"? Are we going to eliminate, just like that, the invasions of evil in our society, in the name of aspirations for a good social life—such as peace, democracy, stability—and pretend to continue our lives as if evil had never touched us? But, does this not condemn us to spread a new and perhaps more treacherous form of "banality of evil"?

However plausible it may seem, this venerable political argument seeks to expel the suffered ills from the social memory, and thereby to eliminate all the demands for a good life. However plausible, this argument produces cer-tain perplexities. Although every history is a story of commemorations, a past of social terror begins to oppress people if one decides to turn one's back on it and try to evade it, if one tries to remain ignorant of those ills that one knows that one must know. This is not the only puzzlement, for while it is true that not all memories can liberate us, the "mandate to forget" binds us; it ties us to that imposed or self-imposed oblivion; it sacrifices that past full of ills which, in a contradictory movement, at once knows and denies itself.

Thus, the official "mandate to forget" yields a form of arrogant reason that pervades people and communities, a reason which knows but does not want to know when and how the mechanism of excessive self-assertion and disdain turned this contempt for the others into the kind of radical evil con-stituted by "abstract hatred": a hatred that had a license for everything, even a license to torture and a license to kill. How can we forget the abstract hatred propagated by the terrorism of the dictatorship that governed Argentina between 1976 and 1983? How to expel from our social memory the license for everything that led to the "flights of death" organized by the Argentinean navy, in which fourteen hundred people, naked and drugged, were thrown into the sea from airplanes, and in which fifteen hundred officers were implicated? How can we forget that Santiago de Chile's stadiums turned into extermination camps?

In addition to these remarks on the ills involved in a mandate to forget, I would like to point to the fact—which the champions of the political strategy also insist on—that the past is often not a closed past; it can also be a past that is still present: an effective past. People do not only dwell among the living, they also roam among ghosts, and are sometimes besieged by them. And social memory, including the social memory of evil, belongs somehow to personal memories. This is the reason why, when a trial is carried out, people are already formed or deformed by a certain past, and even sometimes they find themselves in a constant dialogue with it.

Thus, in order not to forget about ourselves, should we never forget? Above all, should we never forget the wrong we have done or the wrong other people have done to us? But, is not an unqualified mandate never to forget as harmful to life, as paralyzing, as the no-less-unqualified mandate to forget?

Perhaps this is one of those moments in which we must confront the proposed alternative—or maybe we should say the imposed alternative—"trial and punishment" versus "forgetfulness and oblivion." I wonder whether the choice thus articulated is nothing more than a simplifying vertigo.

I think that we have let ourselves be confused with that vertigo, this time under the influence of the law. For the law is not the only way to settle social conflicts: it contains only one of the vocabularies with which one can conceive of a community. To be sure, law is an indispensable tool for any civilized way of life; however, it does not exhaust either the personal or the social possibilities of judgment.

In a democracy one can only judge individuals in a trial by providing conclusive evidence in accordance with the law. However, in most cases, perhaps what is more important in relation to a social past made up of horror is, if not to forget and judge, to make use of the technique of reformulating problems in order to be able to pass from a narrowly legal reconstruction of the problem raised by the impunity of human rights violators to a restatement of the problem, mainly in political terms. As Pablo de Greiff proposes, the aim is to "depersonalize the judgment" and to resist the understandable desire for revenge, among other temptations. (We should always bear in mind that revenge is sown in the wind. The desire for revenge for a suffered wrong somehow continues this wrong; it transforms us into its slave as long as we keep working in its favor, especially if, in vain, we strive to recuperate what is lost—if delusion demands that somebody "pay" a debt that we know is unpayable.)

What does this political restatement of judgment require from us? It forces us to abandon the sphere of pure law and to institutionalize in public life the social memory of those ills we arrogantly refuse to acknowledge.

Every history chooses how to start, what to tell, and when to end: every history remembers and forgets. After social catastrophes such as a military dictatorship or a civil war, we must redo the "national histories," and include in them the suffering of the victims: reconsidering it as part of our past, of our own tradition and even—tough as it is—as a latent menace forever.

Thus, to retell those histories obliges us to take part in a moral battle to decide what should be recuperated and, sometimes, what we wish to suppress. It is a way of using the tortures and crimes to construct monuments which warn us, and which, therefore, are not directed toward the past.

II

Nonetheless, we should be careful not to invest—perversely—these arguments with the character of complete generality. For no argument of this sort can replace specific discussions, full of variables and particularities. A debate with a medium level of generality, such as the one I have sketched, is often useful as a "map" of possible routes of argumentation. And the conclusions drawn from these debates do not usually amount to more than a prima facie or "in principle" proposal. But, in addition to debates of this kind, there will be many local discussions that will introduce hitherto neglected data, which perhaps will confirm good reasons to go against the prima facie conclusion. For instance, regarding massive assassinations, there might have been one or several people who made most of the political decisions, a tyrant responsible for them—although he himself, as we will see, may ignore the fact by "not thinking" about it—and, in that situation, it is perhaps well justified to bring him to trial, especially if, as in the Nuremberg trials or in the 1998 case of the Spanish judges and Pinochet, the trial is carried out by an external authority that does not belong to the community in conflict—so it may probably not risk the "transition" efforts of that community (although this will always be a matter of debate that will have to be discussed *in situ*).

What should be demanded in this kind of situation, of course, is the formation of real international courts, in order to prevent the state to which these courts belong from succumbing to the paternalist temptation of the worst "good conscience"—of arrogant reason. (But, it may be objected, what about countries? And what about national sovereignties? This seems to be a strange "nationalist" arrogance, common to those who defend that there should be no borders for business, but that there should be borders for justice, as if money were a good that enjoyed privileges—extraterritorial rights, for instance—which goods such as human rights lacked.)

So let us avoid the arrogance of the general standpoint—of the more abstract perspectives—which encourages us to believe that the more or less wide-ranging discussions solve "everything" and "forever," as well as the arrogance of the particular standpoint of the local perspectives, where we are forced to think that each situation is so unique, so specific, and so closed, that we can learn nothing from analogous situations or from more general points of view. But, is not productive argumentation rather a matter of establishing reciprocal illuminations between discussions with various degrees of generality? In a different, but perhaps analogous way, is there an interdependence between punishment and forgiveness, memory and oblivion, a time for dwelling on the past and the time for overcoming the old, for reviving, for starting again?

III

I return now to a couple of remarks introduced incidentally in the first section. To a certain extent, they preside over and even generate this train of thought. While discussing the arguments against the motto "forgiveness and oblivion" I asked myself: But, does this not condemn us to spread a new and perhaps more treacherous form of banality of evil? I tried later to warn against the mechanism of excessive self-assertion and the disregarding attitude which transforms this contempt for others into the kind of radical evil constituted by abstract hatred.

Let us focus in detail—although from a more general standpoint than before—on both remarks. The first one refers to different forms of banality of evil. What are these?

Allow me to make a detour at this point. In 1946, Karl Jaspers sent to his former pupil and lifelong friend Hannah Arendt his book *Die Schuldfrage* (The Guilt Question) where he discusses the Nazi crimes and German guilt. While commenting on the book, Arendt was somehow irritated with the word "crime," which seemed to her inaccurate to designate the monstrous acts of the Nazis. Jaspers's reply is categorical:[1]

> You say that what the Nazis did cannot be comprehended as "crime." I'm not altogether comfortable with your view, because a guilt that goes beyond all criminal guilt takes on a streak of "greatness"—of satanic greatness—which is for me as inappropriate for the Nazis as all the talk about the "demonic" element in Hitler and so forth. It seems to me that we have to see those things in their total banality, in their prosaic triviality, because that's what truly characterizes them. Bacteria can cause epidemics that wipe out nations, but they remain bacteria. I regard any hint of myth and legend with horror.[2]

This diagnosis is still valid against all "postmodern fashions" trying to surround with "myth and legend" the "brilliant degenerations" of Heidegger, Ernst Jünger, and many others, including the outrages of the charismatic Latin American patriarch in turn. As for Arendt, she must have forgotten Jaspers's precise words—she never quotes them—but, to be sure, she learned the lesson well. Almost twenty years later, on 16 February 1963, the first of her five articles on Eichmann's trial was published in the *New Yorker.* In May of that year they were collected in *Eichmann in Jerusalem: A Report on the Banality of Evil.* Since this indispensable book, the phrase "banality of evil" has become the name of a whole strategy for reconstructing problems. It started being used and discussed, and it aroused heated debates, thus becoming relatively independent from the use Arendt gave to it.

I think that this demystifying rhetoric on evil, and all deflationary strategies, are useful. They recast facts that tend to be surrounded with an aura of greatness—in this case of "depraved greatness," if there is such a thing—from the point of view of baseness.[3]

The adoption of this point of view is, to be sure, a technique used by comic writers from Aristophanes and Molière to the best cartoons in journals, which are able to uncover, with only a few strokes, the twisted behavior of politicians. But also the tradition of the essay and its search for a "casual tone of voice" sometimes achieves this effect.

On the other hand, this deflationary technique, and perhaps even the phrase "banality of evil," had already been used by the political discourse of the anti-Nazi resistance, among others by Brecht, either when in plays such as *Der aufhaltsame Aufstieg des Arturo Ui* (The Irresistible Ascent of Arturo Ui) Hitler is compared with a simple gangster transformed by the circumstances into something more, much more, or when Brecht depicts *Die Geschäfte des Herrn Julius Caesar* (The Business of Julius Caesar) as the career of a shrewd and corrupt businessman.[4]

But, what sense can we make, generally speaking, of the slogan "banality of evil"? What is that kind of rhetoric? According to Arendt a banality of evil emerges as a consequence of a deep inability to think about the atrocious acts that are being committed, so the agent does not realize what he transforms into when he commits these acts. As to Eichmann, Arendt comments: "The longer one listened to him, the more obvious it became that his inability to speak was closely connected with an inability to think, namely to think from the standpoint of somebody else."[5]

The last phrase, "to think from the standpoint of somebody else," is of course the second maxim introduced by Kant in paragraph 40 of the *Critique of Judgment,* "On taste as a kind of *sensus comunis.*" The point there is how to learn to think and to think about ourselves by adopting the point of view of the third person—the virtue of impartiality.[6] In order to exercise this ability we need (among other virtues, both theoretical and practical) those virtues which are pointed out by the other two maxims of paragraph 40: "to think by oneself," or virtue of autonomy, and "to always think according to oneself," or virtue of integrity.

It goes without saying that the kind of thinking that follows such maxims or virtues is characteristic of "reflexive judgment": according to Kant, it is the judgment that is able to judge from a particular standpoint without any subsumption of general or universal rules. Kant had in mind here aesthetic judgments, while Arendt is especially interested in moral judgments: the ability to judge in a given situation where the agent can hardly appeal to universal rules for guidance.

So now we have a first meaning for banality of evil: people do wrong without thinking, and even without any particular reasons for doing so. So they merely do it because they are unable to acknowledge what they are doing when they do wrong: "Except for an extraordinary diligence in looking out for his personal advancement, he had no motives at all. . . . [Eichmann] merely, to put the matter colloquially, never realized what he was doing."[7]

I am not interested in discussing whether Eichmann did not really have any personal reasons to do what he did. Let us suppose that Arendt's picture is correct. Moreover, surely there are many cases that fall into this first type of "banality of evil."

However, regardless of Arendt's approach, I would like to consider three more possible types of banality of evil. A second type can be discerned when people do have reasons, whether significant or trivial, to do wrong, but this wrongdoing becomes a catastrophe under certain social circumstances that they do not take into account, or rather deny to take into account. Anyone who has been through a situation of political terror knows that the most trifling reasons—for instance, a quarrel over cutting a tree in the boundary of two properties, or even an old grudge, the product of an unrequited love—may lead a decent person to become an informer, someone who accuses his neighbors or acquaintances, without thinking about the fatal consequences those accusations may have.

Let us turn back for a moment to Jaspers's letter. There is also in it a metaphor about bacteria that cause wide epidemics. This metaphor is like that of a wheel which by itself is not very significant, but which produces the movement of a machine when put together with other mechanisms, each one insignificant by itself. I can think that what I am doing is a bad deed, although it may be a small evil in which—I tell myself—"everybody" participates. Besides, whether I do that deed or not, the institutions of my society, the "system," will remain the same; and anyhow, I would be the only one affected if I put up any resistance.[8] For, as is well known, "that's how things are," "that's how institutions are," "that's how people are." In other words: "that's what we are."

With regard to this third kind of banality of evil, the resignation to institutions considered unavoidable, one may also speak, with Seyla Benhabib, of a "routinization of evil."[9] (This is the kind of banality of evil that is usually used to justify corruption in most countries.)

In my opinion, one can find very frequently in the recent dictatorships of Latin America—Argentina, Brazil, Chile, Uruguay—especially the last two kinds of "banality of evil": people many times let themselves be carried by mean reasons, or merely give up any form of resistance that could make them seem suspicious or exclude them from the "system."

On the other hand, I maintain—against Arendt—that the three kinds distinguished here are ideal kinds of "banality of evil." In the real world they are usually degrees of a continuum, and one can often move easily from one kind of evil to another: evil as an inability to think and to think for myself; evil as a lack of discernment of the immediate and later consequences of one's own reasons and deeds; and evil as a form of resignation to the "routinization" or "normalization" of evil.

To repeat: I think that there is in those three kinds of trivialization a banality of evil connected with the first person, the agent of action: the individual who does the wrong. We are not dealing here with "monsters," "satanic greatness," "bewitched auras," nor "witches' sabbath to Lucifer." But, I must insist, is not all this imagery of evil nothing more than fantasies: projections of our fears and frustrations, or of our wishes and jealousy in the very depths of our hearts? We are facing individuals who are not smart enough and are not willing enough to become martyrs—just like most of us. These people under different, less tragical social circumstances could have been our kind neighbors, or at least ordinary citizens.

But—and with this I close my long digression—there would be a fourth kind of banality of evil if we turn from agents to those who, once all is done, establish a relation with past deeds and simply declare "forgiveness and oblivion." This is the sense I would like to underline here: there is not only a possibility of trivializing evil by doing it—from the standpoint of the first person—but also by evaluating it, when we judge it from the standpoint of the second and third persons. The homogeneous "mandate to forget" embedded in the expression "forgiveness and oblivion" is exactly a way of trivializing an unforgivable evil.

Therefore—turning back to my discussion in section I—anybody who, faced with the military terror in Latin America, declares "forgiveness and oblivion" is burdened with a fractured social memory that he unsuccessfully tries to ignore. The acceptance of impunity regarding the systematic violation of human rights ends up contaminating with that very evil the inner lives of individuals and societies.

Thus, the pain we have suffered or inflicted on other people pervades our wishes, beliefs, feelings, and emotions. And the cowardice involved in denying them—in obeying the "mandate to forget"—often distorts judgment. Taken to a limit, it makes us ignore who we are. And, sometimes, to forget is to forget oneself.

The last sentence reasserts the common attributes in the four kinds of banality of evil under consideration: they are all generated from an imposed and/or self-imposed mandate to forget, from an inability to think about what I must think about. This is, in other words, a neglect of those epistemic and practical virtues mentioned in paragraph 40 of the *Critique of Judgment*—impartiality, autonomy, and integrity—and thus it is a way to succumb to their respective vices: narrowness, servility, and corruption.

However, let us turn now to the second remark and to the proposed relation between radical evil and what I called "abstract hatred." My hypothesis is the following: sooner or later we tend to forge, as a justification of the four kinds of banality of evil, a suicidal combination with abstract love and abstract hatred.

First of all, let us point to the fact that an abstract hatred usually exhibits in contrast an abstract love. Here are some well-known oppositions: Jews versus Aryans, foreigners versus natives, Protestants versus Catholics, barbarism versus civilization, despotism versus liberty, liberals versus socialists, the bourgeoisie versus the revolutionaries, westerners versus easterners, Spanish versus Basques, ungovernability versus progress, moral versus politics, in short, them against us. If my conjecture is correct, anybody who feels an abstract hatred in relation to the first term of the opposition will most surely experiment an abstract love toward the second.

What do I mean here by abstract hatred and abstract love? When we come across one or the other we are facing the following:

(*a*) Homogeneous beliefs; that is, no aspects are distinguished in the objects of our love or hatred, so there are no details in the beliefs contained in our love or hatred, nor any particularities, nuances, ambiguities, or doubts. Jews are "bad," Aryans are "good"; foreigners are "bad," fellow countrymen are "good," and so let us defend our nation! Let us solemnly declare, as is declared in so many national anthems: "our country or the grave!" Of course, this hatred or love is ruled by the "all or nothing" mechanism.

(*b*) We also find unlimited wishes. That is why in the case of abstract love "anything is permitted in order to defend the object of love." And regarding abstract hatred, "anything is permitted in order to attack the object of hatred." From the standpoint of an abstract hatred or an abstract love, no effort is in vain if we are to defend our cause, whether it be the cause of Civilization, Liberty, Revolution, the Church, the Party, or whatever. Any wish will be approved if it aims to destroy Barbarism, Despotism, and so forth.

So these are absolute attitudes that do not even need to be joined by specific emotions, for, unlike our particular loves and hates, they conform to general attitudes, or perhaps better, general suppositions that we forbid ourselves to examine from case to case. We all know the old slogans: "Everything is permitted under Civilization; nothing is permitted against Civilization"; "Everything is permitted under the Revolution; nothing is permitted against the Revolution." Hence, from the standpoint of abstract hatred the diagnosis is always the same: "Everything is wrong." And from the standpoint of abstract love we inevitably always hear "Everything is fine." Nothing there can be negotiated, discussed, or argued. Many times there is nothing to calculate, not even from the economic point of view. (It makes one shiver just to think about it, but has anybody ever calculated the economic disaster of the Nazis', or Stalin's, concentration camps? Did the Argentinean navy have any cheaper method of assassination other than putting people on planes and throwing them into the sea?)

It may be objected that perhaps it is inadequate to think that in the first three kinds of banality of evil there operates, as an ultimate justification, or at least as an ultimate explicit justification, the combination of an abstract hatred with an abstract love. From the Nazi leaders to the military of Argentina, Chile, Brazil, or Uruguay, who imprisoned their neighbors, one can surely describe a large part of their behavior in terms of the three kinds of "banality of evil": if we asked those different agents why they did what they did, they would probably appeal to one of the oppositions mentioned above: Jews versus Aryans, foreigners versus fellow countrymen, despotism versus liberty.

Let us suppose the last paragraph is correct. Nonetheless, in what sense can one justify the slogan "forgiveness and oblivion" with a combination of abstract love and abstract hatred?

I think that when this attitude is rationalized as "imposed by political requirements," we get tangled up again in an "abstract love," and such requirements serve to avoid detailed examination. After all, sometimes the decision to break away from the self-deception—which is represented by the immediate advantages of the "mandate to forget"—and to restore the social memory of the many atrocities, impels us to restructure the present and design new life projects. Wounds often heal faster in the open air.

But, if some of these remarks and arguments are accepted, what can be done?

IV

To repeat: how can we get rid of this harmful inclination toward abstract love and abstract hatred, of this tendency which is not only at the root of "state terrorism"—which is essentially what I have been discussing—but is, more generally, at the root of any terrorism, and perhaps of any radical evil?

The answer is not at all new; on the contrary, it is old and simple: unfortunately, I suppose, there are no magical solutions, only the slow and toilsome activity of critical thinking. Let me explain myself. I think that the old and familiar term "critical thinking" is clarified with expressions such as "disruptive thinking" or "dislocating thinking," that is to say, thinking that produces ruptures and uncertainty, which easily "gets on one's nerves." If I am right, then a genuinely critical thinking challenges, ruins, or disturbs our customary ways of feeling, believing, speaking, and acting. Spellbound, we tend to invoke the vocabularies of vicious reason: the stereotypes, slogans, enthusiasm, and sentimentalism which seek to delight in the attitude of "more of the same is always good." Hence the pressing need of a thinking capable of collecting or producing opposing aspects such as counterexamples, anomalies, oblivions, findings, surprises, innovations, and alternatives. In the first and second parts of this paper I have tried to implement a couple of these techniques.

In the first part I recalled a technique of critical thinking which invites us to reformulate problems, discussions, and judgements; in this case, in order to avoid the simplifying vertigo, I tried not to reduce the issues regarding the judgment of the former violators of human rights to the sphere of moral and law, and I tried to formulate them in relation to the policy of public memory.

In the third part I insisted—from the rhetoric of the banality of evil—on a different technique of critical thinking, a deflationary technique: a form of redescription of an issue in a "more superficial" way, usually in order to indicate that "there is nothing behind those surfaces." Or, in more concrete terms, a form of thinking was pursued which, by supressing all pompous rhetoric, used the point of view of baseness to pull to pieces the aura of the sublimity of evil.

Therefore, the techniques of reconstruction of problems and discussions have a therapeutic effect in relation to the simplifying vertigo. And deflationary techniques neutralize the allure of the vertigo of sublimity.

So, perhaps it might still be adduced that the inability to think critically that underlies abstract love and abstract hatred, eliminates the responsibility of agents in all kinds of banality of evil. In other words: the acts in the four kinds of banality of evil emerge from homogeneous beliefs and certain unlimited wishes. But are these not, in their turn, grounded in some character traits—vices such as narrowness, servility, or corruption?

For example, according to Hitler's biographer Allan Bullock: "Hitler's was a closed mind, violently rejecting any alternative view, refusing to criticize or allow others to criticize his assumptions. He read and listened, not to learn, but to acquire information and find additional support for prejudices and opinions already in his mind."[10]

From these remarks by Bullock, J. M. Montmarquet puts forward the following difficulty:

> If the real source of Hitler's culpability lies in his intellectual character, it must lie in something for which he possesses surely no direct responsibility. The road from responsibility for action to responsibility for belief now takes a fur-

ther turn, and it seems in some ways to be a rather unhappy one for the defender of doxastic responsibility. How to prevent responsibility for belief— I must now worry—how to prevent this from dissolving into the mists of time and the murky origins of our "personalities"?[11]

How then can we rescue a concept of responsibility if it would seem that "responsibility for action" would derive both from "responsibility for belief" and from "responsibility for wishes," and these responsibilities, in their turn, would seem to derive from the "responsibility for our virtues and vices," that is, from the slightly murky "responsibility for character"?

As is well known, according to Aristotle—a point confirmed by a significant part of contemporary psychology—a person acquires his virtues and vices by turning certain ways of behaving into habits. Thus, an individual becomes autonomous by behaving in an autonomous way: by acting a way that avoids being servile to the power of people, institutions, or his incontinence. Or the individual becomes impartial by learning to adopt, in appropriate occasions, the point of view of the third person; to avoid narrowness and to defend those institutions where impartiality is honored, promoted, and even demanded.

However, does all this imply that responsibility should be ascribed again only to the level of action and not to the level of wishes and beliefs? Let us try to avoid once again false oppositions and consider all these responsibilities equally.

If this proposal is correct, or at least partly correct, then we can defend the following: First, the agents are as responsible in the four examples of banality of evil as in the case of their more conscious and reflective acts; and second, more generally speaking, responsibility—especially responsibility for a wrong—is not a simple phenomenon. Quite on the contrary, we are constituted in such a way—and we live in a world constituted in such a way—that provokes responsibilities to ramify, intertwine, and interact: responsibility for our deeds involves responsibility for our virtues and vices, both epistemic and practical—responsibility for our epistemic and practical character. And these in their turn send us back again to responsibilities for our wishes and beliefs, which, in their turn, remit us to responsibility for our institutions, which lead us to other responsibilities, one after the next. None of these responsibilities is, in principle, more fundamental than the others, more basic, or primitive: to become a person is to honor all of them.

PART FOUR

Narratives of Evil

14

"Happy Endings"/Unendings
Narratives of Evil

Carol L. Bernstein

One of the problems in theorizing the relation of cultural memory to the Holocaust emerges from the delicate relations between mechanisms for preserving memory and the effectiveness with which the Holocaust destroyed practices for preserving memory—at least those which conflicted with the dominant German culture. If such practices include maintaining narrative communities, grouped around the figure of the storyteller, such communities were in significant measure eradicated in the camps, as Geoffrey Hartman points out.[1] The burden falls upon the survivors not only to bear witness but to assume the role of the storyteller: to find a way to reestablish the narrative base that would restore and convey traumatized memories. The very language the survivors used—their difficulty in speaking words for ordinary things, which had become extraordinary, or their inability even to speak, sometimes for decades—challenges the authority of the storyteller and his responsibility for communicating both the suppressed stories of the immediate past and the now-distant stories of an unreachable past. Even the traditional figures of rhetoric come into question, their functions redefined. Irony, for example, seems to be too urbane a form of denial, insofar as it makes commensurate what is incommensurate. Images, we infer from the schools of Adorno and Lyotard, are not to function as aides-mémoire. How, then, to put the memories of a period, banned by both suffering and theory, into narrative, especially—or even— when narrative turns to fiction? The delicacy lies not so much in the claim of the individual to speak for the group, which derives from the act of witnessing, but in the writing of imaginative narratives that will retain a fine balance between fidelity to historical events and cultural experience on the one hand, and on the other to the structures and norms of artworks, whatever they will be in any one instance. The question of cultural memory becomes still more pronounced when the testimony is at best "archival," the text a product of research into surviving documents of fragmented lives, or when the children and grandchildren of survivors must communicate in words what has been belatedly or silently communicated to them. I raise these issues in the context of evil, which has assumed new meaning since the Holocaust, and which has affected not only the subjects of narratives but its forms, as the ambiguity in my title may imply. To begin, I will review the controversy over the representation of the Holocaust as a prelude to a discussion of traditional literary representations of evil; from there I will move on to a formalist account of evil in narrative; and I will conclude with a discussion of several contemporary narratives.

By now anyone seriously interested in the Holocaust must be aware of the continuing debate, not only over what kinds of representations are possible, but over the possibility of any representation at all. We know of Adorno's comments on writing poetry after Auschwitz. In one version, he writes: "Perennial suffering has as much right to expression as a tortured man has to scream; hence it may have been wrong to say that after Auschwitz you could no longer write poems."[2] He remarks in the same essay, however, that "There is no word tinged from on high, not even a theological one, that has any right unless it underwent a transformation" (367). Later he adds, "Beckett has given us the only fitting reaction to the situation of the concentration camps—a situation he never calls by name, as if it were subject to an image ban. What is, he says, is like a concentration camp" (380). If Adorno's ambivalence over what is permissible in language finds a base in Beckett, it turns elsewhere to ethical and rhetorical prescriptions. Lyotard's claim that postmodernism demands an aesthetics of the unrepresentable has been anticipated by major authors.[3] Insofar as the postmodern, post-Auschwitz writer turns to the camps, she is subject to restrictions both moral and formal. Although Adorno advances a moral injunction, and Lyotard an aesthetic prescription derived from the Kantian sublime, both remind—or admonish—us that representation of the Holocaust and similar evils cannot adopt conventional forms and modes. A strict interpretation of Adorno and Lyotard would then suggest that what we can know about such horrors is that they are unavailable for aesthetic representation. Yet the half-century since the end of the Second World War has produced a body of poetry, fiction, and nonfictional narrative concerned with the evils of the Holocaust. What theory prohibits, writers have written: often, however, in forms that do indeed seem to observe the caution against representation. Turning away from their traditional practices, narratives about evil have relied upon such strategies as ellipsis, or saying too little, as is common in Appelfeld's novels; allusion, or speaking indirectly; and fragmentation. Representations of human actions and events relating to the Holocaust have in significant instances proceeded without the conventions of continuity and connection, without the temporal fictions—and the fictions of community—so central to cultural narrative. What Walter Benjamin wrote between the two world wars of the storyteller's disappearance returns to us now as an uncanny anticipation of the storyteller's second death: a minor apocalypse then and later. It is important to acknowledge, however, that not all post-Holocaust narratives have conformed to this metanarrative of aesthetic transformation and concealment. This fact alone reminds us that poetry and representation are, after all, possible, that the urgent, unrestricted, or popular account of extreme events may, for high or low purposes, follow singular *or* well-worn paths of communication. The films *Shoah* and *Schindler's List* have become the metatexts, the poles that determine debate. In the former, trains arrive at the gates of Auschwitz and other concentration camps—but what the camera finds inside are only ruins, the detritus of history. From this point, narrative proceeds but representation stops: the banishment of visual images increases the burden upon narrative. *Schindler's List,* disregarding prohibitions, takes us farther than any previous film has dared to go, Janet Maslin remarks in her review in the *New York Times*.[4] Since what we see, however, is not a gas chamber but a shower room, this happier outcome qualifies the cinematic daring. Although the difference in degree is immense, both films retain reasonably straightforward narrative techniques and assume that what appears on the screen is related to verbal accounts: the one by refusing to recreate a visual past, the other by appropriating the verbal into the visual, or, as Miriam Hansen remarks in her analysis of the film, by using the visual to refute the verbal—as when scenes of Jewish daily life challenge Goeth's boast that the destruction of the ghetto marks the end of Jewish history.[5] Although they lock horns in an aesthetic debate, both films project a Jewish cultural memory, the one bringing forth words from ruins, the other transferring memory to film when memory cannot speak.

Oddly enough, it is the more conventional works that remind us that narratives of evil have not always been in straits so dire. Before this contemporary dilemma, provoked by the "double dying" of man and the idea of man, evil was both the origin and the subject of major cultural narratives.[6] *Paradise Lost,* Milton's great epic of the introduction of evil into human life, an epic which traces the fall of Satan from Heaven and Adam and Eve's expulsion from Eden—"O Eve, in evil hour" (IX, 1067) was Milton's notorious punning lament at the moment of crisis—contrasts the immediacy of life in Paradise with the introduction of allegory after the Fall. Adam, under the tutelage of the Archangel Michael, must learn to interpret visions of the future: he needs instruction about the many shapes of sin, death, and pain. He must learn, for example, that the reveling on the Plain, where "Nature seems fulfill'd in all her ends" (XI, 602), comes from the Tents of wickedness, dwelling places of the atheistic sons of Cain. More than two centuries later, Lukács, in *The Theory of the Novel,* maintained that the novel is the art-form of a world abandoned by God, that the psychology of its hero occupies the domain of the demonic, and that its constitutive element is time.[7] These elements look suspiciously like those we noted above in Milton's epic. Lukács, in the wake of Marxist theories of alienation, suggests that one consequence of the industrial revolution was the separation of human labor from its products—for which the assembly line may serve as an image. The fictional representation of an alienated human life deprived of immanent meaning was thus directed toward allegory. Temporality, the novel's great contribution to literary form, was thus allied with allegory and the necessity of interpretation. Evil, in one case both cause and effect of individual moral action, and in the other, the result of industrial capitalism, thus has decisive consequences for narrative fiction, for it determines both its form (broadly allegorical) and the response to it (interpretation). In other words, without some forms of evil, we are not likely to have encountered many if not all of the dominant forms of narrative. Insofar as narrative is a vehicle for cultural memory, the latter has long been on familiar terms with evil.

This line of reasoning suggests that the most radical consequences of evil are already present in modern narrative fiction, the one a paradoxically direct result of economic development, the other an after-the-fact explanation of origins: the need for interpretation results from Adam and Eve's sin and the consequent introduction of evil into the world. The line of interpretation is problematic, however. Depending on how you feel about it, the figurative baggage of narrative will look like metaphor, or semblance, or deception, for example; or, alternatively, ellipsis, or strategic silence, or evasion. The fine line between benign and sinister rhetoric—between "elevation" and "manipulation"—depends, then, upon the community of listeners and readers to which it turns. The Longinian sublime may turn defeat into victory; Dickensian low-life characters are adept at "working [language] round": which is more innocent, which more evil?[8] Even in a temporal sense, narrative cannot be simply straightforward, insofar as its verbal account of events at best *refers* to what "really happened," a more or less distant series of referents whose linear sequence depends upon the projections of the narrative as it is related. Whether we think of narrative strategies as evidence of the fall into evil, or as attempted movements toward redemption in a world made sinful by divine fiat or human action, narrative form seems inextricable from evil. In the worst scenario, narrative looks less like an unwilling witness to evil than the willing accomplice to deception. Some Victorian readers—and, I suspect, some contemporary readers as well—considered narrative fiction the devil's own work. But then, the Victorians might have had in mind their romantic precursors, who perceived the close ties between imagination and the demonic. (Shelley models his Prometheus after Milton's Satan, minus the latter's pernicious casuistry: creative imagination is not in question.) Historically, then, evil and creativity have been partners, and their partnership has informed, and indeed helped to form, Western cultural memory.

Not surprisingly, their relation has been ambiguous. To ally narrative fiction and especially its temporal forms with evil can lead on the one hand to endowing form with a moral dimension, and on the other to restricting evil to a formal category. Something like the latter happens in Northrop Frye's *The Secular Scripture*. If the Bible presents a major Western religious mythology, the structures by which subsequent experience is determined and interpreted, romance does the same for secular scenarios. A genre study, Frye's book is concerned with the structures of romance. In his book, evil reaches its greatest reduction. At one point Frye distinguishes between Sir Walter Scott's novels and the history upon which they are based, here medieval: in *Ivanhoe*, the Jewess Rebecca escapes a trial for sorcery, which is redefined as "medical skill," although the same conflation condemns the Jew from whom she learned it to martyrdom. "It seems clear," Frye comments, "that appeals to God, by virtuous characters threatened with evil, may be of little use unless God has a secretary to handle such calls in the form of a good-natured novelist, backed by a sentimental public."[9] In such novels, we may add, the reality of evil is surely tempered by its position in a plot: the formal alternative named above. What makes such an alternative difficult to dismiss is Frye's comment, immediately following, upon happy endings.

> The happy endings of life, as of literature, exist only for survivors. When confronted with something profoundly evil in life like the Nazi regime in Germany, we may say that after all it did collapse in a few years. This fact was of no help to the millions of people it tortured and murdered before it fell, and yet it is true, however smug it may sound, that the survivors have the more complete perspective. Hence the modern world may accept comic mythologies . . . although the benefits of such happy endings are only for those living in a remote future. (135–36)

Survivors necessarily "have the more complete perspective," although there is no reason to link it with a conventionally understood happy ending. Many writers have testified to the lack of closure after the Holocaust, to finding no redemption in remembering the dead. As Hannah Arendt writes, "*This ought not to have happened.* And I don't mean just the number of victims. I mean the method, the fabrication of corpses and so on—I don't need to go into that. This should not have happened. Something happened there to which we cannot reconcile ourselves. None of us ever can."[10]

II

It is with these passages from Frye that our discussion of narratives of evil must take a radical turn. If the evil in the first passage about Scott is radically

reductive, the treatment in the second is all the more astonishing because
it places the horror of modern history in a literary frame, thus foreground-
ing the gulf between subject and representation. Have we forged a link
between a formalism that brackets the Holocaust, and Lyotard's thesis on
the unrepresentable—insofar as the latter's practical effect looks curiously
like a form of bracketing?

Frye's remark is curious for several additional reasons. We should note
first that it occurs at a point where Frye wishes to shift his focus from the
conventional happy endings of romance to the desire for happy endings felt
by readers of romance, together with "the unending, irrational, absurd persistence of the human impulse to struggle, survive, and where possible
escape." Still, Frye's argument does not require him to turn here from the
literary structures that are his primary concern to historical events. To be
sure, his theory does include a mythic element, insofar as it represents
explanatory categories developed by the collective mind of a nation or religious group, deriving from the assumption that literary structures are the
products of collective beliefs or cosmological explanations. Thus the happy
endings to *Paradise Lost* or Dante's *Divine Comedy* are the resolution to the
evil resulting from the fall of Satan from Heaven and the ensuing events, or
to the sufferings of the sinners Dante reviews, but leaves behind in the circles of Hell. The happy endings in both works are visionary, however, projected into a future as yet unrealized. Dante stopping at the top of the
mountain and Adam and Eve embarking on the journey that will lead to a
paradise within represent a theological chronology in which a happy ending
is associated with the end of time as we know it. Such a chronology is not,
apparently, what Frye refers to when he envisages the survivors of the
Holocaust experiencing happy (historical) endings.

Second, Frye's comment on "we, the survivors" names an indeterminate
figure: one who has outlived the Holocaust but who has not necessarily
experienced any of its evils firsthand, or even secondhand, as they are transmitted from those who actually experienced the evil to succeeding generations. Thus the inclusiveness of his terminology blurs the distinction
between survivors and witnesses, and those whose lives were contempora-
neous to but not directly affected by the Holocaust: a distinction crucial to
narratives of the Holocaust and other instances of political persecution and
genocide.

Third, even if we allow for the generic mode to operate within human
actions (Marx's comment on revolution as tragedy and then farce comes
easily to mind), Frye's characterization of the Holocaust as a narrative with
a happy ending leaps over the testimony of many survivors (and witnesses)
for whom, consciously or unconsciously, the Holocaust has not ended.

Fourth, the problem for literature is what shapes authors can draw from,
or impose upon, the experience of evil. For all his acknowledgment of psy-

chological categories, Frye tends to treat them with a set of fine distinctions whose dynamics are subordinate to a structural model.

Fifth, Frye's treatment of evil as part of a generic scenario makes it seem like a counter, part of an elaborate structure whose parts are less individually distinct. In other words, evil tends to lose its enormity, its absoluteness, when it becomes a more or less predictable element in a recurring scenario. And the absolute quality is precisely what is at stake here.[11] Recurrence is not a problem, neither as virtually obsessive repetition nor as what appears in Blanchot's question: "Wouldn't the disaster be, then, the repetition—the affirmation—of the singularity of the extreme?"[12] It is when it defies categorization that evil is most recognizable in all its "singularity" as "the unverifiable, the improper" (6), as Blanchot goes on to say.

Our topic thus far suggests that in the Western literary tradition—and the mythic and formal structures with which it is deeply implicated—evil falls into a narrative pattern that envisages redemption, even if not for the sinner, who has been complicit with evil; or it falls into a narrative pattern that concludes in a happy ending for survivors. Here too, the results are ambiguous, for those who do not survive enjoy no such happy end—and those who do may undergo a double suffering from repetition of the event in memory or the effort to understand the incomprehensible.[13] If, as we noted earlier, literature in its "formal" modes displays a deep complicity with evil, in some scenarios it may also subordinate the individual to a recurring pattern in which she or her successors will arrive at a distant happy end. Fredric Jameson projects a vision of history as the end of class struggle. Conversely, Brecht's play about a mobster converted by a Salvation Army lass (it anticipates both Damon Runyon's story and the musical *Guys and Dolls*) ironizes its title, *Happy End,* reminding us that the fable of evil redeemed by morality is too neat and too unlikely.

III

Let us turn, then, from what some people call "good evil," that which is distant or literary, or both, and which exercises an attraction, often associated with romantic literature as the source of individuality, defiance of authority, and the aesthetic, to the more immediate narratives associated with the Holocaust. In these narratives, evil becomes far more problematic. It is not simply a matter of position, of who happens to occupy the place of the other, nor is it easy to contain. Contrary to Lukács, for whom memory tends to play a redemptive role, the effects of evil in Holocaust fiction resonate in unconscious as well as conscious memory. In such a context, however, memory itself is extremely problematic, not least because of its alliance with metaphor.[14] How, then, can we reconcile the set of contradictions arising from (1) the need to rethink the terms of contemporary narratives of evil as opposed to conventional constructions of evil; (2) the need to bear witness against the desire for closure—or happy endings; (3) the persistence of memory within the repetition of evil; (4) the literary drive to verbalize liminal experiences, which resist structure and literary strategy; and (5) the need to distinguish between bans on representation and conspiracies of silence? One way to begin to answer these questions is to turn to the texts that evoke and address these contradictions.

Longer narrative fictions confront evil in a more radical way than poetry; to them, the evils of the Holocaust and similar disasters pose special dangers. Gertrud Koch, concerned to draw "Moral Conclusions from Narrative Closure," points to the danger to the historical frame of reference from the "perspectival" view: "The obsession with details, stories, closures and stasis in fiction cuts out a perspectival view which works as a symbol for the whole," causing "the monstrosity of the event" to "disintegrate into fragments" recomposed by the dictates of our emotions.[15] Read one way, the need for closure or what Nietzsche called metaphysical comfort may weaken the narrative's obligation to historical veracity, resulting in what Saul Friedländer calls "phantasms."[16] From another perspective metonymy and symbolism, indeed the entire stock-in-trade of imaginative fiction, are threatened. Once again *Shoah* and *Schindler's List* enter the discussion as exemplary illustrations of redundancy or double entendre. While one adopts the mode of interminability, the other ends with a ritual in Jerusalem where "Schindler's people," their progeny, and the actors who played them place stones on his tomb. The message is the "redemptive scenario" in which "He who saves the life of one man, saves the whole world." Koch tells us that in Spielberg's judgment, justice has been done: the happy end of the day of judgment, the end of history, has been advanced to the present. Such a scene may intimate that the need for memory has diminished.

With these comments, we have turned away from representation to the different but related problem of narrative closure: of what it means to attach a happy or redemptive ending to post-Holocaust narratives of evil. From a classical perspective, it seems that *Schindler's List* trumps its great predecessors, not only by its decisive ending, but by its temporal foreshortening. Its literary and religious presumption, one might argue, equals its egregious historical position. Is scale alone what is at stake here? Would a smaller redemption, less sublime in its cinematographic vocabulary, be more appropriate? Or do the film and its critics pose other challenges to narrative, the former by popularizing and perhaps confusing great redemptive scenarios, the latter by refusing to allow a "perspectival" representation of evil events?

The dangers to narrative also appear deceptively casual in a treatment of the way present-day Berliners remember the Nazi era. In Armando's *From Berlin*, glimpses of the Holocaust appear decades later in fragments of street talk:

"a friend of mine . . . told me that during the war she had been evacuated because of the air raids, and she wound up somewhere . . . near Auschwitz. . . . She didn't know exactly what was going on there, but she heard people talking and she saw the transports. . . . Once she was back in Berlin, she said to her friends: Something's going on there, we don't know exactly what, but something's going on there, something terrible. A few days later she was picked up for questioning and interrogated for hours. She was told that if she ever said another word about what was going on there, she'd be put in a camp where she'd have to work until she died." (83–84)[17]

The Nazi ban on talk about Auschwitz—on conversational narrative, as it were—is revealing for the way it affects discourse around 1990, the year it was heard: "something" was "going on"—still unnameable. At no time can either side name evil. Have we reached some impasse where evil is taboo for both perpetrators and victims?

IV

Let us turn to a series of recent post-Holocaust narratives, all of which direct our attention to the problem of closure. Once again, it is *Shoah* that presents the problematic. One of its major recurring images is that of trains running on the tracks to concentration camps: time and again, they lead us to the gates, where the voices of survivors take up a narrative whose visual accompaniment is what remains of the camp in question. Repetition is thus a crucial part of the film, a visual metaphor for interminability and annihilation. For in fact, there is no representation, only repetition. The Czech locksmith whose compatriots enjoin him not to accompany them into the gas chamber weeps as his narrative ends—and he will continue to weep with each showing of the film. Similarly, the Polish agent smuggled into the Warsaw ghetto will continue to voice his horror at a cityscape that did not belong to this world. It becomes part of a symbolic structure informing us that the grass growing over sites of mass graves does not cover them peacefully. The disruption between representation of the present and meaning itself is marked. Repetition, a metaproperty of film, assures us that no commonplace temporality can be restored.

Train tracks form a similar structure of meaning in the novels of Aharon Appelfeld. In *Badenheim 1939,* the guests and staff at a summer spa find their liberties increasingly restricted, until they board "four filthy freight cars" for an "emigration" to Poland. The train's "appearance was as sudden as if it had risen from a pit in the ground. . . . And the people were sucked in."[18] "'If the coaches are so dirty,'" someone remarks at the end of the novel, "'it must mean that we have not far to go'" (148). In *To the Land of the Cattails,* the protagonist returns to the country of his birth, only to learn of the departure of the Jews. At the end of the novel, he joins a group of Jews, too many for the previous train stopping at that remote station, who are waiting for a train to carry them away. It arrives with a "festive whistle . . . an old locomotive, drawing two old cars—the local, apparently. It went from station to station, scrupulously gathering up the remainder."[19] And in *The Iron Tracks,* the narrator has been traveling the same train route for several months each year "since the end of the war." He "possesses an entire continent," repeating his journey every year: "And in this repetition lies a strange hopefulness, as if our end were not extinction but a sort of constant renewal."[20] He has developed both a strange cosmopolitanism and a powerful memory (9). Every 27 March he begins the journey to Wirblbahn station: "In this accursed place," he remarks, "my life ended and I was reborn. The Germans brought our train to this remote station and left us here" (13). If the memory of that time after the train doors opened and the passengers "went to work" is painful, it is nevertheless part of his journey. The narrator stops at various places, speaking with people whose brief appearances help him to reconstruct his past. Over the years, he has collected and sold Jewish artifacts, material repositories of memory. After forty years, however, he has disposed of them. After he locates and kills the Nazi officer who murdered his parents, he returns to Wirblbahn and announces his intention to burn it to the ground. Yet he is aware that his life has come to an end. "If I had a different life, it wouldn't be happy. As in all my drawn-out nightmares, I saw the sea of darkness, and knew that my deeds had neither dedication nor beauty. I had done everything out of compulsion, clumsily, and always too late" (218).

Although Tim O'Brien's *In the Lake of the Woods* concerns the war in Vietnam, and shifts our focus from victims to perpetrators, the dynamic based upon trauma is related to our concerns. John Wade, a Vietnam veteran and a politician whose star has risen rapidly, loses the senatorial primary by a landslide; some terrible revelation has ruptured his career. Over the course of the novel, we piece together his former life, for which the defining event has been the massacre at My Lai, in which American troops slaughtered several hundred Vietnamese in one terrible morning. Wade kills an old man and an American soldier, testifies to Lt. Calley's warped, self-serving version of the event, and is haunted by the memory of that day. The narrative proceeds by a form of collage, in which memories, testimonials, court evidence, and trauma theories interact with the main narrative in which Wade and his wife, Kathy, go off for a postprimary vacation and she disappears. Wade's recurring memory of a "final" scene rounds off the action by speculating about what she must have done. She is never found, and the narrator disclaims knowledge of her fate. What we learn in a fragmented way is that John is responsible for her horrible fate, that his mental instability has become total, that he himself vanishes in a wilderness of Minnesota lakes and trees.[21]

In both Appelfeld's and O'Brien's novels, the individual's participation in a collective trauma is responsible for the persistence of fragmented memory, for its horrible images, its pressures, and its interminability. In "Analysis Terminable and Interminable," Freud writes that analysis has a better chance of achieving closure when trauma predominates over instinctual factors.[22] Yet in the novels, trauma and deeper instinct persist in some destructive pattern, here the compulsive repetition that had helped Freud develop the theory of the death instinct in the years prior to 1919. Both novels represent the slow, fragmentary recovery of memory as a problem in which rhetoric and ethics are entangled. From the literary point of view, repetition (or saying too much) and ellipsis (or saying too little) form a fraught partnership. Neither trauma nor instinct can speak without some kind of figure or metaphor; here repetition and ellipsis overcome their antithetical relation. As Cathy Caruth points out, rhetorical figures "bear witness to some forgotten wound."[23] Like memory itself, they testify in forms of "speaking silence." They remind us that memory is neither analytic nor committed to the direct representation of the truth.

But what happens when the rhetorical figure is that of reading itself? In Bernard Schlink's *The Reader*, the narrator, Michael Berg, has an affair with a woman twice his age. He knows only that she is a streetcar conductor in his town. Their encounters follow a pattern in which he reads to her from texts of the Western canon before they make love. The affair ends, she disappears from town, and the next time he sees her, she is on trial along with four other former concentration camp guards, accused of allowing a group of women prisoners, during a death march toward the end of the war, to burn to death in a church where they have been locked for the night, and which is bombed. During the trial it emerges that Hanna often took some of the frailest prisoners into her house and had them read to her before they were sent to their deaths. The narrator, by then a law student observing the trial process, notices the numbness common to everyone involved in the trial. He continues,

> At the same time, I ask myself . . . what should our second generation have done, what should it do with the knowledge of the horrors of the extermination of the Jews? We should not believe we can comprehend the incomprehensible, we may not compare the incomparable, we may may not inquire because to inquire is to make the horrors an object of discussion, even if the horrors themselves are not questioned, instead of accepting them as something in the face of which we can only fall silent in revulsion, shame and guilt. Should we only fall silent in revulsion, shame and guilt? To what purpose? It was not that I had lost my eagerness to explore and cast light on things which had filled the seminar, once the trial got under way. But that some few would be convicted and punished while we of the second generation were silenced by revulsion, shame and guilt—was that all there was to it now?[24]

Michael may be saying too much about revulsion, shame, and guilt. As he realizes, however, his repetition extends to the act of reading, as it does to the knowledge that the verbal shibboleths of the postwar period have brought him to an ethical and rhetorical impasse. He can say neither too much nor too little. If he acknowledges the horror and awe-fulness of the injunctions, then he should not speak. Silence, however, will permit the punishment of relatively few perpetrators while leaving the succeeding generation burdened with "shame and guilt." Although he has committed no atrocities, he has loved someone who is deeply implicated in them.

During the trial, Hanna's behavior provokes, among other things, the resentment of the other guards. When the judge asks her if she helped to select the weakest prisoners at the labor camp to be sent to Auschwitz to their deaths, she replies, "What else could I have done?"—as if asking the judge for an answer. The other guards accuse her of having written a falsified report of the burning, and Hanna finally admits to having done so. But there is something perplexing about her behavior which Michael cannot read or interpret. Only after a series of Sunday walks in the woods, where his mind goes "round and round in the same tracks week after week," does he come to the uncanny realization: "the familiarity of the surroundings allowed what was truly surprising, what . . . had been growing inside my self, to be recognized: 'Hanna could neither read nor write.'" Hanna is sentenced to life in prison. Over the years, Michael suffers the aftermath, not simply of the affair with Hanna but of collective German guilt and of his own "complicity," however opaque or unknown to him, because of his love for Hanna. The complicity and guilt of his own generation are so entangled with love for their parents that ethical choices look like no-win affairs.

In this novel, reading—or lack of reading—is not only the metaphor for cultural understanding: it is the figure for cultural negotiation. If, like Hanna, you cannot read, you will not know how to respond to the complex signals and signs of a courtroom. Still, the narrator's—Michael's—father, a philosophy professor, makes his reading the medium of abstraction and retreat from human affairs. For his part, Michael can read the classical texts, but until that moment in the forest he is unresponsive to the signals of Hanna's illiteracy. As representatives of their respective generations, Michael and his father are skilled at reading classical texts—his father has written books on Kant and Hegel—but they are less able to read contemporary signs. However one reads this ambiguity, both men relate ambiguously to German or European culture. If we return to that passage we read earlier on the catchphrases of contemporary ethics and aesthetics, it would seem that Michael's opacity is the underside of a sublime in which he is indeed unable to comprehend the incomprehensible, in which he is entrapped by the words that shield the past and quarantine it in the name of horror. He has not experienced evils like those that assail the narrators of *The Iron Tracks* or *In the Lake of the Woods,* but he is, nevertheless, challenged by the same aesthetic injunction. If it does not undergo verbal reduction, the sublime may elevate a postwar generation to the noumenal world, but it is not likely to redeem those who suffered or those who seek to understand that suffering.

What these post-Holocaust novels reveal is a general cultural breakdown apparent in repetition, exemplified in figures of trains, tracks, streetcars, and in the emotional ellipses of silence, the cognitive ellipses of unrecognized knowledge. What theory, what analysis can be commensurate with such narratives? Literary theory often systematizes that which resists system and category: thus the attraction of the sublime, even as a negative sublime. Yet Michael's words remind us that any post-Auschwitz aesthetic terms can diminish into catchwords. What we may need to do is read and reveal with a knowledge of how slippery resonant words, as well as memory, can be. In this context, let us turn to a passage from Blanchot:

> Knowledge which goes so far as to accept horror in order to know it, reveals the horror of knowledge, its squalor, the discrete complicity which maintains it in a relation with the most insupportable aspects of power. I think of that young prisoner of Auschwitz (he had suffered the worst, led his family to the crematorium, hanged himself, after being saved at the last moment—how can one say that: *saved?*—he was exempted from contact with dead bodies, but when the SS shot someone, he was obliged to hold the victim's head so that the bullet could be more easily lodged in the neck). When asked how he could bear this, he is supposed to have answered that he "observed the comportment of men before death." (82)

One thinks back some millenia to the comportment of Sarpedon and Glaucus during the Trojan War, as they anticipate death in battle. Here is Sarpedon, speaking to Glaucus in the archaic and contained style of Alexander Pope's translation:

> Cou'd all our Care elude the greedy Grave,
> Which claims no less the Fearful than the Brave,
> For Lust of Fame I shou'd not vainly dare
> In fighting Fields, nor urge thy Soul to War.
> But since, alas, ignoble Age must come,
> Disease, and Death's inexorable Doom;
> The Life which others pay, let Us bestow,
> And give to Fame what we to Nature owe;
> Brave, tho' we fall; and honour'd, if we live;
> Or let us Glory gain, or Glory give!

The young man at Auschwitz, claiming to observe "the comportment of men before death," reminds us how such words slip into history. Here is the remainder of Blanchot's passage:

I will not believe it. As Lewental, whose notes were found buried near a crematorium, wrote to us, "The truth was always more atrocious, more tragic than what will be said about it." Saved at the last minute, the young man of whom I speak was forced to live that last instant again and each time to live it once more, frustrated every time of his own death and made to exchange it every time for the death of all. His response ("I observed the comportment of men . . .") was not a response; he could not respond. What remains for us to recognize in this account is that when he was faced with an impossible question, he could find no other alibi than the search for knowledge, the so-called dignity of knowledge: that ultimate propriety which we believe will be accorded us by knowledge. And how, in fact, can one accept not to know? We read books on Auschwitz. The wish of all, in the camps, the last wish: know what has happened, do not forget, and at the same time never will you know. (82)

If Blanchot's words—his parable—can evoke the memory of men facing death at an earlier time, then they speak to the persistence of cultural memory despite attempts to negate it. Memory confronts its double and its antithesis: it knows, knowing that it does not know. At this moment, we glimpse the specter of Northrop Frye, for whom literary continuity overcomes historical chaos. But if honor redeems the death of ancient heroes, what can we say of Auschwitz? In Blanchot's passage, survival refuses both terms of "happy endings." Whether we cast it in terms of a knowledge of evil that is never sufficient, or of a collective memory too "deep" to be retrieved, endings entail foreclosures without allowing for interest: the human interest of inquiry. Although genres seem to require endings, the newly prominent modes of the memoir and testimony (about evil) bring pressure upon narrative to leave its endings open. The issue here is not one in which life refuses the abrupt closure of literary form. Rather, memoir, the form that memory takes, requires a new complicity with narrative, whose very "literariness" leads it to approach endings asymptotically, its figures uncertain pledges of redemption at some other time.

Narrating Evil

A Postmetaphysical Theory of Reflective Judgment

María Pía Lara

No philosophy, no analysis, no aphorism, be it ever so profound, can compare in intensity and richness of meaning with a properly narrated story.
HANNAH ARENDT, "ON HUMANITY IN DARK TIMES"

THE FAILURE TO CONCEPTUALIZE EVIL

There are thousands of books on evil,[1] yet not one of them presents a satisfying theory of it. Some attempt to define historically evil's philosophical roots. Others focus on different approaches to evil and, by critically contrasting them, seek to clarify one tradition among others. Some introduce semantic definitions; others, typically anthropological and psychoanalytical, concentrate on revealing the dark side of human behavior and culture. Recently, there has been a new interest, not in such theorizing or description per se, but in what I will call "telling stories" about evil. I believe, in fact, that this marks an important new trend in philosophy, as well as in social sciences, and that this new orientation can take consideration of evil in a fundamentally new direction. I want to suggest, therefore, that our starting point should be an attempt to answer the question: Why do stories seem to offer a better approach to evil than abstract or formal theories? I hope to develop some arguments in this essay that begin to provide answers to this question.

In the past, theologians and experts on religion were the only people really interested in the subject. Even philosophy was dependent on the capacity of religion to create a space for different kinds of answers to the problem of evil. When Kant wrote his important contribution on the subject, *Religion within the Limits of Reason Alone*,[2] he correctly acknowledged that evil lies in free human agency, or as he claimed, in "the wickedness of human nature or of the human heart," which fully reveals our human frailty.[3] It is that frailty that has been explored by religious treatises, which have searched for possible ways of understanding cruelty, suffering, undeserved pain, and all kinds of human losses.

The problem is that neither religion nor religiously indebted philosophy can theorize evil without metaphysical banisters. It is for that reason that traditional religious narratives have always been defensive and ambiguous. Their problem has derived from their attempt to reconcile the belief in an all-good deity with the recognition that there is evil in the world. As one contemporary theologian has recently put it, "humanity reaches the extreme limit—confronting the decisive question of the meaning of life, of the sense and nonsense of reality."[4] This fundamental challenge has made the problem of evil central to what has traditionally been considered the philosophy of religion. Theodicies were philosophical theories that sought to articulate credible explanations that rested on theistic truths and insights. Augustine's theodicy, for example, conceptualized evil as a metaphysical degradation.[5] By attributing evil to the "wrong choices" of a free rational will, Augustine sought not to make evil acts contingent, and thus to restore responsibility, but to save the Christian God from any blame.[6] In fact, he was unable to explain why a good human being could perform an evil action, and he was forced to conclude that "there are mysteries that God provides by filling up every level of creation," up and down the scale, and by making our world full and diverse. Augustine claimed that his principle of "plenitude" helped him explain what evil meant to "creaturely finitude."[7]

Leibniz created the first explicitly philosophical theodicy in order to demonstrate that God could not be blamed for the existence of evil. While reality will always contain some kind of evil, Leibniz wrote, "this world" was the best of all possible worlds.

It is revealing that both Leibniz's and Augustine's accounts opened a space for the aesthetic to play a significant role in thinking and interpreting evil. They describe evil as a necessary element of a diverse and harmonious world. "All goods being created"—Augustine's claim[8]—was echoed in Leibniz's own formula, "the best world possible." Both interpretations aimed at conceiving evil as a part of a whole complex reality. As Leibniz put it, "God seeks to produce richness and quality in the world."[9]

While theodicies conceived suffering as a central theme, I wish to argue that their tendency to aestheticize meant that these kind of theories asserted the necessity of evil, and thus implied some kind of reconciliation with it. The goal, instead, should be to offer a way to understand why this necessity has come to be seen as such a vital part of human life, and thus to suggest some kind of moral responsibility for avoiding it. Only if we begin to think of evil as a moral rather than an aesthetic problem can we move from necessity to the question of "why." In the Irenean theodicy suffering becomes such a truly moral problem because it is regarded as central to "soul" making, that is, to the reconstruction and improvement of the spiritual capacities of the human self.[10] This is the starting point of the story of Job, which, in historical narrative terms, marks the real origin of the moral approach to evil.

As the history of its many interpretations testifies, this biblical narrative has been accorded its unique status because it dealt with the question of how to bear undeserved suffering. The story of Job became central to philosophers' efforts to answer the question: Why should the just suffer?[11] Most philosophers interpreted Job as a theodicy, as demonstrating evil's inextricable link to human finitude. But the story of Job has also pushed beyond the boundaries of theodicy. In the work of the psychoanalyst Carl Jung, for example, it has led to reconceptualizing God as representing good and evil at the same time.[12] Jung is more audacious than appears at first glance, for he claims that, through his suffering, Job has attained a knowledge of God that God himself does not possess. For Jung, in other words, God and humanity reflect each other, the failures of one can only be learned from the human point of view: "Yahweh's dual nature has been revealed, and somebody or something has seen and registered this fact."[13] For Jung, then, the knowledge obtained through consciousness entails a higher stage of moral learning than traditional theodicy, for humanity "can make no progress with himself unless he becomes very much better acquainted with his own nature."

But if theodicies failed to give a philosophically acceptable account of the existence of evil, as Kant argued, stories like Job's possess the possibility for multiple interpretations that can lead to a recognition of the necessary relation between suffering and human learning. Such an interpretation opens up the idea of suffering as something justified or unjustified in a moral sense, and thus as something therapeutic, pedagogical, or redemptive. We can thematize evil within the moral realm by developing an understanding of the universal conditions of suffering via the interpretation of stories that have been taken, in the historical or sociological sense, as having what Hannah Arendt called "exemplary validity." In developing such a "post-metaphysical" moral understanding of evil, we will be able to connect stories about evil to the moral accountability that is produced by the exercise of "reflective judgment."[14] It is in this sense that our task will be eminently philosophical.

CONCEPTUALIZING EVIL THROUGH STORYTELLING

While evil actions and stories about them have been with us since the beginning of human time, we have only recently become conscious of the power of storytelling. Each story seems to bring something new into the realm of experiencing human suffering, throwing a different light on the link between the doer and sufferer of evil deeds and on what is important to remember. Through this process we build up a "negative" moral example, learning about fragility, about our weaknesses and wickedness, in sum, about ourselves in relation to our own moral ambitions and expectations.

Some philosophers have used the relationship between literature and ethics to understand human nature and morality.[15] While literary narratives have been connected to judgment through the positive appraisal of moral values, moral examples, and "positive" exemplary validity, it is important to think more precisely about exactly what it is that makes them significant in conceptualizing and understanding evil. I wish to claim that narratives about evil must accomplish two different functions. They must relate concrete and compelling experiences of evil, and they must also have the power to shape our moral perceptions of evil over historical time.

I will illustrate both these functions by offering a philosophical analysis of different interpretations of the Greek tragedies. Let us begin with Aristotle's conception of tragedy. He argues that "the most important element is the arrangement of the events, for tragedy is a representation not of human beings but of action and a course of life" (1450a15–20). However, what tragedy teaches us about ourselves is not only related to our feelings of "pity" or "fear," both of which have been often portrayed as the most important feelings provoked by Greek tragedies, but something that goes on between the interaction of the experience and different stages of moral learning. Indeed, tragedy says something unique about the unavoidable nature of conflict in moral life. Moral conflicts make universality inseparable from the particular localization of a specific story. This is what allows tragedies to become such powerful vehicles of exemplary validity.

Tragedies can also be conceived as creating a gap "between tragic wisdom and practical wisdom," as Paul Ricoeur has argued.[16] While tragedy shows the unavoidable human suffering created by evil deeds, at the same time it condemns the spectator to reorient his or her actions at his or her own risk, "in the sense of a practical wisdom that best *responds* to tragic wisdom."[17] But if tragedies provoke catharsis in the spectator, as Aristotle explained, one can rightly conclude that our expressive side, the emotions and feelings such as pity and fear, become parts of our *moral* responses to our interpretations of the meaning of tragedy. In this sense, argues Martha Nussbaum, "emotions have a cognitive basis."[18] Thus, we can conceive tragedy as "a mimesis of pitiable and fearful things" that provide us with moral knowledge.[19] Pity and fear are connected to the universality of human suffering and to the particularity and contingency of different contexts of human action. Conceptualized as such, we can think of tragedies as representing the negative sides of action and thus as cases where evil is seen as a negative example of "exemplary validity." In this sense, Martha Nussbaum's interpretation of Aristotle's conception of tragedy reveals the interconnection between the expressive side of our reactions and the dimension of moral learning, for as Nussbaum claims, Aristotle "connects the requirement that plots unfold 'according to necessity or probability' with poetry's ability to show general human possibilities." Thus, negative "exemplary validity" is related to conceiving the narrated experience of others' suffering as something that may happen to me, while also acknowledging the complex interplay that actions have between the necessity and contigency of evil deeds.[20]

Greek tragedies also exemplify the second function of narratives of evil insofar as they have shaped our moral understanding of certain evil deeds. One way to illustrate this dimension is by showing how tragedies have expanded our moral vocabularies. Tragedies have invented words—concepts that acquire moral content when situated within a specific story—which have helped shape our visions of who we are, of our own basic fragility and weaknesses. This is a dimension that Bernard Williams has revealed with his analysis of the concepts of "responsibility," "guilt," and "shame" in his book *Shame and Necessity*.[21] Responsibility, for example, is described by Williams through the tragedy of Oedipus:

> The whole of the *Oedipus Tyrannus,* that dreadful machine, moves to the discovery of just one thing, that he did it. Do we understand the terror of that discovery only because we residually share magical beliefs in blood-guilt, or archaic notions of responsibility? Certainly not: we understand it because we know that in the story of one's life there is an authority exercised by what one has done, and not merely by what one has intentionally done.[22]

The link that Williams develops through a historical interpretation of "responsibility" shows how there are two sides of action, "that of deliberation and that of result, and there is a necessary gap between them."[23] This is precisely the "empty" space filled by the moral content of a story when being told. Thus, we can conclude that the suffering in the lives of tragic heroes and heroines becomes the territory of understanding and learning.[24]

In the same manner, Martha Nussbaum analyzed the concept of "pity" taken from Aristotle's *Poetics.* She too uses tragedies to highlight the moral dimension of the fragility of our lives. Nussbaum claims that Aristotle's conception of pity is "a painful emotion directed toward another person's pain or suffering. It requires, then, the belief that the other person is really suffering, and, furthermore, that this suffering is not trivial, but something of real importance. These sufferings he then divides into two groups: painful and injurious things, and substantial damages caused by luck." Thus, tragedies provide the possibility to explore the vulnerability of human action and evil deeds through a moral scope.[25]

THE EXPLANATORY POWER OF STORYTELLING

Habermas's well-known criticism of the blurring of genres between literature and philosophy, between science and normative discourses, aimed to restore validity claims to different disciplines and discourses and to preserve the epistemic relations between subjects and worlds.[26] Habermas blamed

Heidegger for creating a notion of language that came to be regarded as "an occurence of truth."[27] By radicalizing Heidegger's idea of language, argues Habermas, post-structuralists treat "all validity claims" as "immanent to particular discourses."[28] Thus, post-structuralists have erased "transcendental subjectivity," in Habermas's view, and that step has allowed for an undifferentiation of "world relations, speaker perspectives, and validity claims that is inherent in linguistic communication itself. Without this reference system, however, the distinction between levels of reality, between fiction and reality, between everyday practice and extra-ordinary experience, and between the corresponding kinds of texts and genres becomes impossible and even pointless."[29]

While Habermas is right in highlighting the need to differentiate between genres and validity claims, I think his critical approach needs to distinguish between the philosophical discourses that consider themselves only narratives, and philosophical discourses that need to use a connection to narratives in order to configure a moral theory. I want to propose a "normative bridge" between narratives and the effect they produce on the reader by elaborting a theory of "reflective judgment." Before describing such a bridge, allow me first to bring into view some examples of the relation of narratives to philosophy and social sciences.

Gadamer, for example, has related literature and philosophy to religion because of the "existential" bond between them. In his essay "Rainer Maria Rilke's Interpretation of Existence: On the Book by Romano Guardini,"[30] Gadamer calls our attention to a hermeneutic requirement, "being struck by," while interpreting literary texts. Gadamer is concerned here with the "religious" dimension of human existence that strikes us as something deeply connected with our own fears, which can only be rationally recaptured through a careful hermeneutic. According to Gadamer, "we can never fully comprehend a text unless it is related to the context of our own life as a possible answer to an existential question."[31] Thus, Gadamer insists on the possibility of establishing a permanent dialogue between philosophy and literature. He sees it as a process of *Ausbildung*, something that will help our self-education. In this way, the cultivation of intellectual and moral virtues creates a context where human judgment has a chance of becoming "meaningful."[32]

In the same manner, Walter Benjamin sought something in the relation between philosophy and literature that could elevate our consciousness of moral responsibility. He chose the power of storytelling because "the storyteller takes what he tells from experience—his own or that reported by others. And he in turn makes it the experience of those who are listening to his tale."[33] But what the storyteller takes from others' experiences or from his or her own can only be preserved by creating a moral space, a space we call "memory" or "recollection," that Benjamin linked to "moral responsibility."

Benjamin privileges the role of storytellers because the effect they create on the people is immediate; the spectators are "struck" by their own personal need to repeat the story to others. Thus, argues Benjamin, "the more completely will be his inclination to repeat it to someone else someday, sooner or later,"[34] the more he or she will care to understand it and the better he or she will remember it. It is this connection between stories and the moral space of memory that Benjamin brings to the moral textures of storytelling. Memory becomes what Benjamin has called the "epic faculty" par excellence. "Only by virtue of a comprehensive memory can epic writing absorb the course of events on the one hand and, with the passing of these, make its peace with the power of death on the other."[35] What the story must achieve, then, is a connection with the singularity of the experience of suffering, while at the same time becoming a part of the experience of others. Thus, Benjamin allows us to see the redemptive power of storytelling. That is precisely why Benjamin claims that storytellers have in common the "freedom with which they move up and down the rungs of their experience as on a ladder. A ladder extending downward to the interior of the earth and disappearing into the clouds is the image for a *collective experience* to which even the deepest shock of every individual experience, death, constitutes no impediment or barrier."[36]

Going one step beyond Benjamin, Hannah Arendt was the first thinker to understand the importance of narratives in relation to evil and its redemptive powers, while conceiving stories as the only way to rewind what has happened, that is, to begin anew. After understanding that there could be no redemption from evil deeds but only a proper ending and a new beginning, Arendt theorized about the faculty of forgiveness. "Forgiving," says Arendt, "serves to undo the deeds of the past, whose 'sins' hang like Damocles' sword over every new generation."[37] Everything that can be punished can be forgiven, insists Arendt, except "those offenses which, since Kant, we call 'radical evil' and about whose nature so little is known, even to us who have been exposed to one of their rare outbursts on the public scene."[38]

Those offenses, which Arendt portrayed as mechanisms that have completely stripped away every sort of human spontaneity, point to her persistent concern with twentieth-century totalitarianism's organization of mass murder and extermination. As Richard J. Bernstein has eloquently concluded, Arendt conceptualized "radical evil" neither as punishable nor forgivable, because "punishment and forgiveness presuppose what radical evil eradicates: that is, human action."[39] Faced with this stark impossibility, Arendt envisioned storytelling as a different way to come to terms with past evil. Not by punishing or forgiving, but by creating new understandings of what happened, it is possible to recover humanity. For humans "are not born in order to die but in order to begin."[40] With Arendt's judgment on Eichmann, she provides us with the "first" story, which allows us to see the two functions of narratives while understanding the specificity of evil in the twentieth century. First, in the exemplary validity of the story she tells us, "Eichmann appears as an example of a new kind of evildoer," one who comes into existence with twentieth-century totalitarianism. For with that development, Arendt claims, we are able to grasp a new stage in the moral history of humanity and evil actions. Something specifically linked to our historical times is recovered by Arendt in her analysis of the concrete character of totalitarian evil, something that affected both the agents and their victims by stripping away their humanity.[41] Second, her conceptualization of the banality of evil is historically linked with totalitarianism, as Berel Lang claims, "what was distinctive for her about totalitarianism, which was epitomized for her in one feature in particular: that here, for the first time, appeared an idea of evil which called for the extinction of man as an individual."[42] This is directly connected with the idea of Eichmann as being incapable of discernment or judgment—"the perpetrator himself also was affected." Thus, Arendt creates her own vocabulary to describe an era where negative exemplary validity is conceptualized as the "politics of evil." Our century has witnessed evil as a system where individuality was erased: "Totalitarianism had produced a change not only in how people acted toward each other, but in human nature itself, in what man was."[43]

UNDERSTANDING EVIL THROUGH REFLECTIVE JUDGMENT

Understanding evil seems to lead us toward the realm of interpretation, for actions are understood and linguistically shaped through our moral horizons. If we need interpretation, then we are forced to exercise our capacity for some kind of judgment, and as Hannah Arendt argued, judgment is "the most political of man's mental abilities."[44] But even if "people draw meaning and value from the particular," as Barbara Herman argues, "moral judgment is not the first step in moral deliberation."[45] The first step is how we tell our story, and it is precisely how we perceive a world with specific moral features that situates us in the realm of making or not making a possible judgment This step moves us to what Herman calls a clarifying concept, which she develops as the rules of moral salience.[46]

What exactly judgment, and specifically "reflective judgment," is will be clarified while critically thematizing Kant's and Arendt's notions of reflective judgment in my forthcoming book *Narrating Evil: A Postmetaphysical Theory of Reflective Judgment*. For now, it is sufficient to say that we consider "reflective judgment" the basic moral tool for understanding evil, and that it is through storytelling that we are able to configure a "judgment" that is capable of capturing the particularity and uniqueness of action. The concept of action is developed into what Arendt called "exemplary action," a category that refers to providing examples that help us recognize the specificity of evil action through moral lenses. Judgment, in other words, is provided in the construction of meaning; it is captured in the narration of evil. This brings us back to the interrelation between the moral and the political realms. By creating concrete examples of "evil-actions," we can conceptualize evil's diverse meanings as understanding historical stages of moral learning.

To achieve this, we need to focus on stories that display experiences where evil appears as intersubjectively constructed. We need to show how the symbolic elements in evil narratives are related to the findings of anthropology, sociology, religion, and literature. Finally, we need philosophy to avoid relativism,[47] laying the ground for a universalistic approach to evil so we can morally condemn it. The goal of our philosophical approach cannot be fulfilled without the connection to anthropology,[48] to sociology,[49] to psychology,[50] to literary criticism,[51] and to religion.[52] In building these interdisciplinary connections, we will use the discussion about narratives in recent theories of literature, as well as aspects of storytelling that have been explored by anthropological and sociological experts. We will use the tools that have been provided by religious traditions and by the hermeneutics of religion that have clarified how to interpret the stories of the sacred and their binary definitions.

For example, recent sociological research has shown how illuminating it can be to focus on how people narrate their actions, and in particular how actions and moral "evaluations" are inextricably linked through a "narrative order." Karen A. Cerulo's book, *Deciphering Violence: The Cognitive Structure of Right and Wrong*,[53] focuses on narratives in which individuals think, describe, and evaluate violence. Cerulo argues that she has identified "a menu of sequences—four distinct temporal formats that drive narrators' verbal and visual accounts of violence," and offers evidence of why "narrators come to adopt one sequence over another. Such analyses reveal that storytellers, while not necessarily conscious of their actions, invoke the four sequences of violence in highly regular and predictable ways—ways that tranform storytellers' perceptions of audience morality."[54] Cerulo concludes that her "research indicates that the way in which storytellers sequence a violent account can influence audience assessments of violence as right, wrong, or something in between."[55] Cerulo's work makes us aware that sequences in telling a story prove to be essential to understanding and judging.

The link between narratives and sociology thus appears important and useful for us because "data derived from interviews with those who construct violent narratives and those who read and see them, as well as content analysis of the accounts themselves, suggest that story sequences come to signify a matrix of good and evil." Cerulo shows the connection between narration and the perspective imposed by an account's sequence which is already framed under a moral scenario.[56]

We can see, then, how sociological research supports the conclusion that we have reached through our earlier interpretations of theology and philosophy—in "ordering" a story into a sequence, a narrative, we step inevitably into the moral realm of action. Thus meaning becomes a significant element connecting morality and culture,[57] and, in making this connection, we are led to the possible role of judgment: "Attention to story sequencing may diminish the number of acts now typically evaluated as acceptable or justifiable. If certain storytelling methods can successfully reduce public tolerance for violence, then attention to narrative style ultimately may prove an important tool in reducing the incidence of violent behaviors."[58]

C. Fred Alford's work with inmates' experiences of evil complements Cerulo's findings. Alford claims that "doing evil is" already "telling a story," and he concludes, "how we tell our stories about evil is as important as what we tell."[59] What these stories reveal is how the "particular" is connected to something of a larger significance. Hannah Arendt beautifully described this connection as "the meaning of a committed act [which] is revealed only when the action itself has come to an end and become a story susceptible of narration." This connection provides the possibility for judgment and a certain kind of moral mastery.

> Insofar as any "mastering" of the past is possible, it consists in relating what has happened; but such a narration, too, which shapes history, solves no problems and assuages no suffering; it does not master anything once and for all. Rather, as long as the meaning of the events remains alive—and this meaning can persist for very long periods of time—"mastering of the past" can take the form of ever-recurrent narration.[60]

Stories about evil are thus stories in need of being retold; while reexperiencing them we aim not only at understanding but also at weaving a moral understanding of the past. Alford's psychoanalytic accounts of storytelling highlight this morally redemptive power.

> Ms. Gans knows that her crime tells a story. "I know it means something. It's even kind of funny, if you know what I mean. But it's been two years, and I just can't crack the code." When she finally cracks the code she will have done more than figure out the meaning of her act. She will have entered another conceptual world, in which symbols are more abstract, less embodied and thinglike. Feeling what she is talking about will replace acting it out (or reciting its acting-out, what she was doing in the group).[61]

Through narrations, we see how new meanings change our understanding of the past, how the past "is reintrepreted, yes, but more than that, it is reorganized, repopulated. It becomes filled with new actions, new intentions, new events that caused us to be as we are."[62]

From an anthropological perspective too, storytelling has been rooted in culture since early times. Consider, for example, the Hebrew scriptures and the Jewish religion. Richard Kearny describes the classic case of biblical Israel as a "historic spiritual community formed on the basis of foundational narratives (especially Genesis and Exodus)," through which successive generations recount and reinterpret[63] the Jewish people's sufferings and deeds. The scriptures were concrete narratives where "the Jewish Bible, like the body of Greek myth, simply told a series of stories about human beings and their interaction with a character, God, about whose metaphysical status little or nothing was said."[64] These were stories about suffering and losing, about good and evil. However, it is the subsequent readings of these texts that open them to further stages of moral learning, enriching our interpretations, and allowing us to reorient our future. These "socially constructed meanings," always transforming themselves through continued readings, deal with "those constraints that the text bears within itself and that have to do in large part with its *Sitz im Leben* and, on the other hand, [with] the different expectations of a series of communities of reading and interpretation that the presumed authors of the text under consideration could not have anticipated."[65]

But if narratives bring certain elements needed in assessing moral judgment, we still need to consider the moral validity of what is recounted, that is, we need to recognize that the site of "factual truth" is a vulnerable space. As Kirstie M. McClure has argued about the danger of reconstructing actions through stories, such a space "is vulnerable to time as memory fades, an exigency that charges the historian with the task of remembrance; but it is vulnerable as well to politics—a contingency that can press the activity of historical writing toward the gap between past and future."[66] Thus, one last problem we need to face is, if narratives contain facts and fiction, why is it that they can still help to configure a normative ground for developing "reflective judgment"?

The answer is related to a process of circularity that takes place in the practical domain, something that Arendt knew when she connected her ideas of judgment to the realm of political praxis. This is why evil can be thematized only through the connection of storytelling and "reflective judgment."[67] Storytelling can become an institutional space where we build up our collective memory, the debts to our past, and reorient ourselves to face the injustices committed against others. How narratives help to reconfigure and reshape reality is important to us, for narratives can morally "construct" their readers[68] and reorient their conduct. Thus, the importance of being affected by different narratives of the past must include critical and reflective activities of appropriation, negation, and differentiation as refigurative possibilities.[69] It is for that reason that in stressing the importance of narratives, we do not seek scientific explanations or factual accuracy; what we acquire, rather, is the possibility of building a bridge, a philosophical horizon, where reflective judgment can situate us within the domain of moral learning. What are judged in narratives are the historical and specific meanings of evil, which help us acquire the wisdom to achieve moral orientation vis-à-vis the particularities of the present.

NOTES

INTRODUCTION

1. See Martha C. Nussbaum, *The Fragility of Goodness: Luck and Ethics in Greek Tragedy and Philosophy* (Cambridge: Cambridge University Press, 1986), esp. section 2, "Plato: Goodness without Fragility?" pp. 87–117

2. Cabrera (chapter 1) argues that her essay's purpose "is not to solve the problem of theodicy, but to dissolve it by arguing that, on the one hand, the stock solutions turn out to be unsatisfactory and, on the other, the problem is generated by the acceptance of a conception of God that is not the only possible nor even the most attractive one."

3. This a good term coined by Martha Nussbaum to relate the origins of Greek tragedy and later developments of human frailty with Aristotle in her book *Fragility of Goodness*, pp. 318–72.

4. Arendt explains in her essay "On Humanity in Dark Times: Thoughts about Lessing" that "the antithesis to compassion is not envy but cruelty, which is an affect no less than compassion, for it is a perversion, a feeling of pleasure where pain would naturallly be felt." In *Men in Dark Times* (New York: Harcourt, Brace and Co., 1968), pp. 3–32, esp. p. 15.

5. Immanuel Kant, *Religion within the Boundaries of Mere Reason, and Other Writings*, ed. Allen Wood and George di Giovanni, introduction by Robert Merrihew Adams (Cambridge: Cambridge University Press, 1998), pp. 54–55.

6. Joan Copjec, "Introduction: Evil in the Time of the Finite World," in *Radical Evil*, ed. Joan Copjec (London: Verso, 1996), pp. vii–xxvii, esp. p. xi.

7. Copjec (ibid., p. xi) argues that "one of the consequences of this redefinition of evil is that it burdens us with full responsibility for our actions; we are no longer able to exonerate ourselves by claiming to be victims of our passions and thus of external circumstances."

8. Ibid., p. 32.

9. Ibid., p. 35.

10. There is new research in this field; see G. Felicitas Munzel, *Kant's Conception*

of Moral Character: The "Critical" Link of Morality, Anthropology, and Reflective Judgement (Chicago: University of Chicago Press, 1999).

11. Wellmer concludes: "But we do know of a paradigm in which this gulf is closed in that it is, so to speak, transferred to the interior of the image, and the **claim** to be saying something with the image disappears. That paradigm is the **aesthetic** image. My surmise is that a myth of the kind that Jonas is telling is only possible as a **literary** image" (*Endgames*, trans. David Midgley [Cambridge: MIT Press, 1998], p. 265).

12. Richard, J. Bernstein, "Did Hannah Arendt Change Her Mind? From Radical Evil to the Banality of Evil," in *Hannah Arendt Twenty Years Later*, ed. Larry May and Jerome Kohn (Cambridge: MIT Press, 1996), pp.127–46, esp. p. 127.

13. Hannah Arendt, *The Origins of Totalitarianism* (New York: Harcourt Brace Jovanovich, 1975), p. 459.

14. Ibid.

15. As Dana Villa argues in his essay "Terror and Radical Evil," "what gives her analysis an urgent contemporary relevance is Arendt's insight into the form of political evil created by totalitarian regimes, an evil that she designated as 'radical' in order to distinguish it from the more familiar horrors perpetrated by political regimes throughout the centuries" (in *Politics, Philosophy, Terror: Essays on the Thought of Hannah Arendt* [Princeton: Princeton University Press, 1999], pp. 11–38, esp. p. 13).

16. Arendt claims that "true understanding does not tire of interminable *dialogue* and 'vicious circles,' because it trusts that *imagination* eventually will catch at least a glimpse of the always frightening light of truth" ("Understanding and Politics," in *Arendt: Essays in Understanding, 1930–1954*, ed. Jerome Kohn [New York: Harcourt, Brace and Co., 1993], pp. 307–27, esp. p. 322; my emphasis).

17. Ibid., p. 323.

18. Ibid., p. 322.

19. Arendt to Kenneth Thompson of the Rockefeller Foundation, 31 March 1969, Arendt Collection, Manuscripts Division, Library of Congress.

20. Arendt, *Origins of Totalitarianism*, p. 433.

21. Villa, "Terror and Radical Evil," p. 16.

22. To follow this process in Argentina, see Carlos Santiago Nino, *Radical Evil on Trial* (New Haven: Yale University Press, 1996).

23. Ronald Beiner argues that "as I interpret Arendt, her writings on the theme of judgment fall into more or less distinct phases: early and late, practical and contemplative. . . . The point of the division, however, is to draw attention to the fact that in, say, the discussion of 'representative thinking' in 'Truth and Politics' there is as yet no concern with judging as distinct mental activity (namely, as one of the three articulations of mental life); here Arendt is concerned only with judging as a feature of political life" (in Hannah Arendt, *Lectures on Kant's Political Philosophy*, ed. with an interpretive essay by Ronald Beiner [Chicago: University of Chicago Press, 1982], pp. 89–156, esp. p. 92.

24. See Hannah Arendt and Karl Jaspers, *Hannah Arendt, Karl Jaspers: Correspondence, 1926–1969*, ed. Lotte Kohler and Hans Saner, trans. Robert and Rita Kimber (New York: Harcourt Brace Jovanovich, 1992).

25. See Dana Villa, "Conscience, the Banality of Evil, and the Idea of a Repre-

sentative Perpetrator," in *Politics, Philosophy, Terror: Essays on the Thought of Hannah Arendt* (Princeton: Princeton University Press, 1999), pp. 39–60.

26. Arendt and Jaspers, p. 62.

27. See, for example, the essay on this subject by Bernstein, "Did Hannah Arendt Change Her Mind?" pp. 127–46.

28. Richard J. Bernstein, *Hannah Arendt and the Jewish Question* (Cambridge: MIT Press, 1996).

29. Hannah Arendt, "Nightmare and Flight," in *Essays in Understanding,* pp. 133–35.

30. Dana Villa makes a very similar point in "Conscience," p. 40.

31. Hannah Arendt and Mary McCarthy, *Between Friends: The Correspondence of Hannah Arendt and Mary McCarthy, 1949–1975,* ed. Carol Brightman (New York: Harcourt, Brace and Co., 1995).

32. Villa, "Conscience," p. 45.

33. As Dana Villa argues, "this theme makes *Eichmann in Jerusalem* a work of moral philosophy, at least implicitly. It is by no means a merely theoretical concern, since it bears directly on the issue of how to preserve responsibility for actions in those circumstances where the struggle of conscience with 'base motives' can no longer be honestly (or accurately) invoked" (ibid., p. 46).

34. Hannah Arendt, *Eichmann in Jerusalem: A Report on the Banality of Evil* (New York: Penguin Books, 1994), p. 24.

35. Arendt writes to Mary McCarthy on 20 September 1963: "You write that one hesitates to claim the right to define my ideas. As I see it, there are no 'ideas' in this Report, there are only facts with a few conclusions, and these conclusions usually appear at the end of the chapter" (*Between Friends,* p. 148).

36. Schmitt was an advocate of this theory of seeing societies as only being capable of defining themselves in terms of "friends and enemies." See Carl Schmitt, *The Concept of the Political,* trans. George Schwab (New Brunswick: Rutgers University Press, 1976).

37. Arendt says, "we became aware of the existence of a right to have rights (and that means to live in a framework where one is judged by one's actions and opinions) and a right to belong to some kind of community, only when millions of people emerged who had lost and could not regain these rights of the new global political situation" (*Origins of Totalitarianism,* p. 297).

CHAPTER 1. IS GOD EVIL?

This essay was translated by Douglas McDermid.

1. In what follows I speak of the "Judeo-Christian tradition," well aware that the differences—not only between Jews and Christians, but also within each of these groups—are many, and are, on the whole, more important than the points of agreement. Nevertheless, I believe that in general all of them share a conception of God that allows us to speak, for the purposes of this essay, of one religious tradition.

2. See especially chapters 5 and 11.13–21. In the former, the Decalogue is expounded; in the latter Yahweh's promise to bless the obedient is repeated, as is the threat to visit suffering upon those who do not abide by the terms of the Covenant.

3. *Ecclesiasticus* 2: 4–5.

4. Douglas MacDonald, *Unspoken Sermons,* cited in C. S. Lewis, *The Problem of Pain* (London: Fontana Books, 1957), p. vi.

5. R. Otto, *The Idea of the Holy* (Oxford: Oxford University Press, 1967).

6. B. Spinoza, in the appendix to the first book of his *Ethica, ordine geometrico demostrata.*

7. I believe that all those authors who, implicitly or explicitly, have followed Otto's stress on religious experience would agree on this point. I refer to van der Leeuw, Michel Meslin, Mircea Eliade, Martin Buber, and (in the Spanish-speaking world) José Gómez Caffarena, Martín Velasco, Luis Villoro, and Ramon Xirau. Of course, each of them has their peculiar features, but any one of them could exemplify the conception of God to which I am referring.

8. See H. Fingarette, "The Meaning of Law in the Book of Job," in *Revisions,* ed. S. Hauerwas and A. MacIntyre (London: Notre Dame Press, 1983).

9. I defend this reading in much greater detail in chapter 3, "El Dios de Job," of my book *El lado oscuro de Dios* (Barcelona and Mexico City: UNAM-Paidós, 1998).

10. "A Masque of Reason," in *Job: A Case Study,* by Robert Frost, ed. Raymond Breakstone (New York: Bookman Associates, 1964), pp. 224–25.

11. *La entraña humanista del cristianismo* (Navarre: Verbo Divino, 1998), p. 287.

CHAPTER 2. WHAT'S THE PROBLEM OF EVIL?

1. See Susan Neiman, "Metaphysics, Philosophy: Rousseau and the Problem of Evil," in *Reclaiming the History of Ethics: Essays for John Rawls,* ed. A. Reath, B. Herman, and C. M. Korsgaard (Cambridge: Cambridge University Press, 1997).

2. *Critique of Practical Reason,* Ak. 13.

3. See, for example, J. B. Schneewinds, *The Invention of Autonomy* (Cambridge: Cambridge University Press, 1998) or the work represented in A. Reath, B. Herman, and C. M. Korsgaard, eds., *Reclaiming the History of Ethics: Essays for John Rawls* (Cambridge: Cambridge University Press, 1997).

4. *Saemtliche Schriften,* vol. 5, p. 509.

5. Walter Benjamin, *Theses on the Philosophy of History,* in *Illuminations* (New York: Schocken, 1969).

6. Benjamin, *Illuminations,* p. 253.

7. See Karl Loewith, *Meaning in History* (Chicago: University of Chicago Press, 1949) and Jacob Taubes, *Abendlaendische Eschatologie* (Munich: Francke, 1947), for the original statements of these claims as well as Hans Blumenberg, *Die Legitimitaet der Neuzeit* (Frankfurt am Main: Suhrkamp, 1966), for the most interesting attempt to answer them. Further discussion can be found in Odo Marquard, *Schwierigkeiten mit der Geschichtsphilosophie* (Frankfurt am Main: Suhrkamp, 1973), as well as Robert Pippin, *Idealism as Modernism* (Cambridge: Cambridge University Press, 1997).

8. As close friend to David Hume, Smith had heard many drafts of the *Dialogues Concerning Natural Religion*—the most devastating attack on the notion of Providence ever written—read aloud. Its publication was entrusted to his care in Hume's last letter, written two days before his death. One must wonder how Smith thought

about transferring to the material world the careful intervention his friend had banned from the cosmos.

9. *The Philosophy of Leibniz* (London, 1937), emphasis in original.

10. Max Horkheimer, *Gesammelte Schriften*, vol. 6, *Kritik der instrumentellen Vernunft*, 2 (Frankfurt am Main: Fischer Taschenbuch Verlag, 1991).

11. Susan Neiman, *The Unity of Reason: Rereading Kant* (Oxford: Oxford University Press, 1994).

12. To make this argument convincing one would have to distinguish between redemption, which is something you cannot do on your own, and a more limited form of salvation—the latter being something sought at least by earlier forms of analytic philosophy, which hoped that patience and restraint would make intelligible some of the structures of an unintelligible world.

13. For further discussion see Susan Neiman, "Jean Améry," in *The Yale Companion to Jewish Writing and Thought in Germany, 1096–1996*, ed. S. L. Gilman and J. Zipes (New Haven: Yale University Press, 1997).

14. See Jean Améry, *Über das Altern: Revolte und Resignation* (Stuttgart: Klett Cotta, 1968). Alfred Andersch called this book Améry's poem on the Lisbon earthquake.

15. See Susan Neiman, "Theodicy in Jerusalem," in *Hannah Arendt in Jerusalem*, ed. Ascheim (Berkeley: University of California Press, forthcoming).

16. Hannah Arendt, "Nightmare and Flight," in *Essays on Understanding* (New York: Harcourt, Brace and Co., 1994).

17. Hannah Arendt and Kurt Blumenfeld, *Die Korrespondenz* (Hamburg: Rotbuch Verlag, 1995).

18. Hannah Arendt, "Understanding and Politics," in *Essays on Understanding* (New York: Harcourt, Brace and Co., 1994).

CHAPTER 3.
"RADICAL FINITUDE" AND THE PROBLEM OF EVIL

1. Published in English as *Of Human Freedom*, trans. J. Gutman (Chicago: Open Court, 1936).

2. See Slavoj Žižek, *The Indivisible Remainder: An Essay on Schelling and Related Matters* (London: Verso, 1996); idem, *The Plague of Fantasies* (London: Verso, 1997); and the various contributions in Joan Copjec, ed., *Radical Evil* (London: Verso, 1996). Also Alenka Zupančič, *Ethics of the Real: Kant, Lacan* (London: Verso, 2000), esp. chapters 5 and 6. For a reevaluation of the idealist theory of evil from a somewhat different angle, see Rüdiger Safranski, *Das Böse oder das Drama der Freiheit* (Munich and Vienna: Carl Hanser Verlag, 1997). The Lacanian influence stems from Lacan's unorthodox reading of Kant, which argues the possibility of a disinterested commitment to evil. See the famous essay "Kant avec Sade," in *Écrits* (Paris: Éditions du Seuil, 1966), and *The Seminar of Jacques Lacan*, book 7, *The Ethics of Psychoanalysis*, ed. Jacques-Alain Miller (London: Routledge, 1992).

3. An exception is Henry Staten's tonic and informative article "Radical Evil Revived," *Radical Philosophy* 98 (November–December 1999): 131–43, which traces the continuities between neo-Lacanian discourse on evil and the Christian theological tradition with which the Lacanians imagine they have broken.

4. Jürgen Habermas, "Metaphysics after Kant," in *Postmetaphysical Thinking: Philosophical Essays* (Cambridge, England: Polity Press, 1992), p. 15.

5. Hans Jonas, "The Concept of God after Auschwitz," in *Morality and Mortality: A Search for the Good after Auschwitz*, ed. Lawrence Vogel, pp. 131–43 (Evanston, Ill.: Northwestern University Press, 1996); Albrecht Wellmer, "Der Mythos vom leidenden und werdenden Gott. Fragen an Hans Jonas," in *Endspiele: Die Unversöhnliche Moderne* (Frankfurt am Main: Suhrkamp, 1993), pp. 250–56.

6. Hans Jonas, "Mind, Matter, and Creation: Cosmological Evidence and Cosmogonic Speculation," in *Mortality and Morality: A Search for the Good after Auschwitz* (Evanston, Ill.: Northwestern University Press, 1996), p. 188.

7. Ibid., pp. 189–90.

8. Hans Jonas, "Immortality and the Modern Temper," in *Mortality and Morality: A Search for the Good after Auschwitz* (Evanston, Ill.: Northwestern University Press, 1996), p. 129.

9. See Jürgen Habermas, "Metaphysics after Kant," in *Postmetaphysical Thinking: Philosophical Essays* (Cambridge, England: Polity Press, 1992), p. 15.

10. Albrecht Wellmer, "Der Mythos vom leidenden und werdenden Gott. Fragen an Hans Jonas," in *Endspiele: Die Unversöhnliche Moderne* (Frankfurt am Main: Suhrkamp, 1993), p. 253.

11. Ibid.

12. Ibid., p. 254.

13. Jonas, "The Concept of God after Auschwitz," p. 139.

14. Wellmer, "Der Mythos," p. 255.

15. Jonas, "The Concept of God after Auschwitz," pp. 139–40.

16. Wellmer, "Der Mythos," p. 255.

17. Ibid.

18. Paul Ricoeur, *La Critique et la conviction: Entriten avec François Azouvi et Marc dee Launay* (Paris: Calmann-Levy, 1995), p. 168.

CHAPTER 4. RADICAL EVIL

Emphasis in all quotes is original, except where noted.

1. Hannah Arendt, *Essays in Understanding, 1930–54,* ed. Jerome Kohn (New York: Harcourt, Brace and Co., 1994), p. 134; Hannah Arendt, *The Origins of Totalitarianism,* 3d ed. rev. (New York: Harcourt Brace Jovanovich, 1982), p. 459; Hannah Arendt, *Essays in Understanding,* p. 14.

2. This is T. M. Greene and H. H. Hudson's translation of the title, *Die Religion innerhalb der Grenzen der blossen Vernunft.* In the new Cambridge edition of the works of Immanuel Kant, George di Giovanni translates the title as *Religion within the Boundaries of Mere Reason* (trans. G. D. Giovanni, ed. A. W. Wood [Cambridge: Cambridge University Press, 1998]). References are to the Greene and Hudson translation (New York: Harper Torchbooks, 1960), which is still the standard. It contains an introduction by John R. Silber, "The Ethical Significance of Kant's *Religion.*"

3. An English translation of this essay is published as an appendix to Michael Despland, *Kant on History and Religion* (Montreal: McGill-Queen's University Press, 1973).

4. In "On the Failure of All Attempted Philosophical Theodicies" Kant says that "theodicy is not a task of science but is a matter of faith" (p. 293). He does discuss the Book of Job, and (consistent with his understanding of moral faith) writes: "Job proved that he did not base his morality on his faith but his faith on his morality" (p. 293).

For a study of the development of Kant's understanding of evil and his views about the traditional theological problem of evil see Oliver Reboul, *Kant et le Problème du Mal* (Montreal: Presses de l'Université de Montréal, 1971). A decade before the publication of the *Religion*, Kant, in his *Lectures on the Philosophical Doctrine of Religion*, says: "Thus evil in the world can be regarded as *incompleteness in the development of the germ [Kiem] toward the good*. Evil has *no special* germ; for it is *mere negation* and consists only in the *limitation of the good*. It is nothing beyond this, other than incompleteness in the development of the germ to the good out of uncultivatedness" (in *Religion and Rational Theology: The Cambridge Edition of the Works of Immanuel Kant*, trans. G. D. Giovanni, ed. A. W. Wood [Cambridge: Cambridge University Press, 1996], p. 411).

5. See the discussion of Reinhold's criticism of Kant (and a similar recent criticism by Gerold Prauss) by Henry E. Allison in *Kant's Theory of Freedom* (Cambridge: Cambridge University Press, 1990), pp. 133–36.

6. Kant sometimes uses *Wille* in a broad sense and sometimes in a narrow, more technical sense. When used in the broad sense it refers to the entire faculty of volition. In the narrow, more technical sense it refers exclusively to the norm that is the moral incentive for our free choice or adoption, i.e., for the *Willkür*. For a discussion of the *Wille/Willkür* distinction, see Allison, *Kant's Theory of Freedom*, pp.129–36, and Silber, "Ethical Significance," pp. xciv–cvi. I have followed the procedure of always adding the German word to the English translation in order to indicate when Kant uses "*Wille*" and "*Willkür*." For a discussion of the English translations of these terms (and their cognates), see Ralf Meerbote, "Wille and Willkür in Kant's Theory of Action," in *Interpreting Kant*, ed. Moltke S. Gram (Iowa City: University of Iowa Press, 1982), pp. 69–89.

7. Allison, *Kant's Theory of Freedom*, p. 129.

8. Silber, "Ethical Significance," p. civ.

9. Allen Wood, *Kant's Moral Religion* (Ithaca: Cornell University Press, 1970), p. 211.

10. Christine Korsgaard, *Creating the Kingdom of Ends* (Cambridge: Cambridge University Press, 1996), pp. 55–67. In my text I have cited her translations from Kant's *Groundwork*.

11. Ibid., p. 55.

12. Ibid., p. 58.

13. Ibid., p. 60.

14. According to this "rigoristic" analysis Kant would not hesitate to condemn philosophers from Hume to Annette Baier to Richard Rorty who claim that we ought to be guided by our sense of benevolence and our sympathy for our fellow human beings. They are not simply misguided. They are recommending the adoption of *evil maxims*—maxims which give priority to nonmoral incentives.

15. Allison, *Kant's Theory of Freedom*, pp. 147–48.

16. Many of Kant's contemporaries (including Goethe and Schiller) were extremely critical and skeptical of his introduction of the concept of radical evil.

They took it to be a a misguided concession to Christian orthodoxy. Schiller called Kant's essay "scandalous," and Goethe wrote: "Kant required a lifetime to purify his philosophical mantle of many impurities and prejudices. And now he has wantonly tainted it with the shameful stain of radical evil, in order that Christians too might be attracted to kiss its hem." (For the references and a discussion of these criticisms, see Emil Fackenheim, "Kant and Radical Evil," *University of Toronto Quarterly* 23 [1954]: 340.) The question may be raised: What is the relation between radical evil and the Christian doctrine of original sin? The answer to this question depends on one's understanding of original sin (and radical evil). Kant does think that his concept of radical evil reconstructs the *rational core* of the Christian doctrine of original sin. But one should not underestimate the extent to which Kant categorically rejects many of the theological claims about original sin. So it is possible to interpret radical evil as a sharp repudiation of an orthodox understanding of original sin. (See Fackenheim, "Kant and Radical Evil.") Why did Kant so late in his career feel the need to take up the question of radical evil? There are several reasons. There is no doubt that Kant wanted to extract and defend what he took to be the rational core of a (Christian) religious faith. But I also think that there is a deeper philosophical reason for investigating radical evil. Without compromising his moral stance that human beings are responsible for their good and evil deeds, Kant's understanding of human nature is that we are neither angels nor devils. He also rejected the idea that we are born *morally* good and become corrupted, as well as the idea that we are intrinsically *morally* evil, that we are born sinners and cannot escape from *actually* sinning. This understanding of human nature as intrinsically neither *morally* good nor *morally* evil also has significant consequences for Kant's understanding of human history and progress. Kant seeks to walk a fine line. On the one hand he is skeptical of the idea of moral progress whereby human beings can (and will) achieve human perfection. But on the other hand, although human beings never can escape from the propensity to evil—a propensity constitutive of their species nature, there can be moral progress in history insofar as human beings can become actually good by virtue of their freedom. Kant's faith in (limited) moral and political progress is played out against a dark background, a realistic appraisal of "crooked humanity." In this respect, then, Kant departs significantly from some of the more naive and optimistic Enlightenment conceptions of human progress (for example, Condorcet). Many of the tensions and problems in Kant's theory of radical evil can be traced back to his attempt to *reconcile* the claim that human beings are evil by their very nature with the claim that, despite this propensity, human beings—even the most wicked—can *become* morally good.

17. Arendt, *The Origins of Totalitarianism*, p. 459.

18. For an analysis of what Arendt means by radical evil, see Richard J. Bernstein, *Hannah Arendt and the Jewish Question* (Cambridge: MIT Press, 1996), chap. 7, "From Radical Evil to the Banality of Evil," pp. 137–53.

19. Silber, "Ethical Significance," p. xcvii.

20. Korsgaard, *Creating the Kingdom of Ends*, p. 160. See also Henry E. Allison, *Kant's Transcendental Idealism* (New Haven: Yale University Press, 1983), and Wood, *Kant's Moral Religion*.

21. Wood, *Kant's Moral Religion*, pp. 210–11.

22. It is difficult to find proper English equivalents for *Anlagen, Gesinnung,* and *Hang.* Even the new Cambridge translation follows the standard translation of *Anlagen* as "predispositions," *Gesinnung* as "disposition," and *Hang* as "propensity." But the differences among these concepts, especially the *major* distinction between *Anlagen* on the one hand and *Gesinnung* and *Hang* on the other hand is absolutely crucial for understanding radical evil. This distinction is the basis for *denying* that man is good by nature and *affirming* that "man is evil by nature."

23. Silber, "Ethical Significance," p. cxv.

24. Ibid., p. cxxvii.

25. See Daniel O'Connor, "Good and Evil Disposition," *Kant-Studien* 76 (1985): 288–302. O'Connor brings out many of the difficulties in Kant's analysis of *Gesinnung* and his analysis of evil. With some reservations, I find myself in basic agreement with him when he writes: "There is something odd about Kant's whole discussion of evil, for even if we accepted Kant's contradictory notion of an evil disposition which is freely chosen outside time, we would by his own admission gain nothing in the way of understanding. The 'rational origin of the perversion of the will . . . remains inscrutable to us, because this propensity itself must be set down to our account and because, as a result, that ultimate ground of all maxims would in turn involve the adoption of an evil maxim [as its basis]'" (p. 299). See Allison, *Kant's Theory of Freedom,* pp. 136–45, where he attempts to answer O'Connor's criticisms and to give a plausible account of *Gesinnung.* See also Gordon E. Michalson Jr.'s helpful discussion of the difficulties and instabilities in Kant's understanding of radical evil as an innate propensity (*Fallen Freedom* [Cambridge: Cambridge University Press, 1990], pp. 40–51, 62–70).

26. Here we touch upon one of the most complex and intensely controversial topics in Kant scholarship—the precise meaning and role of maxims. In this context, I simply want to note that, in the *Religion,* Kant clearly commits himself to the idea of a hierarchy of maxims—to the idea of a "supreme maxim" that governs more specific maxims. This raises difficult issues concerning the precise relation between these different levels of maxims. If *all* maxims are freely chosen, if they are manifestations of "the exercise of freedom," then it is not entirely clear what is the relation (causal, logical, or conceptual) between a supreme maxim and the more specific maxims that it presumably influences. Radical evil is a "corrupt propensity," i.e., a supreme maxim that corrupts more specific maxims, but it is not clear precisely how this corruption takes place. How does one freely chosen maxim (no matter how general or ultimate it may be) corrupt another freely chosen maxim? For discussions of meaning and role of maxims see Allison, *Kant's Theory of Freedom;* Onora O'Neill, *Acting on Principle: An Essay on Kantian Ethics* (New York: Columbia University Press, 1975); idem, "Kant After Virtue," *Inquiry* 26 (1983): 387–405; idem, "Universal Laws and Ends in Themselves, *Monist* 73 (1989): 341–61; Barbara Herman, *The Practice of Moral Judgment* (Cambridge: Harvard University Press, 1993); and Korsgaard, *Creating the Kingdom of Ends.*

27. I do not think it is appropriate to ignore or exaggerate Kant's prejudices. Kant, who insisted on public criticism, would expect one to expose prejudices—even when they are exhibited by Kant himself. Kant does not give any evidence for his claim that "all savage peoples have a propensity for intoxicants." He seems to think that this is an obvious truth.

A careful reading of the *Religion* shows how Kant displays numerous anthropological and religious prejudices—some of which are horrendous and very damaging. Kant shows his prejudice (and ignorance) about religions other than Christianity, when he claims that the Christian religion is one true natural and learned religion which is the religion that possesses "the prime essential of the true church, namely the qualification for universality" (Rel 145). Furthermore, Kant also says: "of all the public religions that have ever existed, the Christian alone is moral" (Rel 47). Presumably, Christianity (when rationally understood and divested of extraneous theological elements) is the one and only universal rational moral religion.

28. One might think that although the *Willkür* is not causally determined, it is at least influenced by the propensity to evil—an influence which it must resist. But if "influenced" means "causally influenced" then this suggestion is incompatible with Kant's understanding of human freedom and free choice (*Willkür*).

29. I am tempted to say that the concept of radical evil is not only innocuous, it is "banal"—although I do not mean this is the sense of banality that Hannah Arendt intends when she speaks about the "banality of evil." Nevertheless, Sharon Anderson-Gold, in her discussion of radical evil does say: "There is a certain parallel between Kant's concept of radical evil and Hannah Arendt's concept of 'banal' evil in *Eichmann in Jerusalem* . . . although Arendt would not treat evil as a species character" ("Kant's Rejection of Devilishness: The Limits of Human Volition," *Idealistic Studies* 14 [1984]: 48, n. 30).

30. In the litany of examples that Kant gives to show why we do not need a formal proof that "man is evil by nature," we once again find evidence of Kant's prejudices based upon limited and selective anthropological sources. Kant writes:

> If we wish to draw our examples from that state in which various philosophers hoped preeminently to discover the natural goodness of human nature, namely, from the so-called *state of nature*, we need but compare with this hypothesis the scenes of unprovoked cruelty in the murder-dramas enacted in Tofoa, New Zealand, and in the Navigator Islands, and the unending cruelty (of which Captain Hearne tells) in the wide wastes of northwestern America, cruelty from which, indeed, not a soul reaps the smallest benefit; and we have vices of barbarity more than sufficient to draw us from such an opinion. (Rel 28)

31. Allison, *Kant's Theory of Freedom*, p. 154. I have several problems with Allison's attempt to justify—to give a deduction of what he characterizes as the synthetic a priori postulate that human beings are radically evil. In the first place, there is not the slightest indication that Kant himself ever provided such a deduction or thought it was necessary. Of course, there can be no objection to try to improve upon Kant, to rectify Kant's omission, as long as we fully recognize that this is not Kant, and that indeed, Kant himself clearly states that no such "formal proof" is required. Nevertheless, when Allison begins his deduction, he tell us that "the key to this deduction is the impossibility of attributing a propensity to good to finite, sensuously affected agents such as ourselves (either to the race as a whole or to particular individuals)" (p. 155). But given what Kant understands to be a propensity I do not find Allison's reasoning persuasive. If a propensity is a supreme maxim, "a subjective determining ground of the will" that "springs from our freedom," then why cannot there be a propensity to good. After all, possessing such a propensity does not mean that we will *become* morally good unless we adopt good maxims, just as acquiring and possessing

the propensity to evil does not mean that we will *become* morally evil unless we adopt evil maxims. This reinforces a point that I have made earlier. Kant frequently reiterates that a disposition *(Gesinnung) may* be good or evil, but he does not explain why a propensity *(Hang)* is *only* evil. O'Connor, in his critique, also asks, "Why not a propensity towards good?" He also says: "The lack of symmetry in the two aspects of moral motivation must arouse suspicions about the very notion of a *moral* propensity" (O'Connor, "Good and Evil Disposition," p. 297). There is an unresolved tension that runs throughout Kant's discussion of disposition *(Gesinnung)* and propensity *(Hang).* When Kant discusses these concepts and is drawing upon empirical characteristics, then he himself suggests that there are good and bad moral characters, dispositions, and propensities. And this is what we would expect insofar as these terms are intended to designate features of our moral character for which we are responsible. But when Kant turns explicitly to radical evil as a species concept he drops any suggestion of a symmetry between good and evil propensities.

There is still a further very serious problem. Consider the following claims that Kant effectively makes: *(a)* Radical evil is a propensity to moral evil. *(b)* This propensity is innate and universal in the human species. *(c)* This propensity "must spring from freedom," i.e., from "the exercise of freedom whereby the supreme maxim . . . is adopted by the will *[Willkür]*" (Rel 26). But these three claims entail what (on Kantian grounds) is an absurd—indeed, a self-contradictory—conclusion. All human beings (the human race or species) *necessarily* freely choose the propensity to moral evil.

32. See John R. Silber, "Kant at Auschwitz," in *Proceedings of the Sixth International Kant Congress,* ed. Gerhard Funke and Thomas M. Seebohm (Washington, D.C.: Center for Advanced Research in Phenomenology and University Press of America, 1991), pp. 177–211, esp. p. 180.

33. It is uncanny how close Eichmann came to getting Kant right. Before his trial, in his interview with Avner Less, the Israeli police interrogator, Eichmann said that he lived by duty according to the categorical imperative, "the demand by Kant which I long assumed as my guiding principle. I fashioned my life according to this demand." At the trial, when Judge Raveh asked Eichmann what he meant by his statement, Eichmann replied, "That the basis of my will and the pattern of my life should be such that at all times I should be a universal example of lawfulness. This is what I more or less understood by it." Judge Raveh then asked, "Would you say, then, that your activities within the framework of the deportation of the Jews was consistent with Kant?" Eichmann then gave a very sophisticated Kantian answer. "No, certainly not. For I did not mean as I was living then, under the pressure of a third party. When I talked of the categorical imperative, I was referring to the time when I was my own master, with a will and aspirations of my own, and not when I was under the domination of a supreme force." And he added, "Then I could not live in accordance with this principle [the categorical imperative]. But I could include in this principle the concept of *obedience to authority.* This I must do, for this authority was then responsible for what happened." (These passages from Eichmann's testimony are cited and discussed by Silber in "Kant at Auschwitz," pp. 183–85.)

34. Ibid., p. 185.

35. Ibid., p. 191.

36. Both of these passages from Kant are cited by Silber, ibid., pp. 186, 189. See

Silber's discussion of these (and other closely related passages) in "Kant at Auschwitz." See also Thomas Seebohm's discussion of Kant's uncompromising position in "Kant's Theory of Revolution," *Social Research* 4 (winter 1984): 557–87. Hannah Arendt also discusses Kant's enthusiasm for the French Revolution and his judgment that there is never a right to rebellion or revolution. See her *Lectures on Kant's Political Philosophy*, ed. Ronald Beiner (Chicago: University of Chicago Press, 1982).

37. This passage is from Kant's famous essay, "What is Enlightenment?" where he makes a sharp distinction between the public and private use of one's reason (in *Practical Philosophy: The Cambridge Edition of the Works of Immanuel Kant*, trans. M. J. Gregor [Cambridge: Cambridge University Press, 1996], pp. 18–19).

38. To be fair to Kant, it is important to remember that when he argues that there is a duty to obey "a supreme lawmaking power" he is primarily concerned with the nature of civil society and the basis for its legitimation. He was not dealing with a fanatical Führer who was a mass murderer. Nevertheless, Kant's claim that subjects must obey governments that "rule tyrannically by sheer violence" is not qualified in any significant manner. See Silber's discussion of this issue in "Kant at Auschwitz," pp. 185–87. See also Hannah Arendt's comments on Eichmann's appeal to Kant in *Eichmann in Jerusalem: A Report on the Banality of Evil*, 2d ed. (New York: Viking Press, 1965), p. 136.

39. Silber claims that "Kant's theory can comprehend the motivations of an Eichmann, a functionary whose efficiency and zeal were motivated almost entirely by careerist concerns, but it cannot illuminate the conduct of a Hitler" ("Kant at Auschwitz," p. 194).

40. Allison, *Kant's Theory of Freedom*, p. 130.

41. In this context I am not questioning this claim—one that is basic for Kant's moral philosophy. But I do think it should be questioned. Kant, of course, is not making an empirical claim, but an a priori claim. Nevertheless, I do think we should reflect on what Hannah Arendt says happened in Nazi Germany.

> And just as the law in civilized countries assumes that the voice of conscience tells everybody "Thou shalt not kill," even though man's natural desires and inclinations may at times be murderous, so the law of Hitler's land demanded that the voice of conscience tell everybody: "Thou shalt kill," although the organizers of the massacres knew full well that murder is against the normal desires and inclinations of most people. *Evil in the Third Reich had lost the quality by which most people recognize it—the quality of temptation.* (*Eichmann in Jerusalem*, p. 150, emphasis added)

42. Silber, "Kant at Auschwitz," pp. 198–99. In this passage, Silber seems to identify "the deliberate rejection of the moral law" with "knowingly doing evil for its own sake." But these need to be carefully distinguished—especially in light of Silber's claim that "Kant's ethics is inadequate to the understanding of Auschwitz." In fictional portrayals, there certainly have been characters who can be said "to do evil for evil's sake," and to even to exhibit "satanic greatness." But one may seriously question whether this is an adequate characterization of the Nazi leadership— including Hitler. Hitler (and other Nazis) deliberately rejected the moral law, but we must be careful not to aggrandize their motivations by saying they did "evil for its own sake."

In this respect, an interchange in the correspondence between Karl Jaspers and Arendt is relevant. When in 1946 Jaspers sent Arendt a copy of his book, *Die Schuld-*

frage, Arendt objected to his definition of Nazi policy as a crime. She wrote, "The Nazi crimes, it seems to me, explode the limits of the law; and that is precisely what constitutes their monstrousness." Jaspers replied to Arendt:

> You say that what the Nazis did cannot be comprehended as a "crime"—I'm not altogether comfortable with your view, because guilt that goes beyond all criminal guilt inevitably takes on a streak of "greatness"—of satanic greatness—which is, for me, as inappropriate for the Nazis as all the talk about the "demonic" element in Hitler and so forth. It seems to me that we have to see those things in their total banality, in their prosaic triviality, because that's what truly characterizes them. Bacteria can cause epidemics that wipe out nations, but they remain bacteria. I regard any hint of myth and legend with horror.

In a subsequent letter, Arendt conceded that Jaspers was right about his rejection of any suggestion of demonic or "satanic greatness":

> I found what you say about my thoughts on "beyond crime and innocence" in what the Nazis did half convincing; that is, I realize completely that in the way I've expressed this up to now I come dangerously close to that "satanic greatness" that I, like you, totally reject. . . . One thing is certain: We have to combat all impulses to mythologize the horrible. . . .

For a discussion of this exchange and the issues that it raises, see Bernstein, *Arendt and the Jewish Question*, pp. 148–53.

Slavoj Žižek also criticizes Silber for identifying Kant's notion of "diabolic evil" with the "horrible reality of the Nazi Holocaust." Žižek is also critical of those who think that Kantian formalist rigorism serves as a legitimization of the Nazi executioners.

> Our solution to this alternative (the formalist rigorism of Kantian ethics as a possible legitimization of the Nazi executioners; the Nazi evil as a phenomenon which transcends the horizon of Kant's ethical theory) is to reject both its terms. On the one hand, one should fully endorse the notion according to which Kant's rejection of "diabolical evil" is a theoretically incoherent disavowal of the necessary consequence of his own thought: the inherent logic of his thought effectively compelled him to posit "diabolical evil" as the paradox of an evil prompted by no pathological motivations, but just "for the sake of it," which—on a certain level, at least—renders it indistinguishable from the ethical act. On the other hand, against Silber's position, one should categorically deny any connection between Kantian "diabolical evil" and the horrible reality of the Nazi Holocaust: the Nazi Holocaust crimes have nothing to do with the Kantian "diabolical Evil" (with the "demonic" explicit willing of monstrous deeds for the sake of it, because they are evil). (Slavoj Žižek, *The Plague of Fantasies* [London: Verso, 1997], p. 235)

43. Wood, *Kant's Moral Religion*, pp. 212–13.

44. I also think that Wood obscures the basic issue that Silber is addressing when he writes: "Kant is sometimes criticized for rejecting the possibility of an impulse to evil in man, and inclination to rebel against the law or to disobey the law simply for the same of disobedience" (*Kant's Moral Religion*, p. 212). If "impulse" and "inclination" refer to our *sensuous nature*, then, of course, there is not and cannot be a natural inclination to *moral* evil. But Silber is not referring to a (natural) inclination but rather to an *incentive* that is consciously adopted in a evil maxim. The brunt of Silber's criticism is that Kant fails to recognize that there can be such an incentive.

45. Sometimes Kant himself does not pay sufficient attention to his own doctrine that we cannot "observe" maxims, that we can never be absolutely certain what is the

maxim that is determining an agent's action, and that we might even be mistaken in attributing a specific maxim to an agent. If he had, he might have dealt differently with the question of the supposed right to lie. We know for example that during the Second World War, there were many persons—who with great risk to themselves and their families—hid Jews from the Nazis and were prepared to lie (and did lie) when inquiries were made. We admire such people for their moral courage. And indeed, we can reconstruct what their maxims might have been. It was not the blanket claim that lying is permissible or impermissible. Lying as such is not a maxim, it is an action. But a *maxim* such as: "In extreme crisis situations when one can save the lives of innocent victims, it is permissible to lie" is a maxim that can be universalized, and consequently can be rationally defended in a manner consistent with the categorical imperative.

46. See Silber's discussion in "Kant at Auschwitz," pp. 194–201. Sharon Anderson-Gold has attempted to defend Kant against Silber's criticism (as he stated it in an earlier form in his introduction to the *Religion*). She does this by emphasizing that radical evil is a "species character." But insofar as Silber is primarily concerned with those *individuals* whom he characterizes as demonic or diabolical, I do not think she has adequately answered his challenge (see Anderson-Gold, "Kant's Rejection of Devilishness").

47. The recognition that a finite (sensibly affected) rational being still stands in need of a special type of *incentive* in order to will what it ought to do is not a new problem for Kant. In the *Groundwork* Kant already stated, "In order for a sensibly affected rational being to will that for which reason alone prescribes the 'ought,' it is admittedly required that his reason have the capacity to induce a feeling of pleasure or of delight in the fulfillment of duty, and thus there is required a causality of reason to determine sensibility in conformity with principles" (*Groundwork of the Metaphysics of Morals* in *Practical Philosophy: The Cambridge Edition of the Works of Immanuel Kant* [Cambridge: Cambridge University Press, 1996], p. 106). See John R. Silber's perceptive discussion of the nature and role of the moral incentive in "Kant and the Mythic Roots of Morality," *Dialectica* 35 (1981): 167–93. Silber writes: "Moral feeling, the sensible incentive that moves the will *[Willkur]* to fulfillment of duty, does not reduce Kant's theory to one of ethical empiricism, because moral feeling is rationally, not empirically, determined. Moral feeling is the effect of the moral law on the will, not the cause of the moral law" (p. 183).

48. From a very different perspective Slavoj Žižek also raises questions concerning Kant's restrictions on the incentives for adopting evil maxims, and Kant's rejection of diabolical evil. "By rejecting the hypothesis of 'diabolical evil,' Kant retreats from the ultimate paradox of radical Evil, from the uncanny domain of those acts which, although 'evil' as to their content, thoroughly fulfill the formal criteria of an ethical act. Such acts are not motivated by any pathological considerations, i.e., their sole motivating ground is Evil as a principle, which is why they can involve the radical abrogation of one's pathological interests, up to the sacrifice of one's life" (*Tarrying with the Negative: Kant, Hegel, and the Critique of Ideology* [Durham: Duke University Press, 1993], p. 95).

49. See Allison's lucid analysis of the "fact of reason" in *Kant's Theory of Freedom*, pp. 230–49.

50. Although I do think that this is the most basic and fundamental thesis in Kant's moral philosophy, I do not want to underestimate the unresolved problems in making it fully coherent. For Kant's concept of radical freedom (and responsibility) depends upon a coherent analysis of moral agency. And we have seen there is a deep tension in Kant's analysis between the claim that there is "real" continuity and endurance in the moral self—specifically, one's moral disposition *(Gesinnung)* and that this disposition itself is "chosen." Michalson gives a succinct statement of this problem when he writes:

> The problem is how to discuss this primordial agency in a way that protects it as agency (instead of transforming it into a fixed essence), while simultaneously avoiding having this agency dissolve into formless chaos, unrelated to any structure that could underwrite moral valuation. Kant is, as it were, attempting here to get "behind" the self so as to gain a foothold in the structure of the will that will enable him to impute evil or virtue to the moral agent, bit the foothold itself cannot be "fixed." (Michalson, *Fallen Freedom,* p. 57)

CHAPTER 5.
REFLECTIONS ON THE BANALITY OF (RADICAL) EVIL

All references to Kant are to the volume and page of *Kants gesammelte Schriften* (KGS), published by the Deutschen (formerly Königlichen Preuissischen) Akademie der Wissenschaften, 29 volumes (Berlin: Walter de Gruyter [and predecessors], 1902). Specific works cited are referred to by means of the abbreviations listed below. The translations used are also listed below and are referred to immediately following the reference to the volume and page of the German text. Where there is no reference to an English translation, the translation is my own.

Anthro: *Anthropologie in pragmatischer Hinsicht* (KGS 7). *Anthropology from a Practical Point of View,* trans. Mary J. Gregor. The Hague: Nijhoff, 1974.

Gr: *Grundlegung zur Metaphysik der Sitten* (KGS 4). *Groundwork of the Metaphysics of Morals,* trans. H. J. Paton. New York: Harper and Row, 1964.

MS: *Die Metaphysik der Sitten* (KGS 6). *The Metaphysics of Morals,* trans. Mary Gregor. Cambridge: Cambridge University Press, 1991.

Rel: *Die Religion innerhalb der Grenzen der blossen Vernunft* (KGS 6). *Religion within the Limits of Reason Alone,* trans. T. M. Greene and H. H. Hudson. New York: Harper and Row, 1960.

1. Hannah Arendt, *The Jew as Pariah,* ed. Ron H. Feldman (New York: Grove, 1978), p. 251, cited by George Kateb, *Hannah Arendt Politics, Conscience, Evil* (Totowa, N.J.: Rowman and Allanheld, 1984), p. 79.

2. Hannah Arendt, *The Origins of Totalitarianism* (New York: Harcourt, Brace and World, 1951), p. 459.

3. Elisabeth Young-Bruehl, *Hannah Arendt: For Love of the World* (New Haven and London: Yale University Press, 1982), p. 369.

4. Arendt, *The Origins of Totalitarianism,* p. 469.

5. Hannah Arendt, *Eichmann in Jerusalem: A Report on the Banality of Evil* (New York: Viking Press, revised and enlarged edition, 1964), p. 287.

6. Young-Bruehl, *Hannah Arendt,* p. 368.

7. Arendt says this explicitly in *The Human Condition* (Chicago: University of Chicago Press, 1958), p. 241.

8. Ibid., p. 276.

9. Ibid., p. 136.

10. Ibid.

11. See, for example, *Eichmann in Jerusalem*, pp. 93, 136–37, 148–49, 292–93.

12. Ibid., pp. 136–37.

13. Ibid., p. 21.

14. Ibid., pp. 287–88.

15. See, for example, her account of how the judges ought to have addressed the defendant in rendering their verdict (*Eichmann in Jerusalem*, pp. 277–79). On the other hand, she also suggests (ibid., p. 288) that thoughtlessness of the scope of Eichmann's was hardly commonplace.

16. Ibid., p. 288.

17. Ibid., p. 109.

18. Ibid., pp. 47–49.

19. *Lectures on Kant's Political Philosophy*, ed. Ronald Beiner (Chicago: University of Chicago Press, 1982), esp. pp. 70–74.

20. *Eichmann in Jerusalem*, pp. 294–95.

21. Ibid., p. 287.

22. Ibid., p. 49.

23. Ibid., p. 86.

24. Ibid., pp. 51–52.

25. Ibid., p. 52.

26. Presumably, it is in light of this view of evil, as well as the focus of the book on the concrete matter of the judgment of Eichmann and the other Nazis rather than on general metaphysical considerations, that we must understand Arendt's emphatic statement that, of all the things that the book is not, it is "least of all, a theoretical treatise on the nature of evil" (*Eichmann in Jerusalem*, p. 285). If evil is truly as she depicts it, such a treatise would be pointless.

27. Scholem raises this criticism in a letter to Arendt of June 23, 1963. See *The Jew as Pariah*, p. 245.

28. For my discussion of the "Incorporation Thesis," see *Kant's Theory of Freedom*, especially chapter 2, and chapters 8 and 9 of my *Idealism and Freedom* (Cambridge, Cambridge University Press, 1996).

29. See my "Morality and Freedom: Kant's Reciprocity Thesis," *Philosophical Review* 95 (1986): 393–425; and *Kant's Theory of Freedom*, chapter 11, and chapters 8, 9, 10, and 11 of my *Idealism and Freedom*.

30. John Silber, "The Ethical Significance of Kant's Religion," in *Religion within the Limits of Reason Alone*, trans. T. M. Greene and H. H. Hudson, p. cxxix.

31. Allen W. Wood, *Kant's Moral Religion* (Ithaca, N.Y., and London: Cornell University Press, 1970), pp. 210–15.

32. Sharon Anderson-Gold, "Kant's Rejection of Devilishness: The Limits of Human Volition," *Idealistic Studies* 14 (1984): 35–48. I am here basically following Anderson-Gold's analysis.

33. Ibid., p. 48, n. 30.

34. Arendt, *Eichmann in Jerusalem*, p. 52.

35. Ibid., p. 150.

36. Ibid., p. 276.

37. Interestingly enough, Fichte, who in his account of evil follows Kant in the denial of the possibility of devilishness, appeals explicitly to a kind of freely chosen thoughtlessness in the effort to explain how a being who recognizes the authority of the moral law might yet fail to act on it. (See *Das System aer Sittenlehre nach den Principien der Wissenschaftslehre*, 16, IV, *Fichtes Werke*, ed. I. H. Fichte [Berlin: Walter de Gruyter, 1971], vol. 4, pp. 191–98.) In the same context he also emphasizes the role of self-deception.

38. See *Kant's Theory of Freedom*, pp. 158–61.

39. See note 37, above.

40. This notion of moral salience is suggested by the work of Barbara Herman, who develops an account of rules of moral salience and their role in moral judgment. See her "The Practice of Moral Judgment," *Journal of Philosophy* 82 (1985): 414–36; reprinted in *The Practice of Moral Judgment* (Cambridge: Harvard University Press, 1993), chapter 4.

41. This example was suggested to me by Marcia Baron, who used a similar one for a quite different purpose in a symposium on my *Kant's Theory of Freedom*. For my response to Baron's use of this example see chapter 8 of my *Idealism and Freedom*.

42. See, for example, "What Is Enlightenment," 8: 37 and 41.

43. Frederick Beiser, in *Enlightenment, Revolution, and Romanticism: The Genesis of Modern German Political Thought, 1790–1800* (Cambridge: Harvard University Press, 1992), suggests (on p. 36) that Kant temporarily modified his uncompromising views on obedience in *Reflexion* 8055, dating from the late 1780s, only to return to them from 1793 on. But, as Beiser himself acknowledges, since this text is an unpublished fragment, in which Kant may very well be tentatively considering a view rather than firmly committing himself to it, it is difficult to know how much weight to place upon it. Moreover, Beiser ignores both the response to Bouterwork, which dates from after 1793, and the passage from the *Religion*.

CHAPTER 6. THE POLYHEDRON OF EVIL

I would like to thank Dr. María Pía Lara for her invitation to participate in the discussions of the problem of evil which were the basis for the works appearing in this volume. This paper was translated by Laura Gorham.

1. See *Esquisse d'un tableau historique des progrés de l'esprit humain* (Paris: Éditions Sociales, 1972) pp. 211–13, 238, 261ff.

2. Max Weber, *Die Protestantische Ethik*, vol. 1 (Hamburg: Gütersloher Verlagshaus, 1973), p. 20.

3. Max Weber, *Gesammelte Aufsätze zur Wissenschaftslehre*, ed. J. Winckelmann (Tübingen: J. C. B Mohr [Paul Siebeck], 1968), pp. 603ff.

4. Consider, for example, the repulsive effect of the *horrible*, of the *monstrous* found in all spheres of reality: be it in man (for example, in human deformations, sickness, death), in nature (the destruction of the environment), in society and in politics (for example, in brutality, violence, and crime, as well as corruption and repression).

5. The theodicy problem provides the clue for the interpretation of evil within the sphere of theology. The Book of Job provides the classical treatment of this problem. "The Mystery of Evil," which Augustine attempts to explain based on his doctrine of sin (Rom. 7:23) arises in this context. The Augustinian doctrine refers, as we know, to the word of Paul, the "Law of Sin" (Rom. 7:23), linking the phenomenon of evil to the concept of free will of humans acting on their own.

6. Cited according to the Academy's edition *Die Religion innerhalb der Grenzen der bloßen Vernunft* in *Gesammelte Schriften*, vol. 6 (Berlin and Leipzig, der Königlich Preußischen Akademie der Wissenschaften, 1902–23); henceforth referred to as "Rel" with the corresponding page number.

7. "*Religion ist (subjektiv betrachtet) das Erkenntnis aller unserer Pflichten als göttlicher Gebote*" (Rel 153).

8. See *Kritik der praktischen Vernunft* in *Gesammelte Schriften*, vol. 5 (Berlin and Leipzig, der Königlich Preußischen Akademie der Wissenschaften, 1902–23), pp. 34–35.

9. See Rel 36–37

10. See Rel 47.

11. "nichts sittlich (d.i. zurechnungsfähig-) böse, als was unsere eigene That ist" (Rel 31).

12. Rel 32.

13. "... die Geschichte der Freiheit vom Bösen (anfängt), denn sie ist Menschenwerk" *Mutmasslicher Anfang der Menschengeschichte* in *Gesammelte Schriften* (Berlin and Leipzig, der Königlich Preußischen Akademie der Wissenschaften, 1902–23), vol. 8, p. 115.

14. Rel 43.

15. F. W. J. Schelling, *Über das Wesen der menschlichen Freiheit* (Landshut, 1809). Quotes are from the original edition of 1809, according to the exemplar of the Badische Landesbibliothek, Karlsruhe (Classification: Mombert, 1937).

16. Regarding this and what follows, see the illustrative study Horst Fuhrmans included in an edition of Schelling's book based on the 1809 edition (Stuttgart: Editorial Philipp Reclam Jun., 1964).

17. See Schelling, *Über das Wesen der menschlichen Freiheit*, p. 362.

18. See ibid., p. 364. Schelling expressly points out that it is a matter of "the possibility" (*die Möglichkeit*) of evil, since "the reality" (*die Wirklichkeit*) of this would be the subject of another research project.

19. See ibid., p. 366.

20. Ibid.

21. Ibid.

22. See Franz Baader, "Über die Behauptung, daß kein übler Gebrauch der Vernunft sein kann," *Morgenblatt* 197 (1807), and "Über Starres und Fließendes," *Jahrbüchern der Medizin als Wissenschaft*, vol. 3, no. 2.

23. See Schelling, *Über das Wesen der menschlichen Freiheit*, p. 369.

24. G. W. F. Hegel, *Phänomenologie des Geistes*, in *Werke*, ed. Eva Moldenauer and Karl Markus Michel (Frankfurt am Main: Suhrkamp, 1986).

25. Hegel, *Werke*, vol. 3, pp. 75–76, nn. 24–25.

26. Ibid., pp. 78–79.

27. Ibid., pp. 74–76.

28. See Hegel's analysis of Sophocles' *Antigone* in this respect.

29. G. W. F. Hegel, *Grundlinien der Philosophie des Rechts,* in *Werke,* ed. Eva Moldenauer and Karl Markus Michel (Frankfurt am Main: Suhrkamp, 1986) §§ 106 and 107. Henceforth referred to as "Right," followed by the corresponding paragraph(s).

30. G. W. F. Hegel, *Enzyklopädie der philosophischen Wissenschaften,* in *Werke,* ed. Eva Moldenauer and Karl Markus Michel (Frankfurt am Main: Suhrkamp, 1986), §§ 508. Henceforth referred to as "Encyc," followed by the corresponding paragraph(s).

CHAPTER 7. AN EVIL HEART

1. Moral philosophy does not, of course, have to accept the validity of the prevailing normative convictions, no matter how deep seated or how formative of our cultural self-understanding these may turn out to be. The point is that if it does not, it must take on the task of *reorienting* our thinking so that we no longer find the normative ideas in question convincing.

2. In the following I draw on two examples of postmetaphysical thinking: Jürgen Habermas's discourse ethics and Alessandro Ferrara's theory of reflective authenticity.

3. Two contemporary critics of postmetaphysical thinking who affirm the contextuality of knowledge are Michael Theunissen and Dieter Henrich. See, for example, M. Theunissen, "Society and History: A Critique of Critical Theory" and D. Henrich, "What is Metaphysics—What Is Modernity? Twelve Theses against Jürgen Habermas," both available in English translation in P. Dews, ed., *Habermas: A Critical Reader* (Oxford: Blackwell, 1999).

4. Cf. for example, Arendt's essay, "Thinking and Moral Considerations: A Lecture," *Social Research,* 51, no. 1 (1984): 7–37 (first published in 1971). R. Bernstein describes Arendt's concern with the meaning of evil as "a luminous red thread against a dark background . . . that runs through all her thinking" (see R. Bernstein, "Did Hannah Arendt Change Her Mind? From Radical Evil to the Banality of Evil," in *Hannah Arendt Twenty Years Later,* ed. L. May and J. Kohn (Cambridge: MIT Press, 1996), p. 127.

5. H. Arendt, *Eichmann in Jerusalem: A Report on the Banality of Evil* (Harmondsworth: Penguin Books, 1994).

6. Arendt, "Thinking and Moral Considerations," p. 7.

7. Ibid.

8. Ibid.

9. Ibid., p. 29.

10. Ibid., pp. 28–29.

11. By "linguistic turn" I mean a cultural reorientation that draws attention to the world-constitutive functions of language and to the inescapable contextuality and temporality of knowledge.

12. I hold the view that Habermas's inability to account for the unconditionality and universality of the moral "ought"—and to develop a meaningful conception of moral learning—has to do with his rejection of metaphysical thinking. Similarly, Ferrara's inability to account for the normative force of judgments of authenticity may have its roots in his determined agnosticism with regard to ultimate human

motivations (see M. Cooke, "Between 'Objectivism' and 'Contextualism': The Normative Foundations of Social Philosophy," *Critical Horizons* 1, no. 2 [2000], 193–227, esp. pp. 202–5).

13. My discussion of Habermas in the following is based mainly on essays in his *Moral Consciousness and Communicative Action*, trans. C. Lenhardt and S. Weber Nicholsen (Cambridge: MIT Press, 1990), on the essays in his *Justification and Application*, trans. C. Cronin (Cambridge: MIT Press, 1993), and on his essay, "Individuation through Socialization," in *Postmetaphysical Thinking*, trans. W. M. Hohengarten (Cambridge: MIT Press, 1992).

14. See, for example, J. Habermas, "Treffen Hegels Einwände gegen Kant auch auf die Diskursethik zu?" in *Erläuterungen zur Diskursethik* (Frankfurt am Main: Suhrkamp, 1991), pp. 14–15 (originally in *Moralität und Sittlichkeit*, ed. W. Kuhlmann [Frankfurt am Main: Suhrkamp, 1986]); see also J. Habermas, "Wahrheit vs. Richtigkeit," in *Wahrheit und Rechtfertigung* (Frankfurt am Main: Suhrkamp, 1999), p. 310.

15. In his most recent writings, there is some indication that Habermas may be wavering from a strictly proceduralist position. An example of this is his recent admission (see "Wahrheit vs. Richtigkeit," pp. 272–73) that moral feelings can take on the role of reasons in argumentation. Although I see this as a welcome development of his theory, it seems to have potentially far-reaching consequences for his proceduralist approach: for how are such feelings to be adjudicated without reference to the comprehensive moral identities of those who assert them?

16. Cf. M. Cooke, "Habermas, Autonomy, and the Identity of the Self," *Philosophy and Social Criticism* 18, 3–4 (1992): 269–91.

17. Cf. J. Habermas, *Texte und Kontexte* (Frankfurt am Main: Suhrkamp, 1991), pp. 136, 139. For a brief discussion of some difficulties with Habermas's commitment to "methodological atheism" see M. Cooke, "Religion and Critical Theory," in *Philosophy of Religion 2000*, ed. D. Z. Phillips and T. Tessin (London and New York: Macmillan and St. Martin's Press, 2000).

18. Whereas, for Habermas, rational accountability is the core of moral autonomy, he usually ties it to objective moral validity, the test of which is a universal, discursively achieved consensus on the moral issue concerned. See M. Cooke, "Habermas, Autonomy, and the Identity of the Self," pp. 273–80.

19. Arendt, *Eichmann in Jerusalem*, pp. 136–37.

20. In the following, my discussion of Ferrara is based on his *Reflective Authenticity* (London and New York: Routledge, 1998).

21. See, for example, Arendt, *Eichmann in Jerusalem*, pp. 52–55.

22. Jaspers wrote: "The point is that *this* evil, not evil per se, is banal" (see Hannah Arendt and Karl Jaspers, *Hannah Arendt, Karl Jaspers: Correspondence, 1926–1969*, ed. L. Kohler and H. Saner [New York: Harcourt Brace Jovanovich, 1992], p. 542).

23. Ferrara, *Reflective Authenticity*, p. 13.

24. Ibid., pp. 148ff.

25. I. Kant, *Religion within the Limits of Reason Alone*, trans. T. M. Greene and H. H. Hudson (New York: Harper and Row, 1960).

26. Ibid., p. 16.

27. Ibid., p. 32.

28. Ibid., pp. 22–23.

29. Ibid., pp. 31, 42.

30. Ibid., p. 24.

31. Ibid., pp. 28, 32.

32. Kant's equivocation is shown with admirable clarity by R. Bernstein in "Radical Evil: Kant at War with Himself" (chapter 4 in this volume).

33. Kant, *Religion*, p. 24.

34. Ibid., p. 25.

35. See, for example, D. O'Connor, "Good and Evil Dispositions," in *Kant-Studien* 76 (1985). Bernstein's "Radical Evil" is exemplary in this regard.

36. Kant, *Religion*, p. 25.

37. Kant emphasizes that incentives arising from sensuous nature are not in themselves evil, indeed they are good (ibid., p. 51).

38. See Bernstein, "Radical Evil," esp. pp. 65–71.

39. Kant, *Religion*, p. 20.

40. Ibid., p. 18n.

41. A possible difficulty here is that Kant appears to say that a person's *Gesinnung* is not acquired historically (see ibid., p. 20; cf. O'Connor, "Good and Evil Dispositions," p. 292, and Bernstein, "Radical Evil," pp. 65–71). However, this difficulty is bound up with Kant's equivocation regarding the question of whether evil is innate and, on the reading I prefer, can be disregarded.

42. It seems likely that Kant himself maintains the stronger version of the thesis. This is apparent from his insistence that moral conduct alone—mere conformity to the moral law—is not sufficient reason to deem a person moral (see, for example, Kant, *Religion*, pp. 25, 32, and 33). However, for my present purposes, this is unimportant.

43. For example, Z. Bauman's explanation of the evil of the Holocaust in terms of modern, technological-bureaucratic rationality might comprise one element of such an account. See his *Modernity and the Holocaust* (Cambridge, England: Polity Press, 1989).

44. Kant, *Religion*, p. 26.

45. Bernstein, "Radical Evil," p. 83.

46. Kant, *Religion*, pp. 18–19.

47. Ibid., p. 20.

48. This seems to fit well with Arendt's account of Eichmann as someone who was capable of occasional acts of kindness.

49. Theunissen, "Society and History," pp. 260–63.

50. See the essays in Habermas, *Wahrheit und Rechtfertigung*, esp. pp. 48–55, 261–66, and 291–96.

51. When Habermas refers to the "detranscendentalization" or "demotion" of metaphysical theses about human nature, he seems to assume that the most convincing new position on human nature is a (weak) naturalist one (see, for example, his introduction to the essays in his *Wahrheit und Rechtfertigung*, esp. pp. 26–48. I fail to see that there is any necessary connection between "detranscendentalization" and naturalism. Insofar as his argument is based on the need for a fallibilist approach to human knowledge, it seems equally compatible with metaphysical interpretations of human nature and the world (see M. Cooke, "Socio-Cultural Learning as a 'Transcendental Fact': Habermas's Post-Metaphysical Perspective," *International Journal of Philosophical Studies* 8, no. 4 [2000]).

52. Theunissen, for example, argues for an inescapable theological dimension to the idea of absolute objectivity (which is, for him, subject to the constraints of historicity). See Theunissen, "Society and History," p. 263.

53. This is not to deny the self's determination by external influences nor does it imply that all dimensions of subjectivity are rationally retrievable (cf. M. Cooke, "A Space of One's Own," *Philosophy and Social Criticism,* 25, no. 1 [1999]: 23–53, esp. 24–29).

54. See note 1 above.

55. It is important to emphasize that arguments *alone* are unlikely to bring about the kind of fundamental moral reorientation at issue here; furthermore, that arguments can be of very *different types;* and, finally, that a *counterfactual* model of rational argumentation is presupposed. On this model, argumentation is maximally inclusive, participants are able to express their opinions equally and freely, they are motivated solely by concern for the best arguments, no kind of argument is dismissed out of hand as irrelevant or unacceptable, a multiplicity of modes of argument are encouraged, and so on.

56. See, for example, Kant, *Religion,* p. 40.

57. Ibid., p. 17n.

58. Kant himself points in the direction of a social explanation of moral corruption. He offers a brief sketch of how in certain social contexts innocent self-love can degenerate into the craving to win superiority for oneself over others, with its accompanying vices of jealousy and rivalry (ibid., p. 22). Cf. also S. Anderson-Gold, "Kant's Rejection of Devilishness," *Idealistic Studies,* 14 (1984), and H. Allison, "Reflections on the Banality of (Radical) Evil: A Kantian Analysis" (chapter 5 in this volume; first published in *Graduate Faculty Philosophy Journal,* 18, no. 2 [1995]).

59. Kant, *Religion,* pp. 42–44.

CHAPTER 8. UNDERSTANDING EVIL

An extended version of this paper has been published in Robert Fine and Charles Turner, eds., *Social Theory after the Holocaust* (Liverpool: Liverpool University Press, 2000).

1. Hannah Arendt, *Essays in Understanding, 1930–1954* (New York: Harcourt, Brace and Co., 1994), p. 302

2. Rose, *Mourning Becomes the Law: Philosophy and Representation* (Cambridge: Cambridge University Press, 1996), p. 43.

3. Arendt, *Essays in Understanding,* pp. 307–27, originally published in *Partisan Review,* 20, no. 4 (1954).

4. Quoted in J. Roth and M. Berenbaum, *Holocaust: Religious and Philosophical Implications* (New York: Paragon House, 1989), p. 2

5. Jean-François Lyotard, *The Differend: Phrases in Dispute* (Manchester, England: Manchester University Press, 1988), p. 56

6. Ibid.

7. Arendt, *Essays in Understanding,* p. 316.

8. Ibid., p. 233.

9. Ibid., p. 234.

10. Ibid., p. 236.

11. Ibid., p. 308.

12. Primo Levi, *If This Is a Man* (London: Abacus, 1995) and *The Drowned and the Saved* (London: Abacus, 1988); Tadeusz Borowski, *This Way for the Gas, Ladies and Gentlemen* (New York: Penguin, 1976).

13. Hannah Arendt, *The Origins of Totalitarianism* (New York: Harvest, 1976), p. 442.

14. F. Nietzsche, *The Will to Power*, trans. Walter Kaufmann and R. J. Hollingdale (London: Weidenfeld and Nicholson, 1968) §608.

15. Arendt, *Essays in Understanding*, p. 313.

16. Arendt, *Origins of Totalitarianism*, p. 444.

17. Ibid., pp. 439–40.

18. Arendt, *Essays in Understanding*, p. 282.

19. Arendt, *Origins of Totalitarianism*, pp. viii–ix.

20. Ibid., p. 459.

21. Ibid., p. 459.

22. Ibid., p. 443.

23. Ibid., pp. 439–41.

24. Ibid., p. 443.

25. Ibid., p. 445.

26. Ibid., p. 443.

27. Ibid., p. 317.

28. Hannah Arendt and Karl Jaspers, *Hannah Arendt, Karl Jaspers: Correspondence, 1926–1969*, ed. Lotte Kohler and Hans Saner, trans. Robert and Rita Kimber (New York: Harcourt Brace Jovanovich, 1992), p. 69.

29. Arendt and Jaspers, p. 54.

30. Arendt, *Essays in Understanding*, p. 126.

31. Ibid., p. 130.

32. Hannah Arendt, *Eichmann in Jerusalem: A Report on the Banality of Evil* (New York: Penguin, 1994), p. 289, my own emphasis. Alain Finkielkraut picked up a similar theme when he argued in relation to the Barbie trial that though the Holocaust was "from Eichmann to the engineers on the trains . . . a crime of employees . . . it was precisely to remove from crime the excuse of service and to restore the quality of killers to law-abiding citizens . . . that the category of 'crimes against humanity' was formulated" (see Alain Finkielkraut, *Remembering in Vain* [New York: Columbia University Press, 1992], pp. 3–4).

33. See Karl Marx, *Capital*, vol. 1 (Harmondsworth, England: Penguin, 1990) p. 896. Marx writes: "at the end of the 15th and during the whole of the 16th centuries a bloody legislation against vagabondage was enforced throughout Western Europe. The fathers of the present working class were chastised for their enforced transformation into vagabonds and paupers. Legislators treated them as 'voluntary' criminals and assumed it was entirely within their powers to go on working under the old conditions."

34. Hannah Arendt, *On Violence* (London: Allen Lane, 1970), p. 45.

35. See, for example, Christopher Browning, *Ordinary Men* (New York: HarperCollins, 1993).

NOTES TO PAGES 140–142

36. Max Weber, "The Concept of 'Following a Rule,'" in *Selections in Translation*, ed. by W. G. Runciman (Cambridge: Cambridge University Press, 1989), pp. 99–110.

37. Arendt, *Eichmann in Jerusalem*, p. 11.

38. See Karl Jaspers, *The Question of German Guilt* (New York: Capricorn Books, 1961).

39. Arendt, *Essays in Understanding*, p. 32.

40. According to Article 6, "Leaders, organisers, instigators and accomplices participating in the formulation or execution of a common plan or conspiracy to commit any of the foregoing crimes are responsible for all acts performed by any persons in execution of such plan." Article 7 added that "The official position of defendants, whether as Heads of State or responsible officials in Government Departments, shall not be considered as freeing them from responsibility or mitigating punishment." Article 8 added that "The fact that the Defendant acted pursuant to order of his Government or of a superior shall not free him from responsibility, but may be considered in mitigation of punishment if the Tribunal determines that justice so requires." Articles 9, 10, and 11 authorized the Tribunal to declare that a particular organization, like the Nazi party, is criminal and that individuals who join such an organization are personally responsible both for their membership and for their participation in its criminal activities.

41. Arendt and Jaspers, pp. 419ff.

42. It is for these comments that Arendt's account is most remembered by her critics, but she acknowledged the more positive effects of the trial: it encouraged the prosecution of leading Nazis in West Germany, it publicized the Holocaust to the world, it offered a forum for the testimony of victims, it accomplished a touch of justice (she had no compunction, for instance, about the imposition of the death penalty: "no member of the human race can be expected to want to share the earth with a man who supported and carried out a policy of not wanting to share the earth with the Jewish people and the people of a number of other nations").

43. It was this sense of lost opportunity that was echoed some twenty-five years later by Alain Finkielkraut in his celebrated study of the Barbie trial, when he analyzed contemporary trends toward the "banalisation" of crimes against humanity, as it became part of the "competition of memories" between different national movements and was extended to include all those forms of "man's inhumanity to man" of which we might disapprove. Thus in the Barbie case Finkielkraut criticized the decision of the French court to muddy the distinction between the killing of Jews for what they were and the killing of resistance fighters for what they did, and its decision to stretch the concept of crimes against humanity to include both. He also criticized the attempt on the part of Barbie's defense team to diminish the distinction between the extermination of the Jews and the violence of European colonialism. A certain "emotional confusion" arises, he argued, when on the one hand the definition of crimes against humanity expands to include inhuman actions of every sort and on the other hand contracts to exclude those crimes that cannot be ascribed to Western imperialism. In its actual use, Finkielkraut argued along the same lines as Arendt, the concept was serving to reduce "the unmasterable multitude of mankind to an exultant face to face confrontation between Innocence and the Unspeakable Beast," and to rewrite the Holocaust as a "meaningless idiot's tale" which signifies nothing and leaves only a "gaping black hole" (Finkielkraut, pp. 60–61).

44. Arendt and Jaspers, p. 69.

45. Arendt, *Origins of Totalitarianism*, p. 443.

46. Ibid., pp. 438–39.

47. Hannah Arendt, *Life of the Mind* (New York: Harcourt Brace Jovanovich, 1978), p. 5. See the excellent discussion of this in Richard Bernstein, *Hannah Arendt and the Jewish Question* (Cambridge, England: Polity Press, 1996), pp. 146ff.

48. Arendt and Jaspers, p. 62.

49. Ibid., p. 69.

50. Arendt, *Eichmann in Jerusalem*, p. 288.

51. Ibid., p. 3–4

52. Bernstein, *Arendt and the Jewish Question*, ch. 7, "From Radical Evil to the Banality of Evil."

53. Hannah Arendt, *The Jew as Pariah*, ed. Ron Feldman (New York: Grove Press, 1978), pp. 250–51.

54. Theodor Adorno, *Negative Dialectics*, trans. E. B. Ashton (New York: Continuum, 1987), p. 366.

55. Arendt and Jaspers, pp. 240–45.

56. Extracts to be found in Roth and Berenbaum, p. 179.

57. Roth and Berenbaum, p. 175.

58. Ibid., p. 175.

59. Ibid., p. 184.

60. Ibid., p. 187.

61. We know, for instance, that social atomization in Stalinist Russia was far less complete than the concept of totalitarianism might suggest.

62. Dana Villa, *Arendt and Heidegger: The Fate of the Political* (Princeton: Princeton University Press, 1996), p. 257.

63. Nietzsche, *The Will to Power*, p. 9.

64. In a passage from *Untimely Meditations* Nietzsche captured the experience of "devaluation" thus:

> Now how does the philosopher see the culture of our time? Naturally quite differently than those philosophy professors who are satisfied with their state. When he thinks of the universal haste and the increasing speed with which things are falling, of the cessation of all contemplativeness and simplicity, it almost seems to him as if he were seeing the symptoms of a total extermination and uprooting of culture. The waters of religion are ebbing and they are leaving behind swamps or ponds; the nations are again separating from one another in the most hostile manner and they are trying to rip each other to shreds. The sciences, without any measure and pursued in the blindest spirit of laisser faire, are breaking apart and dissolving everything which is firmly believed; the edified classes and states are being swept along by a money economy which is enormously contemptible. Never was the world more a world, never was it poorer in love and good. The educated classes are no longer lighthouses or sanctuaries in the midst of all this turbulent secularisation; they themselves become more turbulent by the day, more thoughtless and loveless. Everything, contemporary art and science included, serves the coming barbarism. (Nietzsche, trans. R. J. Hollingdale [Cambridge: Cambridge University Press, 1983], pp. 148–49)

65. Arendt, *Origins of Totalitarianism*, p. 328.

66. Ibid., p. 334.

67. Ibid., p. 335.

68. Ibid., p. 125.

69. Ibid., p. 137.

70. Ibid., p. 301.

71. Ibid., p. 300.

72. Ibid., pp. 478–79.

73. Hannah Arendt, *Men in Dark Times* (New York: Harcourt Brace Jovanovich, 1983), p. 25.

74. Arendt, *Origins of Totalitarianism*, p. 302.

75. Arendt, *Men in Dark Times*, pp. 13–17.

76. Arendt, *Eichmann in Jerusalem*, p. 233.

77. Bernstein, *Arendt and the Jewish Question*, p. 146.

CHAPTER 9. TOWARD A SOCIOLOGY OF EVIL

1. I refer here to specifically "social" evil. The subject of evil as such—from a metaphysical, existential, moral, or "human" perspective—is not, in a direct sense, the topic of this contribution. These questions are pursued by other contributors to this volume. While I would not wish to conflate the different approaches to evil, I want to suggest that sociological considerations are relevant to the other kinds of questions that may be asked, answers for which are typically provided without considering the sorts of issues I raise here. Until a sociology has been developed, this will undoubtedly continue to be the case.

2. In the United States, typically, one of the three major professional journals in sociology is called *Social Problems,* and it is the voice of a major professional association, the Society for the Study of Social Problems, which holds large annual meetings.

3. Clifford Geertz ("Common Sense as a Cultural System," in *Local Knowledge* [New York: Basic Books, 1983], pp. 73–93) has written that common sense must be viewed as a cultural system. By this, Geertz means to suggest that "common sense" is an organizing symbolic structure that provides cognitive, moral, and emotional frameworks of interpretation; he is arguing against the notion that common sense is a naturalistic phenomenon, a reflection of some "real," everyday reality. To view something within the framework of common sense is, in this sense, precisely not to gain reflexivity about it.

4. Thomas Cushman, "The Reflexivity of Evil" (paper presented at the colloquium "The Question of Evil," University of Virginia, 9 April 1998), pp. 2–3.

> As a moral concept, evil is an ancient and heavily freighted term . . . that sociology has defined itself against in the course of its development as an autonomous discipline. . . . Sociology is characterized by a conscious distancing of itself from the term and a selective appropriation of ideas that fit the nascent discipline's idea of human nature and the positive telos of human evolution. Indeed, evil is sociology's *doppelganger,* always present, but unwelcome, haunting the discipline and its quest for Enlightenment by calling to mind questions of metaphysics, agency, and the 'dark side' of human progress.

5. Alessandro Ferrara, "The Evil That Men Do: A Meditation on Radical Evil from a Postmetaphysical Point of View," this volume, chap. 10. It is not accidental that, in generating this argument, this philosopher draws not from Kant but from the same "late Durkheimian" position I am developing here:

> If the sacred is a projection of us *at our best,* and the world of the profane a representa-

tion of us *as we actually are,* including the manifestations of ordinary evil that we experience, radical evil can be conceptualized as a projection of *us at our worst,* the worst that we can prove to be while still maintaining those characteristics that make us—us as a community, a society, or humanity—what we are.

   In that sense evil, even radical evil, cannot be overcome. Concrete manifestations of it can be overcome—Auschwitz can be driven out of this world, ethnic cleansing hopefully can too—but if evil is a horizion that moves with us, then there will always be a collectively shared symbolic representation of what we, we as a single moral community or we as humans, can be at our worst. The idea of a good society where evil has been eradicated is, from a postmetaphysical standpoint, as meaningless as the idea of a pacified moral world where no conflict of value exists any longer.

   6. Claude Lévi-Strauss, "Structural Analysis in Linguistics and Anthropology," *Structural Anthropology* 1 (1963): 31–54.

   7. Most forcefully stated in Parsons's essay with Edward Shils, "Values, Motives, and Systems of Action," in *Towards a General Theory of Action,* ed. T. Parsons and E. Shils (Cambridge: Harvard University Press, 1951). Because Parsons did not take the next step implicit in this distinction—the cultural turn with its analogy to language—the radicalism of this early position is not often recalled today. It is recalled, however, by Clifford Geertz, the very figure most responsible for moving beyond Parsons and initiating the cultural turn in American social science.

> Until Talcott Parsons, carrying forward Weber's double rejection (and double acceptance) of German idealism and Marxist materialism, provided a viable alternative, the dominant concept of culture in American social science identified culture with learned behavior. [It was thought that] social phenomena were explained by [simply] redescribing them as culture patterns. . . . [In contrast,] the workability of the Parsonian concept of culture rests . . . on the degree to which the relationship between the [differentiated] development of symbol systems and the dynamics of social process can be circumstantially exposed. (Geertz, "After the Revolution: The Fate of Nationalism in the New States," in *Stability and Social Change,* ed. Bernard Barber and Alex Inkeles [Boston: Little, Brown, 1971], pp. 371–72)

   8. In regard to Saussure, I refer to his insistence on the "arbitrary" relationship between the signifier and the signified in his *General Course in Linguistics.* It is only this insistence, and precisely this insistence, that separates structuralism from the pragmatic semiotics of Peirce. The latter, for all its attractiveness in other respects (e.g., its attention to creativity, temporality, and contingency), does not enable cultural analysis of the kind that has informed the cultural turn. For Dilthey's early and still-instructive rendition of the analytical differentiation between culture and social levels, see the following:

> I shall start from the whole range of facts which forms the firm basis for any reasoning about the human studies. Side by side with the sciences a group of studies, linked by their common subject-matter, has grown naturally from the problems of life itself. These include history, economics, jurisprudence, politics, the study of religion, literature, poetry, architecture, music, and of philosophic world views and systems, and, finally, psychology. . . . It cannot be logically correct to distinguish the human studies from sciences on the grounds that they cover different ranges of facts. After all, physiology deals with an aspect of man and is a science. The basis for distinguishing the two classes of disciplines cannot lie in the facts per se. The human studies must be related differently to the mental and physical aspects of man. . . . The study of language embraces the physiology of the speech-organs as well as the semantics of words and sentences. The chem-

ical effects of gunpowder are as much part of the course of modern war as the moral qualities of the soldiers who stand in its smoke. But, in the nature of the group of disciplines with which we are dealing there is a tendency . . . to relegate the physical side of events to the role of conditions and means of comprehension. This is the turn towards reflection, the movement of understanding from the external to the internal. This tendency makes use of every expression of life in order to understand the mental content from which it arises. . . . In history, we read of economic activities, settlements, wars and the creating of states. They fill our souls with great images and tell us about the historical world which surrounds us: but what moves us, above all, in these accounts is what is inaccessible to the sense and can only be experienced inwardly. . . . For all that is valuable in life is contained in what can be experienced and the whole outer clamor of history revolves round it. (Wilhelm Dilthey, "The Construction of the World in the Human Studies," in *Selected Writings*, ed. and trans. H. P. Rickman [Cambridge: Cambridge University Press, 1976], pp. 170–245, esp. pp. 170–73)

9. "The values which come to be constitutive of the structure of a societal system are, then, the conceptions of the desirable type of society held by the members of the society of reference and applied to the particular society of which they are members. . . . A value-pattern then defines a direction of choice, and consequent commitment to action" (Talcott Parsons, "On the Concept of Value-Commitments," *Sociological Inquiry* 38 [1968]: 136).

This approach was elaborated by Robin M. Williams, the most authoritative sociological interpreter of American values in the postwar period: "A value system is an organized set of preferential rules for making selections, resolving conflicts, and coping with needs for social and psychological defenses of the choices made or proposed. Values steer anticipatory and goal-oriented behavior; they also 'justify' or 'explain' past conduct" (Williams, "Change and Stability in Values and Value Systems," in *Stability and Social Change*, ed. Bernard Barber and Alex Inkeles [Boston: Little, Brown, 1971], pp. 123–59, esp. p. 128).

While Parsons and Williams both represent a specific tradition within sociology— the early and middle period of Durkheim and the later, structural-functional school—their equation of culture with the desirable is shared by every other school of sociological thought.

10. See the demonstration of this point in Marshall Sahlins's discussion of polluted food and clothing symbolism: "Le Pensée Bourgeoise," in *Culture and Practical Reason* (Chicago: University of Chicago Press, 1976), pp. 166–204.

11. A clear statement of this Durkheimian position is Roger Caillois, *Man and the Sacred* (1939; reprint, New York: Free Press, 1959), in which Caillois criticizes Durkheim for not distinguishing clearly enough between the sacred, the profane, and the routine.

12. Two of the most compelling contemporary, neo-Aristotelian analyses of "evil-versus-good" in cultural narratives are Northrop Frye, *The Anatomy of Criticism* (New York: Princeton University Press, 1957), and Vladimir Propp, *Morphology of the Folktale* (1928; reprint, Austin: University of Texas Press, 1969). More recently, see Robin Wagner-Pacifici, *The Moro Morality Play: Terrorism as Social Drama* (Chicago: University of Chicago Press, 1986).

13. In contemporary social science, the most influential analysis of ritual has been Victor Turner, *The Ritual Process* (Chicago: Aldine, 1969).

14. The sacred-profane refers to Durkheim's later "religious sociology," the

promise of salvation to Weber's sociology of religion. For a discussion of these thinkers' contributions in these regards, see Jeffrey C. Alexander, "The Promise of a Cultural Sociology: Technological Discourse and the Sacred and Profane Information Machine," in *Theory of Culture*, ed. Neil Smelser and Richard Munch (Berkeley: University of California Press, 1993), pp. 293–323.

15. Georges Bataille, *Literature and Evil* (1957; reprint, London: Marion Boyars, 1990), pp. 142–45.

16. "It is inherent in our entire philosophic tradition that we cannot conceive of a 'radical evil,' and this is true both for Christian theology, which conceded even the devil himself a celestial origin, as well as for Kant. . . . Therefore we have nothing to fall back on in order to understand a phenomenon that nevertheless confronts us with its overpowering reality" (Hannah Arendt, *The Origins of Totalitarianism* [New York: Harcourt Brace Jovanovich, 1951]).

Richard Bernstein shares this view. "The larger question looming in the background is whether our philosophic tradition—especially the modern philosophic tradition—is rich and deep enough to enable us to comprehend what we are asserting when we judge something to be evil" (Bernstein, "Radical Evil: Kant at War with Himself," this volume, chap. 4, p. 56). After an exhaustive investigation of Kant's thinking, Bernstein's answer is "no." It is a similar perception of this lack in the philosophic tradition that inspires the position María Pía Lara lays out in her own contributions to this volume (introduction and chap. 15).

17. *The Politics*, VII, 1, 13, trans. Ernest Barker (London: Oxford University Press, 1962). In his reconstruction of the republican theory of virtue, Quentin Skinner emphasizes the role of altruistic cultural commitments within it. See his *The Foundations of Modern Political Thought* (Cambridge: Cambridge University Press, 1978).

18. This communicative-normative logic, which so strikingly adumbrates Habermas's later theory, is perhaps most clearly articulated in Dewey's *Democracy and Education* (1916; reprint, New York: Free Press, 1966). Because pragmatism has supplied social science with its theoretical resources for conceptualizing agency and selfhood, this enthusiastic equation of valuation—the act of valuing—with goodness has undermined the ability of social scientists to understand how social creativity, agency, often contributes to evil. Cushman emphasizes the role that agency plays in the social creation of evil in his sociological investigation of Serbian genocide, which also contains a cogent theoretical criticism of the manner in which the pragmatist tradition ignored the agentic capacity for evil.

> Sociological theorists of agency have, like sociological theorists in general, displaced evil. This displacement has much to do with the unbridled political optimism of the progenitors of the pragmatic theories of action [who] simply ignored the idea that the pragmatic, reflexive self could engage in action that was ferocious, malicious, and cruel in its genesis or outcomes. Action and reflexivity was, for these thinkers and their later followers, always considered as progressive. This development was ironic, and perhaps even naïve, since such theories developed in a world historical context in which it was rather evident that agents used the infrastructure of modernity for nefarious rather than progressive ends. This belief in the optimistic and moral ends of agency is very clear [for example] in the work of Anthony Giddens, perhaps the most important contemporary theorist of agency. (Cushman, "The Reflexivity of Evil," p. 6)

Cushman's observations about agency and innocence, made in light of Serbian genocide in the 1990s, eerily dovetail with some remarks I made a decade ago, remarks that were not at all directed to the problem of evil.

> Discussions of agency . . . are celebratory and often heroic. According to one tradition, actors are rational, autonomous, self-sufficient, wily, and clever. According to another, they are knowledgeable, reflexive, self-monitoring, and routinely competent. In the rhetoric of a third approach, actors are endlessly creative, expressive, and meaning-making. [However,] if we do not conflate actors with agents, we are forced to recognize that actors are not nearly as heroic as these accounts imply. They are often befuddled, passive, self-deceptive, thoughtless, and vicious. How can this be so, if "agency" itself can be described in a positive way? The answer is that agency expresses itself only through its cultural and psychological environments, and these latter forces structure agency in open-ended and sometimes extraordinarily harmful ways. (Alexander, "Some Remarks on 'Agency' in Recent Sociological Theory," *Perspectives* 15, 1 [1992]: 4)

Cf. Alexander, "After Neofunctionalism: Action, Culture, and Civil Society," in *Neofunctionalism and After* (New York: Blackwell, 1998).

19. This dichotomy informs, for example, the work of the influential sociological communitarian, Robert Bellah. His collective book, *Habits of the Heart*, is informed by the Republican version of American communitarianism, decrying individualism as evil because it supposedly makes it impossible for Americans to connect to any value outside their selves.

> Americans tend to think of the ultimate goals of a good life as matters of personal choice. . . . Freedom is perhaps the most resonant, deeply held American value. In some ways, it defines the good in both personal and political life. Yet freedom turns out to mean being left alone by others. . . . What it is that one might do with that freedom is much more difficult for Americans to define. . . . It becomes hard to forge bonds of attachment to, or cooperation with, other people, since such bonds would imply obligations that necessarily impinge on one's freedom. . . . The large hope that [one's] freedom might encompass an ability to share a vision of a good life or a good society with others, to debate that vision, and come to some sort of consensus, is precluded in part by the very definition of freedom. (Robert Bellah, Richard Madsen, William M. Sullivan, Ann Swidler, and Steven M. Tipton, *Habits of the Heart* [Berkeley: University of California Press, 1985], pp. 22–24)

Charles Taylor's reply to Bellah is worth noting in this context. "The deeper moral vision, the genuine moral sources invoked in the aspiration to disengaged reason or expressive fulfillment tend to be overlooked," Taylor writes, "and the less impressive motives—pride, self-satisfaction, liberation from demanding standards—brought to the fore" (*Sources of the Self* [New York: Cambridge University Press, 1990], p. 511).

A different version of this communitarian value / no value dichotomy can be found in the more philosophically rigorous position Michael Walzer sets out in *Spheres of Justice* (New York: Basic Books, 1984), which equates particular values with the values of a sphere or community, thus solving the issue of moral rightness through a kind of a priori pluralism. Zygmunt Bauman developed a particularly strong sociological critique of this position in *Postmodern Ethics*, calling it a naïve response to "the cold and abstract territory of universal moral values" associated with modernity. This "'community first' vision of the world," Bauman writes, once "consigned to oblivion by the dominant thought which proudly described itself as 'marching with time,' scientific and progressive," is now so popular in the social sciences that "it comes quite close to being elevated to the canon and uncontested 'good sense' of human sciences" (*Postmodern Ethics* [Oxford: Blackwell, 1993], pp. 42–43).

20. I think this is what Bataille was trying to get at when he called for "the rectification of the common view which inattentively sees Good in opposition to Evil. Though Good and Evil are complementary, there is no equivalence. We are right to distinguish between behavior which has a humane sense and behavior which has an odious sense. But the opposition between these forms of behavior is not that which theoretically opposes Good to Evil" (Bataille, *Literature and Evil*, p. 144).

21. For a sociological consideration of these standard philosophical divisions, and an empirical response to them, see Alexander, "Theorizing the Good Society: Moral, Ethical, and Empirical Discourses," *Canadian Journal of Sociology*, forthcoming.

22. In his *Lectures on the Philosophical Doctrine of Religion*, Kant wrote, "Thus evil in the world can be regarded as incompleteness in the development of the germ toward the good. Evil has no special germ; for it is mere negation and consists only in the limitation of the good. It is nothing beyond this, other than incompleteness in the development of the germ to the good out of uncultivatedness" (in *The Cambridge Edition of the Works of Immanuel Kant* [Cambridge: Cambridge University Press, 1996], p. 411; quoted in Bernstein, "Radical Evil").

It is this Kantian inability to conceptualize what I have called here the *sui generis* autonomy of evil that leads Bernstein ultimately to conclude his investigation of Kant's notion of radical evil by suggesting that, "when we analyze what Kant means, the results are quite disappointing."

> Radical evil seems to be little more than a way of designating the tendency of human beings to disobey the moral law, [that is] not to do what they ought to do. There is a disparity between Kant's rhetoric—his references to "wickedness," "perversity," "corruption"—and the content of what he is saying. . . . Kant's concept of an evil maxim is too limited and undifferentiated. The distinction between a good man and an evil man depends on whether or not he subordinates the "incentives of his sensuous nature" to the moral law as an incentive. (Bernstein, "Radical Evil," p. 84)

The phrase "incentives of his sensuous nature" refers to the egoistic self who is not able to make a connection to values, which themselves are conceived inevitably as representations of the good.

23. For the earlier writings, see, e.g., Habermas, "Labor and Interaction: Remarks on Hegel's Jena *Philosophy of Mind*," in *Theory and Practice* (Boston: Beacon Press, 1973), pp. 142–69. For the prototypical later renditions of this dichotomy, see his *Theory of Communicative Action* (Boston: Beacon Press, 1982–84). I believe that in his most recent writings, those that have tried to articulate the role of culture in the public sphere of "discourse ethics," Habermas has been determined to distance himself from this kind of binary thinking. In my view, he will not be able to do so until he jettisons his narrowly pragmatic approach to discourse as speech acts and incorporates discourse in a broader, more semiotic and hermeneutic sense.

24. Axel Honneth, *The Struggle for Recognition* (London: Verso, 1995). For an expansion of this critique, see Jeffery C. Alexander and María Pía Lara, "Honneth's New Critical Theory of Recognition," *New Left Review* 220 (November–December 1996): 126–52.

25. Quoted in a paper given by Richard Hecht in the conference in Mexico City that initiated the present volume.

26. See Hyam Maccoby, *Judas Iscariot and the Myth of Jewish Evil* (New York: Free Press, 1992).

27. Foucault would seem to be the obvious, and in some ways all important, exception to this argument, as I have indicated above. Foucault, and the postmodernist archeologists of modernity who followed him, found the production of evil, in the form of domination and pollution of the other, to be at the heart of modern thought and practice. Despite this understanding, Foucault did not interpretively reconstruct "evil values" in the manner I am calling for in this paper. Instead, he considered domination and pollution to be the product of "normal" procedures of scientific rational knowledge and the "normalizing" social control accompanying it. In other words, Foucault followed the mainstream tradition in considering evil to follow, as an unintended consequence, from the (however misguided) normatively inspired effort to institutionalize the good. In this regard, Foucault may have been influenced by the spirit of Bataille, but he did not follow the late Durkheimian roots of his thinking.

28. Christopher Lasch, *The Culture of Narcissism* (New York: Norton, 1978).

29. This, of course, is the standard criticism of Parsons's "oversocialized conception of man," but it is connected here not with his functionalism but with a much more general inadequacy in understanding the nature of culture, a problem, I am suggesting, that Parsons shared not only with his anti-functionalist critics but with virtually the entire spectrum of social and political thinkers. For an argument that Parsons can be seen within the Republican tradition, see J. C. Alexander, "Liberalism, Republicanism, and the Crisis of Industrial Society: Talcott Parsons' Search for a New Understanding of His Time," in *At Least Sixty Years Ahead of Its Time? Parsons' Structure and Contemporary Debates*, ed. G. Pollini, D. La Valle, and G. Sciortino (Milan: Franco Angeli, forthcoming).

30. Niklas Luhmann, "Durkheim on Morality and the Division of Labor," in *The Differentiation of Society* (New York: Columbia University Press, 1982), pp. 3–20, esp. pp. 9–10.

> According to Durkheim . . . we are not confronted with factually moral and factually immoral actions. . . . Instead, it has been conceptually decided in advance that, essentially, there is only morality and solidarity, but that under certain regrettable circumstances these can be cut short from their full realization. Durkheim . . . conceives negation as mere deprivation, and to that extent his theory remains Aristotelian. Despite all his understanding for corruption and incompleteness, he expresses an affirmative attitude toward society.

31. See, e.g., Max Horkheimer and Theodor Adorno, *Dialectic of Enlightenment* (1947; reprint, London: Verso, 1972).

32. Zygmunt Bauman, *Modernity and the Holocaust* (Ithaca: Cornell University Press, 1989).

33. Daniel Jonah Goldhagen, *Hitler's Willing Executioners: Ordinary Germans and the Holocaust* (New York: Knopf, 1996). For an earlier historical discussion that also roots Nazism in strongly held "evil" values, see George L. Mosse's closely related and much earlier historical investigation, *The Crisis of German Ideology: Intellectual Origins of the Third Reich* (New York: Universal Library, 1964).

34. As this sentence suggests, the sociological perspective on evil presented here does not aim at making distinctions among different qualities of evil, as philosophers

do, for example, when they distinguish between the banality of evil and radical evil. From a sociological point of view, the structures and processes, both institutional and symbolic, involved in establishing the range of different qualities of evil are the same. Each involves evoking and maintaining a sharp distinction between the pure and the impure.

35. As Ferrara writes: "The criterion for the radicality of radical evil ought perhaps to be internal to us, the moral community, rather than external, objective. Evil then is perhaps best conceived as a *horizon* that moves with us, rather than as something that stands over against us" ("Evil That Men Do," p. 184).

36. For empirical studies of such evil-representing events, their socio-cultural causes, and their subsequent social impacts, see a series of studies undertaken by me and my students. On scandals: J. C. Alexander, "Culture and Political Crisis: Watergate and Durkheimian Sociology," in *Durkheimian Sociology: Cultural Studies,* ed. J. C. Alexander (New York: Cambridge University Press, 1987), pp. 187–224; J. C. Alexander and Ron Jacobs, "Mass Communication, Ritual, and Civil Society," in *Media, Ritual and Identity,* ed. T. Leibes and J. Curran (London: Routledge, 1998), pp. 23–41; Ron Jacobs, *Race, Media, and the Crisis of Civil Society: From Watts to Rodney King* (New York: Cambridge University Press, 2000); for public punishments, Phil Smith, "Executing Executions," *Theory and Society* 25, no. 2 (1996): 235–61; for wars, Smith, "Codes and Conflict: Towards a Theory of War as Ritual," *Theory and Society* 20 (1991): 103–38; J. C. Alexander, "Bush, Hussein, and the Cultural Preparation for War: Toward a More Symbolic Theory of Political Legitimation," *Epoche: Journal for the Study of Religions* 21 (summer 1997): 1–14. For an excellent overview of the phenomenon of moral panics, see Kenneth Thompson, *Moral Panics* (London: Routledge, 1998).

37. For the application of this Aristotle-inspired perspective to the most far-reaching contemporary case of evil construction and institutionalization, see Alexander, "From War Crime to Holocaust Trauma: Progressive and Tragic Narrations of the Nazis' Mass Murder of the Jews," in J. C. Alexander, Ron Eyerman, Bernhardt Giesen, Neil Smelser, and Piotr Sztompka, *Cultural Trauma* (Berkeley: University of California Press, forthcoming).

38. In *Cultural Trauma,* my colleagues and I try to define and create a model for a complex social phenomenon that involves both symbolic and institutional processes in constructing the symbiotic relation of evil to collective identity.

39. This section is drawn from J. C. Alexander, "Citizen and Enemy as Symbolic Classification: On the Polarizing Discourse of Civil Society," in *Where Culture Talks: Exclusion and the Making of Society,* ed. M. Fournier and M. Lamont (Chicago: University of Chicago Press, 1993), pp. 289–308. I have subsequently elaborated this hermeneutic in a number of studies. It informs the cultural dimension of my forthcoming book, *Possibilities of Justice: Civil Society and Its Contradictions.*

40. This is not to say that the attribution of evil to an action, and the subsequent punishment of the agent, is unjustified, either empirically or morally. What is suggested is that such attributions and punishments are arbitrary from the sociological point of view, that is, they do not grow "naturally" from the qualities of the actions themselves. The identification of evil and its punishment are as much determined by social and cultural processes—by context—as by the nature of the actions themselves, though the latter obviously plays an important role.

41. This conception derives from anthropological discussions of taboo, e.g., Franz Steiner, *Taboo* (London: Cohen and West, 1956). In *Stigma* (Englewood Cliffs, N.J.: Prentice-Hall, 1963), Erving Goffman has developed the most general and persuasive treatment of this phenomenon in contemporary social science.

42. Stanley Cohen, *Folk Devils and Moral Panics: The Creation of the Mods and Rockers* (London: MacGibbon and Kee, 1972), and, more generally, Kenneth Thompson, *Moral Panics* (New York: Routledge, 1998). For the notion of boundary danger, see Kai Erickson, *Wayward Puritans: A Study in the Sociology of Deviance* (New York: Macmillan, 1996).

43. Suggested to me by Steven J. Sherwood, personal communication.

44. Other complementary efforts would be investigations into the morality of evil, the genealogy of evil, and the psychology of evil. Regarding the issue of genealogy, Peter Brooks has argued in *The Melodramatic Imagination* (New York: Columbia University Press, 1984) that the transition from a traditional religious society initiated by the French Revolution transferred the consideration of moral good and immoral evil onto the secular plane through the application of the melodrama genre in literature and popular thinking. In *The Great War in Modern Memory* (London: Oxford University Press, 1975), Paul Fussell suggested the melodramatic innocence of nineteenth-century thought gave way, after World War I, to the biting use of "irony" as a way of coping with twentieth-century recognition of the corruption of society by social evil in its modern form, as exemplified, e.g., in Joseph Heller's comic masterpiece, *Catch 22*. The Holocaust evidently initiated another stage in this genealogy, which can be thought of as a series from melodrama to irony to tragedy.

45. Bataille, *Literature and Evil*, pp. 29, 21.

46. The notion of the limit experience is the centerpiece of James Miller's fascinating but one-sided investigation into what he views as the amoral, anti-humane life of Foucault, *The Passion of Michel Foucault* (New York: Simon and Schuster, 1993), e.g., pp. 29, 398 n. 49. Without disputing Miller's moral judgment of Foucault's sexual behavior later in his life, which by several accounts evidenced a lack of concern for spreading HIV, I do question Miller's effort to generalize this accusation to a theoretical and philosophical indictment of Foucault's concentration on evil rather than on the good. Miller takes the notion of the "limit experience" as indicating the moral, even the social endorsement of the anti-good morality that transgression allows. This is not the perspective of Bataille, as I indicate in the following, nor should it necessarily be attributed to the theoretical perspective of Foucault, no matter what the nature of his own personal and idiosyncratic fascination with transgression was.

47. Bataille, *Eroticism*, pp. 68, original italics.

48. Ibid., and also Bataille's *Eroticism: Death and Sensuality* (1957; reprint, San Francisco: City Lights Books, 1986). For discussions of Bataille's life and work, and the context of his time, see Michael Richardson, *Georges Bataille* (New York: Routledge, 1994) and Carolyn Bailey Gill, ed., *Bataille: Writing the Sacred* (New York: Routledge, 1995). The ambiguity and complexity of Bataille's thinking have made it difficult to incorporate his thinking into streams of thought other than French-inspired postmodernist literary theory. While drawing fruitfully from the "later" religious sociology of Durkheim and Mauss (see *Literature and Evil*, p. 208, n. 48),

Bataille also tried, much less fruitfully in my view, to develop a kind of totalizing historical and existential philosophy, which included not only an ontology and a metaphysics, but also a Marxist-inspired political economy. Despite its genuine intellectual interest, the short-lived "College de France," which Bataille initiated with the third-generation Durkheimian Roger Caillois in the late 1930s, had a cultic and antinomian quality that aspired to the status of the Surrealist group of the World War I era. See Michèle Richman, "The Sacred Group: A Durkheimian Perspective on the Collège de Sociologie," in *Bataille: Writing the Sacred*, ed. Gill, pp. 58–76.

49. To be "bad" is to be mean in a precise sense of the term. Badasses manifest the transcendent superiority of their being, specifically by insisting on the dominance of their will, that "I mean it," when the "it" itself is, in a way obvious to all, immaterial. They engage in violence not necessarily sadistically or "for its own sake" but to back up their meaning without the limiting influence of utilitarian considerations or a concern for self-preservation. To make vivid sense of all the detailed ways of the badass, one must consider the essential project as transcending the modern moral injunction to adjust the public self sensitively to situationally contingent expectations.

Jack Katz, *Seductions of Crime: Moral and Sensual Attractions of Doing Evil* (New York: Basic Books, 1988), p. 81. See also Richard Stivers, *Evil in Modern Myth and Ritual* (Atlanta: University of Georgia Press, 1982).

50. Miller, *Passion of Michel Foucault*.

51. Bataille, *Eroticism*.

52. I draw here from "Human Rights Language in Amnesty International," (n.d.), section 4, pp. 24–25. I cannot locate the author of this very interesting manuscript, which, as far as I know, is as yet unpublished.

CHAPTER 10. THE EVIL THAT MEN DO

1. Plato, *Protagoras* 355a–356e.

2. Immanuel Kant, *Religion within the Limits of Reason Alone* , trans. T. M. Greene and H. H. Hudson (New York: Harper and Row, 1960), p. 31.

3. Ibid.

4. Ibid., p. 30. Original emphasis.

5. James Bernauer, "Nazi-Ethik. Über Heinrich Himmler und die Karriere der Neuen Moral," *Babylon* 6 (1989): 46–62.

6. *Hitler's Secret Conversations, 1941–44*, quoted in Bernauer, p. 49.

7. *Goebbels-Reden*, quoted in Bernauer, p. 53.

8. *Hitler's Secret Book*, quoted in Bernauer, p. 54.

9. Quoted in Bernauer, p. 54.

10. G. W. F. Hegel, "Über die wissenschaftlichen Behandlungsaten des Naturrechts," in *Werke*, vol. 2 (Frankfurt am Main: Suhrkamp, 1971), p. 466.

11. Emile Durkheim, "On the Definition of Religious Phenomena," in *Emile Durkheim*, ed. K. H. Wolff (Columbus: Ohio University Press,1960).

12. Emile Durkheim, *The Elementary Forms of the Religious Life* (New York: Free Press, 1967).

13. G. Agamben, *La comunità che viene* (Torino: Einaudi,1990), p. 65.

14. Durkheim, *The Elementary Forms of the Religious Life,* p. 470.

15. Peter Dews, "Disenchantment and the Persistence of Evil," manuscript, 2000.

CHAPTER 11. MAJOR OFFENDERS, MINOR OFFENDERS

1. Marquis de Sade, *Correspondance Inédite* (Paris: Éditions Bourdain, 1929), p. 183.

2. Charles Baudelaire, *Les fleurs du mal,* in *Oeuvres completes* (Paris: Éditions du Seuil, 1968), p. 43.

3. Jean-Paul Sartre, *Genet, comédien et marty* (Paris: Éditions Gallimard), p. 149.

4. Ibid., p. 156.

5. M. Foucault, "La vie des hommes infames," in *Michel Foucault, Dits et écrits,* ed. D. Defert and F. Ewald, pp. 237–53 (Paris: Éditions Gallimard, 1994).

6. George Painter, *Marcel Proust, Biografía 1904–1922,* vol. 2 (Madrid: Alianza Editorial), p. 419.

7. N. Elias and E. Dunning, "The Quest for excitement in Unexciting Societies," in *Deporte y Ocio en el proceso de la civilización,* ed. N. Elias and E. Dunning, pp. 85–116.

CHAPTER 12. ON PAIN, THE SUFFERING OF WRONG, AND OTHER GRIEVANCES

1. In relation to this question Valéry made a wise recommendation: "Fear the person who wishes to have right on their side. In this close relationship the man takes the latter as his wife so as to a keep a close watch over her. But the more this wife is in someone's possession, the less right they have on their side" (*Cahiers*).

2. From Hayek and Popper (to mention two leading representatives of contemporary conservative thinking) to many proponents of the thesis of the perverse effects, many thinkers have taken this line of argument, denying that the majority of great human undertakings (institutions included) are the result of conscious action and are coordinated by individuals. And should anyone interject that on many occasions they have perceived a cause-and-effect relation between human intervention and global results, probably all these authors could avail themselves without fear of contradiction of Nietzsche's famous dictum in Aurora: "All things that endure a long time become progressively steeped in sense to the point that it becomes incredible to believe that they have had their origin in the absurd."

3. A number of references to them can be found in my book *Hacerse cargo. Sobre responsibilidad e identidad personal* (Barcelona: Paidós, 1999).

4. It is no accident that in Spanish, both the adjective *responsible* and the abstract noun *responsibilidad* appeared after 1700. A similar date has been found for the noun responsibility, which, according to the experts on such matters, appeared in English in 1787, and for *responsabilité,* which appeared in French eleven years later.

5. Of course, we should question the extent to which this actually occurs, though this does not affect our argument here. That our attitude to wrongdoing has undergone a change is an assertion that is not falsified by the frustration of our expectations. There is no contradiction in holding the above to be true while admitting that perhaps Kundera was right when he wrote that "most people are deceived by two beliefs, both erroneous: they believe in the eternal memory (of people, of things, of

actions, of nations) and in the possibility of reparation (of acts, of the errors of their ways, of injustices). Both beliefs are false. In reality the reverse is the case: all will be forgotten and nothing will be put right. The role of reparation (of revenge and pardon) leads to oblivion. Nobody will redress the injustices that are committed, rather all injustices will be forgotten" (M. Kundera, *The Joke*).

6. Pascal Bruckner, *La Tentation de l'innocence* (Paris: Éditions Grasset et Fasquelle, 1995).

7. Jonas, *El Principio Responsabilidad*. His thesis is in large part indebted to the work of the theologian Richard Niebuhr, who in his posthumous *The Responsible Self* compared the anthropologies of the human being-as-doer and the human being-as-citizen and the human being-as-respondent. See H. R. Niebuhr, *The Responsible Self: An Essay in Christian Moral Philosophy* (San Francisco: Harper and Row, 1963).

8. It is not always necessary to illustrate one's argument with an authoritative quotation. On an Internet site called "Welcome to Graffiti" (http://www.angelfire.com/de/akitachile) the following can be read: "a computer can make the same number of errors in two seconds as 20 men can in two years."

9. "[W]ith the word and the action we insert ourselves in the human world" or "only the action and the discourse are specifically connected with the fact that living always means living among men" (H. Arendt, "Labor, Trabajo, Acción," in *De la historia a la acción* [Barcelona: Paidós-ICE of the UAB, 1995], p. 103). Although the locus classicus of this opinion is Arendt, *The Human Condition* (Chicago: University of Chicago Press, 1958).

10. If G. H. von Wright will serve as an authority, we could quote a passage from his classic *Explanation and Understanding*, in which he maintains: "What is done is the result of an action; what is caused is the consequence of an action. . . . The connection between an action and its results is intrinsic, logical and not now causal (extrinsic). If the result does not materialize, the action has simply not been carried out. The result is an essential "part" of the action. It would be a grave mistake to consider the action itself the cause of its results" (Ithaca: Cornell University Press, 1971).

11. See M. Cruz, *¿A quién pertenece lo ocurrido?* (Madrid: Taurus, 1995), passim.

12. One of the most stimulating discussions of this in recent times is that contained in Jean Améry's book (translator's note: original title not found) which poses a question that I cannot help identifying with strongly: "Who does the human being belong to?" Although he continues to think that it should belong to the individual—and that, therefore, what he prefers to call voluntary death is a free death and a question for the individual—he astutely notices a contradiction: "on the one hand the cold indifference society shows to the human being, while on the other the deep concern for him when he prepares to abandon voluntarily the society of the living." The question, finally, is whether on the basis of his assertion that at this moment in time the human being is alone, we can conclude, as the author himself does, that "society should keep quiet."

13. The second of these is usually shrouded in misunderstandings, of which the main one might be the tendency to see it as a spurious alternative to justice (an idea expressed in the shameful declaration "we don't want revenge, all we ask for is that justice be done"), when, as we know thanks to the likes of Kant and Hegel, it is included within the latter.

14. Inappropriate content is legion: for example, when the expression is used as a synonym of "be prudent" (as occurs in the political arena when somebody claims not to have made use of certain information "out of a sense of responsibility"), or to mean "obedient," or "polite" (as occurs when parents or teachers say: "this child is very responsible"). I refer to this in *Hacerse cargo,* p. 61ff.

CHAPTER 13. FORGIVENESS AND OBLIVION

1. While I was writing this "detour" I always had on my desk Richard J. Bernstein's excellent book *Hannah Arendt and the Jewish Question* (Cambridge: MIT Press, 1996).

2. Hannah Arendt and Karl Jaspers, *Hannah Arendt, Karl Jaspers: Correspondence, 1926–1969,* ed. L. Kohler and H. Saner, trans. Robert and Rita Kimber (New York: Harcourt Brace Jovanovich, 1992), p. 62.

3. On the point of view of baseness see C. Pereda, "Lo sublime y la bajeza," in *Vértigos argumentales: Una ética de la disputa* (Barcelona: Anthropos, 1994), pp. 225–60, where I discuss texts by Bertolt Brecht, Walter Benjamin, and Nicanor Parra as examples of a rhetoric of baseness.

4. Cf. Bertolt Brecht, *Gesammelte Werke* (Frankfurt am Main: Suhrkamp, 1968).

5. Hannah Arendt, *Eichmann in Jerusalem: A Report on the Banality of Evil* (New York: Viking Press, 1968), p. 49.

6. I. Kant, *Kritik der Urteilskraft,* in *Werke,* vol. 8, ed. W. Weischedel (Darmstadt: Wissenschaftliche Buchgesellschaft, 1968), pp. 388–92.

7. Arendt, *Eichmann in Jerusalem,* p. 287.

8. Arendt rejects emphatically this possible meaning of "banality of evil" in "Personal Responsibility under Dictatorship," *Listener,* 6 August 1964.

9. S. Benhabib, "Hannah Arendt and the Redemptive Power of Narrative," *Social Research* 57, no. 1 (spring 1990): 185.

10. Allan Bullock, *Hitler: A Study in Tyranny* (New York: Harper and Row, 1962), p. 398.

11. James A. Montmarquet, *Epistemic Virtue and Doxastic Responsibility* (Lanham, Md.: Rowman and Littlefield, 1993), p. 13.

CHAPTER 14. "HAPPY ENDINGS" / UNENDINGS

1. See Geoffrey Hartman, *The Longest Shadow: In the Aftermath of the Holocaust* (Bloomington: Indiana University Press, 1996), p. 122.

2. Theodor W. Adorno, "After Auschwitz," in *Negative Dialectics,* trans. E. B. Ashton (New York: Seabury Press, 1973), p. 362.

3. Jean-François Lyotard, *The Postmodern Condition: A Report on Knowledge* (Minneapolis: University of Minnesota Press, 1984).

4. *The New York Times,* November or December 1993.

5. See Miriam Hansen, "*Schindler's List* Is Not *Shoah:* The Second Commandment, Popular Modernism, and Public Memory," *Critical Inquiry* 22, no. 2 (winter 1996): 292–312.

6. Alvin Rosenfeld, *A Double Dying: Reflections on Holocaust Literature* (Bloomington: Indiana University Press, 1980).

7. Georg Lukács, *The Theory of the Novel,* trans. Anna Bostock (Cambridge: MIT Press, 1971).

8. See Longinus, *On the Sublime* 16.2, and Charles Dickens, *Our Mutual Friend* (Oxford: Oxford University Press, 1967), p. 54.

9. Northrop Frye, *The Secular Scripture* (Cambridge: Harvard University Press, 1976), p. 135.

10. Hannah Arendt, *Essays in Understanding, 1930–1954,* ed. Jerome Kohn (New York: Harcourt, Brace and Co., 1994), p. 14, original emphasis.

11. See Hartman, *The Longest Shadow,* pp. 119–20.

12. Maurice Blanchot, *The Writing of the Disaster,* trans. Ann Smock (Lincoln: University of Nebraska Press, 1986), pp. 5–6.

13. See Gertrud Koch, "Moral Conclusions from Narrative Closure," *History and Memory* 9, nos. 1–2 (1997): 393–408.

14. See Dori Laub's discussion of an eyewitness account of the Auschwitz uprising in Shoshana Felman and Dori Laub, *Testimony: Crises of Witnessing in Literature, Psychoanalysis, and History* (New York: Routledge, 1992), pp. 59–60. The eyewitness stated that four chimneys, rather than the historically accurate one, went up in flames. Laub cites the response of a psychoanalyst, who argued that insofar as the increased number testified to "the reality of an unimaginable occurrence," the woman's account could be taken as "'historical truth.'" The numerical transformation in the account thus requires interpretation.

15. Koch, "Moral Conclusions," p. 397.

16. Saul Friedländer, *Reflections of Nazism: An Essay on Kitsch and Death* (New York: Harper and Row, 1984), 12–14.

17. Armando, *From Berlin,* trans. Susan Massotti (London: Reaktion, 1996).

18. Aharon Appelfeld, *Badenheim 1939,* trans. Dalya Bilu (Boston: David R. Godine, 1990), p. 147.

19. Aharon Appelfeld, *To the Land of the Cattails,* trans. Jeffrey M. Green (New York: Harper and Row, 1987), p. 148.

20. Aharon Appelfeld, *The Iron Tracks,* trans. Jeffrey M. Green (New York: Schocken Books, 1998), pp. 4, 5.

21. Tim O'Brien, *In the Lake of the Woods* (New York: Penguin Books, 1995).

22. Sigmund Freud, "Analysis Terminable and Interminable," in *The Standard Edition of the Complete Psychological Works of Sigmund Freud,* vol. 23, ed. and trans. James Strachey (London: Hogarth Press, 1953–74).

23. Cathy Caruth, *Unclaimed Experience: Trauma, Narrative, and History* (Baltimore: Johns Hopkins University Press, 1996).

24. Bernard Schlink, *The Reader,* trans. Carol Brown Janeway (New York: Pantheon Books, 1997), p. 104.

CHAPTER 15. NARRATING EVIL

1. "Barry Whitney recently published a bibliography of over 4,200 philosophical and theological writings on the topic, all published from 1960 to 1990" (Daniel

Howard-Synder, ed., *The Evidential Argument from Evil* [Bloomington: Indiana University Press, 1996], p. ix).

2. Immanuel Kant, *Religion within the Limits of Reason Alone*, trans. Theodore M. Geene and Hort H. Hudson (New York: Harper Torchbooks, 1960).

3. Ibid., p. 24.

4. Michael L. Peterson, *God and Evil: An Introduction to the Issues* (Boulder, Colo.: Westview Press, 1998), p. 10.

5. Richard Swinburne defines it as "Theodicy is the enterprise of showing that appearances are misleading: that evils of the kind and quantity we find on Earth are neither incompatible with nor render improbable the existence of God, we may still have stronger evidence to show that there is a God which outweighs the counterevidence, which suffices to make it rational for us to believe that there is a God." Richard Swinburne, "Some Major Strands of Theodicy," in *The Evidential Argument from Evil*, ed. Daniel Howard-Snyder (Bloomington: Indiana University Press, 1996), pp. 30–39, esp. p. 30.

6. Augustine, *City of God*, trans. Marcus Dods, George Wilson, and J. J. Smith (New York: Random House, 1950). See also Augustine, *The Nature of Good*, in *Augustine: Earlier Writings*, ed. and trans. J. H. S. Burleigh (London: S.C.M. Press, 1953), p. vi.

7. Augustine, *The Nature of Good*, p. 91.

8. Ibid., p. 93.

9. Gottfried Wilhelm von Leibniz, *Theodicy: Essays on the Goodness of God, the Freedom of Man, and the Origin of Evil*, trans. C. M. Huggard from C. J. Gerhardt's edition of the collected philosophical works (1875–90) (New Haven: Yale University Press, 1952), paragraph 201.

10. This type of theodicy can be traced to Bishop Irenaeus (c. 130–c. 202). The most articulate contemporary proponent of Irenaean theodicy is John Hick. Irenaean theodicy looks to the future in terms of God's plan for the development of humanity.

11. I. Kant, G. W. F. Hegel, Søren Kirkegaard, Martin Buber, Simone Weil, and Carl G. Jung wrote important essays on the story of Job. See Isabel Cabrera, ed., *Voices en el Silencio: Job: Texto y Comentarios* (Mexico City: Universidad Autonoma Metropolitana, Iztapalapa, 1992).

12. "This is perhaps the greatest thing about Job, faced with this difficulty, he does not doubt the unity of God. He clearly sees that God is at odds with himself— so totally at odds that he, Job, is quite certain of finding in God a helper and an 'advocate' against God. As certain as he is of the devil in Yahweh, he is equally certain of the good" ("Answer to Job," in *Encountering Jung on Evil*, ed. Murray Stein [Princeton: Princeton University Press, 1995] p. 125).

13. Ibid., p. 137.

14. "Reflective judgment" is a term used first by Kant in his *Critique of Judgment* to characterize "aesthetic judgment" or "judgment of taste" and to differentiate it from "empirical judgment" or "judgment of the sense." Judgment in a Kantian sense meant that there ought to be the inclusion of a particular into a universal. Kant argued that judgment's more important concern lies in matching particulars and universals. In the case of "determinant judgment," Kant argued, the universal exists prior and it is independent from the particular, suggesting that this exercise supplies schemata for concepts furnished by the understanding. In the case of "reflective

judgment," on the other hand, Kant argues that one must find the universal when one is confronted with the particular. Thus, the capacity to respond to the situation is the relation of "reflective judgment." Hannah Arendt used Kant's notion of "reflective judgment" to develop her own conception of it in the political domain. What she meant with "reflective judgment" has never been entirely clarified, because she died before writing her projected work on the subject. Many scholars have developed ideas about her conception of judgment.

15. See, for example, Martha Nussbaum, *Love's Knowledge: Essays on Philosophy and Literature* (Oxford: Oxford University Press, 1990). Also: Wayne Booth, *The Company We Keep: An Ethics of Fiction* (Berkeley: University of California Press, 1988).

16. Paul Ricoeur, *The Symbolism of Evil*, trans. Emerson Buchanan (Boston: Beacon Press, 1967), p. 229.

17. Ibid., my emphasis.

18. Martha C. Nussbaum, *The Fragility of Goodness: Luck and Ethics in Greek Tragedy and Philosophy* (Cambridge: Cambridge University Press, 1986), p. 273.

19. Martha C. Nussbaum, "Tragedy and Self-sufficiency: Plato and Aristotle on Fear and Pity" in *Essays on Aristotle's Poetics,* ed. Amélie Oksenberg Rorty (Princeton: Princeton University Press, 1992) pp. 261–90, esp. p. 276.

20. Martha Nussbaum concludes (ibid., p. 278):

> If I witness a person similar to me being struck down in a manner that I find utterly mysterious and arbitrary, I will have no idea whether or not this is the sort of thing that might happen to me; I will simply not understand it, and I will tend to see the events as too weird for identification. If, on the other hand, I see the causal mechanisms at work, and see them as obeying laws of necessity or probability, then the events will strike me as things that could affect my own life.

21. Bernard Williams, *Shame and Necessity* (Berkeley: University of California Press, 1993).

22. Ibid., p. 69.

23. Ibid.

24. Williams claims that "they have a life that is exposed to fortune on that scale, and this is simply manifest: they do not have to explain it to anyone or argue about it" (ibid., p. 74).

25. Nussbaum concludes that there "is a close connection between the listed occasions for pity and Aristotle's reflections about our vulnerability to the external in the ethical works" (*The Fragility of Goodness,* p. 383).

26. "Every connotation of self-consciousness, self-determination, and self-realization has to have been exorcised from the basic concepts of philosophy before language (instead of subjectivity) can declare independence in this way—whether as an epochal destining of Being, as the frenzy of signifiers, or as a shoving match between discourses, the borders between literal and metaphorical meaning, between logic and rhetoric, and between serious and fictional speech are washed away in the flow of a universal textual occurrence" (Jurgen Habermas, "Philosophy and Science as Literature?" in *Postmetaphysical Thinking: Philosophical Essays* [Cambridge: MIT Press, 1996], pp. 205–27, esp. p. 207).

27. Ibid., p. 209.

28. Ibid.

29. Ibid., p. 210.

30. Hans-Georg Gadamer, *Literature and Philosophy in Dialogue: Essays in German Literary Theory* (Albany: State University of New York Press, 1994).

31. Robert H. Paslick, translator's introduction to *Literature and Philosophy in Dialogue: Essays in German Literary Theory,* by Hans-Georg Gadamer (Albany: State University of New York Press, 1994), pp. vii–xii.

32. Ibid., p. ix.

33. Walter Benjamin, "The Storyteller: Reflections on the Works of Nikolai Leskov," in *Illuminations: Essays and Reflections,* ed. Hannah Arendt (New York: Harcourt Brace Jovanovich, 1968), pp. 83–110.

34. Ibid., p. 91.

35. Ibid., p. 97.

36. Ibid., p. 102, my emphasis.

37. Hannah Arendt, *On Human Condition* (Chicago: University of Chicago Press, 1958), p. 237.

38. Ibid., p. 241.

39. Richard J. Bernstein, *Hannah Arendt and the Jewish Question* (Cambridge: MIT Press, 1996), p. 149.

40. Arendt, *On Human Condition,* p. 246.

41. Berel Lang, "Hannah Arendt and the Politics of Evil," in *Hannah Arendt: Critical Essays,* ed. Lewis P. Hinchman and Sandra K. Hinchman (Albany: State University of New York Press, 1994), pp. 41–56, esp. p. 50.

42. Ibid., p. 50.

43. Ibid., p. 51.

44. Hannah Arendt, *The Life of the Mind* (New York: Harcourt Brace Jovanovich, 1978), p. 192.

45. Barbara Herman, *The Practice of Moral Judgement* (Cambridge: Harvard University Press, 1993), pp. 74, 76.

46. "Typically they are acquired in childhood as part of socialization; they provide a practical framework within which people act. When the rules of moral salience are well internalized, they cause the agent to be aware of and attentive to the significance of 'moral danger.' They are not learned as bits of information about the world, and not as rules of guidance to use when engaged in particular sorts of activities (moral ones). The rules of moral salience constitute the structure of moral sensitivity" (ibid., p. 78).

47. C. Fred Alford argues "more often relativism is a defense against experience, the overwhelming emotional and moral experience of evil" (C. Fred Alford, *What Evil Means to Us* [Ithaca: Cornell University Press, 1997], p. 9).

48. J. S. La Fontaine, *Speak of the Devil: Tales of Satanic Abuse in Contemporary England* (Cambridge: Cambridge University Press, 1998).

49. Karen A. Cerulo, *Deciphering Violence: The Cognitive Structure of Right and Wrong* (New York: Routledge, 1998).

50. Alford, *What Evil Means to Us.*

51. Peter Levine, *Living Without Philosophy: On Narrative, Rhetoric, and Morality* (Albany: State University of New York Press, 1998). See also Colin MacGinn, *Ethics, Evil, and Fiction* (Oxford: Clarendon Press, 1997) .

52. Paul Ricoeur, *The Symbolism of Evil* (Boston: Beacon Press, 1967). And from

the same author: *The Conflict of Interpretations* (Evanston, Ill.: Northwestern University Press, 1974).

53. Cerulo, *Deciphering Violence.*

54. Ibid., p. 3.

55. Ibid.

56. Ibid., p. 7.

57. "My work poses a symbiotic relationship between the social and the cultural. For example, in carefully charting the narrative sequences of violence and the ways in which these sequences become institutionalized, I argue that social structure can influence the shape and substance of culture. I also note several factors and conditions that can both facilitate and constrain narrators' use of these cultural conventions. However, my work is equally concerned with the ways in which culture can influence social action, particularly when such action strays from expectation" (ibid., p. 9).

58. Ibid., p. 10.

59. Alford, *What Evil Means to Us*, p. 13.

60. Hannah Arendt, "On Humanity in Dark Times: Thoughts about Lessing," in *Men in Dark Times* (New York: Harcourt, Brace and Co., 1968), pp. 3–31, esp. p. 21.

61. Alford, *What Evil Means to Us*, p. 12–13.

62. Ian Hacking, *Rewriting the Soul: Multiple Personality and the Sciences of Memory* (Princeton: Princeton University Press, 1995), p. 6.

63. Richard Kearney, "Remembering the Past: The Question of Narrative Memory," *Philosophy and Social Criticism* 24, nos. 2/3 (1998): 49–60, esp. p. 54.

64. Levine, *Living without Philosophy*, p. 151.

65. Andre La Cocque and Paul Ricoeur, *Thinking Biblically: Exegetical and Hermeneutical Studies* (Chicago: University of Chicago Press, 1998), p. xi.

66. Kirstie M. McClure, "Speaking in Tenses: Narrative, Politics, and Historical Writing," *Constellations* 5, no. 2 (1998): 234–49, esp. p. 234.

67. "Transforming private emotions into public—or better, publicly communicable—affect, the 'political function' of the storyteller converges with that of Aristotle's poet. In both Arendt discerns 'the operation of a catharsis, a cleansing or purging of all emotions' that could prevent individuals from acting. Whether as historian or as novelist, 'the political function of the storyteller is to teach acceptance of things as they are.' On Arendt's view, however, this acceptance is not a matter, Hegelianwise, of acquiescing in the reality of the rational and the rationality of the real. Rather, it is the wellspring of the 'faculty of judgement'" (ibid., p. 243).

68. "The activity of reading, on his view, thus completes the circle of narrativity by returning it to the world of praxis. That return, however, is double mediated—in the first instance by selective judgement of writers in the activity of configuration, in the second by its readers' similarly selective activity of refiguration" (ibid., p. 244).

69. All these terms were developed by Paul Ricoeur. See: Ricoeur, *Time and Narrative*, 3 vols., vols. 1–2 trans. Kathleen McLaughlin and D. Pellauer, vol. 3 trans. Kathleen Blamey and D. Pellauer (Chicago: University of Chicago Press, 1984–88).

CONTRIBUTORS

JEFFREY C. ALEXANDER is professor of sociology at Yale University. He is a sociologist of major international stature. Since his multivolume *Theoretical Logic of Sociology* (1982–83), he has published numerous books and articles, most recently edited, with Steven Seidman, *The New Social Theory: Contemporary Debates* (2001). In recent years he has concentrated on the problems of culture and civil society and he is currently preparing for publication a book entitled *Possibilities of Justice: Civil Society and Its Contradictions*.

HENRY E. ALLISON is currently professor of philosophy at Boston University and professor emeritus at the University of California, San Diego. His major books include *Kant's Transcendental Idealism* (1983) and *Kant's Theory of Freedom* (1990), *Idealism and Freedom* (1996), and *Kant's Theory of Taste* (2001).

CAROL L. BERNSTEIN is Mary E. Garrett Alumnae Professor of English and Comparative Literature at Bryn Mawr College. Her books include *Precarious Enchantment: A Reading of George Meredith* and *The Celebration of Scandal: Toward the Sublime in Victorian Urban Fiction*. She is currently working on cultural memory and the ethics of narrative, as well as Walter Benjamin and the trajectory of the sublime.

RICHARD J. BERNSTEIN is Vera List Professor of Philosophy and Chair at the Graduate Faculty of the New School University. His recent books include *Beyond Objectivism and Relativism: The New Constellation, Hannah Arendt and the Jewish Question* and *Freud and the Legacy of Moses*. He is currently working on the problem of evil.

ISABEL CABRERA is professor of philosophy at the Institute for Philosophical Research, Universidad Nacional Autónoma de México. She is the author of *El Lado oscuro de Dios* (1998), and editor of *Voices in Silence: Job, Text and Commentaries* (1992), and of *Religion and Suffering* (1996).

MAEVE COOKE is a senior lecturer in the Department of German at University College Dublin, Ireland. She is author of *Language and Reason: A Study of Habermas' Pragmatics* (985) and editor of a collection of Habermas's writings on language and communication: *On the Pragmatics of Communication* (1998). She has published a number of articles in the areas of political and social philosophy. Her current research projects include books on self-realization and on evil.

MANUEL CRUZ is professor of philosophy at the University of Barcelona. His most recent books are: *Filosofía de la historia* (1991), *¿A quién pertenece lo ocurrido?* (1995), and *Hacerse cargo* (1998). He has edited the books: *Individuo, Modernidad e Historia* (1992), *Tiempo de subjetividad* (1995), and *Tolerancia o Barbarie* (1998). He is editor of the philosophy series "Pensamiento Contemporáneo" and "Biblioteca del Presente" and co-director of the series "Filosofía hoy y Biblioteca Iberoamericana del Presente."

PETER DEWS is professor of philosophy at the University of Essex. He has held visiting positions at the University of Konstanz, and at the Graduate Faculty, New School for Social Research. He is the author of *Logics of Disintegration* (1987), and *The Limits of Disenchantment: Essay in Contemporary European Philosophy* (1995). He has also edited *Autonomy and Solidarity: Interview with Jürgen Habermas* (1986), and *Habermas: A Critical Reader* (1999). His current research concerns the relation between religious and philosophical discourse in modernity.

ALESSANDRO FERRARA is associate professor in the Faculty of Letters and Philosophy at the University of Parma. He is the author of *Modernity and Authenticity: A Study of the Social and Ethical Thought of Jean-Jacques Rousseau* (1993), *Reflective Authenticity: Rethinking the Project of Modernity* (1998), and *Justice and Judgement* (1999). He is currently working on problems of authenticity and evil.

ROBERT FINE is director of the Social Centre at the University of Warwick. He is the author of *Democracy and the Rule of Law: Liberal and Marxist Critiques* (1985), *Beyond Apartheid: Labour and Nationalism in South Africa* (1991), coeditor of *People, Nation, and State: The Meaning of Ethnicity and Nationalism* (1999), and of *Social Theory after the Holocaust* (2000). A version of this paper has been published in *Social Theory after the Holocaust*, ed. Fine and Turner (2000). His latest book is *Political Investigations: Hegel, Marx, Arendt* (2001).

MARÍA PÍA LARA is professor of philosophy at the Universidad Autónoma Metropolitana, México. She has published *La democracia como proyecto de Identidad Etica* (1992), *Moral Textures: Feminist Narratives on the Public Sphere* (1998). Her current research is on the problem of evil and on the normative foundations of democracy and globalization.

GUSTAVO LEYVA is professor of philosophy at the Universidad Autónoma Metropolitana, México. He is director of the postgraduate studies of political philosophy at Universidad Autónoma Metropolitana, Iztapalapa. He has worked on the philosophy of Kant and published several articles in this field.

SUSAN NEIMAN is Director of the Einstein Forum, Postdam. She has also been professor of philosophy at Yale University and Tel Aviv University, and is the author of *Slow Fire: Jewish Notes from Berlin* (1992), *The Unity of Reason: Rereading Kant* (1994), as well as numerous essays. Her next book is *Evil in Modern Thought* (2001, forthcoming).

CARLOS PEREDA is professor of philosophy at the Institute for Philosophical Research, Universidad Nacional Autónoma de México. He has published *Debates* (1987), *Conversar es Humano* (1991), *Vértigos Argumentales* (1993), *Razón e Incertidumbre* (1994), *Sueños de vagabundos: Un Ensayo sobre filosofía, moral y literatura* (1998), and *Crítica de la Razón Arrogante* (1998).

SERGIO PÉREZ is professor of philosophy at the Universidad Autónoma Metropolitana. He has been dean of humanities and social sciences at Universidad Autónoma Metropolitana, Iztapalapa (1992–96), and head of the Department of Philosophy at UAM-I (1985–89). He has published numerous books and articles on Hegel and Foucault. His most recent book is *Sobre el Mentir* (1998).

INDEX

Villa, Dana, 10, 146, 252n15, 253n33
Violence, 183, 197; badass and, 285n49;
    narratives of, 247; in totalitarian terror,
    133–34; and will to power, 148
Vivaldi, Antonio Lucio, 26
Volition. *See* Will; *Willkür*
Voltaire (François-Marie Arouet), 27, 28, 36,
    38, 41

Wade, John, 234
Walzer, Michael, 280n19
War, 167–68
Warsaw ghetto, 233
Washington, George, 166
Watergate, 168
Wealth of Nations, The (Smith), 34
Weber, Max, 102–3, 140, 277n7
Wellmer, Albrecht, 5, 7, 51, 47–52, 252n11
Wickedness, 70–71, 76, 84, 93, 96, 98–99,
    194, 239
Wiesel, Elie, 30, 132
Will/*Wille*, 194; Augustine on, 240; to
    destroy, 146–49; diabolical, denial of,

91, 94, 95; freedom of, see *Willkür*; Kant
    on, 3–4, 57–60, 65–76, 78, 91, 92,
    122–24, 174, 175, 257n6, 259n25,
    261n31; radical evil and, 174–75;
    Schelling on, 107; subjective, right
    of, 110–11; vs. *Willkür*, 58–59, 79–80,
    83–84, 257n6
Williams, Bernard, 243, 291n24
Williams, Robin M., 278n9
Willkür, 58-59, 65, 69, 70–73, 76, 78, 81–
    85, 92, 109, 122, 123, 128, 257n6,
    260n28, 261n31; *Gesinnung* and, 66–67;
    Hegel on, 111
Will to Power, The (Nietzsche), 135, 147
Wittgenstein, Ludwig, 155, 203
Wood, Allen, 60, 63, 65, 80, 94, 263n44
Wright, G. H. von, 287n10

Yahweh. *See* God
Young-Bruel, Elizabeth, 86, 87
Yugoslavia, former, 178, 184

Žižek, Slavoj, 46, 263n42, 264n48

Text:	10/12 Baskerville
Display:	Baskerville
Compositor:	BookMatters
Printer/binder:	Maple-Vail Book Manufacturing Group